Bob Vila's Guide to Historic Homes of the Midwest and Great Plains

Bob Vila's Guides to Historic Homes of America

Bob Vila's
Guide to Historic Homes of
the Midwest and
Great Plains

LINTEL PRESS

QUILL
WILLIAM MORROW
New York

ISBN: 0-688-12495-X

Library of Congress Catalog Card Number: 93-086127

Printed in the United States of America

First Quill Edition

1   2   3   4   5   6   7   8   9   10

MANAGING EDITOR — JILL TARDIFF
CONTRIBUTING EDITORS — BARBARA WINARD AND PAUL KOZLOWSKI
LAYOUT AND DESIGN BY EVA JAKUBOWSKI

Acknowledgment

$\mathcal{I}$ would like to acknowledge all of the people who helped make the idea of this book become a reality. To my wife Deborah who shares my enthusiasm for everything about history and whose idea of a vacation is incomplete without visiting every historic house along the way. Her encouragement and determination to see every room in every house gave me the idea for this series of guides.

To Ron Feiner who brought us all together long ago and by doing so enriched us all. To Bob Sann and Hugh Howard whose path findings led us to our publishers, a special thanks for enabling us to be spared the normative agony of attempting to get published. Through Hugh's excellent relationships we hope to benefit all.

To my brother Seth, whose expertise in the publishing business facilitated my limited understanding of the industry.

To Jill A. Tardiff, Barbara Winard, and Paul Kozlowski who worked so tirelessly and professionally to make this a reality. I could not have found more skillful people whose strengths complemented my weaknesses.

To my partner Barry Weiner, whose unfailing support allowed us to open the checkbook when the possibility of returns were vague.

To Eva Jakubowski, who makes books and computers come together. If I ever figured out what you do I'd probably thank you even more.

And finally, to my mother Miriam, who aside from being a librarian demonstrated to me at a very early age that a universe of knowledge could be found between the covers of that most marvelous and wonderful of all things...books.

— *Jonathan Russo*
Lintel Press

Table of Contents

Publisher's Note

We hope that this book will serve as more than a conventional guide to historic homes. For while we set out to create a detailed, informative, and unique guide, devoted exclusively to historic houses, we also had higher goals. For those among you who enjoy, and are devoted to, preservation, architecture, decorative and fine arts, what we have attempted will be self-evident. For those who are first becoming interested in the world of historic Americana, we will try to give you a helping hand. For all those venturing across these historic thresholds, we invite you in, knowing that you will not be disappointed.

The following pages contain a wealth of information on the fascinating people—both the famous and not so famous—who lived in these houses, as well as descriptions of the houses and their remarkable collections. What can also be found within this book, beyond the listings of locations, hours, and tour information, is the most elusive of all things—wonder. For behind each and every house listing lies a world of wonder. Not the manufactured kind, packaged and sold to replace the imagination. Not the superficial kind which manipulates the emotions at the expense of the intellect. But wonder on a higher plane.

The first wonder is that any of these houses still exist and that anyone cares at all. Our society has often achieved its enviable position of affluence by focusing on the new and disposing with the old. The desire for the latest architectural styles, furnishings, and conveniences has often meant a bulldozing of the past, to the point where even the recent past is endangered. Of course, this has always been so; Colonial homes were remodeled into Greek Revivals at the expense of their original architecture. But the changes are far more devastating now, instead of remodeling the houses, we are tearing them down altogether. Time after time, when we went to a historic house in a small city or village, our guide's first statement was that the historic society had been formed to prevent the house from being torn down, often to make room for a parking lot. Historic houses have been made into rooming houses, beauty parlors, or high rises. As we walked through a fifteen room, four-story house built in 1840, complete with irreplaceable architectural details, the enormity of the "let's tear it down" mentality became overwhelming.

Of course the houses themselves possess more wonder than anything else. It is a sorrowfully calloused person who cannot experience the past in a historic house. To tour the prosperous ship captain's house in historic Newport, Rhode Island is to wonder at the riches of furniture, decorations, textiles and food stuffs that ships and winds provided. To tour the 18th-century stone houses of Washington, Pennsylvania with their two-foot thick walls is to wonder at the fortitude of their inhabitants as they struggled against attacks and defended themselves against the cold winters. The very cosmopolitanism of mercantile families in Greenwich Village, New York permeates the air of the historic houses there. One can sense the refinement these people must have felt when they sipped brandy and smoked cigars in their impressive parlors. To be told why people used fireplace screens —so that the wax women used as a cosmetic to fill in their pockmarked faces would not melt—is an explanation of a common object that brings the past alive in a personal and wonderful way. The treasures of art, architectural details, furniture, household implements, and costumes contained in these homes also makes us pause in reflection. Things were viewed very differently when they were made by hand and scarce. There is an education for all of us living in a throw-away culture.

So it is to the individuals, organizations and societies who are saving, preserving and displaying historic America that our sense of wonder and gratitude is directed. Sometimes, we would drive by a mall and see endless cars, stores and shoppers, and know that the energy of the town was now clearly centered at the mall. Then we would arrive at our destination, the local historic house, and find we were the only visitors. Despite this daunting competition from today's faster paced entertainments, our guide was cheerful, patient and full of enthusiasm for the wonder of the house.

We admire the volunteers who fundraise, lobby, catalogue, lecture, and guide their fellow citizens. As visitors, we enrich ourselves because of the efforts of the organizations and individuals who have labored to restore and revitalize these fine houses. We wish to thank the individuals who have given us their time and energy on these tours, and have given us their cooperation in putting this book together. If, in some small way, this guide helps you in your efforts, please consider it a thank you.

— *Jonathan Russo*
Lintel Press

Editor's Note

*O*ur thanks go to all of the individuals and organizations who have dedicated themselves to preserving America's architectural and historical heritage as exemplified in her residential structures and from whom we received the brochures, photographs, histories, drawings, suggestions, and enthusiastic encouragement without which there would be no book. We only hope that we have been faithful to their stories, their houses, and their mission.

We have tried to make the entries as easy to use as possible, and have included the latest and most accurate information made available to us by the homes themselves. Even so, we highly recommend that you contact a house before planning a visit to verify its hours of operation, scheduled activities, and especially its wheelchair access status—for many older structures, wheelchair access means limited access to the first floor only. Wherever possible we have made mention of other houses located in a given city or town that are worth visiting; these homes appear under the heading "Additional Information."

Though the book is necessarily incomplete—after all, every human habitation is in some sense historical and none are truly permanent—we have tried to include as many of America's most noteworthy homes as possible. If we have omitted any of your favorites, please let us know.

Introduction

All buildings have character, some seem friendly while others have a forbidding feel. Many big buildings demand your attention, while more than a few small ones seem content to let you pass by them unnoticed. Buildings can be eccentric, exotic, familiar, unassuming, warm and welcoming, or cold and sinister; but their individuality is there for all who choose to recognize it.

Since the Bicentennial celebration, millions of Americans have come to appreciate another element of the architectural personality. Like people of a certain age, antique buildings have survived wars and changes and visitors, wanted and unwanted alike. Their very characters are reflections of times past. Some buildings, like some people, have aged gracefully; some have seen happy and sad times, but all of them have something to teach us, about their histories and even ourselves. The truth is that all old houses have something in common with your house and mine.

I fell in love with houses and buildings early in my life—I studied architecture long before *This Old House* and *Bob Vila's Home Again* introduced millions to some intriguing rehabilitation jobs with which I've been involved. My fondness for buildings in general and my experience with old houses in particular only heightens my appreciation of the houses you'll meet in these pages, and the uncompromising approach the many historical societies, community organizations, individuals, and groups have taken to getting the houses restored just right.

These houses represent an immense range of the American experience. Every one has a story to tell, whether it's of the people who built the house or those who lived there; the community that is the context for the place; or even the events that led to its preservation; which so often involve battles with developers or others insensitive to the value and merit in a tumbledown, antique structure.

Each of these houses provides a unique opportunity to step back in time, to learn about how our ancestors lived. Which is another way of saying, these houses offer a glimpse of history, that wonderful state of mind that explains, in part, why and who we are today. I hope in some way we can help inspire you to visit these houses and those other eras that have so much to teach us.

—*Bob Vila*

Arkansas

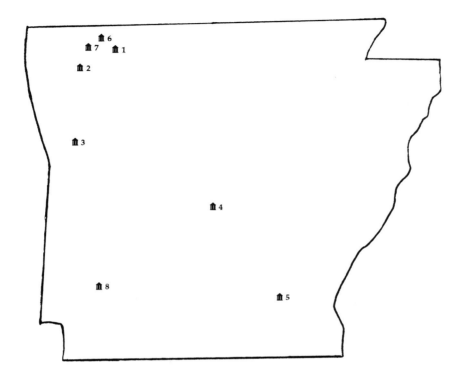

1. **Eureka Springs**
   Calif House
   Quigley's Castle

2. **Fayetteville**
   Headquarters House–
   The Tebbetts House
   Sarah B.N. Ridge House

3. **Fort Smith**
   W. H. H. Clayton House

4. **Little Rock**
   Brownlee-Noland House
   Pike-Fletcher-Terry House
   "Villa Marre"

5. **Monticello**
   Garvin Cavaness House

6. **Pea Ridge**
   Elkhorn Tavern

7. **Rogers**
   Hawkins House

8. **Washington**
   John D. Trimble House

Calif House

95 South Main Street
Eureka Springs, AR 72632
(501) 253-9417

Contact: Eureka Springs Historical Museum
Open: Mar.-Dec., Tues.-Sun.
9:30 a.m.–4 p.m.; Jan. and Feb.
closed Sunday
Admission: Adults $2.00; students free;
special group rates
Activities: Group tours, introductory video
available
Suggested Time to View House:
45–60 minutes
Facilities on Premises: Gift shop

Description of Grounds: Small city lot
located in the heart of the Eureka Springs
Historic District
Best Season to View House: Year round
Number of Yearly Visitors: 5,000
Year House Built: 1889
Style of Architecture: Modified Late Second
Empire
Number of Rooms: 8
On-Site Parking: Yes **Wheelchair Access:** No

Description of House

By the time Samuel Calif built this fine Second Empire-style residence in Eureka Springs, the town was already a well-known health resort attracting thousands of visitors annually. Its salubrious waters were discovered by the pioneer doctor Alvah Jackson and made popular by his friend, Judge J. B. Saunders, who took "the cure" in 1879; it is conjectured that the community got its name when the Judge's son exclaimed, "Eureka! I have found it (the cure)!" A spur of the railroad was brought into town and the older wooden structures began to be replaced by more permanent and luxurious brick and stone buildings. Scarcely ten years later, Calif—a merchant from Illinois—came to Eureka Springs with his family and operated a grocery store out of his home.

The three-story structure is built out of limestone quarried from the White River. The main floor porch and covered balcony protect two entrances: one leads into Calif's store and the other leads to the private quarters. The upper two floors served as a rooming house. The exterior features molded cornices, decorative brackets, heavy quoins, spindle-like railings and supports on the porch, and paired dormer windows with elaborate surrounds. The house is furnished in an eclectic mix of period antiques—primarily Victorian—decorated by local residents.

In 1980, the Calif House was given to the Eureka Springs Historical Museum Association by the Ozark Folk Festival Inc. This non-profit corporation, made up of community members whose chief activity is sponsoring the famous local festival of the same name, had purchased the house some years before and turned it into a museum.

Notable Collections on Exhibit

Among the items on display here are a collection of home furnishings, photographs, and documents relating the lives of the area's early settlers. There is also a fine collection of china dolls and a fully outfitted pioneer kitchen. One of the rooms was established and is maintained by the Abendschone Chapter of the Daughters of the American Revolution, founded locally and named in honor of one of the first families to settle here.

Additional Information

The Calif House lies within the Eureka Springs Historic District-South Main Street which is listed on the National Register of Historic Places.

Quigley's Castle

Contact: Quigley's Castle

Open: Apr.-Oct., Mon.-Wed., Fri. and Sat. 8:30 a.m.–5:00 p.m.

Admission: Adults $4.00; children (under 15 with parent) free; group rates (20 or more) available

Activities: Guided tours

Suggested Time to View House: 30 minutes

Best Season to View House: Early spring and mid-summer

Description of Grounds: European-inspired perennial gardens with unique rock sculptures, arboretum, aquarium and fish ponds complete the landscaping

Number of Yearly Visitors: 16,000

Year House Built: 1945

Style of Architecture: Folk Eclectic

Number of Rooms: 12

On-Site Parking: Yes **Wheelchair Access:** No

Description of House

Quigley's Castle, which bills itself as the Ozark's strangest dwelling, is largely the creation of one woman, Elise Quigley. In 1943, this wife and mother of five had a vision of a house that approximates "living in the world instead of a box." Thus she tore down the family's existing three-room family house and began construction on this eclectic dwelling. Elise's husband, Albert, who worked in a nearby sawmill, cut and planed lumber from their own property for use in structure, the whole family completed the carpentry and masonry themselves, and they only spent $2,000 on manufactured materials and outside labor. (The house was subsequently valued at $60,000 in 1944 dollars!)

Mrs. Quigley's house has two unique features which immediately attracted the curious: the exterior is entirely covered with rocks and fossils—part of an enormous collection begun by Mrs. Quigley when she was a girl of nine—of every shape and size imaginable; visitors now spend hours marveling at this rock "skin." The second feature is on the inside: Mrs. Quigley directed that a three-foot-wide channel of raw soil be left exposed just inside three of the dwelling's four outer walls. Into this soil she planted flora from around the world, thereby effectively bringing the "world" into her house. With the twelve four-by-six windows letting in a great deal of light these plants have flourished, and many have reached the second story in height. The second story is supported with oak pillars bolted to the edge of the first floor; the interior walls of the house are wood and display natural tongue-and-groove joinery.

Mr. Quigley died in 1972 and Elise twelve years later; the house is now owned and operated by a granddaughter. It is a regular tourist stop on the petroleum industry's Ozark Frontier Trail.

Notable Collections on Exhibit

As might be expected, the Quigley Castle is full of marvelous and unusual objects; of special note are the unique rock, arrowhead, and butterfly collections.

Headquarters House– The Tebbetts House

118 East Dickson Street
Fayetteville, AR 72701
(501) 521-2970

Contact: Washington County Historical Society

Open: Jan.-Mar., Mon.-Fri. 1–4 p.m.; Apr.-Dec. Tues.-Sat. 1–4 p.m.; other times by appointment; closed holidays

Admission: Donation requested

Activities: Self-guided tours with volunteers available, annual "Gay Nineties" Ice Cream Social

Suggested Time to View House: 30 minutes

Facilities on Premises: Historical society publications for sale

Description of Grounds: Period landscaped yard

Best Season to View House: Spring and fall

Number of Yearly Visitors: 5,000

Year House Built: 1853

Style of Architecture: Greek Revival

Number of Rooms: 10, 7 open to the public

On-Site Parking: Yes **Wheelchair Access:** No

Description of House

The superb example of the Greek Revival style—one of the finest such structures in Arkansas—was built in 1853 by Jonas March Tebbetts, a native New Englander who migrated west, studied law, and was admitted to the bar at twenty-two. Over the next two decades, he traveled the region intensively, acting as lawyer, sometimes special judge, and serving in the legislature; in 1852, he helped found Arkansas College. His wife was Matilda Winlock, a graduate of Miss Sophia Sawler's Fayetteville Female Seminary.

When the Civil War broke out, Tebbetts—known to be a "Union man"—was arrested as a spy by Confederate General Ben McCulloch. After McCulloch's death in the Battle of Pea Ridge, Tebbetts won release and fled to the Union lines in Missouri. In 1862, he returned to Fayetteville to fetch his family; he would never live in the house again. During the remainder of the war, it served as the headquarters for whichever army was occupying the town. After the war, and before it was acquired by the Historical Society in 1965, the house passed through the hands of four owners, most notably Charles Whiting Walker—a prominent local attorney and one of the first persons ever born in Fayetteville—and Charles Appleby, who bought it in the 1920s with the intention of restoring it to its former glory.

This one-and-a-half-story residence features a full-height entry porch, dentil trim around the eaves, a front door with transom and sidelights, pilasters at the corners, and a impressive portico with fluted columns supporting a decorated pediment. The original floor plan included a parlor, library, and two bedrooms placed symmetrically about a central hall, and two small bedrooms upstairs; a separate rear wing housed the kitchen. The house suffered some damage during the Battle of Fayetteville. When the restoration of the house was begun, the rear wing and porch were removed and replaced with a full basement and other additions. The interior has been interpreted to the period between 1853 and 1863—its authenticity is based on a journal kept by one of Tebbetts' daughters.

Notable Collections on Exhibit
The Tebbetts House contains a fine collection of donated period furniture; the only thing which belonged to the family is a silver service set.

Additional Information
The Tebbetts House is listed on the National Register of Historic Places. It stands in Fayetteville's Washington-Willow Historic District—also on the National Register—which itself is worth an extended visit. The Washington County Historical Society publishes a pamphlet detailing a self-guided tour of the eighty houses which make up the district; so well-preserved are they that the 1981 television movie *The Blue and The Gray* was partially filmed here.

Sarah B.N. Ridge House

230 West Center Street
Fayetteville, AR 72701
(501) 521-2970

Contact: Washington County Historical Society

Open: Year-round, Mon.-Fri. 9 a.m.–5 p.m.; access to certain areas by appointment only

Admission: Free

Activities: Viewing only

Suggested Time to View House: 15 minutes

Facilities on Premises: Rental offices

Description of Grounds: Simple yard with native grasses surrounded by picket fence

Style of Architecture: Folk "dog-trot" log cabin, later modifications rural Greek Revival and Saltbox styles

Number of Rooms: 8 with central hall open to the public

Best Season to View House: Spring and fall

Year House Built: 1836, additions c. 1839 and c. 1859, remodeled 1877

On-Site Parking: Yes **Wheelchair Access:** No

Description of House

This house—originally built in 1836 by Dr. M. H. Clark—is named for Mrs. Sarah Bird Northrup Ridge who purchased it in 1839 after fleeing the Oklahoma Indian Territory with her children and missionary friend, Sophie Sawyer. Mrs. Ridge's Indian husband had been killed by those within the Cherokee Nation who were angered by his participation in the signing of the treaty which ceded Cherokee lands in the Eastern United States to the federal government. The family lived here until 1839, when Mrs. Ridge's son Aeneas died.

After the Civil War, the house was owned by Judge David Walker and J. W. Pettigrew, then Mr. and Mrs. Zebulon Pettigrew. After the couple's death, it was turned into an apartment house. In 1971, the Washington County Historical Society purchased the house and saved it from demolition.

Mr. Clark's original two-pen "dog-trot" log cabin was remodeled, added to, and enlarged several times by subsequent owners: first by the Ridge family who added a frame second floor over the two-pen and a one-story ell at the rear, then by the Pettigrews in 1877, when four rooms were added to the main block, thereby doubling its size. At the time, the roofline was altered to resemble the saltbox design. The house features a full-height, two-story entry porch and balcony, four chimneys, and four-over-four simple sash windows.

In 1975 a fire damaged much of the structure; the second floor, roof, and rear half of the house had to be reconstructed. During this work, a cellar—completely filled in with trash—was discovered and excavated by University of Arkansas archaeologists. In the entrance hall of the house the artifacts recovered in the digs are kept on exhibit. The Sarah B. N. Ridge House is listed on the National Register of Historic Places.

W. H. H. Clayton House

514 North Sixth Street
Fort Smith, AR 72901
(501) 783-3000

Contact: Fort Smith Heritage Foundation, Inc.

Open: Summer, Tues.-Fri. 10 a.m.–4 p.m.; winter, Tues.-Fri. Noon–4 p.m.; year-round, Sat 10 a.m.–4 p.m. and Sun. Noon–4 p.m.; Mondays by appointment

Admission: Adults $2.00; children (12-18) $1.00; children (under 12) free; special group rates

Activities: Guided tours, Victorian theme and antique-related lectures and socials, annual "Clayton Family at Christmas"

Suggested Time to View House: 45 minutes

Description of Grounds: Small city lot located in the Belle Grove Historic District. Flower gardens are reminiscent of those popular in the late 1880s; a side herb garden features culinary, fragrant, medicinal, and Shakespearean varieties

Best Season to View House: Early spring-late fall

Number of Yearly Visitors: 2,000

Year House Built: 1852, expansion 1882

Style of Architecture: Transitional Gothic Revival and Italianate

Number of Rooms: 14

On-Site Parking: Yes **Wheelchair Access:** Yes

Description of House

In 1864, twenty-four-year-old native Pennsylvanian William Henry Harrison Clayton moved to Pine Bluff, Arkansas; three years later he studied the law and was soon appointed Superintendent of Public Instruction over a seven-county school district. By the time he'd left office in 1870, Clayton had established thirty schools. He was then admitted to the bar and began a long and distinguished public career. His posts included: Prosecuting Attorney, Judge of the First Judicial Court, U. S. District Attorney, and Judge of the U.S. Court of the Indian Territory. In 1874, Clayton—who by then had married "Southern belle" Florence A. Barnes—moved to Fort Smith and into this house. In addition to his legal career, Clayton attained several high offices in the Masonic Lodge. He died in Oklahoma in 1920.

This three-story frame house, with its asymmetrical design, steeply-pitched roof, and gabled dormers, has been restored to appear exactly as it did during the years when Judge Clayton and his family lived here. Exterior details include: an exaggerated over-hang roof, paired window arrangements, a partial front porch, several one-story bay extensions, spindle-like balustrades on the porch and bay roof lines, and "punched"-design porch and foundation fillers. The chimneys, when viewed from the attic, are seen to be "warped" some two feet out of plumb; perhaps this configuration helped draw air up into the four fireplaces feeding into each chimney.

The interior features hand-carved wood work throughout, a beautiful black walnut staircase, handmade iron nails, elaborate coal-burning fireplaces, and fully reconstructed frescoes in the music room. The furniture dates from the 1880s ; much of it in the Rococo Revival-style, almost all of it donated by Agnes Oglesby.

Notable Collections on Exhibit

Four portraits hang in the foyer of the Clayton House: William H. H. Clayton and his three brothers, Judge Thomas J. Clayton (who lived and died in Pennsylvania), Powell Clayton (Governor of Arkansas during Reconstruction), and John Middleton (who was assassinated while running for Congress).

Brownlee-Noland House

Third and Scott Streets
Little Rock, AR 72201
(501) 324-9351

Contact: Arkansas Territorial Restoration
Open: Mon.-Sat. 9 a.m.–5 p.m., Sun.
1–5 p.m.; closed Easter, Thanksgiving,
Christmas Eve and Day, New Year's Day
Admission: Adults $2.00; seniors (65 and
over) $1.00; children (16 and under) $.50;
special youth group rates
Activities: Guided tours, "living history"
program, audiovisual presentations,
special events including the Craft Show
and Festival, and Christmas Open House
Suggested Time to View House: Museum
complex-1 hour
Best Season to View House: Year round

Facilities on Premises: Visitor center and
shop, art and craft gallery
Description of Grounds: City block
consisting of restored historic buildings
including the Hinderliter Grog Shop
(c. 1820s), the Brownlee-Noland House,
the McVicar-Conway House (c. 1840s),
and the pre-Civil War Plum Bayou Log
House
Number of Yearly Visitors: 50,000
Year House Built: c. 1840s
Style of Architecture: Federal
Number of Rooms: 3
On-Site Parking: Yes **Wheelchair Access:** Yes

Description of House

The Arkansas Territorial Restoration Project—spearheaded by Mrs. Louise Loughborough, a descendant of Arkansas's last territorial governor—began in 1939 with the restoration of the historic buildings on Block 32 of the original city of Little Rock and was opened to the public in July, 1941.

One of the buildings on the site is this simple, one-story Federal-style brick residence. It was built in the 1840s by Robert Brownlee, a Scottish stonemason, for his brother James, who lived in it while recovering from a mining accident. It is thought to be Brownlee's first attempt at building a brick structure; he would go on to build the Old State House in Little Rock. The walls are three bricks thick and the house features double-end chimneys and six-over-six windows on the east face only (to keep the house cool in summer and warm in winter). The interior has three rooms—a central hallway flanked by a bedroom on one side and a living/dining room on the other. All of the doors and mantels are original; the mantels are "marbleized."

Robert Brownlee who, with his brother, later moved to California, kept a detailed diary which was referred to extensively during the restoration process. After Brownlee's departure, the house is thought to have been lived in by C. F. M. Noland, a territorial legislator and writer—creator of the popular character Pete Whetstone—during the decade of the 1850s. It is currently furnished with appropriate period pieces.

Additional Information

Another important house at the Restoration is the Hinderliter Grog Shop. This structure—the oldest standing house in Little Rock—was built in the 1820s by Jesse Hinderliter who lived in it until 1834. The tavern he ran was a very popular local "watering hole"; it is also thought to be the site where the Territorial legislature last met in 1835.

Pike-Fletcher-Terry House

411 East Seventh Street, P.O. Box 2137
Little Rock, AR 72203
(501) 372-4000

Contact: Arkansas Arts Center Decorative Arts Museum

Open: Mon.-Sat. 10 a.m.–5 p.m., Sun. Noon–5 p.m.; holidays Noon–5 p.m.; closed Christmas Day

Admission: Free

Activities: Guided tours on Sun. at 1:30 p.m. and Wed. at Noon, group tours, educational programs, Regional Craft Biennial and the National Objects Invitational Biennial

Suggested Time to View House: 45 minutes

Best Season to View House: Early spring

Facilities on Premises: Museum with catalogues, art books and cards relating to the collection and exhibitions on sales

Description of Grounds: Landscaped grounds

Number of Yearly Visitors: 25,000

Year House Built: 1840, interior remodeled 1916

Style of Architecture: Exterior-Greek Revival, interior-Period Colonial Revival

Number of Rooms: 9

On-Site Parking: Yes **Wheelchair Access:** Yes

Description of House

The Pike-Fletcher-Terry House is considered the most significant house in Arkansas; when the Greek Revival-style structure was built in 1840 by Albert Pike what is now downtown Little Rock was forest and only two other buildings of consequence stood in the fledgling city—the State Capitol (Old State House) and the Arsenal Building. The Pike family lived here until 1871 but, during the last two years of the Civil War, it was occupied by Union troops and its contents pillaged. After the war, Albert Pike himself moved to Memphis, Tennessee, then Washington, D.C.

In 1871, Pike's daughter Lilian rented the house to the Arkansas Female College; fifteen years later, she sold it to one of that institution's teachers, Miss Lou Krause. When the College moved to smaller quarters, Miss Krause sold the house to her sister Adolphine and her husband, Colonel Fletcher. The couple had three children. In 1910—the year the Fletchers died—their daughter and her husband, David C. Terry, took possession of the house. The Terrys had been married in the front parlor of the house and lived here for the rest of their lives; they celebrated their fiftieth wedding anniversary in 1960. The house was given to the City of Little Rock by Mrs. Terry and her sister to be used by the Arkansas Arts Center. It underwent a thorough renovation in 1981.

The house that Albert Pike built had a symmetrical floor plan and the formal proportions and characteristic details of the Greek Revival style. These include the beautiful full-facade porch with its Ionic Order volutes and unfluted columns, and the main entry's elaborate entablature with decorative frieze work. The brick employed on the rear and side walls is distinctly inferior to the fine brick on the front facade; as such, it had to be painted to conform to the better material. The house was set amid fine formal gardens and the property had a number of outbuildings, many for the Pike slaves.

The floor plan featured four rooms on each floor flanking a wide center hallway; interior details include: pocket doors, oak flooring, and hallway moldings. Over the next century a number of alterations were made to the house, but the front downstairs rooms remain relatively unchanged. When the house was used by the College, the back porch was eliminated and classroom wings were added. The Fletchers removed these additions, altered the roof, and redecorated the interior in the late Victorian style. In 1916, the Terrys commissioned the prominent architect George R. Mann to do a thorough remodeling. Both of these major alterations can be clearly seen in the house today, since no attempt was made to return its appearance to that of the Pike years.

Notable Collections on Exhibit

Collections on display in the house include contemporary crafts by regional and national artists, European and American glass of the late 19th and early 20th centuries, and contemporary toys designed by artists. In addition, the museum is a leading exhibitor of many fine traveling shows.

Additional Information

The Pike-Fletcher-Terry House is listed on the National Register of Historic Places.

"Villa Marre"

1321 South Scott Street, P.O. Box 165023
Little Rock, AR 72216
(501) 374-9979

Contact: Quapaw Quarter Association
Open: Mon.-Fri. 9 a.m.–1 p.m., Sun. 1–5 p.m.
Admission: Adults $3.00; children (under 12)
  $2.00; senior group rates available
Activities: Guided tours
Suggested Time to View House: 30 minutes
Description of Grounds: Small city yard
  with trees and shrubs

Best Season to View House: Year round
Number of Yearly Visitors: 7,500
Year House Built: 1881, remodeled c. 1910
Style of Architecture: Transitional Italianate
  and Second Empire
Number of Rooms: 12
On-Site Parking: Yes **Wheelchair Access:** Yes

Description of House

The "Villa Marre"—which gained national recognition when it was used as the interior design studio on CBS's *Designing Women* television series—was built in 1881 by an Italian immigrant and saloon-keeper, Angelo Marre. He originally came from Italy to Memphis, Tennessee, as a young boy and moved to Little Rock at the age of thirty. Here he owned and operated a tavern and billiards parlor at 122 West Markham, now the site of the Excelsior Hotel and Convention Center. After his death in 1889, Marre's wife, Jennie, remarried and continued to live in the house. For the last four years of her life, it was rented out; one of the tenants was Arkansas Governor Jeff Davis.

In 1905, after Jennie's death, the house was purchased by Edgar Burton Kinsworthy, a lawyer who had served as Attorney General of Arkansas. Kinsworthy and his wife, Mary, hired the well-known local architect Charles L. Thompson to direct an extensive remodeling of the interior which is still visible in the southern rooms on the first and second floors. After the Kinsworthy years ended in 1929, the house fell into a thirty-five period of decline. Finally, in 1964 it was rescued by James W. Strawn, who engaged the architect John Truemper and led the first restoration of a Victorian property in Little Rock. Strawn named the house "Villa Marre" and dedicated its renovation to his mother; he donated it to the Quapaw Quarter Association in 1980.

Though the house was repaired and remodeled several times before being bought by Strawn and remodeled, many original details remain intact: the 19th-century kitchen cabinets, the Italianate-style front porch with its tiled floor, a reconstructed curved staircase featuring the original banister and some balusters, the parquet floor, and much of the decorative stenciling. The Kinsworthy-remodeled drawing room and dining room feature mantel pocket doors, crown molding, Craftsman-influenced paneling, and a beamed ceiling. The Penzel Sewing Room on the second floor has an unusual "crazy quilt"-pattern parquet floor.

The house is furnished in an eclectic array of pieces from the mid-19th to the early 20th century; many of these were collected by James Strawn from Little Rock's many fine Victorian-era homes.

Notable Collections on Exhibit

On display here is a collection of oil paintings done by Little Rock artist Benjamin Brantley.

Garvin Cavaness House

**404 South Main Street
Monticello, AR 71655
(501) 367-7446**

Contact: Drew County Historical Society
Open: Tues.-Fri. 1–5 p.m., Sat. and Sun.
2–5 p.m.; closed New Year's Day, Fourth
of July, Thanksgiving, Christmas Eve and
Day
Admission: Free
Activities: Guided tours, annual Christmas
Candlelight Tour
Suggested Time to View House: 1 hour
Facilities on Premises: Southeast Arkansas
Research and Archives Center

Description of Grounds: Shaded yard with
plantings located in the Monticello
Historic District. A relocated historic
smokehouse built in 1832 and the Peter
Rives Cabin built in 1820 are sited also on
the property.
Best Season to View House: Spring
Number of Yearly Visitors: 3,000
Year House Built: 1907
Style of Architecture: Eclectic Neoclassical
Number of Rooms: 12
On-Site Parking: Yes **Wheelchair Access:** No

Description of House

In 1907 Monticello businessman Garvin Cavaness built this unusual Neoclassical-style mansion for his new bride. In 1969 it was acquired by the Drew County Historical Society; two years later, primarily through the efforts of Mr. and Mrs. Eric Hardy, the Society opened their museum here.

The Cavaness House is unusual because it is built out of unusually-produced cement brick: when a train derailed nearby, it spilled its load of cement on the tracks. The cement was then hauled to the building site where Cavaness ordered the contractor to use it to make his bricks! The house he built features a full-width, full-length porch with Ionic columns, simple sash window treatments with squared hood molds, and a main entry glazed door and side panels highlighted by a large elliptical fanlight almost Palladian in style.

The house contains many wonderful period furnishings, including a rosewood bed and wardrobe made in Kentucky in 1843 and a chair that converts into a table.

Notable Collections on Exhibit

The Museum contains many fascinating objects, including: handkerchiefs handmade by local women in the late 1800s, an Edison gramophone, a set of hand-painted French china, a "Doctor's Room" full of late 19th-century medical paraphernalia, a collection of antique quilts, and an extensive collection of Native American artifacts and pottery.

Additional Information

The Garvan Cavaness House is listed on the National Register of Historic Places. It stands in the Monticello Historic District which comprises forty-two buildings, including the Joe Lee Allen House at 713 North Main Street—sometimes called the "Ghost House."

Elkhorn Tavern

Highway 62 East
Pea Ridge, AR 72751
(501) 451-8122

Contact: National Park Service and the Pea Ridge National Military Park
Open: Summer, park hours daily 8 a.m.–5 p.m.; house closed winter months
Admission: Adults $1.00; seniors and the disabled free
Activities: Self-guiding auto tour
Suggested Time to View House: 30 minutes
Facilities on Premises: Park visitor center

Description of Grounds: Park featuring Civil War battlefied in western Arkansas
Best Season to View House: Summer
Number of Yearly Visitors: 140,000
Year House Built: Original-1830, new construction-1865
Style of Architecture: Federal
Number of Rooms: 5, upstairs rooms closed to the public
On-Site Parking: Yes **Wheelchair Access:** Yes

Description of House

The Federal-style Elkhorn Tavern—so named for the elk antlers mounted under the building's eaves—stands in the Pea Ridge National Military Park. The Battle of Pea Ridge was fought on March 7 and 8, 1862, and proved to be one of the decisive battles in the Western Theater of the Civil War; in it, Union forces under General Samuel Curtis routed the Confederate troops commanded by General Earl Van Dorn and thereby effectively ended the possibility that Missouri would come under Rebel rule. It was also the battle in which the popular Confederate General Ben McCulloch fell.

The tavern was at the very eye of the fighting—it is reported that the bodies of Confederate dead were stacked on its porch like firewood—and was burned to the ground shortly after the battle by guerrillas. It was rebuilt by the Cox family, who had owned it at the time of its destruction. Members of the family lived here until 1905 when it was acquired by Lorenza Scott. Melinda Cox Scott was the last occupant of the tavern before it was taken over by the National Park Service in 1960.

The present structure was completely rebuilt by the National Park Service based on photographs taken around 1880. It is thought that the structure is an accurate reproduction of the pre-Civil War tavern; it is a two-story structure featuring a full-height and width front porch and balcony, and a sloping shed roof at the rear of the house. There are also two end-gable chimneys made of native stone. Inside, there are two public rooms downstairs connected by a door and two staircases leading to the upper rooms which are separated by a partition.

Notable Collections on Exhibit

Because the tavern and its contents were burned after the Battle of Pea Ridge, none of the items currently on display here can be said to be original. They are, however, period pieces which accurately reflect life in the Ozarks in the latter decades of the 19th century. The visitor center at the park entrance has a fine exhibit of Civil War weapons and uniforms.

Hawkins House

322 South Second Street
Rogers, AR 72756
(501) 621-1154

Contact: Rogers Historical Museum
Open: Year-round, Tues.-Sat. 10 a.m.–4 p.m.;
closed major holidays
Admission: Free
Activities: Guided and holiday theme tours,
exhibits, annual Victorian Christmas
Open House
Suggested Time to View House: 15 minutes
Facilities on Premises: Museum and gift shop

Description of Grounds: Front and side
yard with foundation plantings, patio
garden with perennials
Best Season to View House: Spring-fall
Number of Yearly Visitors: 12,000
Year House Built: 1895
Style of Architecture: Folk Victorian, brick
Number of Rooms: 5
On-Site Parking: Yes **Wheelchair Access:** Yes

Description of House

The Hawkins House was built in 1895 by the Matthews brothers who
are credited with erecting many of Rogers's buildings. It was built for
Alexander Oakley, a local businessman. Five years later, the house was
purchased by Francis C. Hawkins and his family. It stayed in the Hawkings
family for some seventy-nine years. Hawkins, the owner of a livery stable,
was a well-respected member of the community; after he died, his son Frank
moved his family into the house to be with his mother. Frank was a former
professional baseball player and umpire who'd become a teacher. Many of
the town's residents who attended his classes back in the 'thirties and 'forties
remember him fondly to this day. After his widow Lillian died in 1979, the
Hawkins family gave up the home to be used as the Rogers Historical
Museum.

The Hawkins House is a fine example of a typical brick folk Victorian-
style cottage belonging to a turn-of-the-century middle class family in this
region of the country. Although it is modest in scale, it conveys a sense of
proportion and solidity which many larger, more grandiose residences
never achieve; it has also been the subject of much historical investigation.

The house is currently interpreted as a typical residence of the area; it
features off-white wood molding, wallcoverings in various then-popular
revival styles, a front gable with decorative vergeboards, a modified
pyramidal ridged roof line, and two porches—one open and one screened.
The furnishings are mostly factory-made pieces in one of three styles:
Eastlake, "cottage," and Revival.

Additional Information

In 1995, on the one-hundredth anniversary of the its construction, the
museum is planning a grand re-opening of historic Hawkins House.

John D. Trimble House

Washington Street and Highway 195
P.O. Box 127
Washington, AR 71862
(501) 983-2828

Contact: Pioneer Washington Restoration
Foundation, Inc.

Open: Year-round, daily 9 a.m.–4 p.m.;
closed Thanksgiving, Christmas, New
Year's Day

Admission: Adults $4.50; children (6-12)
$2.50 plus state sales tax; group
discounts available

Activities: Guided tours

Suggested Time to View House: 30 minutes

Number of Yearly Visitors: 80,000

Description of Grounds: Restored
outbuildings and yard

Year House Built: c. 1847

Number of Rooms: 5

Best Season to View House: Spring and
summer

Style of Architecture: Greek Revival

On-Site Parking: Yes **Wheelchair Access:** No

Description of House

The oldest continuously operating post office in the State of Arkansas—established on February 23, 1820—is in the historic Village of Washington. Here John D. Trimble made a name for himself as one of the settlement's early and most successful merchants and built this fine Greek Revival-style home around 1847. Three more generations of the Trimble family followed John D. in living here before the house, its grounds, and its contents were given to the Pioneer Washington Restoration Foundation.

The house that Trimble built is a one-story frame structure with a full-height entry porch. Other exterior details include: wide band trim, paired, square columns, a pyramidal-shaped roofline, and six-over-six window treatments with shutters. Inside, there are many fine reproductions of period decorative elements, especially the window coverings and wallpapers, including a Richard Thibaut reproduction in the entrance hallway.

Many of the furnishings on display are original to the house; pieces include: a hand-painted plantation desk with faux-mahogany graining, an Empire-style Mallard tester bed, and a 1920 oak sideboard in the style of the Arts and Crafts Movement.

Additional Information

One of the finest and most extensive historic sites in the United States is the Old Washington Historic State Park. It comprises an entire district of both public and private buildings, most of which were built between 1830 and 1880. The log and wood frame structures are predominantly in the Greek Revival style; a complete tour takes at least half a day. For more information, please write or call. The address is Highway 4 North and Interstate 30 Exit 30, P.O. Box 98, Washington, Arkansas 71862; the phone number is (501) 983-2684.

Illinois

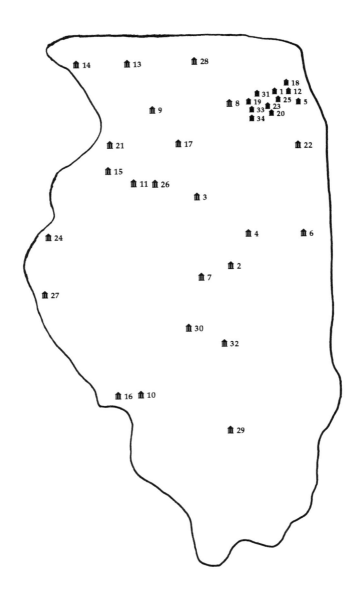

1. **Arlington Heights**
   Banta House
   Muller House

2. **Bement**
   *Bryant Cottage State Historic
   Site*

3. **Bloomington**
   *David Davis Mansion State
   Historic Site*

4. **Champaign**
   Wilber Mansion

5. **Chicago**
   Frederick C. Robie House
   Henry B. Clarke House
   John J. Glessner House

6. **Danville**
   *Dr. William Fithian Home–
   Vermilion County Museum*
   Lamon House

7. **Decatur**
   James Millikin Homestead

8. **DeKalb**
   Ellwood House Museum

9. **Dixon**
   Ronald Reagan Boyhood Home

10. **Edwardsville**
    John Weir House

11. **Elmwood**
    Lorado Taft Museum

12. **Evanston**
    Charles Gates Dawes House

13. **Freeport**
    *Oscar Taylor House–
    "Bohemiana"*

14. **Galena**
    Daniel A. Barrows House
    *U. S. Grant Home State
    Historic Site*

15. **Galesburg**
    *Carl A. Sandburg State
    Historic Site*

16. **Granite City**
    *Historic Emmert House and
    Old Six Mile Museum*

17. **Hennepin**
    Pulsifer House

18. **Highland Park**
    Francis Stupey Log Cabin
    Jean Butz James Museum

19. **LaFox**
    1846 Garfield Inn

20. **Lockport**
    *Illinois and Michigan Canal
    Commissioner's Office and
    Residence*

21. **Moline**
    Butterworth Center, "Hillcrest"
    Deere-Wiman House, "Overlook"

22. **Momence**
    Momence Historical House

23. **Naperville**
    *Martin-Mitchell Mansion at
    Naper Settlement Museum
    Village*

24. **Nauvoo**
    Brigham Young Home
    Heber C. Kimball Home
    John Taylor Home
    *Joseph Smith Homestead and
    Mansion House*
    Sarah and Hiram Kimball Home
    Wilford Woodruff Home

25. Oak Park
Frank Lloyd Wright Home
and Studio

26. Peoria
John C. Flanagan House
Pettengill-Morron House
Museum

27. Quincy
Governor John Wood Mansion

28. Rockford
Erlander Home Museum
Tinker Swiss Cottage

29. Salem
William Jennings Bryan
Birthplace

30. Springfield
Frank Lloyd Wright's Dana-
Thomas House State Historic Site

Lincoln Home National
Historic Site

31. St. Charles
Dunham Hunt House–
"Oaklawn"

32. Taylorville
James Canty Morrison House

33. West Chicago
Kline Creek Farm at Timber
Ridge Forest Preserve
Kruse House Museum

34. Westmount
William L. Gregg House Museum

Banta House

Contact: Arlington Heights Historical
Society and Museum

Open: Sat. and Sun., guided tours 2 p.m.,
3 p.m., Mon.-Fri., guided tours for
groups

Admission: Adults $1.00; children $.50

Activities: Guided tours, exhibits, classes
and special events throughout the year

Suggested Time to View House: 1 hour

Facilities on Premises: Gift shop

Description of Grounds: 1 acre yard
surrounded by decorative fencing

Best Season to View House: Year round

Number of Yearly Visitors: 5,000

Year House Built: 1908

Number of Rooms: 8

Style of Architecture: Prairie School

On-Site Parking: No **Wheelchair Access:** Yes

Description of House

This restored Craftsman/Prairie-influenced house was built in 1908 for Wilhelmina Müller and Nathaniel Banta. The property adjoins that of the Müller home where Wilhelmina grew up; the two houses, taken together, along with some other structures belonging to the Müller family, now comprise the Arlington Heights Museum.

The house is a typical Prairie-style American foursquare structure designed by the Elgin architect, E. Abel. It has been completely restored to the period just before the First World War, 1908 to 1916, and the interior is furnished with donated Mission, Arts & Crafts, and Colonial Revival furniture, all of which is appropriate to the period.

Notable Collections on Exhibit

On display in the Banta House are several Wallace Nutting prints and the Martha Mills Doll Collection.

Müller House

500 North Vail Avenue
Arlington Heights, IL 60004
(708) 255-1225

Contact: Arlington Heights Historical
Society and Museum
Open: Sat. and Sun., guided tours at 2 p.m.
and 3 p.m., Mon.-Fri., guided tours for
six or more by appointment only
Admission: Adults $1.00; children $.50
Activities: Guided tours, exhibits, classes
and special events throughout the year
Suggested Time to View House: 1 hour
Facilities on Premises: Gift shop
Description of Grounds: 1 acre yard
surrounded by decorative fencing
Best Season to View House: Year round
Number of Yearly Visitors: 5,000
Year House Built: 1882
Number of Rooms: 13

Style of Architecture: Folk Victorian
On-Site Parking: Yes **Wheelchair Access:** No

Description of House

Built in 1882 for F. W. Müller, an Arlington Heights manufacturer of soda pop, this house is a good example of the Victorian style of the last two decades of the nineteenth century. Interestingly enough, before Müller constructed a soda factory in 1906 on his adjacent property, the basement of this house served that function. Nearby is the coach house where the horses and wagons used to deliver the soda pop were kept and, as mentioned in the entry for the Banta House above, the entire complex now serves as a museum.

This two story brick house with its English basement was originally a one story structure; the second floor was added in 1896. The simple roof is supported with brackets. Inside, the authentic wall coverings—the parlor is wallpapered in gold and olive and the office in a deep burgundy—and the many pieces of period furniture give an accurate representation of a typical Victorian interior of the 1890s.

Two other structures at this location are worth mentioning. The first floor of the former soda pop factory has become the Country Store, a fine antiques and collectibles shop, and the nearby Log Cabin, constructed of hand-hewn logs and shake shingles, is a representation of a typical home of those early settlers who founded the community of Arlington Heights.

Additional Information

The Müller House is listed on the National Register of Historic Places.

Bryant Cottage State Historic Site

Contact: Illinois Historic Preservation
Agency
Open: Wed.-Sat. Noon–4 p.m.
Admission: Donations accepted
Activities: Guided tours
Suggested Time to View House:
20–40 minutes
Description of Grounds: .3 acre lot
Best Season to View House: Spring-fall
Number of Yearly Visitors: 8,500
Year House Built: 1856
Number of Rooms: 4

146 East Wilson Street, P.O. Box 41
Bement, IL 61813
(217) 678-8184

Style of Architecture: Greek Revival
On-Site Parking: Yes **Wheelchair Access:** Yes

Description of House

At the age of fifteen Francis E. Bryant moved from New Hampshire to Ohio with his parents, then came to Illinois four years later. On July 4, 1840, he married Sarah E. Briscoe and the couple began a family; in 1856 they moved to Bement. Here Bryant opened the first bank in the village and a store specializing in grain, coal, lumber, and salt; he also built his cottage here just a hundred feet from the railroad tracks. The successful businessman soon became a successful politician, serving two terms in the state legislature, and as mayor and postmaster of Bement. Bryant became a close friend of Senator Stephen A. Douglas and headed a group of business leaders who supported the "Little Giant" in his race against Abraham Lincoln; the agreement between Lincoln and Douglas to engage in a series of debates was hammered out in the parlor of Bryant's cottage. The cottage remained in the family until the end of the 19th century when it was sold and moved. In 1925, Bryant's grandson, John Sprague, bought the house and returned it to its original site; in 1947 it was given to the state.

This modest four-room frame house features a small entry porch with Victorian spindle-work posts; the floor plan consists of a bedroom, sitting room, parlor, and kitchen. Interior details include carpets laid over the plank floors, a cast-iron stove used to heat the house, and wallpaper in three of the rooms. The interior has been fully restored to interpret the period from 1850 to 1880 and the furnishings—some of which are original—are period pieces dating to the same era.

David Davis Mansion State Historic Site

1000 East Monroe Street
Bloomington, IL 61701
(309) 828-1084

Contact: Illinois Historic Preservation Agency

Open: Wed.-Sun. Noon–4 p.m.; closed Thanksgiving, Christmas, New Year's Day

Admission: Free

Activities: Guided tour, pretour presentation, annual holiday event

Suggested Time to View House: 90 minutes

Facilities on Premises: Gift shop

Description of Grounds: 4 acres of park-like lawns and formal flower gardens

Style of Architecture: Italianate with Second Empire elements

Best Season to View House: Spring-fall

Number of Yearly Visitors: 30,000

Number of Rooms: 14

Year House Built: 1872

On-Site Parking: Yes **Wheelchair Access:** Yes

Description of House

This impressive house was built in 1872 for David Davis (1815-1886), an Illinois lawyer who was appointed to the United States Supreme Court by Abraham Lincoln in 1862. Davis, who had been Lincoln's political mentor, friend, and campaign manager, served on the high court until 1872. In that year, the Judge was chosen to be the Presidential nominee for the newly formed National Labor Reform Party; his withdrawal from that nomination helped cause that party's collapse. Davis was executor of Lincoln's estate and legal guardian of the slain President's son, Todd. His wife was Sarah Walker, daughter of the Massachusetts judge William Walker.

This completely restored Italianate-style mansion, with its stucco overlaid solid brick exterior featuring delicate wrought-iron cresting on the balconies and peak, and characteristic heavy quoins, is an excellent showplace for the comforts that the newly industrialized economy afforded its beneficiaries. It features three bathrooms, running water, a coal-burning central heating system, and two communications systems. The furnishings, many of which are original to the home, are mostly in the style of the Renaissance Revival.

Additional Information

The David Davis Mansion is listed on the National Register of Historic Places.

Wilber Mansion

709 West University Avenue
Champaign, IL 61820
(217) 356-1010

Contact: Champaign County Historical Museum

Open: Guided tours, Wed.-Sun. 1–4 p.m.; closed between Christmas and New Year's Day, month of January

Admission: Adults $2.00; children (under 12) $.50

Activities: Guided tours, audiovisual presentations, demonstrations, May Heritage Program for children

Suggested Time to View House: 30–60 minutes

Facilities on Premises: Gift shop with books

Description of Grounds: Large yard with herb garden

Best Season to View House: Spring and summer

Style of Architecture: Victorian Queen Anne, brick

Number of Yearly Visitors: 8,000

Year House Built: Between 1904 and 1907

Number of Rooms: 17 open to the public

On-Site Parking: Yes **Wheelchair Access:** No

Description of House

The Wilber Mansion was built by Roger Sloan Wilber and his wife, Elizabeth, who had come to Champaign from New York in the 1860s. Evidence suggests that the Wilbers built the house for their then-single, thirty-five-year-old daughter, Ella, an expert china painter. Roger, who, with his son's help, had made the transition from being a farmer and drayman to becoming a successful coal dealer and merchant, died in 1910. Three years later, Ella married William Wallace Paul, a shoe store owner, and they lived in the house with Ella's mother, brother, and sister-in-law. The Pauls had to mortgage the house after suffering financial difficulties in the Great Crash of 1929; eventually, they lost it. In 1934, it was bought by Dean C. M. Thompson, head of the Commerce Department at the University of Illinois. The last private owners were Dr. and Mrs. H. Ewing Wachter, who lived here from 1964 to 1974, when it was sold to the Champaign County Historical Museum.

This large and graceful Queen Anne-style mansion is constructed of glazed red brick and concrete blocks; therefore the exterior lacks some of the surface details found on the more typical Queen Anne-style homes built of wood. It does have the bow windows, bays, and gables common to the style.

The leaded glass doors and windows are set into frames having brass studs, and the brass door-knobs are embossed with the letter "W." Interior details include: fireplaces framed by hand-painted ceramic tiles, the original copper and marble sinks, an old ice box in the butler's pantry, original lighting fixtures in the bathrooms, and curved radiators. The furnishings have all been collected from the turn-of-the-century period.

Notable Collections on Exhibit

The Mansion is now the Champaign County Historical Museum; the Museum's collections consist of approximately 10,000 artifacts relating to the history of the county from the 1850s to the present.

Frederick C. Robie House

5757 South Woodlawn Avenue
Chicago, IL 60637
(312) 702-8374

Contact: Universtiy of Chicago
Open: Daily Noon-1 p.m.; closed national holidays
Admission: Adults $5.00; seniors and students with I.D. $1.00
Activities: Guided tour
Suggested Time to View House: 1 hour
Facilities on Premises: Gift shop and book store
Best Season to View House: Year round

Description of Grounds: Corner city lot with small enclosed courtyard and motor court
Number of Yearly Visitors: 8,000
Year House Built: Between 1908 and 1910
Style of Architecture: Prairie School
Number of Rooms: 17, 3 rooms open to the public
On-Site Parking: No
Wheelchair Access: No

Description of House

This house, designed and built by Frank Lloyd Wright for the bicycle manufacturer Frederick C. Robie and his wife, Lora, is one of the landmarks of American Prairie-style architecture and one of three structures which Wright himself designated as his favorites. Commissioned in 1906 and completed in 1910, the house was lived in only briefly by the couple and their two young children. In 1909, Frederick Robie's father had died, leaving his son with a crushing debt which forced him to sell the house in 1911 to the David Taylor family who sold it a year later to Marshall Dodge Wilbur, a former commodore of the Chicago Yacht Club. Wilbur, who lived here with his family until 1926, is said to have been fascinated by Wright's prairie schooner. After the Wilburs, the house was owned by the Chicago Theological Seminary which could not make good use of the facility—in 1941 it was slated for demolition and only the onset of World War II saved the house. When the Seminary announced demolition plans again in 1957, the Robie House was bought by the contracting firm Webb & Knapp. Six years later, it was donated to the University of Chicago where it now serves as the home of that school's Alumni Association.

In the Robie House one sees all of the hallmarks of Wright's mature Prairie style: elongated horizontal planes, limestone bands, exaggerated roof overhangs, hidden balconies, and a flowing interior floor plan highlighted by massive stone fireplaces and the use of art glass as a decorative element. The sculptural shape, the use of unpainted brick and natural oak, and the wall of windows all serve to create an oasis in the metropolis. The apparent unity of design goes beyond the aesthetic into the very mechanics of the space: Wright filled the house with engineering innovations such as natural air-conditioning, self-watering planters, a central vacuum system, and a three-car garage. He also designed all of the furniture, lighting fixtures, window treatments, and rugs so as to create a total environment. The original pieces have been removed from the house and replaced by reproductions taken from Wright's designs.

Notable Collections on Exhibit

The original Wright-designed furnishings which were removed from the Robie House are kept on display at the University of Chicago's Smart Museum.

Additional Information

The Frederick C. Robie House is listed on the National Register of Historic Places. Those who enjoy their visit to this house should travel to the Chicago suburb of Oak Park and see the Frank Lloyd Wright Home and Studio, which is also listed in this guide.

Henry B. Clarke House

Contact: Chicago Architecture Foundation
Open: Guided tours, Wed. and Fri., Sat. and Sun. at Noon, 1 p.m., 2 p.m., 3 p.m
Admission: Adults $5.00/$8.00 if touring Glessner House
Activities: Guided tours, school group tours
Suggested Time to View House: 60–90 minutes
Best Season to View House: Summer

Facilities on Premises: Gift shop and tour center at the Glessner Carriage House
Description of Grounds: Public park and adjacent to the John J. Glessner House
Number of Yearly Visitors: 8,000
Year House Built: 1836
Style of Architecture: Greek Revival
Number of Rooms: 9
On-Site Parking: Yes **Wheelchair Access:** Yes

Description of House

The Henry B. Clarke house is the oldest house in Chicago and the city's only surviving example of Greek Revival architecture. It was built by Henry and Caroline Clarke who'd moved to the three-year-old pioneer town in 1835, purchased some twenty acres on the shore of Lake Michigan near Fort Dearborn, and erected a small log cabin on the site. The following year, they began construction on their "real" house. In 1837, the Clarkes lost all their money in the infamous Bank Panic of that year and construction stopped. During those hard times, the unfinished rooms in the house were hung with the carcasses of the game that Henry hunted for survival's sake. He died in the cholera epidemic of 1849 but his widow sold off some of the 20 acre property and completed the house before the Civil War. Particularly impressive is the Italianate-style cupola added to the roof. The house survived the Great Chicago Fire of 1871 and a move 40 blocks south of its original site before the City of Chicago bought it, moved it again—to its present location only three blocks from where it originally stood—and completely restored it, winning an award from the American Institute of Architects in the process.

The two-story white frame house was constructed employing the post-and-beam method even though balloon frame construction was more commonly used in Chicago at that time. The exterior is chiefly noted for the cupola which Mrs. Clarke added in the 1850s; that detail, and the size of the house, lead some to level the charge of pretension at the Clarkes, who were certainly not among Chicago's wealthy elite. Inside, the parlors are finished with carved woodwork and plaster ceiling medallions. The house has been furnished by the National Society of the Colonial Dames in the State of Illinois; the pieces, all of which are original to the 1830-1850 period, include nothing which actually belonged to the Clarkes.

Additional Information

The Henry B. Clarke House is located in Chicago's Prairie Avenue Historic District near the site of the 1812 Fort Dearborn Massacre. It is listed on the National Register of Historic Places.

John J. Glessner House

1800 South Prairie Avenue
Chicago, IL 60604
(312) 922-3432

Contact: Chicago Architecture Foundation

Open: Guided tours, Wed. and Fri., Sat. and Sun. at Noon, 1 p.m., 2 p.m., 3 p.m.

Admission: Adults $5.00/$8.00 if touring Clarke House

Activities: Guided tours, school group tours

Suggested Time to View House: 60–90 minutes

Facilities on Premises: Museum, gift shop and tour center at the Glessner Carriage House

Description of Grounds: Located in the Prairie Avenue Historic District and adjacent to the Henry B. Clarke House

Best Season to View House: Summer

Number of Yearly Visitors: 8,000

Number of Rooms: 33, 16 open to the public

Style of Architecture: Richardsonian Romanesque

Year House Built: c. 1880

On-Site Parking: Yes **Wheelchair Access:** Yes

Description of House

In 1886, John J. Glessner, one of Chicago's wealthiest citizens, commissioned the famous American architect Henry Hobson Richardson to design this Prairie Avenue house. What he got was something radically different from other houses then being built, an elegant and unique residence which broke the bounds of tradition and came to be called Richardson's "finest urban residence." The Glessners lived in the house until their deaths in the 1930s. When it was threatened with demolition in 1966, a foundation was formed to save it; it was restored to its 1890s grandeur and now boasts the distinction of being the only Richardson house in the United States open to the public and the first building in Chicago to be both declared a National Historic Landmark and listed on the National Register of Historic Places.

The simple pink granite exterior of the house has a marked resoluteness and sense of substance, especially in contrast to its neighbors. It is a powerful statement of Richardson's idea of a modern "American" architecture—an idea which would fuel the work of his successors, John Root, Louis Sullivan, and Frank Lloyd Wright. The interior floor plan, with its main rooms that are turned inward to face a sun-filled courtyard, also turns its back on tradition. Many rooms have been restored using reproductions of the English Arts & Crafts wallpapers and fabrics made by the William Morris Company. There are many Glessner family pieces on display; in addition to furniture made by Richardson's own Boston firm, there are pieces made by the Herter Brothers of New York and some intricate hand-carved items fashioned by Isaac E. Scott of Chicago.

Additional Information

Like the Henry B. Clarke House listed above, the Glessner House is in the Prairie Avenue Historic District on the site of the 1812 Dearborn Massacre. It is also listed on the National Register of Historic Places.

Dr. William Fithian Home– Vermilion County Museum

**116 North Gilbert Street
Danville, IL 61832
(217) 442-2922**

Contact: Vermilion County Museum Society

Open: Tues.-Sat. 10 a.m.– 5 p.m.,
Sun. 1–5 p.m.; closed major holidays

Admission: Adults $1.00; children $.50

Activities: Guided tours by appointment,
special exhibits and contests, seasonal
events including Lincoln's Birthday Open
House and July Quilt Show

Suggested Time to View House: 1 hour

Facilities on Premises: Gift shop

Description of Grounds: Nationally
recognized herb garden

Best Season to View House: Spring
and summer

Number of Yearly Visitors: 6,000

Number of Rooms: 14

Style of Architecture: Italianate with Greek
Revival modifications

Year House Built: 1855, addition c.1895

On-Site Parking: Yes **Wheelchair Access:** No

Description of House

Dr. William Fithian, prairie legislator, horseback doctor, Civil War surgeon and friend to Abraham Lincoln, settled in Danville in 1830. Here he would live and practice for the next 60 years. In 1850, the fifty-year-old doctor married Josephine Culbertson and five years later they built the house which now bears his name. On September 21, 1858, in the midst of his historic senatorial campaign against Stephen A. Douglas, Abraham Lincoln visited Danville for a political rally; while here, he delivered an informal speech from the balcony of his friend's house and stayed the night. The upstairs room in which the future President spent the night has been restored to appear as it would have then—its furnishings even include the original canopied bed upon which Lincoln slept. In 1880, at the age of eighty-one, Dr. Fithian finally set up an office in the house which he would use for his practice until his death in 1890. The home was then used as a rooming house until Charles Feldkamp bought it in 1895. The Feldkamps, who added the front porch and windows on the south side of the house, lived here for the next forty-eight years.

The house is a symmetrical, center-gabled mixture of the Greek Revival and Italianate styles; it has a columned porch and a hipped roof with side balconies extending from the second floor. The interior rooms of note include the doctor's office, the parlor, the den, the maid's room and, of course, the famous Lincoln Room. The furnishings include some original pieces, but the majority are late Victorian. The Dr. William Fithian Home is listed on the National Register of Historic Places.

Notable Collections on Exhibit

The Fithian Home now serves as the Vermilion County Museum and features an extensive collection of personal artifacts belonging to many of Danville's prominent citizens, including those of Joseph G. Cannon, member of the U. S. House of Representatives and Speaker of that body from 1903 to 1911.

Lamon House

Lincoln Park on North Logan Avenue
Danville, IL 61832
(217) 442-2922

Contact: Vermilion County Museum Society
Open: May-Oct. Sun 1:30–4:30; other times
by special appointment
Admission: Adults $1.00; children $.50
Activities: Individual and group guided
tours available
Suggested Time to View House:
30 minutes
Facilities on Premises: Conference room
Description of Grounds: Located in
park setting
Best Season to View House: Spring-fall
Year House Built: 1850 with later additions
Style of Architecture: Rural Greek Revival
Number of Rooms: 6

On-Site Parking: No **Wheelchair Access:** No

Description of House

Melissa Beckwith, daughter of Daniel Beckwith, after whom the town of Danville is named, married Joseph Lamon and, in 1850, they built this frame house. Joseph's cousin was Ward Hill Lamon, a local attorney who had been Abraham Lincoln's law partner and confidant, and who followed the newly elected President to Washington to act as his bodyguard during the Civil War. In the 1850s, when Lincoln and his partner were riding Illinois's Eighth Judicial Circuit, it is quite likely that they stopped in Danville and stayed at this house on more than one occasion.

The simple, one-story structure is thought to be the oldest frame house in Danville. The Lamon House has been restored to the 1850 to 1875 period, furnished with local antique pieces and decorated with appropriate period wallpaper motifs.

Additional Information

Prior to relocation, the Lamon House served as law offices to two local attorneys, the Wright Brothers, who gave the house to the Vermilion County Museum Society.

James Millikin Homestead

125 North Pine Street
Decatur, IL 62522
(217) 422-9003

Contact: James Millikin Homestead, Inc.
Open: Mar.-Oct., last Sunday 2–4 p.m.;
daily, guided group tours by
appointment
Admission: Free; nominal fee for groups
Activities: Victorian Christmas Open House
Suggested Time to View House:
45–60 minutes
Description of Grounds: 5 acres of lawn
and restored gardens with carriage house
Best Season to View House: Year round
Year House Built: Started 1875, completed
1876, remodeled 1883
Style of Architecture: Italianate, towered
with Second Empire influence
Number of Rooms: 11, 9 open to public
On-Site Parking: Yes
Wheelchair Access: No

Description of House

In 1849 James Millikin and his father, a prosperous Pennsylvania farmer, began herding livestock west from Pennsylvania to Indiana and Illinois. The business was quite successful and, by the mid-1850s, James began purchasing large tracts of land in Illinois and Iowa. In 1856, he moved to Decatur and married Anna Bernice Aston on New Year's Day 1857. During the first years of their marriage, they traveled extensively, collecting many pieces of art along the way. In 1860, Millikin divested himself of his holdings and founded the bank which he'd been persuaded Decatur needed; two years later, he purchased the 22 acre tract that includes the present homestead site. Here the couple built their home and practiced their philanthropy: Anna helped establish the 1880 Decatur Art Class and James founded the well-regarded university which bears his name. After he died in 1909, and his wife in 1913, the home stood vacant for many years, though it was pressed into service as an emergency hospital during the flu epidemic of 1918. It was deeded to Millikin University in 1942 and served as the school's Art Institute until 1969.

The exterior of this large, red brick house features a square, three-and-a-half-story mansard-roofed tower, a veranda, oriel windows, modillions on the second-story pediments, and iron cresting on the roofs. Inside, the floor plan resembles that of Millikin's Pennsylvania birthplace—a first floor comprised of a large central hall, two parlors, a dining room, a library, the kitchen and breakfast room, and a second floor consisting entirely of bedrooms. The elaborate interior details include: plaster ceiling reliefs throughout the first floor, a walnut and butternut staircase, muslin-covered ivory walls in the parlors, acid-etched camphor glass doors, and an Art

Nouveau stained glass window in the north bay of the breakfast room. Beneath the stained glass oriel window on the landing of the relocated staircase is a bench that seats ten. The northeast bedroom was known as the "Snowball Room" because of the painted hydrangeas which once graced the ceiling.

Notable Collections on Exhibit

There is a small photography exhibit in the breakfast room focusing on the Millikins. Furnishings are of the same period as the house; most of the major pieces, including the Eastlake dining room set, belonged to the Millikins and are original to this home.

Additional Information

The James Millikin Homestead is listed on the National Register of Historic Places.

Ellwood House Museum

509 North First Street
DeKalb, IL 60115
(815) 756-4609

Contact: Ellwood House Association
Open: Apr.-Dec., Tues.-Fri. guided tours
1 p.m, 3 p.m.; Sat. and Sun. guided tours
1 p.m., 2 p.m., 3 p.m.
Admission: Adults $3.50;
children (6-14) $1.00
Activities: Guided tours, lecture series,
special seasonal events including July Art
Fair, August Ice Cream Social and
Christmas Open House
Suggested Time to View House: 90 minutes
Facilities on Premises: Small gift shop
Description of Grounds: 9 acres of grounds
and gardens
Style of Architecture: Mix of Gothic Revival
with later additions of Colonial Revival

Best Season to View House: Spring
Number of Yearly Visitors: 10,000
Year House Built: 1879, additions 1898
and 1911
Number of Rooms: 30
On-Site Parking: Yes **Wheelchair Access:** Yes

Description of House

Isaac Ellwood (1833-1910) was the principal manufacturer of barbed wire fencing in DeKalb, the city where the barbed wire industry began with Joseph Glidden's 1874 patent in which Ellwood had purchased a one-half interest. He quickly became one of the richest men in all of Illinois. In 1879, he commissioned Chicago architect George O. Garnsey to design a house commensurate with that wealth to be built on his 1,000 acre estate. His son, Perry Ellwood, inherited the house in 1910 and lived here with his wife until 1964.

The three-story Gothic Revival structure features elaborate dormers topped with decorative pinnacles and iron cresting around the roof. A Colonial Revival-style portico was added in 1898. The most impressive interior features are a three-story "rotunda" with spiral staircase and the Jacobean-style living room, created in 1911 when the two parlors were combined. The furnishings are all originals belonging to the two generations of Ellwoods.

On the grounds of the Ellwood house is a feature of extraordinary interest: a Victorian playhouse, originally designed as a builder's model and parade float, first installed for Isaac's grandchildren. Called "The Little House," it has been faithfully restored to its original appearance, that of a completely authentic miniature Gothic Revival house with Victorian and Queen Anne details—its decorated vergeboards, elaborate Eastlake spindlework, and wood shingles are quite remarkable.

Notable Collections on Exhibit

The house boasts a large collection of Victorian Staffordshire figurines and American costumes from the years 1850 to 1930.

Additional Information

The Ellwood House Museum is listed on the National Register of Historic Places.

Ronald Reagan Boyhood Home

816 South Hennepin Avenue
Dixon, IL 61021
(815) 288-3404

Contact: Ronald Reagan Home Preservation Foundation

Open: Mar.-Nov., Mon.-Sat. 10 a.m.-4 p.m., Sun. 1-4 p.m.; Dec.-Feb., Sat. 10 a.m.-4 p.m., Sun. 1-4 p.m.; closed New Year's Day, Easter, Thanksgiving, Christmas

Admission: Free

Activities: Guided tour, introductory video

Suggested Time to View House: 45 minutes

Facilities on Premises: Visitor center, gift shop

Description of Grounds: Small park

Best Season to View House: Spring-fall

Number of Yearly Visitors: 12,000-14,000

Year House Built: 1891

Style of Architecture: Victorian Queen Anne

Number of Rooms: 7

On-Site Parking: Yes **Wheelchair Access:** No

Description of House

In 1920, the Reagan family—Jack, his wife, Nelle, and their two sons, Neil and nine-year-old Ronald—moved into this smart Queen Anne-style home in Dixon, one of the oldest towns on the Mississippi in the State of Illinois. The house had been built in 1891 by William C. Thompson on a piece of land originally owned by Father John Dixon, after whom the town is named. The Reagan family lived here for close to nineteen years; here is where Ronald went to school, attended church, gave his first public recitations, and served as a lifeguard in the summers down by the river. After Ronald had achieved a measure of success out in California, he sent for his parents who joined him there in the late 1930s. When the Reagans left the house it was turned into a two-unit apartment building. In 1980 a group of concerned local citizens—led by a letter carrier—bought the house for $31,500, paid off the mortgage within a year, and completed its restoration just in time for President Reagan's birthday visit on February 6, 1984. The restoration was made possible through the efforts of many citizens; when the roof needed to be redone in wood shingles to reflect its appearance in the 1920s, money was raised by "selling" these shingles at fifty cents each. A record was kept of each donor as they bought and signed their shingle—over 8,400 people bought a piece of the roof, people from all fifty states and over fifty different countries.

The two-story house features cross-gabling, a full-width front porch, a smaller porch off the rear kitchen, decorative bands of textured shingles, simple sash-style windows, and triangular air vents in the attic. The floor plan consists of three bedrooms upstairs and a parlor, sitting room, and dining room on the main floor. A fully restored barn also stands on the property. Some of the period furnishings have been donated by the Reagan Home Volunteers; they are authentic to the period of the 1920s.

Notable Collections on Exhibit
On display at the Reagan home is a 1919 Model T Ford.

Additional Information
The Ronald Reagan Boyhood Home is listed on the National Register of Historic Places.

John Weir House

715 West Main Street
Edwardsville, IL 62025
(618) 656-7562

Contact: Madison County Historical Society Museum

Open: Wed., Thurs., Fri. 9 a.m.–4 p.m., Sun. and first Sat. 1 p.m.–4 p.m.; closed major holidays, month of January

Admission: Free

Activities: Guided tours, slide presentation

Suggested Time to View House: 90 minutes

Facilities on Premises: Research library and archives, gift shop

Description of Grounds: Small town front and backyard

Best Season to View House: Year round

Number of Yearly Visitors: 5,000

Year House Built: 1836, addition 1929

Style of Architecture: Federal, brick

Number of Rooms: 10

On-Site Parking: Yes **Wheelchair Access:** Yes

Description of House

John Weir, born in South Carolina of Scotch-Irish parents, attended Phillips Academy in Andover, Massachusetts, graduated with a degree in medicine from Harvard University in 1835, and, later that year, moved to Illinois with his first wife. In 1836, he built the house which would be home to Weir family for the next one hundred and twenty-seven years. During the Civil War, the doctor attended those Confederate soldiers incarcerated at the federal prison in Alton, Illinois. He and his second wife, Mary Hoxey, had one son, Edward, who also became a doctor. Edward married Ann Frances Terry in 1875 and the couple had five daughters.

The Federal-style house is a two-and-a-half-story rectangular structure built from Philadelphia row house plans that Dr. Weir had brought with him from the east. The walls are constructed of locally manufactured brick—the Weir House is the second oldest existing brick residence in Edwardsville—and the peg-fastened trusses and beams are oak. On the facade, five second-story windows sit above the four windows and beautifully detailed inset door of the first floor in delightful harmony. Inside, four rooms on each of the first two floors open off the center hall and stairway; the first-floor rooms include Dr. Weir's office and two parlors connected by arched openings. An addition completed in 1929 includes a kitchen and a maid's room with bath. The parlors and bedrooms are decorated in fabrics, wallpaper and paints authentic to the period c.1830 to 1855. The furnishings represent a mix of periods, from Empire to Victorian to Eastlake and later. The fully restored house is in superb condition inside and out.

Notable Collections on Exhibit

The Madison County Historical Society Museum collection includes: the Native American artifact collections of John Sutter and Raymond P. Smith; early toys and dolls including a c.1860 Mary Todd Lincoln China Head Doll; early firearms; historic costumes and fans; antique dishes, quilts, and needlework. Noteworthy objects on display include: an 1815 Sheraton piano which belonged to Elijah P. Lovejoy; a primitive painting of the prehistoric Cahokia Mounds; and an 1893 sewing cabinet with wood inlay.

Additional Information

The John Weir House is listed on the National Register of Historic Places.

Lorado Taft Museum

302 North Magnolia Street
Elmwood, IL 61529
(309) 742-7791

Contact: Elmwood Historical Society
Open: Mar.-Nov., Wed. 1–4 p.m
Admission: Donations accepted
Activities: Guided tours by
  appointment only
Suggested Time to View House: 90 minutes
Facilities on Premises: Books of local
  history on sale
Description of Grounds: Yard with barn
Best Season to View House: Summer
Number of Yearly Visitors: 600
Year House Built: 1875
Style of Architecture: Victorian
  Queen Anne
Number of Rooms: 9
On-Site Parking: No **Wheelchair Access:** No

Description of House

Lorado Taft, the well-known Beaux-Arts sculptor, was born in Elmwood and this Taft family house contains much memorabilia associated with the artist. In addition to his art, Taft is remembered as the author of the first serious survey of American sculpture, *The History of American Sculpture*, published in 1903. Built in 1875 and occupied by three generations of the family until 1950, the house has changed little since its early days. In fact, much of the woodwork is in its original condition.

Dishes in the dining room and a desk and chair in the office are original to the house; the remaining furnishings have been collected and are appropriate to the period.

Notable Collections on Exhibit

One room of the house is devoted entirely to the life and work of Larado Taft, displaying personal effects as well as pieces of his sculpture.

Charles Gates Dawes House

225 Greenwood Street
Evanston, IL 60201
(708) 475-3410

Contact: Evanston Historical Society
Open: Mon. and Tues., Thurs.-Sat. 1–5 p.m.; closed Wed., Sun. and major holidays
Admission: Adults $3.00; seniors and students $1.00
Activities: Guided tours, audiovisual presentations, annual 1920s Croquet Tournament
Suggested Time to View House: 45–60 minutes
Facilities on Premises: Headquarters for the Evanston Historical Society and Museum

Description of Grounds: Large city yard with coach house, and decorated with stone ornaments and gargoyles retrieved from various public and private buildings
Best Season to View House: Spring and summer
Number of Yearly Visitors: 500
Year House Built: 1895
Style of Architecture: Eclectic Chateauesque
Number of Rooms: 28
On-Site Parking: Yes **Wheelchair Access:** No

Description of House

Charles Gates Dawes (1865-1951), Vice President of the United States under President Calvin Coolidge, gained world-wide recognition when he was awarded the 1925 Nobel Peace Prize for devising and implementing his plan for European economic recovery. Dawes, who gained early attention fighting discriminatory railroad rates as a lawyer in Nebraska, moved to Chicago in 1893 with his wife, the former Caro D. Blymyer. His public career commenced in 1897 when he served as Comptroller of the Currency under President McKinley. Over the next four decades, Dawes would serve as Brigadier General during World War I, first Director of the Bureau of the Budget, and Ambassador to Great Britain from 1929 to 1932, in addition to his term as Vice President. In 1909, he purchased the lakefront mansion at 225 Greenwood Street for $75,000. The house had originally been built in 1894 for Dr. and Mrs. Robert Sheppard. Dawes lived here until his death in 1951; after his widow died in 1957, ownership of the house passed to Northwestern University. Eventually it became the headquarters and museum of the Evanston Historical Society.

Designed by the noted New York architect Henry Edwards-Ficken, this twenty-eight-room mansion reflects Mrs. Sheppard's fondness for the chateaux of France. The exterior is of varicolored orange and tan brick and features an entrance flanked by two voluminous two-story towers with single belt courses. Their "candle snuff" style roofs are mimicked by the pinnacled dormer set between them. Inside, the house has nine bedrooms, seven bathrooms and fourteen fireplaces; of the other rooms, the more interesting are: an English Tudor dining room with a molded plaster ceiling and musicians' gallery, the Jacobean-style Great Hall dominated by a massive oak stairway, and the Renaissance library paneled in cherry. The furnishings are original to the house, dating from the years 1925 to 1929 when Dawes served as Vice President.

Notable Collections on Exhibit

Among the many objects on display are five Louis Comfort Tiffany lamps, several Oriental rungs, bronzes, and autographed photographs of the Presidents under whom Dawes served.

Additional Information

Henry Edwards-Ficken also designed the Ferry Houses and Shops of Hoboken and the Henry Finn House of Montclair, both in New Jersey; the C. F. Robert Lodge of Oakdale, Long Island; the Stone Trust Association Building of New Haven and the Ferguson Memorial Library of Stamford, in Connecticut. He also designed some of the interiors at Grey Tower, a Chateauesque mansion designed by Richard Morris Hunt in Milford, Pennsylvania. That house, like the Dawes house, has been declared a National Historic Landmark and is listed on the National Register of Historic Places.

Oscar Taylor House– "Bohemiana"

Contact: Stephenson County
Historical Society
Open: Fri.-Sun. 1–4 p.m.; other times by
appointment; closed major holidays
Admission: Donations accepted
Activities: Guided tours, special events
Suggested Time to View House: 30 minutes
Description of Grounds: Arboretum with
various trees, shrubs and flowers
Best Season to View House: Year round
Number of Yearly Visitors: 1,500
Year House Built: 1857
Number of Rooms: 8 open to the public

**1440 South Carroll Avenue
Freeport, IL 61032
(815) 232-8419**

Style of Architecture: Italianate
On-Site Parking: Yes **Wheelchair Access:** No

Description of House

In 1857, when Oscar and Malvina Taylor built this home in Freeport, the issue of slavery was on everybody's mind. The Taylors, who abhorred the institution, are thought to have put their beliefs into practice by assisting runaways passing through the town on the way to freedom. In addition, the Taylors were also passionate about gardening: they were great experimenters in the cultivation and breeding of shrubs, flowering plants, and trees—especially those varieties not native to Illinois. Today one can view the results of their interest in plants at the Taylor Arboretum. The couple were also known as warm and gracious hosts; over the years, their guests included Horace Mann, James Russell Lowell, Horace Greeley, Ralph Waldo Emerson, Mark Twain, and Artemus Ward.

The Taylor House features a number of elements common to the Italianate style: a square cupola (lantern), narrow and hooded windows showing a full arch, a low pitched roof with elaborate brackets, and a two-story extended side bay. The exterior walls and foundation are built of limestone; cut into the walls above the main entry is a characteristic double window grouping. Inside, one of the rooms has been interpreted to the years between 1857 and 1909 when the house was occupied by the Taylors; a second room reflects the period of the 1930s and the Frank and Clarissa Taylor Bass residency.

Notable Collections on Exhibit

In addition to the furnishings in the rooms noted above, "Bohemiana" houses a collection of antique toys, Civil War memorabilia, and Dirksen Silver.

Additional Information

The Oscar Taylor House, "Bohemiana," is listed on the National Register of Historic Places. When visiting the Arboretum in the historic town of Dixon, one should also view the One-Room School (1910-1920), the Farm Museum (1850-1920), the 1850 Irish Homestead of the John Hogan family, and the Industrial Museum. The corner of Douglas and State Streets in downtown Freeport was the site of the second round of the Lincoln-Douglas Debates.

Daniel A. Barrows House

211 South Bench Street
Galena, IL 61036
(815) 777-9129

Contact: Galena-Jo Daviess County
Historical Society and Museum

Open: Daily 9 a.m.–4:30 p.m.; closed New
Year's Day, Easter, Christmas

Admission: Adults $3.00; children $2.00;
children (under 10) free; group rates
available

Activities: Audiovisual presentations,
special seasonal events

Suggested Time to View House:
30–45 minutes

Facilities on Premises: Gift shop

Description of Grounds: Terraced hillside
behind building

Best Season to View House: Year round

Year House Built: 1858, addition 1922

Number of Rooms: 8

Number of Yearly Visitors: 20,000
Style of Architecture: Italianate
On-Site Parking: No **Wheelchair Access:** No

Description of House

In 1858, Daniel A. Barrows, a prominent early Galena merchant who owned a confectionery store, distillery and lumber yard in town, built this Italianate mansion. His architect, William Dennison, was the same man who also designed the U. S. Grant Home in Galena. Today, the house serves as the county history museum, featuring thousands of artifacts and exhibits pertaining to life in Galena and the surrounding communities.

The house is a two-story structure with the typical center gable; the porticoed front porch has been completely restored. Inside, the features include the original marble fireplaces, decorative ceiling moldings, and a wooden spiral staircase. Recently, the woodwork in the entry and two front parlors has been "woodgrained" in the popular style of the 1860s. None of the present decorative materials or details are original to the house, but all are authentic to the period and lend the house greater historic importance.

Notable Collections on Exhibit

As befits a museum in Galena, the collection concerns U. S. Grant: there is a Civil War exhibit featuring the Thomas Nast painting "Peace in Union," depicting Lee's surrender to Grant, and there are some original leather goods from the Grant Leather store. Just steps away, on South Main Street, equally interesting collections can be seen on exhibit at the Old General Store Museum.

Additional Information

The town of Galena is a treasure-trove of historical homes and buildings, all of which highlight the role of northwestern Illinois in the development of the frontier. The Dowling House built on 1826 located at 220 Diagonal Street, and the Belvedere Mansion and Gardens built in 1857 located at 1008 Park Avenue, both offer to the visitor a glimpse of these bygone days.

U. S. Grant Home State Historic Site

500 Bouthillier Street
Galena, IL 61036
(815) 777-0248

Contact: Illinois Historic Preservation Agency
Open: Daily 9 a.m.–5 p.m.; closed Thanksgiving, Christmas, New Year's Day
Admission: Free
Activities: Self-guided tour
Suggested Time to View House: 30 minutes
Description of Grounds: State park grounds available for picnics located across the street

Best Season to View House: Spring and summer
Number of Yearly Visitors: 165,000
Year House Built: 1860
Style of Architecture: Italianate, bracketed
Number of Rooms: 9
On-Site Parking: Yes
Wheelchair Access: Yes

Description of House

When Ulysses S. Grant moved to Galena in 1860, he did so out of necessity, for the only real talent he seemed to show in the years since leaving the military was that of being able to lose money with some regularity. Grant had his family—dear Julia, as always, stood by him—but having to come to work for his younger brothers as a clerk in his father's store was like admitting defeat, and defeat ran counter to his very nature. Had he reached the pinnacle of success as a lieutenant in the Mexican War? The Grants rented a modest brick house on the western bank of the river and Ulysses satisfied his restlessness by traveling throughout what was then called the Northwest—Wisconsin, Minnesota, and Iowa—selling to customers.

Then came the war and everything changed. Grant, carried from obscurity to international renown by circumstance, and his own talent for waging war, would return to Galena a genuine hero of the republic, perhaps, after Lincoln, the most famous man in America.

In August of 1865, four months after General Robert E. Lee had handed his sword to General Grant in the parlor of Wilmer McLean's Appomattox home, Galena's hero came back home. The town went wild with jubilation, capping their celebration by presenting the Grants with this handsome furnished home. It had been built in 1860 for Alexander J. Jackson, former City Clerk; at the war's end, a group of local Republicans purchased it for $2,500 for presentation to the Grants. In Julia's words, it was "a lovely villa exquisitely furnished with everything good taste could desire." In succeeding years, the Grants actually spent very little time in the house, although it was always kept ready for their visits to Galena.

Designed by William Dennison, the house is a two-story Italianate-style structure with typical projecting eaves, elaborate bracketed trim, a low pitched roof, and balustrade balconies over covered porches. Much of the furniture is original and was used by Grant and his family. A wash house, added in 1880, was removed in the 1930s because it was not in place during the Grant years. The house has been restored to match its appearance in the November 14, 1868, issue of *Frank Leslie's Illustrated Newspaper*.

Additional Information

The U. S. Grant Home is listed on the National Register of Historic Places.

Carl A. Sandburg State Historic Site

331 East Third Street
Galesburg, IL 61401
(309) 342-2361

Contact: Illinois Historic Preservation
Agency
Open: Daily 9 a.m.–5 p.m.; closed
major holidays
Admission: Free
Activities: Guided tours, audiovisual
presentation
Suggested Time to View House: 30 minutes
Facilities on Premises: Bookstore
Description of Grounds: Small wooded
park where the ashes of Carl A.
Sandburg are buried
Style of Architecture: National, frame
workman's cottage
Best Season to View House: Summer
Number of Yearly Visitors: 15,000
Number of Rooms: 3

Year House Built: 1870
On-Site Parking: Yes **Wheelchair Access:** No

Description of House

On January 6, 1878 Carl Sandburg, poet of the prairies and chronicler of American lives, folkways, and history, was born in this three-room cottage to two Swedish immigrants, August and Clara Anderson Sandburg. A year later, August, who worked in a blacksmith's shop, moved his family to a larger house in Galesburg. His modest beginning, the hard, low-paying jobs he had to endure, and the years he spent on the road as a kind of hobo created in Sandburg a deep and abiding sympathy for the working poor of our society. This passion for justice led to his efforts at union organization and journalism but he was, first and foremost, a writer and not a social reformer. Sandburg wrote many works of enduring fame, but is perhaps best remembered for his multi-volume biography of Abraham Lincoln, his poetry, and his book of children's tales, *Rootabaga Stories*. Though he moved far from Galesburg in his life, ultimately settling in North Carolina, Carl Sandburg never forgot the home where he was born and, after his death on July 22, 1967, his ashes were returned to the little park behind the white cottage at 331 East Third Street. The poet's grave is marked by a red granite boulder, his Remembrance Rock.

The small, front-gabled workman's cottage is painted white with black shutters. In its modest size, and with its original furnishings, some of which belonged to the Sandburgs, the house is a fair representation of a typical residence of a late 19th-century working class family.

Historic Emmert House and Old Six Mile Museum

3279 Maryville Road
Granite City, IL 62040
(618) 931-3023

Contact: Old Six Mile Historical Society
Open: Every Sunday 1–4 p.m., special tours available anytime
Admission: Free; donations accepted
Activities: Guided tours, rummage sales, special seasonal events including Apple Butter Days, and Christmas Open House
Suggested Time to View House: 45 minutes
Facilities on Premises: Bookstore

Description of Grounds: 1¾ acres with summer kitchen and smoke house
Best Season to View House: Summer and fall
Style of Architecture: Federal, later Folk Victorian-style farmhouse
Number of Yearly Visitors: 500
Year House Built: 1837, remodeled c. 1865
Number of Rooms: 6
On-Site Parking: Yes **Wheelchair Access:** No

Description of House

In the 1830s farmers began to settle the rich prairie bottomland six miles northeast of St. Louis and their settlement came to be called Six Mile Prairie. The area, once known as "The Garden Spot of the State," grew rapidly into today's Granite City where the Emmert House, now surrounded by apartments, houses, a church, and a school, is virtually the only vestige left of the historic original settlement. Mr. Emmert began construction on his Federal-style house in 1833, the same year that the Lincoln House in Springfield was built, perhaps using the same plans as that famous dwelling. It was completed in 1837 and remained unchanged until the end of the Civil War, when it got a Victorian facelift. In 1884, Emmert sold the house to the Zippels, a German immigrant family. Shortly thereafter, they added the smokehouse and a guest bedroom over the kitchen. The property was purchased by the Old Six Mile Historical Society in 1984, restored, and opened to the public as a museum.

The farmhouse interior features a living room and hall covered with the rich red wallpaper popular in the post-Civil War period.The furnishings are period antiques donated by the descendants of those pioneer families who settled the Six Mile Prairie.

Notable Collections on Exhibit

In addition to the pioneer relics on display, there is an exhibit showing the various granite products made in Granite City.

Pulsifer House

Power Road
Hennepin, IL 61327
(815) 925-7560

Contact: Putnam County Historical Society
Open: Tues.-Fri. 9 a.m.–4 p.m.
Admission: Free
Activities: Guided tours, audiovisual presentation
Suggested Time to View House: 30 minutes
Facilities on Premises: Gift shop, carriage house
Best Season to View House: Spring-fall

Description of Grounds: ½ acre with smoke house and summer kitchen
Style of Architecture: Late Georgian and Federal-style townhouse with Greek Revival interiors
Number of Yearly Visitors: 500
Year House Built: 1844
Number of Rooms: 11
On-Site Parking: Yes **Wheelchair Access:** No

Description of House

Edward F. Pulsifier, native Vermonter, moved to Ohio, got married and fathered two sons, continued west, and settled in the newly-hatched town of Hennepin. The year was 1839 and the ambitious twenty-six-year-old Pulsifier was hoping that his new hometown would become the chief transportation and trading hub of the Midwest. Setting himself up as a commission merchant and dry goods dealer, he soon branched out into real estate, bill collecting, and, as a stockholder in the *Hennepin Tribune*, newspaper publishing. By 1844, he was successful enough to be able to purchase a bank-owned tract of land and build this impressive Georgian townhouse. Here he lived until 1863 when, owing to an economy severely curtailed by the Civil War, his business flagged and he moved to Chicago. The house was purchased by William Thomas in 1904 and it stayed in the Thomas family until 1979 when it was deeded to the Village of Hennepin.

Built of locally-fired brick on a limestone foundation, the Pulsifier House is unquestionably the finest surviving example of the Federal style in Putnam County, if not in the State of Illinois. This style, in a confident vernacular interpretation, is well illustrated by the treatment of the gables and chimneys, the off-center entrance, restrained ornamentation, "Beverly L"-shaped floor plan, typical six over six fenestration, and the Greek Revival-style interiors. Perhaps the house was built by a local carpenter from an available pattern book or builder's guide; in any case, its integrity is evident in every detail, from the exquisite door moldings to the original beveled woodwork throughout. The woodwork in the ladies' parlor is in the Egyptian Revival style; in the men's parlor the style is Greek Revival—the fireplace and light ring are decorated with carved acanthus leaves. All furnishings have been donated or purchased. These include three Empire-style pieces in the men's parlor, Victorian furniture purchased at the Rousseau House sale in 1928, and an 1830s Empire-style mahogany sideboard in the dining room. In the attic, three steel rods run the east-west length of the house with the purpose of keeping the structure plumb.

Notable Collections on Exhibit
Among the objects on display are a set of Pulsifier family portraits.

Additional Information
The Pulsifer House is listed on the National Register of Historic Places.

Francis Stupey Log Cabin

Laurel Park at 1750 Block and
St. Johns Avenue
Highland Park, IL 60035
(708) 432-7090

Contact: Highland Park Historical Society
Open: May–Oct., Sun. 2–4 p.m.; other times
  by appointment
Admission: Free
Activities: Viewing only
Suggested Time to View House: 30 minutes

Description of Grounds: Located in park
  setting
Best Season to View House: Summer
Year House Built: 1847
Style of Architecture: National, log cabin
Number of Rooms: 1
On-Site Parking: No **Wheelchair Access:** No

Description of House

This pioneer log cabin is the oldest standing structure in Highland Park,
the suburban lakefront community situated on Lake Michigan some twenty-five miles north of Chicago. When the cabin was moved to its present
address and restored to its original appearance, the interior was furnished
with authentic 1850s pieces. The Stupey cabin has belonged to the Highland
Park Historical Society since 1966; the Society also operates the Jean Butz
James Museum, built in 1871, and the Walt Durbahn Tool Museum, built in
1910. All three, taken together, present an interesting survey of the settlement and development of the town.

Jean Butz James Museum

326 Central Avenue
Highland Park, IL 60035
(708) 432-7090

Contact: Highland Park Historical Society
Open: Mon.-Fri. 9:30 a.m.–12:30 p.m., Sat. and Sun. 2–4 p.m.; closed major holidays
Admission: Free
Activities: Guided tours
Suggested Time to View House: 30–60 minutes

Description of Grounds: Large garden
Best Season to View House: Summer
Number of Yearly Visitors: 2,000
Year House Built: 1871
Style of Architecture: Late Italianate, brick
Number of Rooms: 10
On-Site Parking: Yes **Wheelchair Access:** No

Description of House

This house, like the Francis Stupey Log Cabin listed above, is operated by the Highland Park Historical Society as a museum. Originally built in 1871 by the Highland Park Building Company, the asymmetrical two-story Italianate home features a parlor furnished in the period of the 1880s, a children's playroom decorated c. 1895 with many antique toys on display, and a room devoted to the history of the Ravinia Festival, the summer home of the Chicago Symphony Orchestra.

Notable Collections on Exhibit

Some of the Society's more than 6,000 items of local historical interest are always featured in the Museum's changing display rooms; of particular interest are the Ladies' Fashion Parlor-room featuring clothing from the Victorian Era, the Walt E. Durbahn Tool Room, the Sewing Room, and the Military History Room.

Additional Information

The Jean Butz James Museum is listed on the National Register of Historic Places.

1846 Garfield Inn

3N016 Garfield Road, P.O. Box 403
LaFox, IL 60147
(708) 584-8485

Contact: Garfield Farm and Tavern Museum
Open: June–Sept., Wed. and Sun. 1–4 p.m.;
year-round by appointment
Admission: Adults $3.00; children
(under 13) $1.50
Activities: Guided tours, prairie hikes,
special seasonal events including Fall
Festival, Heirloom Garden Show and
Candlelight Reception
Suggested Time to View House:
60–90 minutes
Best Season to View House: Spring-fall
Description of Grounds: 250 acre 1840
farmstead with five outbuildings
Number of Yearly Visitors: 8,000
Number of Rooms: 11

Style of Architecture: Federal, brick tavern
with elements of Greek Revival style
Year House Built: 1846, remodeled 1875
On-Site Parking: Yes **Wheelchair Access:** Yes

Description of House

In 1841 Timothy Garfield brought his wife and eight children to Illinois from Rutland County, Vermont; here, in what is now Campton Township, they purchased a 440 acre farm on the Chicago-St. Charles-Sycamore Road. Over the next five years, they expanded the farm and began providing food and shelter to the teamsters who were hauling grain to Chicago. By 1846, the growing business of providing "good custom" to travelers necessitated building a tavern-inn which soon garnered the reputation of being one of the best between Chicago and the Rock River. Unfortunately, the business was short-lived; when the railroad became the preferred transport for hauling crops, road traffic died, and the Garfields had to fall back on farming for their livelihood. Timothy died in 1859 and his son Robert took over the farm, moving it away from a crop-growing operation to dairying. He married Hannah Mitchell of Plano, whose parents had also come west from Vermont. After Robert died in 1901, Hannah had the idea of preserving the farm and tavern for posterity.

The tavern, built of native brick, is a good example of a New England farmstead transplanted to the prairie, with its grained woodwork and shelf chimneys. The house consists of a ladies' parlor, dining room, tap room, a second floor ballroom, and several other rooms, including a winter, and a summer, kitchen. The whole has been faithfully restored to its 1890s appearance, which features many original furnishings belonging to the Garfield and Mitchell families and on the wall of the master bedroom hang portraits of the original residents, Timothy and Harriet Garfield.

Additional Information

The entire farm is in the process of restoration; once done it will serve as an 1840s living history farm and museum. The 1846 Garfield Inn is listed on the National Register of Historic Places.

Illinois and Michigan Canal Commissioner's Office and Residence

803 South State Street
Lockport, IL 60441
(815) 838-5080

Contact: Will County Historical Society
Open: Daily 1–4 p.m.; closed major holidays, Thanksgiving week, December 15 to January 2
Admission: Free
Activities: Guided tours by costumed docents, local history video presentation
Suggested Time to View House: 1 hour

Description of Grounds: Former canal site
Best Season to View House: Spring-fall
Number of Yearly Visitors: 50,000
Year House Built: 1837
Style of Architecture: Greek Revival
Facilities on Premises: Small gift shop
Number of Rooms: 14
On-Site Parking: Yes **Wheelchair Access:** Yes

Description of House

Before the railroads came to the Midwestern prairie, the hauling of grain and other goods was accomplished primarily over the region's waterways, natural and man-made. One particularly well-trafficked waterway was the Illinois and Michigan Canal; begun in 1836 and completed in 1848, this canal ran from LaSalle on the navigable Illinois River—a direct link to the Mississippi—to the small settlement of Chicago on Lake Michigan. The town of Lockport, which began life as a collection of huts on the Lone Star Indian Trail, owed its very existence to the canal and today can boast of being the best preserved canal town in the nation. During the years of the canal's heyday, the I & M Canal Commissioner's Office and House rivaled the state capitol in importance, receiving many official visitors, serving as the social hub of Northern Illinois, and, of course, standing as headquarters for the planning, construction, and operation of the canal.

Except for the upper part at the south end of the building, which was completed after the Civil War, the structure was built in 1837. The north wing was used primarily as the office of the Canal Commission, whereas the south wing served as the living quarters for the canal officials and their guests. It is this part of the house, now the Illinois-Michigan Canal Museum, which is laid out to show the typical household artifacts found in a 19th-century kitchen, dining room, parlor, and bedroom. Though the structure itself is largely in the Greek Revival style, the interiors are Victorian and mostly reflect life at the turn of the century.

The I & M Canal was abandoned in 1933 but, thirty-six years later, a group of dedicated and concerned citizens successfully restored the building—winning a commendation from the American Association for State and Local History—and established the Illinois-Michigan Canal Museum. The Museum now draws over 50,000 people a year and the building it is housed in has been listed on the National Register of Historic Places.

Notable Collections on Exhibit

The Canal Museum features many permanent exhibits which depict the history of the canal, Lockport, Will County, and the lives of the occupants of the house. Chief among these exhibits is the fully restored office of Dr. Dougall, the physician who tended the canal workers, and the family parlor which includes, among its furnishings, a locally-manufactured Evans organ and a three-hundred-year-old cradle.

Additional Information

The Illinois and Michigan Canal Commissioner's Office and Residence is listed on the National Register of Historic Places.

Butterworth Center, "Hillcrest"

1105 Eighth Street
Moline, IL 61265
(309) 765-7971

Contact: William Butterworth Memorial Trust
Open: Mon.-Fri. by appointment only; July and Aug., Sun. 1–4 p.m.; closed major holidays, week between Christmas Eve and New Year's Day
Admission: Free
Activities: Guided tours, special seasonal events including Spring and Christmas Open Houses
Suggested Time to View House: 45 minutes

Description of Grounds: Beautiful gardens with many labeled plants and flowers includes a greenhouse, gazebo, walkways and rose gardens
Best Season to View House: Spring-fall
Number of Yearly Visitors: 6,000
Year House Built: 1892, addition 1917
Style of Architecture: Victorian Queen Anne and Stick Style
Number of Rooms: 35
On-Site Parking: Yes **Wheelchair Access:** Yes

Description of House

Katherine Deere Butterworth (1866-1953), was the granddaughter of John Deere, well-known inventor of the steel plow and founder of the company which bears his name; this house was built for her by her parents when she married in 1892. Her husband was William Butterworth (1864-1936), a native Ohioan and son of Benjamin Butterworth, United States Senator and head of the U. S. Patent Office. William took a position with Deere & Company, eventually becoming its third president in 1907, then Chairman of the Board. He retired in 1928 and served as president of the U.S. Chamber of Commerce for three years. Katherine was active in the Daughters of the American Revolution, a myriad of philanthropies, and numerous community affairs. It was she who created the Butterworth Trust which, upon her death, refurnished the house, allowed non-profit organizations to use it for meetings, and opened it to the public.

The family made many alterations to the Queen Anne-style wood-sided house completed in 1892; architects from Chicago designed the interior Gothic Revival-style detailing in Circassian walnut, the carved stonework and plasterwork, the Italian Renaissance-style library, and the two-story living room. In 1905, an elevator and a central vacuum system were installed. In 1909, the family added a garage (which includes a squash court), a greenhouse, and installed a twenty-six-rank pipe organ in the living room. Finally, in 1925, the basement gaming rooms (the Oak Room, Billiards Room and Card Room) were remodeled in the Arts & Crafts Movement style, using bull's-eye glass in the windows and typical light fixtures.

Only ten percent of the furnishings belonged to the Butterworths; the rest are purchases made by the trust Mrs. Butterworth established for that purpose.

Notable Collections on Exhibit
Perhaps the most notable item on display is the ceiling painting in the library; the ceiling was purchased whole from the Hotel Danieli in Venice and the painting is thought to be by Tiepolo.

Additional Information
The house museum of the Rock Island County Historical Society located at 822 Eleventh Avenue was, at one time, occupied by members of the Deere family. The twelve-room, Victorian-style frame house was built in 1877. It now houses a historical research library and exhibition space featuring local pioneer history. Call the historical society for hours at (309) 764-8590.

Deere-Wiman House, "Overlook"

817 Eleventh Street
Moline, IL 61265
(309) 765-7971

Contact: William Butterworth Memorial
Trust
Open: Mon.-Fri. by appointment only; July
and Aug., Sun. 1–4 p.m.; closed major
holidays, week between Christmas and
New Year's Day
Admission: Free
Activities: Guided tours, special seasonal
events including Spring and Christmas
Open Houses
Suggested Time to View House: 45 minutes
Facilities on Premises: Archives
Best Season to View House: Spring-fall
Description of Grounds: 7 acres of lovely
gardens
Number of Yearly Visitors: 5,500
Number of Rooms: 25

Style of Architecture: Originally Victorian
Stick Style "Swiss Villa"
Year House Built: 1872, remodeled 1899
On-Site Parking: Yes **Wheelchair Access:** Yes

Description of House

Charles Deere (1836-1907) was the son of inventor John Deere and president of the company that his father founded from 1886 to 1907. In 1872, he hired Chicago architect William Le Baron Jenny to build the Stick-style house which would "Overlook" the town of Moline, the Mississippi River, and the John Deere Plough Works. Charles lived here until his death; his wife, May, died in 1913 and the house was briefly used by their daughter, Anna, and her husband. In 1920, Anna's eldest son, Charles Deere Wiman, moved into the house and lived here until his death in 1955. After his widow died in 1976, the house was given to the William Butterworth Memorial Trust.

The original 1872 building has undergone some structural changes; these include moving some of the walls and fireplaces, adding stucco to the exterior, and eliminating the decorative vergeboards. Most of the major structural changes occurred after an 1899 fire which damaged parts of the house. Even so, a number of characteristic exterior features remain: the extended bays, candle-snuff roof, and wrap-around porch. Inside, the house features nine bathrooms, an elevator, a spa shower c. 1900, and a beautiful, open center staircase which extends the full three stories. Ninety percent of the furnishings belonged to the residents and most are in the Victorian style.

Notable Collections on Exhibit

Among the items on display, there is an 1860 edition of Audubon prints, a costume collection ranging from the 1830s to the 1940s, and many fine decorative pieces featuring French porcelains dating from the 1760s.

Additional Information

"Overlook" is one block from "Hillcrest," the house that Charles had built for his daughter, Elizabeth.

Momence Historical House

117 North Dixie Highway
Momence, IL 60954
(815) 472-2001

Contact: Momence Historical Board
Open: Call for current hours
Admission: Donation welcome
Activities: Guided tours, rotating exhibits
Suggested Time to View House: 30 minutes
Description of Grounds: Town yard
surrounded by a white picket fence

Best Season to View House: Summer
Number of Yearly Visitors: 500
Year House Built: 1860
Style of Architecture: Early Victorian
Number of Rooms: 5
On-Site Parking: Yes **Wheelchair Access:** No

Description of House

During the late 19th century, Momence, a prosperous community on the Kankakee River, was said to be the "Eden of Illinois." Though much has changed since then, the Momence Historical House still stands, both as a testament to the longed-for virtues of the simpler life in 1880s small town America, and as an evocation of that life. This simple front-gabled frame house, standing behind a white picket fence, has been fully furnished to recreate the period of 1870 to 1900; these furnishings have been donated or loaned by Momence residents. One of the bedrooms contains an 1840 cannonball rope bed with its trundle. A tour through the Momence Historical House is an exercise in nostalgia—objects from a bygone era abound—that one wishes would never end.

Martin-Mitchell Mansion at Naper Settlement Museum Village

201 West Porter Avenue
Naperville, IL 60540
(708) 420-6010

Contact: Naperville Heritage Society
Open: May-Oct. Wed., Sat., Sun.
1:30–4:30 p.m.; call for winter schedule
Admission: Adults $4.00; seniors and students $2.00; family $10.00; children (under 5) free
Activities: Guided student programs, special seasonal events including Annual Antiques Show and Sale, "Christmas in the Village," Joe Naper Day, and Civil War Encampment
Suggested Time to View House: House-45 minutes, museum village-3 hours
Description of Grounds: 12 acre living history museum; several outbuildings dating from early 19th century including a log house, Fort Payne, the Naper-Haight House, the Daniels and Murray Houses, the Blacksmith shop, and the Stone Carver's Shop

Facilities on Premises: Museum store and archives
Best Season to View House: Spring-fall
Year House Built: 1883
Style of Architecture: Victorian Queen Anne, brick
Number of Rooms: 17
On-Site Parking: Yes **Wheelchair Access:** No

Description of House

George Martin emigrated to the United States from Scotland, settled in Naperville, just outside of Chicago, and made his fortune exploiting the area's native clay and limestone—materials used in producing the bricks, blocks, and tiles which were needed to build Chicago's first skyscrapers. In 1883, he built the house which would symbolize his great wealth and the fulfillment of every immigrant's dream: to achieve worldly success by joining in the bustle of a rapidly growing America.

The Victorian brick mansion is of an asymmetrical design which features a full two-story bay, a partial front porch with elaborate Eastlake spindlework railings and columns, a small side entrance porch, and ornate wrought-iron cresting atop the roof line of both house and porch. The roof is designed with alternating rows of straight-edged black tiles and scalloped beige tiles, and the windows are in the double sash style.

The house is furnished entirely in the style of 1880s Victorian; most of the furniture is made of dark woods and many of the wall coverings and draperies are done in the heavy velvet typical to the period.

Additional Information

The Martin-Mitchell Mansion is listed on the National Register of Historic Places.

Brigham Young Home

Corner of Kimball and Granger Streets
Nauvoo, IL 62354
(217) 453-6648

Contact: Nauvoo Restoration, Inc.
Open: Summer, Memorial Day-Labor Day, Mon.-Sat. 9 a.m.–6 p.m., Sun. Noon–6 p.m.; winter, Mon.-Sat. 9 a.m.–5 p.m., Sun. Noon–5 p.m.
Admission: Free
Activities: Guided tours
Suggested Time to View House: 15 minutes
Facilities on Premises: Nauvoo Visitor Center located at the north end of Main Street

Description of Grounds: Backyard with vegetable and flower gardens, orchards and above ground root cellar; stonewalk in front of house
Style of Architecture: Federal, brick with step front gables
Best Season to View House: Spring-fall
Number of Yearly Visitors: 22,426
Year House Built: 1843
Number of Rooms: 5
On-Site Parking: Yes **Wheelchair Access:** No

Description of House

The Brigham Young Home is only one of the many fully restored structures which make up the Nauvoo Restoration, one of the largest and most important such restored communities in the United States. This forty-four-acre site on the Mississippi was settled in 1839 by Joseph Smith and his followers, the Church of Jesus Christ of Latter-day Saints, commonly known as the Mormons, and it flourished in the following decade to become the tenth largest city in America. However, Nauvoo, the Hebrew word for "beautiful place," was also the site of Joseph Smith's martyrdom, where the persecution of the Mormons forced their eventual exodus west. Soon after, the French Icarians conducted an experiment in communal living here—and it failed. Then, after almost a century of quiet obscurity, the town of Nauvoo rose, phoenix-like, as descendants of the original settlers began to buy up properties and bring them back to their mid-19th century glory. All of the homes listed in Nauvoo—this lovely town of orderly streets, ample greenery, and restored Federal-style brick houses—have their own histories, but they all share in the greater history of the town itself.

After the murder of Joseph Smith in 1844, Brigham Young became leader of the Mormons and ultimately led the church on the largest single migration to cross the Mississippi in the history of the United States. Along the way, he founded, or helped found, over three hundred cities and towns across western America, as well as numerous religious and educational institutions. He even served as the first governor of the Territory of Utah from 1850 to 1858.

Young, his wife, Mary Ann Angell Young, and their six children moved into the Nauvoo area in 1839. In the latter part of that year, however, he was sent to the British Isles as a missionary, and did not return until 1841. An accomplished carpenter, he built this house for his family in 1843; three years later, when the Mormons were forced to leave Nauvoo, it was sold at auction. Brigham Young died in Utah in 1877.

The house Brigham Young built was a front-gabled, two-story structure in the Federal style. In the summer of 1844, two one-story side wings were added; the west wing became the children's bedroom and the east wing served as Young's office and a council room for the Nauvoo community. The house has been restored with pine woodwork woodgrained to look like oak and the original brick floor. The downstairs includes a kitchen and dining room which feature a huge cooking hearth and "bustle over" stove. The collected furnishings reflect the 1840s period and include rope string beds, a "nanny" bench, a dry sink, a walnut council table with eight matching Windsor chairs, and a dough bin. The children's room features a seventy piece hand-carved wooden Noah's Ark set.

Notable Collections on Exhibit

During the excavation, archaeologists uncovered what is believed to be the largest collection of intact ceramic artifacts ever taken from a 19th-century American site. Many of the objects—banded creamware, ironstone, poonah, featheredge, and porcelain—are on display.

Additional Information

Restoration of the Brigham Young home was begun in 1965 and completed in 1969. Historic Nauvoo is listed on the National Register of Historic Places.

Heber C. Kimball Home

Corner of Munson and Partridge Streets
Nauvoo, IL 62354
(217) 453-6648

Contact: Nauvoo Restoration, Inc.
Open: Summer, Memorial Day-Labor Day, Mon.-Sat. 9 a.m.–6 p.m., Sun. Noon–6 p.m.; winter, Mon.-Sat. 9 a.m.–5 p.m., Sun. Noon–5 p.m.
Admission: Free
Activities: Guided tours
Suggested Time to View House: 20 minutes
Facilities on Premises: Nauvoo Visitor Center located at the north end of Main Street

Description of Grounds: White picket-fenced yard with flower gardens and several outbuildings
Best Season to View House: Spring-fall
Number of Yearly Visitors: 19,765
Year House Built: 1845, addition 1867
Style of Architecture: Federal, brick with some elements of Greek Revival style
Number of Rooms: 8
On-Site Parking: Yes **Wheelchair Access:** No

Description of House

In 1954, this house was purchased by Dr. J. LeRoy Kimball, a great-grandson of the original owner; when he began to restore it for use as a vacation home, news spread rapidly and the house became a tourist attraction. Dr. Kimball had unwittingly started the Nauvoo Restoration Project, the largest such effort in the Midwest; the total number of houses brought back to their original condition and open for public viewing has now grown to twenty-six, and another twenty-eight are either undergoing restoration or serve as private residences.

Dr. Kimball's great-grandfather, Heber C. Kimball, lived here from 1839 to the Mormon exodus in 1846. A blacksmith and potter by trade, he also served as First Counselor to Brigham Young during Young's First Presidency of the Church of Latter-day Saints. Kimball and his wife, Vilate, had six children.

This two-story Federal-style house includes an addition constructed out of hand-made bricks; exterior features include a rubble stone foundation, double chimneys, wood roof shingles, stone sills and lintels, six-over-six fenestration, and a partial wooden porch with rounded columns and incised railings that match those on the widow's walk. The house originally had two sets of shutters; the inner were of glass, and the outer were of wood. Inside, the woodwork is painted a slate blue-gray color and the reproduction carpets faithfully replicate the original needlepoint. One of the upstairs rooms has been left in an unretouched state to illustrate the restoration process itself.

Notable Collections on Exhibit

Heber Kimball spent much of his life as a missionary and many artifacts gathered on his travels reflect this vocation. From Vauxhall, England—site of Kimball's first missionary work—there is a gaslight fixture, a coatrack, and a stair-post ornament. Other items include a razor belonging to Joseph Smith, a Book of Mormon presented by Smith to Josiah Quincy, a rare Nauvoo Temple plate, a drum and fife which belonged to William Clayton, and an English Staffordshire china Temple plate. One of the more charming collections is a series of ten drawings called "Scenes Along the Mississippi and other Mormon Sites" dated 1853 and signed by Frederick Percy.

Additional Information

Historic Nauvoo is listed on the National Register of Historic Places.

John Taylor Home

Contact: Nauvoo Restoration, Inc.
Open: Summer, Memorial Day-Labor Day, Mon.-Sat. 9 a.m.–6 p.m., Sun. Noon–6 p.m.; winter, Mon.-Sat. 9 a.m.–5 p.m., Sun. Noon–5 p.m.
Admission: Free
Activities: Guided tours
Suggested Time to View House: 20 minutes
Best Season to View House: Spring-fall

Facilities on Premises: Nauvoo Visitor Center located at the north end of Main Street
Description of Grounds: Picnic area with tables
Number of Yearly Visitors: 14,217
Year House Built: 1842
Style of Architecture: Federal
Number of Rooms: 4
On-Site Parking: Yes **Wheelchair Access:** No

Description of House

John Taylor, a well-educated immigrant from Great Britain, served as the editor of two Nauvoo publications, the newspaper *Times and Seasons* and a weekly periodical called the *Nauvoo Neighbor*. His home was used as both the community's post office as well as its print shop. John Taylor was in the Carthage Jail cell with the Prophet Joseph Smith and his brother, Hyram Smith, when the two were killed in 1846. Taylor himself was reported to have been hit five times by gunfire, but his pocket watch stopped the one bullet which would have proved fatal. Years later, when the Mormons settled in Utah, he became the third President of the Church.

The house has brick parapet walls built on a stone foundation, with stone sills and lintels. On the first story, large Georgian-style windows hung nine-over-six both front and back give the interior plenty of light; on the second story, the windows are hung six-over-six in the Adam style. All the windows are capped with flat lintels. Inside, the woodwork is painted tan and the flooring is mostly original; the upstairs bedrooms feature closets with doors, an element rarely seen in houses of this period. Of the furnishings currently on display, we know that the oak shaving stand with its adjustable mirror and the American bar back, rawhide chair belonged to Taylor; the rest are authentic to the 1860s. Of these, the Kimball Organ c. 1865 located in the parlor is particularly noteworthy. Most touching is the needlepoint scene of "Rebecca at the Well" given to Taylor by his sister.

Additional Information

Historic Nauvoo is listed on the National Register of Historic Places.

Joseph Smith Homestead and Mansion House

Main and Water Streets
P.O. Box 338
Nauvoo, IL 62354
(217) 453-2246

Contact: Restoration Trail Foundation
Open: Memorial Day-Labor Day, daily 9 a.m.–7 p.m.; Labor Day-Memorial Day, daily 9 a.m.–5 p.m.
Admission: Free
Activities: Guided tours, audiovisual presentations
Suggested Time to View House: 45–60 minutes
Facilities on Premises: Visitor center, gift and book shop
Best Season to View House: Year round
Number of Yearly Visitors: 65,000

Description of Grounds: Complex consisting of three historic buildings pertaining to the life and work of Joseph Smith, Jr.
Year House Built: Homestead-1803 with additions c. 1840s and 1850s, mansion-1842
Style of Architecture: Homestead-Folk log cabin and Federal, mansion-modified Greek Revival with latent Georgian features
Number of Rooms: 8
On-Site Parking: Yes **Wheelchair Access:** No

Description of House

Unlike the historic homes in Nauvoo listed above, the Joseph Smith Homestead and Mansion is operated by the Restoration Trail Foundation as a monument to the memory of the founder of the Mormon Church and his son, who was anointed by his father to lead the community of believers. Joseph Smith led his people to Nauvoo in 1839 and took up residence in this modest, though unusual, two-story cabin. It had been built in 1803 out of hand-hewn logs with heavy chinking and featured several elements not typically seen in such structures: double-hung sash windows with a six-over-six pane arrangement, end gables, an asymmetrically placed front door, and visible timber supports which suggest that the building may have once had a full-width porch. During the time that the Smiths lived here, before they moved into their mansion, they added a north wing—a two-story structure with clapboard siding and the same Federal-style windows as the cabin. A west wing was added sometime later, perhaps by the Icarians who inhabited Nauvoo after the Mormons left in 1846.

In 1842 Smith built a mansion on the same property to accommodate guests as well as his own family. The two-story house features several elements of the Georgian style: a double-hipped roof, full-height pilasters of the Doric order flanking the main entrance and end corners, a Greek Revival-style recessed entry, and a plain, wide, divided band as the cornice. The downstairs windows are double-hung, nine-over-six treatments while the second floor windows are the more typical six-over-six arrangement—all of the windows are shuttered. Inside, one sees murals over the mantels in both Smith's office and the reception room and a fine three-part window on the second floor landing; the interior color scheme has been determined by the Foundation after much research.

In the homestead, the furnishings are pieces typical of an early 19th-century pioneer farm; while in the Mansion, the furnishings reflect a more affluent middle-class family.

Notable Collections on Exhibit

In addition to the furnishings and implements on view here which give a real sense of the lives lived by Nauvoo's religious settlers, there are also several fine portraits of Joseph Smith.

Additional Information

The Village of Nauvoo is listed on the National Register of Historic Places. The Restoration Trail Foundation runs a series of worthwhile guided tours which include—in addition to the Joseph Smith Homestead and Mansion—the Red Brick General Store (1841), where the father blessed the ministry of his son, and the Smith Family Cemetery. Here one sees the gravesites of Joseph and Hyrum Smith—both murdered on June 27, 1844—as well as that of Emma Smith, Joseph's beloved wife.

Sarah and Hiram Kimball Home

Young and Marion Streets
Nauvoo, IL 62354
(217) 453-6648

Contact: Nauvoo Restoration, Inc.
Open: Summer, Memorial Day–Labor Day,
Mon.-Sat. 9 a.m.–6 p.m., Sun.
Noon–6 p.m.; winter, Mon.-Sat.
9 a.m.–5 p.m., Sun. Noon–5 p.m.
Admission: Free
Activities: Guided tours
Suggested Time to View House: 15 minutes
Facilities on Premises: Nauvoo Visitor
Center located at the north end of Main
Street
Description of Grounds: Antique flower
garden and an orchard
Style of Architecture: Modified Greek
Revival
Best Season to View House: Spring-fall
Number of Yearly Visitors: 6,053
Number of Rooms: 5

Year House Built: c.1830s
On-Site Parking: Yes **Wheelchair Access:** No

Description of House

Sarah Granger was born in Phelps, New York, in 1818; some fifteen years later, her parents joined the Mormons and moved to the Church's Ohio settlement. Hiram Kimball, a Vermonter born in 1806, met Sarah in Commerce, Illinois, when he was traveling on business. They married in 1840 and moved into the small frame house which lies just outside of Nauvoo. Here she played an important role in the formation of the Relief Society, an charitable organization of Church women. Hiram died in a steamboat accident in 1863, leaving Sarah to raise three sons, a daughter, and an adopted Indian girl. In Utah, she stayed active in both religious and civic affairs, heading the Utah Woman's Suffrage Association in 1890 and acting as that state's Delegate to Washington in 1891. She died in 1898.

The simple, one-and-a-half-story Greek Revival house features a large central fireplace which was used to heat both the kitchen and the parlor, a full cellar, and oak plank flooring in the kitchen. The downstairs walls are painted cream color and show an intricate stenciled border. Most of the furnishings have been donated; among these are an American Empire-style settee, a mahogany secretary, and a Seth Thomas mantel clock. The house, which was fully restored in 1981 through the efforts of the Relief Society of the Church of Jesus Christ of Latter-day Saints—the organization that Sarah helped found—appears as it did in the 1840s.

Additional Information

Historic Nauvoo is listed on the National Register of Historic Places.

Wilford Woodruff Home

**Corner of Hotchkiss and Durphy Streets
Nauvoo, IL 62354
(217) 453-6648**

Contact: Nauvoo Restoration, Inc.
Open: Summer, Memorial Day-Labor Day,
Mon.-Sat. 9 a.m.–6 p.m., Sun.
Noon–6 p.m.; winter, Mon.-Sat.
9 a.m.–5 p.m., Sun. Noon–5 p.m.
Admission: Free
Activities: Guided tours
Suggested Time to View House: 20 minutes
Facilities on Premises: Nauvoo Visitor
Center located at the north end of Main
Street
Best Season to View House: Spring-fall
Description of Grounds: White
picket-fenced yard with gardens
Number of Yearly Visitors: 8,990
Number of Rooms: 8

Style of Architecture: Federal, brick with
double end chimneys
Year House Built: 1843
On-Site Parking: Yes **Wheelchair Access:** No

Description of House

Born in Farmington, Connecticut, in 1807, where he learned to make flour at his father's mill,Wilford Woodruff, from whose personal journals much of Mormon history can be traced, was ordained as one of that Church's Twelve Apostles in 1839, just six years after his conversion to the beliefs of Joseph Smith. Fifty years later, he would become the Church's president. While in Nauvoo during the early 1840s, Woodruff experimented with various crops, most notably cotton and rice, both unusual for the area; years later, in Utah, he formed that territory's first horticultural society and organized the beet sugar industry.

The Woodruff house, a red brick structure with fire-step chimneys located at each end, is considered to be one of the best examples of Federal-style architecture in the state of Illinois. It consists of eight rooms, each with its own fireplace. The front walls have two features not typically found in homes of this period: the large wedge-shaped "arch" bricks instead of of stone or wooden lintels above each of the windows, and the the obvious use of a different brick—one of smoother texture and more uniform color—than is used in the rest of the house. This latter idiosyncrasy can be explained by the fact that, when Woodruff noticed that the bricks to be used in building his house were hardly of uniform quality, he personally laid out all 14,000 of them and selected the best, which he then instructed to be used on the front walls of the house.

The Wilford Woodruff house is the most authentic restoration of all the Nauvoo houses; the original floors, stairways, woodwork, and doors are all still in place. All of the furnishings are from the period of the 1840s. The restoration began in 1967 and was completed two years later.

Additional Information

Historic Nauvoo is listed on the National Register of Historic Places.

Frank Lloyd Wright Home and Studio

951 Chicago Avenue
Oak Park, IL 60302
(708) 848-1500

Contact: Frank Lloyd Wright Home and Studio Foundation

Open: Guided tours, Mon.-Fri. 11 a.m., 1 p.m., 3 p.m., Sat. and Sun. 11 a.m.–4 p.m.; closed Thanksgiving, Christmas, New Year's Day

Admission: Adults $6.00; seniors and children $4.00; children (under 10) free

Activities: Guided architectural tours of Home and Studio and surrounding historic district, educational programs, group and foreign language tours available

Suggested Time to View House: 1 hour

Facilities on Premises: Research center and book shop

Description of Grounds: Small grounds with native prairie plantings and 100 year-old ginkgo tree

Best Season to View House: Spring-fall

Number of Yearly Visitors: 68,000

Year House Built: Home 1889, remodeled 1895, Studio 1898

Style of Architecture: Victorian Shingle Style

Number of Rooms: 14

On-Site Parking: Yes **Wheelchair Access:** Yes

Description of House

It is no exaggeration to say that Frank Lloyd Wright was, and remains to this day, America's most famous architect; the roster of his more than six hundred buildings includes such ground-breaking and wide-ranging works as Taliesin East, Fallingwater, the Unity Temple in Oak Park, Midway Gardens, and Tokyo's Imperial Hotel. His practice of an "organic" architecture, which took as its template Nature's own geometry, palette, and textures, and led to the development of Prairie-style architecture, was uniquely his own; it remains one of the signal developments in the history of the profession.Wright was born in Wisconsin in 1867, initially apprenticed with Joseph Silsbee of Chicago, who worked in the Shingle style, then joined the renowned Chicago firm of Adler and Sullivan. That city, rebuilding after the great fire of 1871 and rapidly fashioning itself into America's "Second City," served as a marvelous laboratory for the development of a truly American architecture. Louis Sullivan, Wright's mentor in those years, was only one of a number of practicing architects who, while erecting the first steel-framed skyscrapers, carried on, in their very designs, an exciting debate—sometimes with themselves—between ornamentation and functionality; a debate which Wright would attend, then extend, in his own work.

The Frank Lloyd Wright Home and Studio was Wright's own architectural laboratory for the first twenty years of his professional career; he lived here with his wife, Catherine Tobin, and their six children, until 1909. The studio, in which Wright designed more than 150 buildings, was added in 1898. The house was originally designed with the prominent gables, window bays, and characteristic dark shingled surfaces of the Atlantic coast Shingle-style homes that Wright admired. Even so, other, more idiosyncratic, elements are on display: the simple overall geometry, broad eaves, window bands, and large open interior spaces which prefigure the Prairie style; and the obvious Japanese influences in the interior, where the oak woodwork, repetitive natural patterns, and earthen colors evoke an almost Zen-like serenity. A live tree growing through the roof of the studio passageway adds to the feeling that somehow nature itself has been incorporated into the house.

The home and studio have been fully restored to their appearance in 1909, the last year of Wright's residency here. The furniture, designed by the architect, is mostly original to the house; if not, the pieces are reproductions based on his designs.

Notable Collections on Exhibit

Many items belonging to the famous architect are on display, including a number of decorative pieces and woodblock prints which he collected on his several trips to Japan; among these is a lovely set of black lacquerware—a tiered foodbox and matching bowls—he acquired on his first trip to that country, in 1905. The set is marked with the red square which Wright adapted as his personal symbol.

Additional Information

On the third weekend of each May, from 9 a.m.–5 p.m., the Annual Wright Plus Housewalk is conducted from the Frank Lloyd Wright Home and Studio; the walk features tours of eight privately owned homes and two public buildings designed by Wright and his contemporaries. The home and studio is listed on the National Register of Historic Places.

John C. Flanagan House

942 Northeast Glen Oak Avenue
Peoria, IL 61603
(309) 674-1921

Contact: Peoria Historical Society
Open: Mon.-Fri. 10 a.m.–4 p.m.; closed
major holidays
Admission: Adults $3.00; children
(15 and under) $1.00
Activities: Guided tours, seasonal events
Suggested Time to View House:
45–60 minutes
Facilities on Premises: Gift shop
Description of Grounds: Grounds offer a
spectacular view of the Illinois River; the
residential yard features a variety of
plants found in the 1850s

Best Season to View House: Spring and
summer
Number of Yearly Visitors: 800
Number of Rooms: 9

Style of Architecture: Federal, brick with
elements of Italianate
Year House Built: c.1837
On-Site Parking: No **Wheelchair Access:** No

Description of House

John C. Flanagan, a lawyer originally from Philadelphia, came to settle
in Peoria with his mother, brother, and two sisters; here he gained renown
as a land developer and city alderman. Flanagan, who remained a bachelor,
lived in the house until his death in 1891; it was left to a niece who sold it
eleven years later.

The John Flanagan House is the oldest residential structure still standing
in Peoria. The front of the Federal-style house, which faces the Illinois River,
is virtually unchanged from its original appearance and condition. It features a center gable, front and back porches decorated with elaborate
wrought-iron posts and railings done in a grapevine design, overhanging
eaves with simple brackets, a U-shaped crown on the top window, and a
slate roof. The whole has been fully restored to appear as it did in the 1850s.

Most of the furnishings are in the Empire Revival style; some pieces
belonged to the Flanagans, but the majority have been collected and
donated—most locally—and are authentic to the period. Carpeting and
wallpapers in the front hall are authentic reproductions of fragments which
were found behind the radiators during the restoration process.

Notable Collections on Exhibit

In addition to the artifacts, furnishings, and implements appropriate to a
mid-19th-century home, the Peoria Historical Society uses the Flanagan house
to display objects which illustrate local history, from the Native American habitation of the region through the early French settlements, up to the present era.

Additional Information

The John C. Flanagan House is listed on the National Register of Historic
Places.

Pettengill-Morron House Museum

1212 West Moss Avenue
Peoria, IL 61603
(309) 674-4745

Contact: Peoria Historical Society
Open: Tues.-Sat. 10 a.m.–4 p.m.;
closed major holidays
Admission: Adults $3.00; children
(15 and under) $1.00
Activities: Guided tours, seasonal programs,
rotating exhibits
Suggested Time to View House: 1 hour
Facilities on Premises: Gift shop

Description of Grounds: 2½ acre park-like
grounds with shrubs and trees
Best Season to View House: Spring and fall
Number of Yearly Visitors: 4,000
Year House Built: 1868, remodeled exterior
1900, remodeled interior 1945
Style of Architecture: Victorian Second
Empire with later Revival-style additions
Number of Rooms: 11
On-Site Parking: Yes **Wheelchair Access:** No

Description of House

Moses Pettengill (1802-1883), born in New Hampshire, son of Benjamin Pettengill, a locally prominent farmer and member of the State Legislature, decided to seek make his fortune as a merchant. From 1827 to 1833, he traveled searching throughout the eastern United States for money-making opportunities and even opened several businesses in New York State. In 1834, he decided to go west, and he and his wife, Lucy, settled in Peoria; here, he began selling hardware and stoves and soon found himself a success. When the Pettengills arrived in Peoria, the town only had a hundred and fifty inhabitants, virtually all of whom lived in log cabins; it was in such a setting that they took it upon themselves to exert a civilizing influence, first by helping found the Main Street Presbyterian Church, then the Pettengill Female Seminary. From the time of Pettengill's death in 1883 to 1953, when Miss Jean Morron purchased the property, the house had gone through at least five owners and two major remodelings.

Miss Jean Morron, daughter of John Herschel Morron and Eleanor Reynolds, and granddaughter of John Reynolds, founder of the meat-packing firm which bore his name, graduated from Smith College and McGill University, then came back to Peoria to teach. She traveled extensively, especially in France, whose language she was fluent in, and volunteered at the Neighborhood House where she worked with disadvantaged children. When she moved into the Pettengill House, she brought with her the iron fence, brass rails from her front porch, silver nameplate, gaslight fixtures, and marble mantelpiece from her former bedroom. Miss Jean Morron died in 1966, without heirs, and the house and its contents was given to the Peoria Historical Society.

The brick Victorian structure has eleven rooms with three large hallways, four stairways, five fireplaces, an attic, and a full basement. The exterior boasts of walls fifteen inches thick and features a partial wrap-around porch with a Neoclassical pediment and columns, probably added in 1900, and a porte-cochere. The house has been restored to the period of Jean Morron's occupancy; though she had donated some pieces to different institutions, many originals belonging to her or the Pettengills remain in the house.

Notable Collections on Exhibit

Among the items on display are a dragonfly lamp from the studios of Louis Comfort Tiffany and a document signed by George Washington.

Additional Information

The Pettengill-Morron House is listed on the National Register of Historic Places.

Governor John Wood Mansion

425 South Twelfth Street
Quincy, IL 62301
(217) 222-1835

Contact: Historical Society of Quincy and Adams County

Open: Apr., Sept., Oct., Sat. and Sun. 1–4 p.m.; June–Aug., Mon.-Thurs., Sat. and Sun. 1–4 p.m.; weekends in December

Admission: Adults $2.00; students $1.00

Activities: Guided tours, orientation program, Christmas Candlelight Tours

Suggested Time to View House: 60–90 minutes

Best Season to View House: Spring-fall

Facilities on Premises: Visitor center, gift shop

Description of Grounds: Grounds have been restored to mid 19th-century appearance

Number of Yearly Visitors: 5,000

Year House Built: Started 1835, completed 1838

Style of Architecture: Greek Revival

Number of Rooms: 14

On-Site Parking: Yes **Wheelchair Access:** No

Description of House

John Wood, a native of New York State, came west in the early 19th century and founded the town of Quincy in 1822. A driving force in early Illinois politics—Wood was an organizer of the Republican Party in the state—Wood served as Lieutenant Governor from 1856 to 1860, when he was elected to the governorship. It is reported that he sponsored the 1858 meeting in Quincy at which his friend Abraham Lincoln was first mentioned as a possible candidate for the Presidency of the United States.

The John Wood Mansion is considered one of the finest examples of Greek Revival architecture extant in the Midwest; it features a front-gabled, full facade porch, two full width two-story porches, four Doric columns, and a triangular pediment with lunette. In 1864, the house was moved to its present location, just across the street from its original site. Even though the distance was short, it took some doing to move the structure: first, it had to be sawed in half; then, twenty teams of horses had to haul it, one half at a time, over a ten-foot ramp which protected Wood's prized Osage Orange hedge. Fortunately, the operation was a success. Now the house is restored in segments, the downstairs to the 1830-1850 period when John Wood lived here and the upstairs to the later period of the 1860s when his son, Daniel, occupied the house. The second floor hallway is suspended above non-load-bearing walls, and the 1865 bathroom features a zinc-lined wooden tub.

Most of the furniture in the house is in the Empire style, notable exceptions being the Hepplewhite and American Chippendale chairs. All pieces, even those not belonging to the Woods, are local to Quincy and authentic to the middle part of the 19th century.

Notable Collections on Exhibit

Among the items on display, there is an 1840 oriental carpet once owned by Walter Chrysler, keys to the Mormon Temple in Nauvoo, a three-story Victorian dollhouse, a table used by Abraham Lincoln, and various portraits done by Chester Harding, a relatively well-known 19th-century painter.

Additional Information

The Governor John Wood Mansion, acquired in 1907 by the Historical Society of Quincy and Adams County, stands as the first example of historic preservation in the state of Illinois. It is listed on the National Register of Historic Places.

Erlander Home Museum

404 South Third Street
Rockford, IL 61104
(815) 963-5559

Contact: Swedish Historical Society of
Rockford

Open: Sun. 2–4 p.m.; other times by
appointment

Admission: $2.00 per person

Activities: Guided group tours, annual
Midsommer's Dag and Lucia Fest
celebrations

Suggested Time to View House: 1 hour

Facilities on Premises: Swedish-made gift
items and books

Description of Grounds: Corner lot with
antique Victorian plantings

Best Season to View House: Spring-fall

Year House Built: 1871

Number of Rooms: 14

Number of Yearly Visitors: 1,700

Style of Architecture: Italianate

On-Site Parking: Yes **Wheelchair Access:** No

Description of House

The home of John Erlander was the first brick house built in Rockford's Haight Village, an early Swedish-American community now designated a National Historic District. Erlander was born in Sweden in 1826 and emigrated to the United States with his brother and sister in 1854. He was a tailor who became a partner in a clothing store and introduced the first sewing machine into town; later, John served as president of both the Union Furniture Company, a furniture manufacturing cooperative founded by Swedish immigrants in 1876, and the Swedish Mutual Fire Insurance Company. He also became quite active in civic and church affairs. Erlander married Inga Stina and the couple had eight children—only three of whom reached maturity. This house remained in the Erlander family until 1951.

This Italianate house is built of a fine red brick hand-made in Rockford; the interiors and the exterior decorative woodwork were designed and executed by Swedish craftsmen. The front hall is wallpapered in a reproduction Victorian design, while the parlor and sitting room feature extensive stenciling on the walls and ceilings. Though the house is extremely well-built and snug, it was never fitted with electricity, gas, or central heating in all the years of its occupancy by the family. Many of the furnishings belonged to the Erlanders, most of them were manufactured in Rockford, and all of them are appropriate to the period of John and Inga's occupancy. The kitchen chairs come from the first Swedish household in Rockford.

Notable Collections on Exhibit

There are items on display here which portray the lives of Rockford's early Swedish settlers: copper kitchen utensils, John Erlander's trunk containing tools, farm implements, pewter, and glass, a *kakelugn* (heating stove) with decorative tiling, and a collection of Scandinavian dolls in native dress. We also see photographs of the Erlander family and Mary Erlander's watercolors.

Tinker Swiss Cottage

**411 Kent Street
Rockford, IL 61102
(815) 944-2424**

Contact: Tinker Swiss Cottage Museum
Open: Wed.-Sun., guided tours at 1 p.m.,
2 p.m., 3 p.m.
Admission: Adults $2.00; seniors $1.00;
children $.50
Activities: Guided tours, group tours by
appointment
Suggested Time to View House:
60–90 minutes
Facilities on Premises: Picnic and
recreation areas
Description of Grounds: Located in public
park-former property of the Tinker
estate-with picnic and recreation areas
Style of Architecture: Exotic Revival Swiss
Chalet cottage
Best Season to View House: Summer
Number of Yearly Visitors: 7,500
Year House Built: Between 1865 and 1877
Number of Rooms: 20
On-Site Parking: Yes **Wheelchair Access:** No

Description of House

Robert Tinker, who worked at the Manny Reaper Company, had taken a world tour in 1862; when he returned to Rockford, he began construction on his Swiss cottage. It stood on Kent Creek just across from Miss Mary Dorr Manny's home. Robert loved Miss Mary and, in 1870, they got married. They maintained both properties until 1886, when her former home was sold to the railroad. After Mary Tinker's death in 1904, Robert then married Jessie Dorr Hurd, Mary's widowed niece who had lived with the couple for some years. Robert died in 1924, but Jessie lived on in the house until her death eighteen years later.

The design of the Tinker Cottage is based on that of a Swiss chalet Robert had visited and admired on his world tour. The exotic five-story structure is constructed of wood and features a two-story octagonal library modeled after that belonging to Sir Walter Scott, an interior porch and balcony, a smoking porch, and a conservatory with a fish pond and fountain. Several of the rooms are decorated with large murals depicting European landscapes, still-lifes, and portraits. All of the furnishings are original to the house and were donated fully intact, along with the building and property, by Jessie Tinker upon her death in 1942.

Additional Information

The Tinker Cottage is a city, state, and national landmark. It is listed on the National Register of Historic Places.

William Jennings Bryan Birthplace

408 South Broadway
Salem, IL 62881
(618) 548-7791

Contact: City of Salem
Open: Daily except Thurs. 1–5 p.m.; closed major holidays
Admission: Donations accepted
Activities: Guided tours, group tours by reservation, annual William Jennings Bryan Annual Birthday Celebration
Suggested Time to View House: 20 minutes

Description of Grounds: Fenced yard
Best Season to View House: Year round
Number of Yearly Visitors: 500
Year House Built: 1852
Style of Architecture: National
Number of Rooms: 8, 3 open to the public
On-Site Parking: Yes **Wheelchair Access:** No

Description of House

William Jennings Bryan—lawyer, statesman, famous orator, and three-time Presidential candidate—was born in this house in 1860, and lived here for the first six years of his life. He was born to Silas and Mariah Bryan who built the house in 1852. Silas was a teacher, lawyer, circuit judge, and congressman who won renown as one of the framers of the Constitution of the State of Illinois. Today William Jennings Bryan is perhaps best known as the prosecuting attorney during the infamous Scopes "Monkey" Trial in Dayton, Tennessee—the trial he lost to Clarence Darrow—immortalized in the movie *Inherit The Wind*.

The floor plan of the Bryan House consists of two rooms upstairs on either side of a central hall sitting above their mirror image on the first floor with the addition of a dining room and kitchen in the rear. The whole interior color scheme is white with varying accents—for example, one of the rooms is done in a blue reproduction wallpaper common to the period. Throughout the house are large floor-to-ceiling windows in a two-over-two sash design; some of these windows still show the original glass. All of the furnishings on display have been donated by the Bryan family. These include: a corner cabinet, a marble-topped washstand, a lawyer's desk, a rocker with a leather bottom, and several can chairs.

Notable Collections on Exhibit

In addition to the furnishings mentioned above, one may also view a collection of vintage clothing and Bryan memorabilia collected in the years of his Presidential campaigns.

Additional Information

The William Jennings Bryan Birthplace is listed on the National Register of Historic Places. If one is interested in America's great speechmaker, another site worth visiting is the Home of William Jennings Bryan in Lincoln, Nebraska. This house is currently undergoing extensive renovation but will be open to the public in the near future. The phone number is (402) 483-3721.

Frank Lloyd Wright's Dana-Thomas House State Historic Site

301 East Lawrence Avenue
Springfield, IL 62703
(217) 782-6776

Contact: Illinois Historic Preservation Agency
Open: Wed.-Sun. 9 a.m.–4 p.m.
Admission: Free
Activities: Guided tours, 10 minute slide program
Suggested Time to View House: 60–90 minutes
Facilities on Premises: Book shop
Number of Yearly Visitors: 100,000

Description of Grounds: Landscaped city yard
Best Season to View House: Summer and fall
Year House Built: Between 1902 and 1904
Style of Architecture: Prairie School, original Italianate-style house (encased) with Victorian interiors
Number of Rooms: 35
On-Site Parking: No **Wheelchair Access:** Yes

Description of House

Remodeled by Frank Lloyd Wright for the Springfield socialite, women's rights activist, and founder of the Lawrence Center for Constructive Thought Susan Lawrence Dana, this home is perhaps the most complete early expression of the the famous architect's Prairie style. Susan, daughter of Rheuna Lawrence, a successful investor in mining ventures and one time mayor of Springfield, lived through much personal tragedy: her first husband, Edwin Dana, with whom she had two children who died in infancy, himself died in a mining accident in Oregon; her second husband, the Danish baritone Lawrence Joergen-Dahl, died suddenly in her presence; her third marriage ended in divorce; and her mother died only a few months after completion of this house. The house which Wright remodeled came into Susan's hands upon the death of her father in 1904. The house was sold to Mr. and Mrs. Charles C. Thomas in 1944; though they made some minor changes—the house was used as their publishing company's offices—much of the house remained intact and the integrity of Wright's design was fully protected.

Wright took the house that Susan's father had built in the Italianate style and completely altered it, except for the original brick foundation and a portion of the original floor plan which includes a Victorian sitting room and marble fireplace. It now shows Wright's characteristic low horizontal roofs, wide overhanging eaves, and row upon row of art glass windows.

Inside there are over one hundred pieces of original Wright-designed furniture. The interior features a musician's balcony, a sixty-foot conservatory hallway, a gallery for entertaining, and a full-scale duck pin bowling alley.

Notable Collections on Exhibit

Original terra cotta sculptures by Richard W. Bock can be found in the vestibule and reception hall and a George Niedecken mural spans the four walls of the dining room.

Additional Information

Frank Lloyd Wright's Dana-Thomas House is listed on the National Register of Historic Places.

Lincoln Home National Historic Site

413 South Eighth Street
Springfield, IL 62701
(217) 492-4150

Contact: National Park Service

Open: Jan.-Mar., daily 8:30 a.m.–5 p.m.; Apr.-May 8:30 a.m.–6 p.m.; May-Sept. 8 a.m.–8 p.m.; Sept.-Dec. 8:30 a.m.–5 p.m.

Admission: Free

Activities: Two 20 minute films in visitor center presenting Lincoln's life and times

Suggested Time to View House: 30 minutes

Facilities on Premises: Visitor center, bookstore

Description of Grounds: Located in historic four block neighborhood consisting of eighteen restored buildings which date from the Lincoln era

Best Season to View House: Late fall-early spring

Number of Yearly Visitors: 500,000

Year House Built: 1839, expanded 1856

Style of Architecture: Greek Revival

Number of Rooms: 11

On-Site Parking: Yes **Wheelchair Access:** Yes

Description of House

This two-story Greek Revival-style house—the only home that Abraham Lincoln ever owned—was originally built as a one-story cottage in 1839 by the Reverend Charles Dresser. The Lincolns, Abe and Mary Todd, lived here from 1844 to 1861 and all four of their boys, Robert, Edward, William and Thomas, were born here. Little "Eddie" died here. Had Lincoln returned from Washington after serving out his second term as sixteenth President of the United States, it would have been to this house. During their years here, the Lincolns made a number of changes to the structure, the chief one being the 1856 enlargement and addition necessitated by the growth of the family and Lincoln's own rise in stature. When the family left for Washington in 1861, the house was rented to Lucian Tilton, president of the Great Western Railroad. After Lincoln's assassination in 1865, the house continued to be held and rented out by the family. Within years, Robert Todd Lincoln became the sole owner of the property; in the 1870s he donated it to the state of Illinois. A century later, in 1972, the National Park Service took responsibility for the house and property, extending the National Historic Site into the surrounding neighborhood.

The house, which may have originally been painted brown, has been fully restored to its appearance in 1860; because the Lincolns held a large sale of their household items just prior to leaving for Washington, many pieces original to the house have gone; in fact, only fifty items on exhibit actually belonged to the family. The rest are genuine period pieces set against authentic reproduction wallpaper, carpeting, and window coverings. These furnishings reflect the influence of the Empire and Late Classical styles of the early 1800s, as well as the popular mid-century Rococo Revival style.

Notable Collections on Exhibit

The massive four-poster bed in the Lincoln bedroom, measuring six-feet-nine-inches long and showing seven-foot posts, is almost certainly a reproduction; the original is thought to have been moved to Chicago along with a number of other Tilton family possessions, where it was ultimately destroyed in the Great Fire of 1871.

Additional Information

This site is listed on the National Register of Historic Places.

Dunham Hunt House, "Oaklawn"

304 Cedar Avenue
St. Charles, IL 60174
(708) 584-7001

Contact: Dunham Hunt Historic
Preservation Society
Open: Wed.-Sun. 1–4 p.m.; closed major
holidays; other times by appointment
Admission: Donation suggested; special
group fee $1.00 each person
Activities: Monthly exhibits
Suggested Time to View House:
30–60 minutes
Facilities on Premises: Gift shop
Description of Grounds: Original gardens
restored
Best Season to View House: Spring and
summer
Number of Yearly Visitors: 1800
Number of Rooms: 7

Style of Architecture: Colonial Early
Classical Revival, red brick
Year House Built: 1840
On-Site Parking: Yes **Wheelchair Access:** No

Description of House

The two-story Dunham Hunt House was built in 1840 by Bela T. Hunt of local brick; since then, it has been occupied by members of only two families: the Hunts and the Dunhams. Mark Dunham, who inherited his father's farm in the 1850s, owned one of the largest breeding farms of Percheron horses in the United States: at any given time, as many as six hundred of these powerful work horses could be found on the Dunham property. Visitors from around the world came to see the breeding establishment, called "Oaklawn." After Mark died, his son, Wirth, continued the operation until 1927. By then, the growing use of tractors on America's farms had begun to render the work horse an anachronism, and the breeding business unprofitable. Jane Dunham purchased the property in 1980 and converted it into a Museum. The property is also used as a riding center and home of the Wayne-DuPage Hunt and Horse Show.

The house features hand-stenciled parquet floors and wall borders, as well as many furnishings which originally belonged to "The Castle," Mark W. Dunham's house which still stands at the corner of Dunham and Army Trails Roads in Wayne, Illinois. The restored interior shows the house as it appeared in latter half of the 19th century.

Notable Collections on Exhibit

Two of the more notable items on display are: an original Rosa Bonheur painting of a Dunham Percheron and an Isidore Bonheur bronze of a race horse which had been given as a prize at the Columbian Exposition of 1893.

Additional Information

The Dunham Hunt House is listed on the National Register of Historic Places.

James Canty Morrison House

Routes 29 and 48 East
Taylorville, IL 62568
(217) 824-6922

Contact: Christian County Historical Society

Open: Apr.-Nov., Wed.-Sun. 11 a.m.–5 p.m.

Admission: General fee $1.00

Activities: Guided tours, special seasonal events including October Open House and Persimmon Party

Suggested Time to View House: 1 hour

Facilities on Premises: Genealogy library and office

Description of Grounds: Complex includes the 1820 Log Cabin, the 1839 Christian County Courthouse, the 1856 One-Room Country Schoolhouse, "Buckeye School," and a picnic area with benches

Style of Architecture: Greek Revival, brick with Victorian interiors

Best Season to View House: Fall

Number of Yearly Visitors: 600

Number of Rooms: 8

Year House Built: 1854

On-Site Parking: Yes **Wheelchair Access:** Yes

Description of House

In 1839, James Canty Morrison came and settled in Taylorville; here he farmed approximately seven hundred acres, built the first jailhouse, and served as the school commissioner. Morrison's sons became local clothing merchants. His daughter was an amateur painter who moved to Oklahoma.

This two-story brick farmhouse stands on the original site of the Morrison farm; the bricks used in its construction were made of clay taken from the property; the walls are of varying thicknesses: the basement is over sixteen inches thick, the first floor twelve inches, and the second story only eight inches. The simple, less than full height, entry porch leads to a beautiful hand-carved walnut railing on the front stairway. An original outbuilding, called the Bee Castle, still stands. All of the furnishings are authentic to the period 1850 to 1870; these include a Victorian velvet settee and matching chairs, and a rosewood Melodeon, all found in the living room. The painting in the parlor was done by Morrison's daughter, Illinois.

Notable Collections on Exhibit

The kitchen in the Morrison House features many domestic utensils and appliances common to an 1850s farmhouse.

Kline Creek Farm at
Timber Ridge Forest Preserve

1 North 600 County Farm Road
West Chicago, IL 60188
(708) 790-4900

Contact: Forest Preserve District of
DuPage County
Open: Year-round, Thurs.-Mon. 9 a.m.–5 p.m.
Admission: Free
Activities: Guided tour, demonstrations
Suggested Time to View House: 90 minutes
Facilities on Premises: Gift shop
Style of Architecture: Folk Victorian-style
farmhouse

Description of Grounds: 1,000 acre preserve
and working c.1890 farm with several
outbuildings, fields and orchards, and
walking paths
Best Season to View House: Year round
Number of Yearly Visitors: 35,000
Year House Built: 1890
Number of Rooms: 5
On-Site Parking: Yes **Wheelchair Access:** Yes

Description of House

The farmhouse at the Kline Creek Farm is only one component of a fully restored 1890s farm complex; the whole provides an unusually detailed view of every aspect of the farm life typical throughout DuPage County 100 years ago. The Kline family, German immigrants who settled here, in the fertile northeastern corner of Illinois, planned their farmstead in accord with the dictum, "A place for everything and everything in its place." The various outbuildings were positioned to save labor, protect crops and take full advantage of Nature's forces, such as wind and water. On the Kline farm today, demonstrations conducted by interpreters in authentic garb complete the portrait of the family's life which the house and other buildings draw for the visitor.

The Klines were a family of some means and the white Victorian farmhouse illustrates the fact well. The exterior features a simple gable front with two-story bays, an L-shaped wing, a small partial front porch accented with a spindlework rail, and jigsaw cut brackets. Inside, there is a parlor, sitting room, dining room, kitchen, and the second floor bedrooms. The very presence of a dining room points to affluence and the decorated kitchen with its water pump confirms it. The house is furnished in a fashion authentic to a late nineteenth century prairie farmhouse; items include a rocking chair and a pump organ c. 1870.

Kruse House Museum

527 Main Street, P.O. Box 246
West Chicago, IL 60185
(708) 231-0564

Contact: West Chicago Historical Society
Open: May–Sept., Sat. 11 a.m.–3 p.m.;
  special guided tours by appointment
Admission: Free
Activities: Guided tours, slide program,
  special seasonal events oncluding Ice
  Cream Social and Holiday Open House
Suggested Time to View House:
  30–60 minutes
Description of Grounds: Expansive yard
  and garden with original garage and
  garden shed
Best Season to View House: Spring-fall
Year House Built: 1917, addition c.1930
Number of Rooms: 11

Number of Yearly Visitors: 500
Style of Architecture: Prairie School
On-Site Parking: No **Wheelchair Access:** No

Description of House

Originally known only as "Junction," West Chicago began life as the village in which three separate branches of the Galena and Chicago Union Railroad (now the C & NW), which started running in 1849, joined: the St. Charles Branch, the Aurora branch, and the Omaha line. By the middle part of the 19th century, the village had become a bustling city whose every activity was centered around the railroad. Today, West Chicago boasts some of the finest exhibits depicting the heyday of the American railroads.

Fred Kruse, a passenger service collector for the C & NW line, lived in this Prairie-style house with his wife, Bertha. Their daughter, Celia, lived here until 1975, when the property was deeded to the West Chicago Historical Society. Many of the furnishings and personal items on display here belonged to the Kruse family and the whole effect of the house, and its contents, is to accurately depict the common life of a typical railroad family living in the early part of this century.

The light beige stucco house features an enclosed front porch which was added c. 1930, leaded glass windows in the main downstairs rooms, plate rail in the dining room, a full basement originally used as the kitchen, and tile floors with oak woodwork throughout the house.

Notable Collections on Exhibit

There are Steuben chandeliers on display, as well as seventeen quilts made by Celia, her mother, and a grandmother. In addition to the household items, the house features, as befits any dwelling in West Chicago, many artifacts and memorabilia pertaining to the railroad.

Additional Information

Located just a short distance away, at 495 Main Street, is Heritage Commons, the city's 1976 Bicentennial project devoted to preserving the living memory of its railroad heritage.

William L. Gregg House Museum

115 South Linden Avenue
Westmount, IL 60559
(708) 960-3392

Contact: Westmount Historical Society

Open: Guided tours for groups by appointment; closed Christmas and New Year's Day

Admission: Free

Activities: Guided tours, Collector's Exhibit, special seasonal events including Valentine's Day, Easter, Christmas Open Houses

Description of Grounds: Located at Veteran's Memorial Park with picnic grove and sports fields

Suggested Time to View House: 20–40 minutes

Best Season to View House: Spring to early fall

Number of Yearly Visitors: 500

Number of Rooms: 9

Facilities on Premises: Gift shop and archives

Style of Architecture: Victorian Second Empire, brick

Year House Built: 1872

On-Site Parking: Yes **Wheelchair Access:** No

Description of House

After Chicago's Great Fire of 1871, with lumber in exceedingly short supply, the manufacture of brick and other building materials proved to be a uncommonly good business to undertake, and many fortunes were made during this period of rebuilding the city. The area around Westmount was ideally suited to such manufacture for two reasons: first, the native clay made fine brick; and, second, the land here was higher in elevation than at Chicago, which meant that the heavy brick only had to be transported downhill. And it was here that William L. Gregg of Philadelphia founded the Excelsior Brick Manufacturing Company and made his fortune. His company did much to bolster the local economy as well, and, during Excelsior's heyday, Gregg was regarded as a hero: today's Cass Avenue was called Gregg's Road, the train station was called Gregg's Station, and the present-day Maercker School was called Gregg's School! Unfortunately, his success was short-lived; by 1883, Gregg had moved out of the area and his company shut down operations in 1890.

The Victorian house was built in 1872 of Excelsior brick and features a straight mansard roof, a wrap-around porch leading to the north entrance, and characteristic arched windows. Since Gregg's departure, the house has served many functions, including that of farmhouse, local speakeasy, community recreation center, funeral parlor, rectory, and convent. It was moved to its present site in Veteran's Memorial Park in 1976 to avoid demolition.

Additional Information

The William L. Gregg House is listed on the National Register of Historic Places.

Indiana

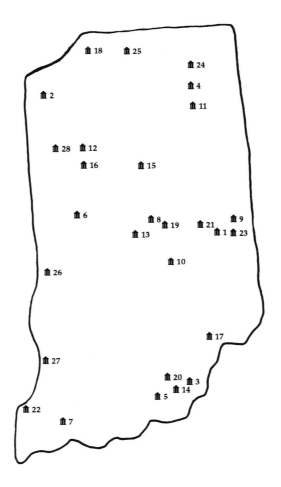

1. **Cambridge City**
   Huddleston House Tavern
   Museum

2. **Cedar Lake**
   Lake of the Red Cedars Museum

3. **Charlestown**
   Thomas Downs House

4. **Columbia City**
   Thomas R. Marshall House

5. **Corydon**
   Posey House Museum

6. **Crawfordsville**
   Lane Place Historic Home

7. **Evansville**
   Historic Reitz Home

8. **Fishers**
   William Conner Estate

9. **Fountain City**
   *Levi Coffin House State
   Historic Site*

10. **Geneva**
    *Limberlost Cabin State
    Historic Site*

11. **Huntington**
    *Chief Richardville House
    Samuel Purviance House*

12. **Idaville**
    Abner Shafer House

13. **Indianapolis**
    *James Whitcomb Riley Museum
    Home*
    *Lilly Pavilion of Decorative Arts–
    "Oldfields"*
    Morris-Butler House
    *President Benjamin Harrison
    Memorial Home*

14. **Jeffersonville**
    Howard Steamboat Museum

15. **Kokomo**
    Seiberling Mansion

16. **Lafayette**
    Moses Fowler House

17. **Madison**
    *Lanier Mansion State
    Historic Site*

18. **Michigan City**
    Barker Mansion

19. **Nashville**
    *T.C. Steele State Historic Site,
    "House of the Singing Winds"*

20. **New Albany**
    Culbertson Mansion

21. **New Castle**
    *William C. Grose Home–
    Henry County Historical
    Museum*

22. **New Harmony**
    *1830 Owen House
    David Lenz House
    Fauntleroy House*

23. **Richmond**
    Andrew F. Scott House

24. **Rome City**
    Cabin in Wildflower Woods

25. **South Bend**
    *John D. Oliver House–
    Copshaholm*

26. **Terre Haute**
    Home of Eugene V. Debs

27. **Vincennes**
    *Old French House
    William Henry Harrison House–
    "Grouseland"*

28. **Wolcott**
    Wolcott House

Huddleston House Tavern Museum

U.S. Highway 40 West
P.O. Box 284
Cambridge City, IN 47327
(317) 478-3172

Contact: Historic Landmarks Foundation of Indiana

Open: Feb.-Dec. Tues.-Sat. 10 a.m–4 p.m.; May-Aug. Sun. 1–4 p.m.; closed major holidays, month of January

Admission: Suggested donation $2.00

Activities: Guided Tours, group tours by appointment, seasonal programs

Suggested Time to View House: 45 minutes

Description of Grounds: Outbuildings and lawn

Best Season to View House: Spring and fall

Number of Yearly Visitors: 5000

Year House Built: 1841

Style of Architecture: Federal

Number of Rooms: 11

On-Site Parking: Yes **Wheelchair Access:** Yes

Description of House

John Huddleston, whose father had come to Indiana from North Carolina with a large group of Quakers in 1816, built this farmhouse around 1840 for his growing family. It was sited on the much-traveled National Road and Huddleston took advantage of this location and built two "travelers' kitchens" into his basement. In addition to renting out these kitchens, he also let rooms for the night. For weary teamsters, drovers, and emigrants—and their animals—the Huddleston Farmhouse and Tavern was a welcome respite from their journey west.

The house that John Huddleston built here is a large Federal-style brick structure with its basement built into a hill. This basement was designed strictly to serve travelers who needed food and shelter as they traveled the National Road, and it contains two kitchens. The house is the centerpiece of a farm complex which also includes the original barn, a smokehouse, springhouse, and carriage barn. The house has been restored to the period of the 1840s, when the Huddlestons lived and worked here, and it is furnished to that period.

Additional Information

Group tours of the Huddleston Farmhouse Inn Museum are available, and the restored barn can be rented for meetings. The museum is listed on the National Register of Historic Places.

Lake of the Red Cedars Museum

7808 West 138th Place
Town Complex Grounds
Cedar Lake, IN 46303
(219) 374-6157

Contact: Cedar Lake Indiana Historical Association
Open: May-Oct., Thurs.-Sun. 1–5 p.m.
Admission: Adults $2.00; children (under 12) $.50
Activities: Guided tours, audiovisual 1927 film, special programs
Suggested Time to View House: 1 hour

Description of Grounds: Located on town park
Best Season to View House: Spring-fall
Number of Yearly Visitors: 2,000
Year House Built: 1895, remodeled 1920
Style of Architecture: National, frame hotel
Number of Rooms: 65
On-Site Parking: Yes **Wheelchair Access:** Yes

Description of House

This sixty-five-room resort hotel—Cedar Lake was a favored retreat for Chicago's high society during Prohibition—began its life in 1895 as a boarding house for workers who cut ice from the lake for the Armour brothers. When the ice business was sold to John Shedd, the family of Chris Lassen, who already owned a restaurant on Cedar Lake, bought the T-shaped structure and had it hauled across the frozen lake in the winter of 1919. From that year until just shortly after the Second World War, the Lassens used the building as a hotel. They then sold it to a Christian youth group. In 1977, the town bought the shabby building and its 26 acre property; instead of demolishing it, they leased it to the Cedar Lake Historical Association, who saved it and opened it as a museum.

The main part of the two-story frame structure was built in 1895 and the north-south wing was added in 1919, the year that the whole was relocated across Cedar Lake. The 16,300 square foot lakefront hotel features a full wrap-around porch and a pyramidical roof. The rooms have been interpreted thematically to display fashions and furnishings from the 1830s to the 1950s.

Notable Collections on Exhibit

Most of the displays at the museum depict the Prohibition period when the hotel was in its heyday as a resort for Chicagoans. Other noteworthy collections include: the only documented set of Dr. Scholl's cobbler tools (Dr. Scholl apprenticed in Cedar Lake), an extensive set of ice-cutting tools as used by the Armour workers, and a letter and land contract written by Declaration of Independence signer Josiah Bartlett.

Additional Information

The Lake of Red Cedars Museum is listed on the National Register of Historic Places.

Thomas Downs House

1045 Main Street
Charlestown, IN 47111
(812) 949-7903

Contact: Clark's Grant Historical Society
Open: Year-round, by appointment only
Admission: Free, donations accepted
Activities: Guided tours, classes and
special presentations
Suggested Time to View House:
30–40 minutes
Facilities on Premises: Small gift items
Description of Grounds: Herb garden and
traditional flowers
Best Season to View House: Spring
Year House Built: 1809
Style of Architecture: Federal
Number of Rooms: 4
On-Site Parking: Yes **Wheelchair Access:** No

Description of House

This Federal-style four-room house is thought to be one of the oldest in Charleston, if not in all of Clark County. It was built at the end of the first decade of the 19th century by Thomas Downs, one of the region's pioneer settlers who farmed the land then became a lawyer and judge. He died in 1832 and it is believed that shortly thereafter his family left Indiana for the Missouri frontier.

The house is built of solid brick and features two front doors; the Clark's Grant Historical Society, which only acquired the property recently, is in the processing of giving it a complete restoration. All of the furnishings on display are collected period pieces.

Notable Collections on Exhibit

Among the items on display here is a drawing of Indiana's first Governor, Jonathan Jennings; several pieces of porcelain dating from before the 1830s; and a decoratively painted rush-bottom chair c. 1815.

Additional Information

The Thomas Downs House is listed on the National Register of Historic Places.

Thomas R. Marshall House

108 West Jefferson Street
Columbia City, IN 46725
(219) 244-6372

Contact: Whitley County Historical Museum
Open: Year-round, Mon.-Thurs.
  10 a.m.–2 p.m.; first Sunday of month
  1–4 p.m.; other times by appointment
Admission: Donation suggested
Activities: Tours, rotating exhibits, special
  seasonal events including Old Settlers Craft
  Round-Up, and Holiday Open House
Suggested Time to View House: 45 minutes
Facilities on Premises: Gift shop
Description of Grounds: Small yard with
  plantings
Best Season to View House: Spring-fall
Year House Built: 1864
Number of Rooms: 10

Number of Yearly Visitors: 2,000
Style of Architecture: Eclectic Italianate
On-Site Parking: Yes **Wheelchair Access:** Yes

Description of House

"What this country needs is a really good five-cent cigar." So spoke Thomas R. Marshall, Governor of Indiana from 1908 to 1912 and Vice President under Woodrow Wilson during the First World War. Marshall, a native Hoosier who moved to Columbia City to be with his parents and practice law, bought this house in 1877 and remodeled it in 1895 for his young bride, Miss Lois Kimsey. He sold it when he was elected Governor. This fine home, now operated as the Whitley County Historical Museum, is fairly redolent of the essential decency and democratic conviviality of its one-time owner and the era he represents—Marshall also said, "A rounded life is a pleasant past, a contented present, and a hopeful future."

This Italianate-style house was built in 1864 for John Rice, bought by Thomas Marshall in 1877, and remodeled in 1895 by the Fort Wayne architectural firm Wing & Mahurin. Inside, it features quarter-sawn oak woodwork, crown moldings, a Masonic staircase, and Italian ceramic fireplace tiles. The first floor has parquet flooring and leaded glass windows. After the Marshalls sold it, the house went through a number of transformations, finally becoming a four-unit apartment building. It has now been restored to its original elegance. A number of the furnishings belonged to the Marshalls and the collected pieces are all appropriate to the period of the Marshalls' occupancy. The Thomas Riley Marshall Home is listed on the National Register of Historic Places.

Notable Collections on Exhibit

In addition to the furnishings on display, the Museum also houses a collection of Thomas Marshall campaign memorabilia, Miami Indian artifacts, quilts and coverlets belonging to early Whitley County settlers, military uniforms and equipment, and—most prized of all—a small cedar cup fashioned by one of the Pilgrims during the historic voyage of the *Mayflower* to America. This cup was donated to the Museum by Simon Peabody, a local lumber mill owner.

Posey House Museum

Contact: Hoosier Elm Chapter, Daughters
of the American Revolution
Open: Year-round, daily Noon–5 p.m.
Admission: Donations appreciated
Activities: Guided tours
Suggested Time to View House: 30 minutes
Facilities on Premises: Gift shop
Description of Grounds: Beautiful yard
with magnolia trees
Best Season to View House: Year round
Number of Yearly Visitors: 1,000
Year House Built: 1817
Style of Architecture: Federal
Number of Rooms: 6

On-Site Parking: Yes **Wheelchair Access:** No

Description of House

Colonel Thomas L. Posey, the son of Indiana's Territorial Governor, was a prominent Corydon citizen whose success as a local merchant and cashier at the Corydon branch of the Bank of Vincennes was followed by service as Harrison County Treasurer and State Adjutant General. This lifelong bachelor was also quite active in his church and managed to raise fourteen orphans. This home was built for him in 1817 at nearly twice its present size. It is now maintained by the Hoosier Elm Chapter of the Daughters of the American Revolution as a museum depicting life here in the early 19th century.

Notable Collections on Exhibit

Most of the furnishings on display are authentic to the region and the era; these include a one-hundred-and-fifty-year-old rosewood piano and pump organ in the parlor, a trundle bed with straw ticking, hand-made quilts, and fancy-work in the bedroom, as well as implements—including several looms—and Civil War relics in the weaving room.

Lane Place Historic Home

212 South Water Street
Crawfordsville, IN 47933
(317) 362-3416

Contact: Montgomery County Historical Society

Open: Apr.-Oct. Tues.-Sun., 1–4 p.m.; closed holidays

Admission: Adults $2.00; children (under 10) $.50

Activities: Bus tours, antique car shows, craft classes, oral history projects, special seasonal events including the Strawberry Festival and Christmas Candlelight tour

Suggested Time to View House: 1 hour
Facilities on Premises: Publications for sale
Description of Grounds: 4 acre lawn
Best Season to View House: Summer
Number of Yearly Visitors: 5,000
Year House Built: 1845
Style of Architecture: Greek Revival
Number of Rooms: 14
On-Site Parking: Yes **Wheelchair Access:** No

Description of House

In June of 1837, Crawfordsville Mayor "Jack" Hawkins and his family moved into the Federal-style cottage which now constitutes the dining room and serving room of the Lane Place Historic Home. One of the Hawkins daughters, Louisa, married Edward R. Canby in the parlor here two years later; Canby and his fellow townsmen, Lew Wallace and John P. Hawkins, became generals in the Union Army during the Civil War. The Hawkins family left town in 1842 and the cottage was purchased by Henry Lane, a popular lawyer and widower who had served as a Congressman and the first Republican governor of Indiana. In February of 1845, Lane married Miss Joanna Elston, the daughter of his next-door neighbor, and she began supervising the construction of the much larger Greek Revival-style house called Lane Place. The house, and its park-like grounds, would become Crawfordsville's Village Green. Here the whole town gathered—for picnics, politics, sugar camps, and all sorts of celebrations. The estate underwent further changes under the guidance of Helen Smith, Mrs. Lane's niece, who inherited the property in 1914.

The construction of 1845, which took the simple Federal-style cottage and built around it an ornate neoclassical house, was executed superbly: the two styles blend extremely well. During the 1870s, a room was added on the southeast corner of the first floor as a library for the Honorable Mr. Lane. The massive two-story gallery, south portico, and the second floor southeast bedroom were all added later still. At the head of the stairs is a small storage attic through which one steps out onto the widow's walk sitting atop a standing-seam copper roof. The deck above the West Portico has served as a balcony for special occasions since it was built in 1845. Most of the furnishings are original purchases made in Cincinnati, New Orleans, New York, and even Europe.

Notable Collections on Exhibit

Among the more interesting items on display are: Joanna Lane's sewing box, the top hat and honorary pallbearer's badge worn by Lane at President Lincoln's funeral, Col. Lane's sword, a cobalt blue cracker jar that President Lincoln dipped into, and a Fashion Doll (1810-1820).

Additional Information

Preservation of this house began in 1983 with the stabilization of the original brick wall of the early cottage. The Lane Place Historic Home is listed on the National Register of Historic Places.

Historic Reitz Home

224 Southeast First Street, P.O. Box 2478
Evansville, IN 47728
(812) 426-1871

Contact: Reitz Home Preservation
Society, Inc.
Open: Feb.-Dec., Wed.-Sun. 1–4 p.m.; other
times by special appointment
Admission: Adults $3.00; students $2.00;
children (under 12) $1.00
Activities: Guided tours, audiovisual
presentations, special programs, annual
Victorian Christmas Tour
Suggested Time to View House:
45–60 minutes

Facilities on Premises: Gift shop
Description of Grounds: Small
Victorian-style backyard garden
Best Season to View House: Spring and
summer
Style of Architecture: High Victorian
Second Empire
Number of Yearly Visitors: 8,000
Year House Built: 1871
Number of Rooms: 17
On-Site Parking: No **Wheelchair Access:** No

Description of House

John Augustus Reitz, a wealthy Evansville lumberman, built this house
in 1871. Both he and his wife, Gertrude, died in the 1890s and ownership of
the property fell to their son and his four sisters; he commenced an extensive
three-year redecoration in the late 1890s. When the last of the Reitz family
died in 1931, a Catholic women's organization called the Daughters of
Isabella took possession of the house and used it as a meeting place. Thirteen
years later, the Diocese of Evansville bought the house for its first head,
Bishop Grimmelsman, and he lived here for twenty-eight years. In 1974, the
Diocese turned the home over to the Reitz Home Preservation Society, which
now maintains it as a museum.

The imposing facade of this three-story Second Empire-style home looms
above the delicate wrought-iron gate which leads into the property. Outside,
one sees the elements typical of the style: a straight mansard roof, cresting along
the roof line, decorative window surrounds on the dormers, quoins, and

bracketed cornice molding. The house is painted white with brown trim. The solid walnut entry door features exquisite leaded glass panels. The opulent interior includes: Moorish-inspired wood-paneled hallways, parquet flooring inlaid with various woods, nine fireplaces—each one different from the rest, light green damask wall coverings, gold leaf on the cornices, and imported gilded chandeliers. About half of the furnishings belonged to the Reitzes and the rest are authentic period pieces; styles represented include the Gothic and Renaissance Revivals, Eastlake, and Exotic Turkish.

Notable Collections on Exhibit

Here one can see two sets of Jelliff furniture in superb condition, huge paintings of the family, needlework done by the Reitz sisters, and a satinwood bedroom set manufactured by the Tobey Company of Chicago.

Additional Information

The Reitz House Museum, which is listed on the National Register of Historic Places, is located in Evansville's Riverside Historic District. The fully restored Carriage House, which includes a kitchen, is now available to rent for meetings.

William Conner Estate

13400 Allisonville Road
Fishers near Noblesville, IN 46060
(317) 776-6000

Contact: Conner Prairie

Open: Apr.-Nov. Wed.-Sat. 10 a.m.–5 p.m., Sun. Noon–5 p.m.; May-Oct., Tues.-Sat. 10 a.m.–5 p.m., Sun. Noon–5 p.m.; historic areas closed Easter and Thanksgiving Day

Admission: Adults $8.00; seniors $7.25; children (6-12) $5.00; children (5 and under) free

Activities: Audiovisual presentation on 1836 Indiana, "living history" demonstrations

Suggested Time to View House: 2–3 hours

Facilities on Premises: Gift shop, restaurant and bakery

Description of Grounds: 250 acres of fields, woods and historic areas including Prairietown, the 1836 village. Some of the grounds are stone paved. Nearby handicapped accessible nature trail and museum center.

Style of Architecture: Federal, brick farmhouse

Best Season to View House: Spring and fall

Number of Yearly Visitors: 300,000+

Year House Built: 1823

Number of Rooms: 5

On-Site Parking: Yes **Wheelchair Access:** No

Description of House

William Conner was one of the very first American pioneers to blaze a trail into the heart of the wilderness that would come to be known as the State of Indiana, living among the Delaware Indians, trading in furs, then trading in land, and finally serving as an early state legislator. He had first come out here in 1800 and built this brick farmhouse some twenty-three years later. In 1934, Eli Lilly, the pharmaceutical tycoon, purchased the home and the surrounding acreage, restored it to its 19th century glory, and donated it to Earlham College to serve as a museum. This typical example of a two-story brick Federal-style home is believed to be the first residence built in New Purchase, Indiana.

The furnishings in the house, which is presently undergoing another restoration, are collected pieces appropriate to the period of Conner's occupancy.

Additional Information

William Conner's brick house forms the centerpiece of the Conner Prairie, a 250 acre living history complex which also includes the Pioneer Adventure Area and Prairietown, a working 1830s Indiana village. The site is listed on the National Register of Historic Places.

Levi Coffin House State Historic Site

115 North Main Street
on U.S. Highway 27
Fountain City, IN 47341
(317) 847-2432

Contact: Levi Coffin House Association, Inc.
Open: June 1-Sept.15, Tues.-Sun. 1–4 p.m.; Sept. 15-Oct. 31, weekends only; closed Nov.-Apr., Mondays and July Fourth. May reserved for school groups.
Admission: Adults $1.00; children (6-18) $.50; school groups $.25 per child
Activities: Guided tour, slide show, annual "Reminiscence Day" first Sunday in June
Suggested Time to View House: 1 hour

Facilities on Premises: Gift table
Description of Grounds: Town lot
Best Season to View House: Spring and fall
Number of Yearly Visitors: 5,000
Year House Built: 1839
Style of Architecture: Modified Federal, brick
Number of Rooms: 8
On-Site Parking: Yes **Wheelchair Access:** No

Description of House

The Levi Coffin House is known chiefly for being the "Grand Central Station" of the Underground Railroad in Indiana. The Coffins, anti-slavery Quakers from North Carolina, built this house in 1839 with the notion that it must serve as a hiding-place for fugitive slaves—hence the secret compartment in the garret off an upstairs bedroom. Even though they moved to Cincinnati in 1847, they held on to the property until 1860. In Cincinnati, they got to know Harriet Beecher Stowe—the character of "Eliza" in Stowe's famous novel, *Uncle Tom's Cabin*, is modeled after one of the slaves who took sanctuary at the Coffins' house. While in Newport, Levi Coffin operated a linseed oil mill at the foot of Mill Street in addition to heading one of the most successful Underground operations in the North. This house was subsequently owned by the Rhetts, who converted it into a hotel, and their daughter, Nola Rupe Brittain, who lived here until 1967, when the State of Indiana bought it.

This simple two-story brick house is built in the Federal style and features seven rooms, including the bedroom with the secret hiding-place. It is probable that the poplar used in framing out and trimming the house and the ash used for the flooring came from the Coffins' property. The library with its built-in bookcase, the living room, and the two second floor bedrooms were largely untouched when the house was converted into a hotel; each of these four rooms has its own fireplace. In the basement, one sees a very unusual interior well located near the ice storage bin. The house has been fully restored to its appearance in 1839; the furnishings on display consist mostly of pieces donated by descendants of the Quakers who settled in the area.

Notable Collections on Exhibit

Among the many implements, household utensils, and furnishings, there are a number of items here of special interest: two portraits of Levi Coffin, one done by Indiana artist Marion Blair, the other based on a picture which appeared in Coffin's autobiography; a set of Phantasia pattern ironware c. 1840; and a drop-leaf desk which bears a shipping label from Coffin's Cincinnati store.

Additional Information

The Levi Coffin House was designated a National Historic Landmark in 1965 and is listed on the National Register of Historic Places.

Limberlost Cabin State Historic Site

200 East Sixth Street, P.O. Box 356
Geneva, IN 46740
(219) 368-7428

Contact: Department of Natural Resources Indiana State Museums and Historic Sites

Open: Mar.15-Dec. 31, Wed.-Sat. 9 a.m.–5 p.m., Sun. 1–5 p.m.; closed state holidays except Memorial Day, Fourth of July and Labor Day

Admission: Fee

Activities: Guided tours, school programs, community outreach programs, special seasonal events including a nature photo contest, lawn social, and Christmas Open House

Suggested Time to View House: 30 minutes

Best Season to View House: Spring and fall

Description of Grounds: ½ city block surrounded by original stone fence, orchard, garden, and log barn

Number of Yearly Visitors: 13,800

Number of Rooms: 13

Style of Architecture: Eclectic mix of Victorian Queen Anne style with log and redwood shingle

Year House Built: 1895

On-Site Parking: Yes **Wheelchair Access:** No

Description of House

Geneva "Gene" Stratton Porter, the renowned Indiana naturalist and author, and her husband, Charles Porter, lived in this Geneva cottage from 1895 to 1913. They built their cabin—really a thirteen-room upper-middle-class home—here because of its proximity to nearby Limberlost Swamp where Gene studied and photographed the native flora and fauna, and because Charles had his businesses here. In addition to her wildlife photography and advocacy of conservation, Gene also wrote a popular series of novels set in nature, one of which is titled *A Girl of the Limberlost*. Today, her works are enjoying a modest revival as environmental consciousness has grown.

Limberlost is a two-story Queen Anne-style log structure which features redwood shingles on the second story and a shake roof. The turn-of-the-century interior is done in the popular American Arts and Crafts style; elements include stenciled ceilings, lincrusta borders (faux leather), and oak paneling. The conservatory off the dining room, and the two porches, bring the outdoors into the house itself, a feature entirely appropriate to a naturalist's home. The furnishings reflect the era of the Porters' occupancy and include an original bedroom set.

Notable Collections on Exhibit

Two distinct displays of note are: Gene Stratton Porter's 1906 butterfly and moth collection and a superb collection of Native American artifacts acquired by Charles Porter on his travels through Mexico and the Southeast United States.

Additional Information

The museum shop at Limberlost offers a wide selection of Gene Porter's works.

Chief Richardville House

U.S. Highway 24 West
Huntington, IN 46750
(219) 356-4218

Contact: Historic Forks of the Wabash, Inc.

Open: Apr.-Oct., Wed.-Sun. 1–4 p.m.

Admission: Adults $3.00; children (6-12) $1.00

Activities: Guided tours, audiovisual programs, Native American and pioneer life demonstrations

Suggested Time to View House: 1 hour

Facilities on Premises: Visitor center, gift shop, reading room

Description of Grounds: Picturesque site on Wabash River and with two miles of trails along the Wabash & Erie Canal

Best Season to View House: Spring-fall

Year House Built: 1833

Number of Rooms: 7

Number of Yearly Visitors: 5,000

Style of Architecture: Greek Revival

On-Site Parking: Yes **Wheelchair Access:** Yes

Description of House

Jean Baptiste-Richardville (1764-1841), Chief of the Miami Indian Nation, was one of the wealthiest Native Americans of the 19th century. He built this house in 1833 and it served as the center for conducting tribal affairs for the next thirteen years. Richardville's mother was Ta-cum-wah, sister to Chief Little Turtle. After Chief Richardville's death, this home was occupied by Francis La Fontaine, the last Miami chief in Indiana.

The house that Chief Richardville built was the first frame house in the region; it is a simple structure—built in a style occasionally referred to as "two-thirds I-house"—which features an exceptionally beautiful and well-proportioned Greek Revival-style entrance with a broken transom light and unaffected entablature. Other exterior details include a shingle roof and six-over-six window treatments. The scrupulously restored interior shows the original color scheme, wood-grained woodwork in the formal rooms, wallpaper documented to the period, an open stairway of solid walnut, three fireplaces, and servants' quarters. The furnishings all reflect the period of the mid-1830s through the 1840s.

Notable Collections on Exhibit

The Chief Richardville House is a storehouse of information related to the Miami Nation, their history and culture.

Additional Information

The Chief Richardville House is listed on the National Register of Historic Places. Prior to living in this house, Chief Richardville lived in a small Greek Revival house which was built for him by the United States Government in 1827 in Fort Wayne. That home is one of the few remaining government homes built for a Native American chief still standing in America; it is also the oldest house in Allen County, if not all of northeast Indiana. It is located at 5705 Bluffton Road in Fort Wayne; although the house is not open for organized tours, you may call (219) 426-2882 to make an appointment to view it.

Samuel Purviance House

Contact: Gernand Enterprises
Open: Open by appointment
Admission: Adults $2.00
Activities: Guided tours
Suggested Time to View House: 1–2 hours
Description of Grounds: Flower gardens
Best Season to View House: Spring-fall
Number of Yearly Visitors: 2,000
Year House Built: 1859
Style of Architecture: Italianate with
  elements of Greek Revival style
Number of Rooms: 10
On-Site Parking: Yes **Wheelchair Access:** Yes

Description of House

The Samuel Purviance House was built by the founder of Huntington's First National Bank in 1841. The bank continues to do business; and the house, which is the oldest south of the river in Huntington, still stands. Purviance was an early settler who led the town into years of growth and prosperity; in addition to banking, he held many local government positions with distinction.

Perhaps the first requirement of a banker's house is that it be solid. The Samuel Purviance House features fourteen-inch-thick brick walls, massive and ornate brackets, heavy quoins, and a symmetrical flat roof—all projecting a comforting solidity. Other exterior details include a fine Greek Revival-style entrance with a full transom light and simple entablature, and a highly ornamented front porch which has double paired columns and pilasters. Inside, one notices a solid cherry winding staircase which turns 180 degrees, parquet flooring, four fireplaces, and the original shutters. The whole has been restored to the mid-19th century and contains numerous antique furnishings authentic to that period. The various rooms each show a different furniture style, from midwestern primitive rope beds to a very fine Eastlake-style spinning wheel. All of the furnishings were owned by the Purviance family.

Notable Collections on Exhibit

In addition to the furnishings noted above, the house contains many items of note: quilts, hand-hooked rugs, vintage garments, teddy bears, and blue granite-ware. It is also a repository of genealogical information on the four families who inhabited the house—the Purviances, the Taylors, the Mitchels, and the Becks.

Additional Information

The Samuel Purviance House is listed on the National Register of Historic Places.

Abner Shafer House

Rural Route 1, P.O. Box 147
Idaville, IN 47950
(219) 826-4163

Contact: Parrish Pioneer Village and Museum
Open: May–Nov., daily 11 a.m.–5 p.m.
Admission: Adults $4.00; children $2.00;
group rates
Activities: Guided tours, programs related to
pioneer life, annual "Old-Fashioned
Fourth of July Quilt Show"
Suggested Time to View House: 90 minutes

Facilities on Premises: Gift shop
Description of Grounds: Herb garden
Best Season to View House: Spring-fall
Number of Yearly Visitors: 20,000
Year House Built: 1850
Style of Architecture: National, frame
Number of Rooms: 6 plus summer kitchen
On-Site Parking: Yes **Wheelchair Access:** Yes

Description of House

When one visits the Abner Shafer House, one can partake of an oral history of the home, Idaville, the surrounding region, and its inhabitants, given by a 100-year-old neighbor. One learns about the Wabash Erie Canal and how this house served as a stop-over for those traveling or hauling freight on that waterway. The house and its history portray pioneer life in northwestern Indiana with exceptional fidelity.

The frame structure is a fine example of early post-and-beam construction and features six-over-six windows, a Cape Cod entrance, wide plank flooring, and two fireplaces. Inside, there is a center hall with a hand-carved open stairway, chair rails, and white-washed walls with Moses Eaton stencils throughout. It took four years to restore the house to its original appearance—the last private owner was using it to store grain—and collect the authentic period furniture.

Notable Collections on Exhibit

Among the antiques on display is a Boston tea-table, an Early Empire-style sofa, Mr.-and-Mrs. Victorian chairs, a Victorian card table, and an 1834 candle stand.

James Whitcomb Riley Museum Home

528 Lockerbie Street
Indianapolis, IN 46202
(317) 631-5885

Contact: Riley Memorial Association
Open: Tues.-Sat. 10 a.m.–4 p.m., Sun
Noon–4 p.m.; closed major holidays, first
week of January
Admission: Adults $1.00; children (12-15) $.25
Activities: Guided tours
Suggested Time to View House: 45 minutes
Facilities on Premises: Gift shop and
bookstore

Description of Grounds: Located on historic
Lockerbie Square
Best Season to View House: Year round
Number of Yearly Visitors: 13,000
Year House Built: 1872
Style of Architecture: Italianate, brick
Number of Rooms: 11
On-Site Parking: Yes **Wheelchair Access:** No

Description of House

James Whitcomb Riley, America's renowned "Hoosier Poet," was born in Greenfield, Indiana, on October 7, 1849, educated locally, and settled in Indianapolis where he wrote for the newspapers. In 1885 he published the most famous of his vernacular poems, "Little Orphant Annie." From then on, he pursued a full-time career composing verse and giving public recitals—including a performance at Carnegie Hall. With "The Raggedy Man," written in 1890, Riley scored another enormous success. For the last twenty-three years of his life—Riley died in 1916—the poet lived in this house as a paying guest of his lifelong friends, the Major and Mrs. Charles L. Holstein. The house had been built in 1874 for Mrs. Holstein's father. Riley shared expenses with the Holsteins and helped to furnish the house as well. After the deaths of Riley and Mrs. Holstein, the contents of the house came into the possession of a favored domestic, Miss Katie Kindell. A group of the poet's friends—including Booth Tarkington and George Ade—purchased the estate and organized the James Whitcomb Riley Memorial Association in 1921.

The two-story Italianate-style house is designed on an asymmetrical plan which features a one-story, partial width porch, window crowns with inverted U-shaped hoods, a slate roof, and paired window arrangements. The house is built of brick on a stone foundation. The interior has been fully restored to the period of Riley's occupancy and all of the furnishings are original. A number of the rooms have been returned to their original use: the kitchen, dining room, serving pantry, and butler's pantry. The wallpaper in the housekeeper's bedroom is a copy of that in Empress Josephine's bedroom—and therefore called "Josephine"—and the ceiling covering in the entry hall is hand-decorated canvas. Other interior features of note include a copper-lined bathtub fashioned out of cherry and fireplaces done in imported Italian marble.

Notable Collections on Exhibit

In addition to several fine Victorian-style pieces on display, the house also contains many of Riley's papers and personal items, including vintage clothing and the poet's top hat. Above one of the fireplaces, there is hung a Wayman Adams portrait of Riley's beloved pet poodle "Lockerbie."

Additional Information

The James Whitcomb Riley Museum Home is listed on the National Register of Historic Places.

Lilly Pavilion of Decorative Arts— "Oldfields"

1200 West 38th Street
Indianapolis, IN 46208
(317) 923-1331

Contact: Indianapolis Museum of Art

Open: Tues.-Sat. 10 a.m.–5 p.m., Sun. Noon–5 p.m.; closed Thanksgiving, Christmas, New Year's Day

Admission: Free

Activities: Guided tours, annual Holiday at the Lilly Pavilion

Suggested Time to View House: 1 hour

Facilities on Premises: Museum gift shop

Year House Built: Between 1910 and 1912, redecorated 1932

Description of Grounds: Located on the grounds of the Indianapolis Museum of Art with informal English-style landscaped gardens

Best Season to View House: Year round

Number of Yearly Visitors: 15,000-20,000

Style of Architecture: French Eclectic in the Chateau manner

Number of Rooms: 9 open to the public

On-Site Parking: Yes **Wheelchair Access:** Yes

Description of House

In 1932 this sumptuous chateau was acquired by Mr. and Mrs. Josiah K. Lilly—it had been built some twenty years earlier—and given a sensitive remodeling by their architect, Frederick Wallick of Indianapolis. Josiah Lilly was the grandson of Colonel Eli Lilly, founder of the pharmaceutical company which bears his name. In 1966, the children of the Lillys donated the house and its contents to the Art Association of Indianapolis.

The Lilly Mansion was designed by Lewis Ketcham Davis in 1910 in the style of a French chateau, with a steep slate roof, dormer windows, projecting wings, and a hipped roof with a ridge. One of Davis' innovative elements was the employment of hollow tile underneath the stuccoed facade as fireproofing. At the time of its completion in 1912, the house boasted a full ballroom in the attic. The grounds—designed by the Olmstead Brothers of Brookline, Massachusetts, in the informal English tradition—were planted in the 1920s. The 1932 remodeling undertaken by the Lillys included the expansion of a small two-story garden room on the south side of the mansion into a Georgian-style library used to house Lilly's collection of rare books; changing the placement of the entry from the northeast wing to the center of the facade; and the replacement of an original wooden staircase with a spiral staircase made of marble and bronze. In 1940, an 18th-century-style recreation house was erected on the grounds and, in the early 1950s, the Loggia Gallery, designed and executed by Douglas Riseborough, with its vaulted ceiling, marble tiling, and marvelous wall murals, was added.

Notable Collections on Exhibit

The Lilly Mansion is a first-class museum exhibiting European and American decorative arts of the last three centuries. As one passes from room to room, one sees collections from different periods and countries: the Main Gallery features French furniture and textiles of the 18th century, the Library is an authentic recreation of an 18th-century English interior with two extremely rare Georgian "rib-band back" side chairs executed in mahogany, the above-mentioned Loggia Gallery features an exhibit of European porcelain, and the Indiana Chapter of the Colonial Dames of America maintains a full wing of American Furniture and Decorative Arts.

Morris-Butler House

1204 North Park Avenue
Indianapolis, IN 46202
(317) 636-5409

Contact: Historic Landmarks Foundation of Indiana, Inc.

Open: Tues.-Sat. 10 a.m.–4 p.m., Sun. 1–4 p.m.; closed major holidays, month of January

Admission: Discounts for students, seniors and groups

Activities: Guided tours on the hour, extensive programs on architecture, decorative arts and social history

Suggested Time to View House: 45–60 minutes

Description of Grounds: Landscaped half-acre surrounding house

Best Season to View House: Winter-late fall

Number of Yearly Visitors: 10,000

Year House Built: Started 1864, completed 1865

Number of Rooms: 16, 14 open to public

Style of Architecture: Eclectic Italianate and Victorian Second Empire, towered

On-Site Parking: Yes **Wheelchair Access:** No

Description of House

In 1865 John D. Morris—Indianapolis businessman and investor—completed this unique three-story house which, in its mixture of disparate architectural elements, clearly shows the transition from the Italianate villa style to the more prominent Second Empire style. It is the only house of its kind in Indianapolis and became the first preservation project of The Historic Landmarks Foundation of Indiana, the largest private statewide preservation organization in the United States. Morris and his family lived here from 1865 to 1878. Sometime later, the house was acquired by Noble Chase Butler, U. S. District Court Clerk and bankruptcy attorney, who lived in it with his wife and seven children until his death in 1933. His daughter Florence remained here until her death in 1958—she'd lived in the house seventy-five years.

The Morris-Butler House is built of brick on a limestone foundation and features an imposing tower which rises four stories above the center of the structure. Other exterior details include two porches on the south side of the house, arched window hoods, and elements of both the predominating Second Empire style as well as the earlier Italianate villa style. The interior is now a museum which recreates the "high" style of the mid-Victorian period as typically found in Indiana and throughout the Midwest. Most of the furnishings are authentic to the period between 1840 and 1890, but few are original to the house. The Morris-Butler House is listed on the National Register of Historic Places.

Notable Collections on Exhibit

Among the pieces on display is a collection of rare Belter & Meeks furniture in the parlor, an Indiana-made Wooten Cabinet Secretary, and a large collection of 19th-century Indiana paintings.

President Benjamin Harrison Memorial Home

1230 North Delaware Street
Indianapolis, IN 46202
(317) 631-1898

Contact: President Benjamin Harrison Foundation

Open: Mon.-Fri. 10 a.m.–4 p.m., Sun. 12:30–4 p.m.; closed Easter, Thanksgiving, Christmas, month of January

Admission: Adults $2.00; students $1.00; preschoolers free; group tours $1.50 per person

Activities: Guided tours, adult workshops, children's programs

Suggested Time to View House: 45–60 minutes

Facilities on Premises: Gift shop, community meeting rooms, and the Harrison Research Library open by appointment

Description of Grounds: Rose garden and herb garden

Best Season to View House: Spring and fall

Number of Yearly Visitors: 35,000

Year House Built: 1875

Style of Architecture: Italianate, brick

Number of Rooms: 16, 10 open to public

On-Site Parking: Yes **Wheelchair Access:** Yes

Description of House

This three-story brick house served as the home of Benjamin Harrison, President of the United States from 1889 to 1893. Harrison, great-grandson to his namesake Benjamin Harrison V, signer of the Declaration of Independence and three-term governor of Virginia, and grandson to William Henry Harrison, President of the United States for one month before succumbing to pneumonia, was born in North Bend, Ohio, on August 20, 1833. He studied law in Cincinnati, then moved to Indianapolis with his wife, Caroline, to establish his own law practice. During the Civil War, he commanded the 70th Indiana in the Atlanta and Nashville campaigns, retiring with the rank of Brigadier General. In 1880 he was elected to the U.S. Senate and eight years later defeated Grover Cleveland for the Presidency of the United States in a close race. In 1892, the same two men contended for the office again and this time Cleveland won. Harrison returned to Indianapolis where he practiced law and taught college. After his wife, Caroline, died, Harrison married her niece, Mary Lord Dimmick. He died in 1901 but his family lived on here until 1913, when it became a boarding house. It is now a National Historic Landmark.

The first and second floors of the house have twelve-and-a-half-foot ceilings and the third floor was apparently used as a ballroom. Interior details include beautiful butternut woodwork and elaborate parquet flooring with cherry inlay on the first floor, an open winding stairway of oak and walnut, and numerous fireplaces, each one different from the rest. The house underwent a major remodeling in the 1890s, at which time indoor plumbing, electricity, and central heating were installed. The front porch—done in the Colonial Revival style popular then—was added at that time as well. Most of the furnishings belonged to the Harrisons and all of them are authentic to the period of the family's occupancy. The President Benjamin Harrison Memorial House is listed on the National Register of Historic Places.

Notable Collections on Exhibit

Many of President Harrison's personal effects are on display, as well as a fine portrait done by T. C. Steele and a number of pieces of furniture which were used in the Harrison White House.

Howard Steamboat Museum

1101 East Market Street
P.O. Box 606
Jeffersonville, IN 47131
(812) 283-3728

Contact: Clark County Historical Society

Open: Tues.-Sat. 10 a.m.–3 p.m., Sun. 1–3 p.m.; closed holidays

Admission: Adults $4.00; seniors $3.00; children and students $2.00; children (under 6) free

Activities: Guided tours and special programs throughout the year

Suggested Time to View House: 60–90 minutes

Facilities on Premises: Small gift shop

Best Season to View House: Spring, summer and fall

Description of Grounds: Surrounded by original limestone-topped brick wall; original fountain; many unusual trees including paulownia, hackberry and gingko

Number of Yearly Visitors: 8,000-10,000

Year House Built: Started 1890, completed 1894

Style of Architecture: Late Victorian Queen Anne, patterned masonry with Richardsonian Romanesque elements

Number of Rooms: 22

On-Site Parking: Yes **Wheelchair Access:** Yes

Description of House

Edmonds J. Howard and his wife, Laura Burke Howard, designed and built this mansion in the early 1890s. Howard was the son of James Howard, the founder of the Howard Shipyards, renowned builders of steamboats. After the couple died in 1919, the house was inherited by their sons Clyde and Jim. Eventually, Jim took sole possession of the house; he was also the last of the family to own the shipyards. The government bought the yards in 1941, but Captain Jim and his wife continued to occupy the mansion with their children. After his death in 1956, his widow Loretta saw to it that the mansion would be turned into a museum—this was accomplished in 1958.

This massive three-story brick mansion was built largely by the carpenters and cabinet-makers who worked at the shipyard turning out the exquisite Howard Steamboats. The exterior features sandstone lintels and relief decoration, seven chimneys, and portions of the original slate roof.

The floor plan consists of a first floor comprising a Moorish parlor, library, dining room, den, and back porch and a second floor of bedrooms and a bathroom; the bathroom and one of the bedrooms have been restored to their original condition and are furnished appropriately—the rest of the second floor rooms are given over to display space for the museum's exhibits depicting riverboat history. Interior details of note include: a grand staircase, leaded glass windows, four carved spandrels, several different mantels and fireplace surrounds, and a solid cherry den. Virtually all of the furnishings in the house belonged to the Howards or were used on their famous steamboats. The mansion is a winning mixture of a solid well-proportioned design executed with the finest possible workmanship.

Notable Collections on Exhibit

The Howard Steamboat Museum features a number of collections concerning the shipyard, the boats produced there, and life along the Ohio River at the turn of the century; these include artifacts, pieces of boats, a superb assortment of model craft, and Captain Jim's wonderfully evocative photographs. His 1898 German-made camera is still here, though not always on display.

Additional Information

The Howard Steamboat Museum is listed on the National Register of Historic Places.

Seiberling Mansion

**1200 West Sycamore Street
Kokomo, IN 46901
(317) 452-4314**

Contact: Howard County Museum
Open: Year-round, Tues.-Sun. 1–4 p.m.
Admission: Donations accepted
Activities: Guided tours, annual
  "Christmas at Seiberling"
Suggested Time to View House: 90 minutes
Facilities on Premises: Gift shop
Description of Grounds: Restored
  Victorian gardens
Best Season to View House: Year round
Number of Yearly Visitors: 10,000
Year House Built: Started 1889, completed
  1891
Style of Architecture: Victorian Queen
  Anne
Number of Rooms: 18

On-Site Parking: Yes **Wheelchair Access:** No

Description of House

Monroe Seiberling of Akron, Ohio, was the founder of the Diamond Plate Glass Company and the Kokomo Strawboard Works. His uncle was Charles Goodyear, the inventor of vulcanized rubber and founder of the internationally known tire company which bears his name. Seiberling built this imposing eighteen-room mansion for the princely sum of fifty thousand dollars.

The three-story house took two years to complete; it features some heavy Romanesque elements in a design of the late Victorian style known as Queen Anne. As was typical of homes built during this period, the first floor consisted of the public rooms, among them the parlor, dining room, and porch, the second floor consisted of the bedrooms and bathroom, and the top floor was used as a ballroom. Outside, the house is utterly dominated by a massive tower with an S-shaped roof and open arches rising over the facade, and another, smaller tower in the rear. Other exterior details include a porte cochere side entrance, windows and doorways that are either hooded or curved, and several stained glass windows. The ornate interior woodwork is executed in numerous different woods: oak, walnut, maple, cherry, mahogany, tulip, and poplar; the various textures and grains are visually compelling. The mansion is furnished appropriately for the period of the 1890s, but none of the pieces are original.

Additional Information

The Seiberling Mansion is listed on the National Register of Historic Places.

Moses Fowler House

909 South Street
Lafayette, IN 47901
(317) 742-8411

Contact: Tippecanoe County Historical Association

Open: Tues.-Sun. 1–5 p.m.; closed major holidays, month of January

Admission: Free

Activities: Guided tours ($.50 per person), audiovisual introduction, lectures, special programs, special events "Toast to Preservation" award ceremony, and "Holiday Happening" theme party for children

Suggested Time to View House: 60–90 minutes

Facilities on Premises: Small gift and book shop

Description of Grounds: Tree-shaded lawns with some plantings and flower urns

Best Season to View House: Spring and summer

Number of Yearly Visitors: 14,000

Year House Built: 1852, remodeled 1916

Style of Architecture: Romantic English Gothic Revival, asymmetrical with later Tudor Revival-style elements

Number of Rooms: 32, 12 open to public

On-Site Parking: Yes **Wheelchair Access:** Yes

Description of House

Moses Fowler—Tippecanoe County pioneer, banker, investor, railroad man, and rancher—played a key role in getting a rail line built to connect Cincinnati, Lafayette, and Chicago. In 1861 he organized the meat packing firm Culbertson, Blair & Co. in Chicago; at the time, he himself owned one of the finest herds of Hereford cattle in the United States. Fowler's wife, Eliza Hawkings Fowler, was one of eleven children whose devout Quaker parents founded Shadeland Farms and helped organize the Farmers' Institute. The Fowlers were well-known for their philanthropy, donating land and money to the Central Presbyterian Church and Purdue University. When Fowler died in 1889, his estate was valued at three million dollars. The house remained in the family until 1941, when it was purchased by the Tippecanoe County Historical Association for use as their museum headquarters.

The Moses Fowler House was designed to evoke images of a European castle, particularly in the stone entryway with its Gothic arches, the lower terrace with its Medusa-head fountain, and in the hand-carved woodwork and exposed beams. The thirty-two-room house, originally built on a grand scale out of brick and timber, was remodeled in 1916 and covered in stucco. At that time the "living porch," kitchen, servants' quarters, and master bedroom wing were all added. The woodwork in the house was all done in native white oak and walnut and the ceiling ornamental work was executed by Italian artisans brought from New York to Lafayette by Fowler.

Notable Collections on Exhibit

Today, twelve of the rooms are open to the public, only one of which is interpreted to the period of the Fowlers' residence—the "Weatherill Memorial Parlor." Most are used as display space for the museum's exhibits: "The Building Years: 1840-1900" which features the growth of Tippecanoe County and its industry; "The Woodland Indian Gallery" depicting the life of local Native American peoples from 10,000 B. C. to their removal in 1838; and the "Hall of Portraits," a gallery showing numerous Lafayette citizens.

Additional Information

The Moses Fowler House is listed on the National Register of Historic Places.

Lanier Mansion State Historic Site

511 West First Street
Madison, IN 47250
(812) 265-3526

Contact: Indiana Division of Museums and
Historic Sites

Open: Tues.-Sat. 9 a.m.–5 p.m., Mon. and
Sun. 1–5 p.m.; closed all major holidays
also day after Thanksgiving, Christmas
Eve and Day, New Year's Eve and Day

Admission: Free; donations welcome

Activities: Guided tours, slide presentation,
annual spring Civil War encampment

Suggested Time to View House: 45 minutes

Facilities on Premises: Gift shop

Description of Grounds: In the process of
restoring an elaborate 1850s garden

Best Season to View House: Early
spring-late fall

Number of Yearly Visitors: 70,000

Year House Built: 1844

Style of Architecture: Greek Revival

Number of Rooms: 17, 13 open to the
public

On-Site Parking: Yes **Wheelchair Access:** No

Description of House

The financier J. F. D. Lanier was instrumental in building Indiana's economy in the decades prior to the Civil War, and then, during that conflict, he saved the state twice from fiscal disaster by loaning it over a million dollars to meet its obligations. After the war, he traveled to Europe as an emissary of the United States Government on a mission to convince leading foreign capitalists to invest in Reconstruction. Lanier built this outstanding Greek Revival house in 1844 near the Ohio River in Madison. It is a superb example of the style of living that wealth and influence could provide in what was then the western frontier of America; in fact, when this home was completed, it was called the "finest such structure in the West."

The Lanier Mansion was designed and built by the noted architect Frances Costigan. It is now owned and operated by the Indiana Division of Museums and Historic Sites, which is currently researching the provenance and history of the various furnishings in the house. Thus far, it appears as though about one-third of the pieces belonged to the Laniers. The Mansion is the most notable structure in the historic town of Madison, which is easily accessible from either Louisville, Kentucky, or Cincinnati, Ohio, and well worth a visit.

Additional Information

The Lanier Mansion State Historic Site has been listed on the National Register of Historic Places. If one is in the southeastern Indiana area, another fine house worth visiting is the Culbertson State Historic Site at 914 East Main Street in New Albany, just across the Ohio River from Louisville. This structure too is operated by the Indiana Division of Museums and Historic Sites.

Barker Mansion

631 Washington Street
Michigan City, IN 46360
(219) 873-1520

Contact: Barker Civic Center
Open: Mon.-Fri. tours 10 a.m., 11:30 a.m.,
1 p.m.; June-Oct., Sat. and Sun. tours
Noon, 2 p.m.
Admission: Adults $2.00; children $.50
Activities: Guided tours, seasonal events
Suggested Time to View House: 1 hour
Best Season to View House: Summer

Description of Grounds: Formal Victorian
gardens
Number of Yearly Visitors: 12,000
Year House Built: 1900, remodeled 1905
Style of Architecture: Eclectic Period
Revival in the English Manor style
Number of Rooms: 38
On-Site Parking: Yes **Wheelchair Access:** No

Description of House

John Barker, Sr. (1814-1878), came from Massachusetts to the Michigan frontier in 1836 where he became a successful grain merchant and owner of a commission house which held goods being transported on the Great Lakes. In 1855, he bought an interest in a small company manufacturing railroad cars; during the Civil War years, business boomed and Barker became a very wealthy man. In 1869, he retired and managership of the company fell to his son, John Henry Barker. Fourteen years later, the younger Barker would become president of the Haskell & Barker Company, which had by then grown to become the largest manufacturer of railroad freight cars in the country. In 1922, Haskell & Barker merged with Pullman Company to form the giant Pullman Standard. After Barker's first wife—and three infant children—died, he married Katherine FitzGerald and they had one daughter, Catherine. In 1900, they commissioned the renowned Chicago architect Frederick Perkins to build this mansion near the lakefront in Michigan City. Both of the Barkers died in 1910, leaving possession of the house to their young daughter. In 1948, the mansion was given to Purdue University for use as a study center; twenty years later, ownership reverted to the Barker Welfare Foundation of which Catherine was president.

This three-story brick mansion is a study in elaborate ornamentation, beginning with the facade, which features cut stone tabs and cast stone casements surrounding the windows, Flemish-style gables, and an arched entry which leads one into the mansion's lavish interior. The exterior also features patterned masonry along the entire frieze line and, off to the left, a two-story, semi-hexagonal bay crowned with a stone balustrade. The floor plan has the public rooms—foyer, library, drawing room, dining room, and kitchen—as well as Mrs. Barker's study and bedroom and the servants' quarters on the main floor, the bedrooms and several of the home's ten bathrooms upstairs, and the ballroom, schoolroom, and governess' bedroom on the third floor. Interior details include Baroque-style plaster ceilings, hand-carved marble fireplace, silver doorknobs and plates, red velvet flocked wallpapers, and an array of exotic woods. Most of the pieces on display in the mansion belonged to the Barkers and had been purchased through dealers in New York.

Notable Collections on Exhibit

Among the many wonderful items on view are several objects made by Louis Comfort Tiffany and two original Baumgarten tapestries.

Additional Information

The Barker Mansion is listed on the National Register of Historic Places.

T.C. Steele State Historic Site– "House of the Singing Winds"

Rural Route 1, southwest
of town off Route 46
P.O. Box 256
Nashville, IN 47448
(812) 988-2785

Contact: Indiana Department of Natural Resources

Open: Mar.-Dec., Tues.-Sat. 9 a.m.–5 p.m., Sat. and Sun. 1–5 p.m.; closed some holidays

Admission: Free, donations welcome

Activities: Guided tours, hiking trails, focus programs

Suggested Time to View House: 30–60 minutes

Facilities on Premises: Gift shop

Description of Grounds: 20 acres of mowed grounds and partially restored gardens, four nature preserve hiking trails

Best Season to View House: Spring and fall

Number of Yearly Visitors: 17,000

Year House Built: 1907

Style of Architecture: National, rustic bungalow

Number of Rooms: 4 open to the public

On-Site Parking: Yes **Wheelchair Access:** No

Description of House

Theodore Clement Steele was a native Indianian who graduated from the Waveland Academy in 1868, went and studied art in Cincinnati and Chicago, moved with his young wife to Michigan where he began to make a name for himself as a portraitist. In 1873, he moved to Indianapolis where a group of wealthy art lovers supported him in a residency abroad which enabled him to study at the Royal Academy in Munich. In addition to his well-known paintings of President Benjamin Harrison and the Hoosier poet James Whitcomb Riley, Steele repaid his benefactors by painting them all. After his wife died in 1899, he traveled to California and the Pacific Northwest before settling in Brown County and marrying a second time. Artists from around the United States came to work with Steele; many stayed and organized the famous Brown County Art Colony.

Though the house is a relatively simple rectangular-shaped bungalow, the site affords a spectacular view of the forested rolling hills of south central Indiana—the view that attracted Brown to Nashville. The house was originally intended as a summer cottage and consists of a dining room, living room, bedroom, changing room, kitchen, porch, and sunroom. The west wing was extended to afford more private space for the family; today only the rooms in the original building are open to the public. The grounds feature a beautifully landscaped garden—developed by Steele's second wife, Selma Neubacher Steele—a barn studio, a guest cottage, and the Dewar log cabin. The furnishings on display in the public rooms are original to the Steeles who lived here until 1945; these pieces represent an eclectic mix of late 19th and early 20th century styles.

Notable Collections on Exhibit

The "House of Singing Winds" boasts a collection of over three hundred paintings done by T. C. Steele, at least sixty of which are on display at any given time, and Mrs. Steele's extensive textile collection.

Additional Information

The T. C. Steele State Historic Site adjoins the Selma Steele State Nature Preserve, named after the artist's second wife. The "House of Singing Winds" is listed on the National Register of Historic Places.

Culbertson Mansion

914 East Main Street
New Albany, IN 47150
(812) 944-9600

Contact: Culbertson State Historical Site
Open: Tues.-Sat. 9 a.m.–5 p.m., Sun.
1–5 p.m.; closed major holidays except
Memorial Day, Fourth of July, Labor Day
Admission: Donations accepted
Activities: Guided tours, special seasonal
events including October "Haunted
House," educational outreach programs
Suggested Time to View House: 30 minutes
Facilities on Premises: Gift shop, picnic area

Best Season to View House: Late
spring-early fall
Description of Grounds: City block with
seasonal flora and large shade trees
surrounded by original wrought-iron fence
Number of Yearly Visitors: 30,000
Year House Built: Between 1867 and 1869
Style of Architecture: HighVictorian Second
Empire
Number of Rooms: 25
On-Site Parking: Yes **Wheelchair Access:** No

Description of House

In 1814 William S. Culbertson was born in New Market, Pennsylvania; at the age of twenty-one he left his hometown to find his fortune. Culbertson went exploring the Western Territory along the Ohio River, settled in the town of New Albany and got a job as a clerk in a dry goods store. Soon the enterprising young man had his own business. By 1868, he was able to retire from the dry goods business and invest his money in new ventures: the Kentucky-Indiana Railroad Bridge Company and his own utility company. He also built this ornate mansion. When Culbertson died in 1892, he was reported to be the richest man Indiana, with a net worth of over three and a half million dollars. His philanthropy was legendary—he served as trustee of the First Presbyterian Church, funded and supervised the Culbertson Old Ladies Home, and founded the Cornelia Memorial Orphans Home. The mansion underwent several changes of ownership until acquired by the state in 1976.

This two-story, asymmetrical Second Empire-style structure features a three-story front bay extension, elaborate wrought-iron cresting along the roof line, bracketed and elongated windows, dormers with decorative surrounds, and exaggerated roof brackets. The roof is flared and the tiles are arranged in a pattern; one-story bays and small porches appear on all exterior faces. The house is now painted a yellow ocher with white trim but the original color was gray. The 20,000-square-foot interior is dark downstairs, light on the second floor; details include two cantilevered staircases, restored frescoed ceilings, a lattice closet, and woodgrained moldings and paneling throughout. The donated furnishings are authentic to the 1870s and 1880s and include pieces in the following styles: Eastlake, Second Empire, and the Renaissance and Rococo Revivals.

Additional Information

The Culbertson Mansion is listed on the National Register of Historic Places.

William C. Grose Home–
Henry County Historical Museum

606 South Fourteenth Street
New Castle, IN 47362
(317) 529-4028

Contact: Henry County Historical Society Inc.

Open: Apr.-Dec, Tues.-Sat. 1–4:30 p.m.;
closed holidays and Mondays; prior
arrangements needed for large groups

Admission: Free, donations appreciated

Activities: Guided tours, special seasonal
events including the Summer Lawn
Social, and Victorian Christmas Tea

Suggested Time to View House: 1 hour

Facilities on Premises: Books and
stationery for sale

Description of Grounds: Large rolling
lawns with benches

Best Season to View House: Spring and
summer

Number of Yearly Visitors: 1,200

Year House Built: 1870

Number of Rooms: 16

Style of Architecture: Italianate

On-Site Parking: Yes **Wheelchair Access:** No

Description of House

General William Grose (1812-1900) made his name as Commander of
the 36th Indiana Infantry during the Civil War. He also had two sons serve
in the Union Army during that conflict. After the war, the General resumed
practicing law here in New Castle and threw himself into politics, becoming
very active in both the city and state governments. He, his wife, Rebecca,
and their children were among the most beloved of New Castle's citizens.

The William C. Grose Home is one of the largest Italianate-style mansions in Indiana. It has been lovingly restored by the Henry County Historical Society so that the major rooms accurately reflect the period of General
Grose's occupancy. Upstairs, one sees the fully furnished master bedroom,
a young person's bedroom, the Clothing Collection Room, Civil War Room,
and Natural History Home. The basement houses the Barber Shop, summer
kitchen, and two Pioneer Tool Rooms. Outside, a pavilion connects the main
house to a smaller annex in which one finds a charming children's museum,
a genealogy library, and a dining room and kitchen used by the Society for
socials. Only a few of the furnishings on display belonged to the original
residents; the majority are collected pieces authentic to the Victorian era.

Notable Collections on Exhibit

Among the notable items shown at the Grose Home are an assortment
of quilts and coverlets, political mementos, pioneer tools, Native American
artifacts, portraits, and some fine examples of primitive art.

Additional Information

The William C. Grose Home was listed on the National Register of
Historic Places in 1983.

1830 Owen House

West Street
New Harmony, IN 47631
(812) 682-4488

Contact: Historic New Harmony

Open: Apr.-Oct., daily 9 a.m.–5 p.m.; Nov.-Mar., call for schedule; closed Thanksgiving, Christmas Eve and Day, New Year's Eve and Day

Admission: Full tour rates: adults $8.00; seniors $7.00; students $4.50

Activities: Guided walking tours, annual Christmas Candlelight Tour

Suggested Time to View House: 15 minutes

Facilities on Premises: Visitor center, gift and book shops, crafts stores, art gallery, restaurants, accommodations

Description of Grounds: Historic 19th-century utopian village with many restored houses and tradesman buildings including the David Lenz House, the Fauntleroy House, the 1830 Owen House, the John Beal House, and the George Keppler House

Best Season to View House: Early spring-fall

Style of Architecture: English Georgian style, brick

Number of Yearly Visitors: 50,000-60,000

Number of Rooms: 8

Year House Built: 1830

On-Site Parking: Yes **Wheelchair Access:** No

Description of House

The 1830 Owen House, and the two houses that follow in this guide, are located in New Harmony, Indiana, one of the most important historical sites in America. The town has its origins in a 30,000 acre land purchase made in 1814 by George Rapp on behalf of a group of Lutheran Separatists called the Harmonie Society. These religious people had come to the United States from Germany ten years earlier and settled in Butler County, Pennsylvania. They built their town on the Wabash in less than a year and, over the next decade, built a model community here which rivaled the large cities of the eastern seaboard in prosperity, scientific innovation, and cosmopolitan cultural awareness.

In 1825, New Harmony was purchased by the Welsh industrialist Robert Owen who wished to establish his version of Utopia here; that it failed is not as important as the fact that the attempt sparked a rich flowering of intellectual, scientific, and spiritual activity which broadened out into the life of America. The community included naturalists, educators, early feminists, geologists (at one time New Harmony was one of the two most important centers for the study of geology in the country), and a host of visiting luminaries in the arts and sciences. Historic New Harmony is now a jointly run program of the University of Southern Indiana and the Division of State Museums and Historic Sites.

The 1830 Owen House, built in 1830 by the contractors Johnson & Bondslay, is thought to have been commissioned by Robert Owen's sons, Robert Dale Owen and David Dale Owen. They owned the house until 1838 but never lived in it; instead, it was rented out to various community families. The two-story, brick Georgian-style house features eight-over-twelve windows, green shutters, two separate entrances on the facade, one centered, one to the far left, and a hipped roof. Inside, the fully restored rooms include a hallway showing an exposed wood ceiling and joists with attached pegs thought to be used for hanging food, a parlor decorated as a formal sitting room, and the 1833 kitchen with the original wood floor, brick hearth and fireplace mantel. The various paints and wallpapers used in the restoration are based on samples found in the house or copied from other homes in the community and the furnishings on display reflect daily life in the post-communal period of 1830 to 1840.

Notable Collections on Exhibit

The collection of household artifacts, utensils, and home furnishings includes several interesting items: an Eli Terry clock c. 1817 with a reverse glass painting of Mount Vernon on the face, a portable metal candle called a "torchaire," a lockable tea caddy, and a "muffinere."

Additional Information

The historic town of New Harmony is listed on the National Register of Historic Places.

David Lenz House

Contact: Historic New Harmony

Open: Apr.-Oct., daily 9 a.m.–5 p.m.;
Nov.-Mar., call for schedule; closed
Thanksgiving, Christmas Eve and Day,
New Year's Eve and Day

Admission: Full tour rates: adults $8.00;
seniors $7.00; students $4.50

Activities: Guided walking tours, annual
Christmas Candlelight Tour

Suggested Time to View House: 15 minutes

Facilities on Premises: Visitor center, gift
and book shops, crafts stores, art gallery,
restaurants, accommodations

Description of Grounds: Historic
19th-century utopian village with many
restored houses and tradesman
buildings including the David Lenz
House, the Fauntleroy House, the 1830
Owen House, the John Beal House, and
the George Keppler House

Number of Yearly Visitors: 50,000-60,000

Year House Built: c. 1820

Best Season to View House: Early
spring-fall

Style of Architecture: Folk, rustic German
frame

Number of Rooms: 6

On-Site Parking: Yes **Wheelchair Access:** No

Description of House

David Lenz, a lawyer and a farmer, was one of the original Harmonists
who settled New Harmony after emigrating from Germany to Pennsylvania. Lenz, whose wife had died in 1815, moved into this house with his
children and brothers. At the time the home stood on a quarter of an acre
plot which included a barn and large Harmonist garden. After he died in
1825, one of his sons became a trustee of the Economy Society. During the
Owen-McClure period in New Harmony, the house was occupied by John
Beal before he built his own house, then by Thomas Mumford, who'd joined
the community in 1828 and married Louisa Maental; Louisa's father lived
his last days in this house. Mumford's descendants donated the house to the
National Society of the Colonial Dames of America and, in 1958, it was
moved to its present location and restored.

The David Lenz House is a typical single-family frame structure built
to the standard specifications of all Harmonist dwellings: it is twenty feet
by thirty feet and contains an upper and lower hall, two sleeping chambers,
a "common" room, and a kitchen. This house also has a root cellar and attic.
These prefabricated homes all had side entrances and individual gardens,

were made of insect-resistant poplar, and were insulated with "Dutch biscuits," boards wrapped in mud and straw which were sun-dried and placed between the ceiling joists. Most of the furniture reflects the period of the 1820s, but little of it belonged to the Harmonists—most of what they had they took with them when the community was sold to Robert Owen.

Notable Collections on Exhibit

There are a number of interesting items on view in the Lenz House: a Harmonist table, pewter plates, a pine blanket chest, a Shaker single bed, a c. 1820 Pennsylvania-made dry sink, an 1817 hand-painted German chest, and a cast-iron stove manufactured in Pittsburgh.

Additional Information

The David Lenz House is part of Historic New Harmony which is listed on the National Register of Historic Places.

Fauntleroy House

West Street
New Harmony, IN 47631
(812) 682-4488

Contact: Historic New Harmony

Open: Apr.-Oct., daily 9 a.m.–5 p.m.; Nov.-Mar., call for schedule; closed Thanksgiving, Christmas Eve and Day, New Year's Eve and Day

Admission: Full tour rates: adults $8.00; seniors $7.00; students $4.50

Activities: Guided walking tours, annual Christmas Candlelight Tour

Suggested Time to View House: 15 minutes

Facilities on Premises: Visitor center, gift and book shops, crafts stores, art gallery, restaurants, accommodations

Description of Grounds: Historic 19th-century utopian village with many restored houses and tradesman buildings including the David Lenz House, the Fauntleroy House, the 1830 Owen House, the John Beal House, and the George Keppler House

Best Season to View House: Early spring-fall

Number of Yearly Visitors: 50,000-60,000

Year House Built: c. 1820, addition 1840

Style of Architecture: Folk, German frame

Number of Rooms: 8

On-Site Parking: Yes **Wheelchair Access:** No

Description of House

Prior to its ownership by the Fauntleroy family, this Harmonist dwelling was home to a succession of community notables: original Harmonie Society member Franz Pfeil, Robert Owen's partner William McLure, and the inventor Oliver Evans. The Fauntleroys took possession of the house in 1840 and raised four children here. When Robert Dale Owen and his family returned to New Harmony after a diplomatic stint overseas, they lived with the Fauntleroys for a while and, in 1859, a literary group called the Minerva Society was organized by Fauntleroy daughter Constance in the parlor. In 1911, another branch of the family moved into the house and lived here until 1925, when it was sold to the Indiana Federation of Clubs who were to keep it intact as a shrine to women's clubs throughout the state.

The Fauntleroy House is one of the original structures built by the Harmonist community—it was known as Dwelling Number 53—according to their rigid standards. That original house now forms the first floor parlor and library and the two bedrooms upstairs of the present building; the door on the north side of the library used to be the front door into the house. The large hall, dining room, and west bedroom wing were added in the 1840s and the sleeping porch in the 1920s. Like most of the community's buildings, the house is a simple frame structure with a front gable and a porch on either end. This house is painted white. Most of the furnishings on display here were collected by Mary Ellen Fauntleroy—who stayed on as caretaker of the property when it was taken over by the Indiana Federation of Clubs—in the late 19th and early 20th century.

Notable Collections on Exhibit

Items of note on display include: a copy of the Minerva Society constitution, Jane Fauntleroy's harp and piano, portraits of family members and Robert Dale Owen, a telescope belonging to Robert Henry Fauntleroy, and an assortment of quilts and coverlets dating from the decades between 1830 and 1870.

Additional Information

The Fauntleroy House, like the two houses mentioned above, is one of the many structures which make up the historic town of New Harmony. The site has been listed on the National Register of Historic Places.

Andrew F. Scott House

126 North Tenth Street
Richmond, IN 47374
(317) 962-5756

Contact: Wayne County Historical Museum
Open: Mon.-Fri. 9 a.m.–4 p.m., Sun.
 1–4 p.m.; other times by request
Admission: $1.00 per person
Activities: Guided tours by reservation
Suggested Time to View House:
 45–60 minutes
Number of Yearly Visitors: 1,000

Description of Grounds: Small city yard
 surrounded by wrought iron fence
Best Season to View House: Spring,
 summer and fall
Year House Built: 1859, remodeled 1869
Style of Architecture: Italianate, bracketed
Number of Rooms: 7
On-Site Parking: Yes **Wheelchair Access:** No

Description of House

Native Virginian Andrew Finley Scott came to Richmond in 1834, a year after the opening of the National Road. The town's population of 1,000 would increase dramatically as thousands of pioneers traveled the road and Wayne County came to be known as a major gateway on the way to the western frontier. Scott pursued several careers in Richmond, including that of teacher, grocer, farmer, real estate investor, building contractor, and Democratic County Clerk. In 1872 he co-founded the Second National Bank and served as its president for some twenty years. Scott was married to Martha McGlathery of Philadelphia in 1839 and the couple had four children. It was their granddaughter, Martha Scott, who bequeathed the house to the Wayne County Historical Society in 1977.

The house that the Scotts moved into in 1860 is a symmetrical two-story brick structure built in the Italianate style. It features a large center gable, elaborate bracketing, and a prominent lantern (cupola). The fenestration is varied: elongated floor-to-ceiling windows on the first floor and a paired arrangement above the entry contrast with the simple shuttered six-over-six windows seen throughout the rest of the house. Other exterior features include an entry door featuring a pedimented surround and simple entablature, and two single-story side porches with unusual paired supports. Inside, the main hall is interpreted to the years 1875 to 1885 with its imitation embossed leather wallcovering and painted grain on the woodwork; the parlor shows hand-worked plaster walls; and the dining room reflects the later period of the 1890s with a Victorian-Eastlake fireplace. The furnishing are a mixture of original pieces and donations made by local residents.

Notable Collections on Exhibit

Some of the collected pieces on view here have stories all their own: a large secretary used by Garr Williams, a Richmond native who drew cartoons for the *Chicago Tribune*, a Renaissance Revival-style armchair which belonged to Richmond's photo-historian Edwin F. Dalby, and a Gothic-style slipper chair which belonged to Indiana Governor Oliver P. Morton. The house also contains some wonderful portraits, including one of Francis A. McNutt, a grandson who grew up here, became Chamberlain to Popes Leo XIII and Pius X, and married the granddaughter of Clement C. Moore, author of *A Visit from St. Nicholas*.

Additional Information

The Scott House is located in Richmond's Starr Historical District, a twenty-five-block residential area containing many superb Victorian townhouses and mansions, among them the Gaar House Museum at 2593 Pleasant View Road. This Second Empire-style home, built in 1876 by local architect John Hasecoster for the Gaars, has been completely restored and features a superb collection of Eastlake-style furniture. It is open to the public; the phone number is (317) 935-8687. Both the Gaar House Museum and the Scott House are listed on the National Register of Historic Places.

Cabin in Wildflower Woods

Southeast of town off Route 9
P.O. Box 639
Rome City, IN 46784
(219) 854-3790

Contact: Gene Stratton Porter State Historic Site-Limberlost, North

Open: Mar. 15-Dec. 31, Tues.-Sat. 9 a.m.–4:30 p.m., Sun. 1–4:30 p.m.; closed Easter, Thanksgiving, Christmas

Admission: Free, donations appreciated

Activities: Guided tours, audiovisual presentations, special programs

Suggested Time to View House: 45 minutes

Facilities on Premises: Gift and book shop

Description of Grounds: 20 acres of woods and formal gardens

Best Season to View House: Early spring-fall

Number of Yearly Visitors: 25,000

Year House Built: 1914

Style of Architecture: National, "rustic" log cabin

Number of Rooms: 14

On-Site Parking: Yes **Wheelchair Access:** No

Description of House

Gene Stratton Porter and her husband, Charles, left their cottage in Geneva, Indiana (see the entry for Limberlost State Historic Site), and moved, north to Rome City where they built this marvelous fourteen-room cabin out of white cedar timber. Porter, who lived here until her death in 1924, won international renown as an author, photographer, and naturalist; eight of her novels, including the famous *A Girl of the Limberlost*, have been made into movies. As our awareness of the importance of protecting the environment has increased, so has our appreciation for Gene Stratton Porter's accomplishments.

The Cabin in Wildflower Woods sits amid a stunning array of formal gardens comprising some thirty-five individual plots divided by a wisteria arbor; these were all designed and planted by the Porters. The interior of the log cabin features exquisite cherry paneling, three unique fireplaces, a conservatory, a library and Porter's darkroom. All of the furnishings either belonged to the couple or were collected to reflect the period of their occupancy.

Notable Collections on Exhibit

The cabin contains many of Gene Stratton Porter's hand-colored photographs and her library houses both the books she wrote as well as her extensive reference collection. There are also collections of shells and Southwestern and Mexican pottery.

Additional Information

The Cabin in Wildflower Woods is listed on the National Register of Historic Places.

John D. Oliver House–
Copshaholm

808 West Washington Avenue
South Bend, IN 46601
(219) 284-9664

Contact: Northern Indiana Historical Society

Open: Year-round, Tues.-Sat.10 a.m.–5 p.m., Sun. Noon–5 p.m.; closed mid January to mid February

Admission: Adults $5.00; seniors $4.00; children (5-18) $2.50; tours $4.00. Leighton Gallery, no admission charge

Activities: Guided tours, slide presentation, garden treasure hunt

Suggested Time to View House: 90 minutes

Facilities on Premises: Gift shop

Description of Grounds: 2 acres of historical formal gardens are being restored

Best Season to View House: Spring-fall

Number of Yearly Visitors: 25,000

Year House Built: 1895

Style of Architecture: Eclectic mix of Victorian Queen Anne and Richardsonian Romanesque

Number of Rooms: 38

On-Site Parking: Yes **Wheelchair Access:** No

Description of House

Mishawaka native Joseph Doty Oliver, whose education was completed in nearby South Bend, took a position as bookkeeper in his father's plow manufacturing plant, was then elected treasurer of South Bend Iron Works in 1868 at the tender age of seventeen, and appointed Director of that firm within four years. In 1884, he was married to Anna Gertrude Wells in Johnstown, New York, and the couple had four children. In 1908, he became president of the Oliver Chilled Plow Works, the internationally known farm equipment company which had grown from his father's business. Oliver was an ardent Republican who helped reorganize his party in 1914 and became good friends with Theodore Roosevelt. After his death at Copshaholm in 1933, members of the family lived on here until 1988, when the mansion was given to the Northern Indiana Historical Society.

This imposing thirty-eight-room mansion was designed by New York architect Charles Alonzo Rich in a heavy Romanesque style leavened by Queen Anne-style details throughout—delicate wooden balustrades meet massive walls built of native granite, a huge stone arch leads to a wide veranda, a magnificent gambrel roof of red clay tiles is seen above Corinthian columns adorning the central second-story window. The texture and visual interest created by this juxtaposition of styles is thoroughly beguiling. The interior of the mansion features an asymmetrical floor plan, parquet floors—each in a different pattern—downstairs, a glass dome on the second floor lit from above, and leaded glass windows throughout. In addition to the hundreds of luxurious details and superb workmanship in evidence, the house was also the first in South Bend to have electricity. The name "Copshaholm" refers to the ancient name of the Scottish town where Oliver's father was born.

Notable Collections on Exhibit

All of the furnishings belonged to the Olivers and the interiors appear exactly as it did when they occupied Copshaholm; many of the fine antiques and art objects were collected by the family on their many trips overseas. Among the pieces on display are first-class collections of European ceramics, silver, glass, prints by Bartolozzi, vintage clothing, and two bronze busts done by Lorado Taft. In the Music Room one comes upon a reproduction of Luca Della Robbia's frieze "Cantoria"—the original is in Florence's Duomo.

Additional Information

In addition to the magnificent house, the site also includes 2 acres of formal gardens, a recently restored tea house, tennis courts, and a sunken garden. Tours of the house involve a good deal of strenuous walking and stair-climbing; reservations are requested and groups of ten or more must reserve at least two weeks in advance. Copshaholm is listed on the National Register of Historic Places.

Home of Eugene V. Debs

451 North Eighth Street
Terre Haute, IN 47807
(812) 232-2163

Contact: Eugene V. Debs Foundation
Open: Wed.-Sun. 1–4:30 p.m.; other times
by appointment; closed national
holidays; week between Christmas and
New Year's Day
Admission: Free
Activities: Guided tours
Suggested Time to View House:
45–60 minutes
Facilities on Premises: Books and
memorabilia for sale
Description of Grounds: Memorial garden
displays and plaques honoring twelve
pioneer labor leaders
Best Season to View House: Year round
Number of Yearly Visitors: 1,000-2,000
Number of Rooms: 8

Style of Architecture: Modified Victorian, frame
Year House Built: 1890
On-Site Parking: Yes **Wheelchair Access:** No

Description of House

A visit to the Eugene V. Debs Home is meant to serve as an vivid
introduction to the history of the American Labor Movement and an inspira-
tion to those for whom Social Reform is still a live issue. In 1990 Eugene V.
Debs, the prominent early labor leader, founder of the American Railway
Union, and co-founder of the American Socialist Party, was included in *Life*
magazine's list, "100 Outstanding Americans of the 20th Century," and
enrolled in the Labor Hall of Fame. These belated acknowledgments of his
contributions to our society—sixty-four years after his death in 1926—cannot mask the fact that Debs is still a character of some controversy in
America, a man of deep conviction who was willing to be imprisoned for
six months for his work in organizing the famous Pullman Strike of 1894.

This wood frame Victorian house served as the home of Eugene and Kate
Debs from 1890 until their deaths. It is situated on a block in Terre Haute where
many of the town's most influential citizens lived. Inside, the living room
features a hand-carved mantel of white oak and the library has bookcases and
a mantel done in solid cherry; the dining room furniture, which was owned by
the Debs couple, is mahogany. The rooms throughout the house have been
filled with period furniture and artifacts pertaining to the labor leader's life.
The Home of Eugene V. Debs is both a Registered National Historic Landmark
and listed on the National Register of Historic Places.

Notable Collections on Exhibit

On the third floor of the house are murals done by the local artist John
Laska which depict the life and struggles of Eugene Debs. There is also a
large and significant collection of his correspondence here, including letters
to and from people such as Upton Sinclair, James Whitcomb Riley, and Carl
Sandburg.

Old French House

509 North First Street, Box 1979
Vincennes, IN 47591
(812) 882-0199

Contact: Old Northwest Corporation
Open: May–Sept., daily 1–4 p.m.
Admission: Adults $1.00; children $.50
Activities: Guided tours
Suggested Time to View House: 45 minutes
Description of Grounds: Small, unadorned lot

Best Season to View House: Summer
Number of Yearly Visitors: 1,000
Year House Built: Between 1786 and 1814
Style of Architecture: French Colonial
Number of Rooms: 4 plus attic
On-Site Parking: No **Wheelchair Access:** No

Description of House

The Old French House is the only surviving example of a French *poteaux-sur-sole* residence in Indiana and, as such, it provides a living link to that chapter of Indiana history which tells of French-Canadian trappers and settlers who traveled down the Ohio and Wabash Rivers to the Mississippi. The house was built at the end of the 18th century by Michel Brouillet, the son of an officer who fought under George Rogers Clark during the American Revolution. Brouillet traded in furs, ran a store in Vincennes, and established a trading post on Brouillette's Creek north of Terre Haute before receiving licenses to trade with the Indians in 1801 and 1804. He married Marie Droulet and the couple had eight children. From 1809 to 1811 he spied on Chief Tecumseh for Governor William Henry Harrison, and during the War of 1812 he served the American cause as a captain in the militia. After the war, he returned to Vincennes, first as a fur trader, then as a tavern-keeper. After Brouillet died in 1838, the property was sold and fell into complete obscurity until it was "discovered" in 1974 encased in a small Victorian cottage. The Old Northwest Corporation bought the house in the following year and restored it as a Bicentennial Project.

Poteaux-sur-sole (posts on a sill) construction had its origins in the half-timber houses built in medieval Normandy as adapted by French-Canadian traders and trappers. A twenty-two-foot by thirty-two-foot sill of foot-thick oak is laid on a sandstone foundation; floor joists are then fitted into the sill, followed by fourteen-foot-high upright posts every sixteen inches or so capped by a horizontal plate. The frame thus created is braced at the corners with angles running from the sill to the posts. The house has three rooms, two bedrooms and a "grande chambre" which served as both a kitchen and living room. Unlike other houses of its time, the Brouillet house also had a plastered loft, probably used as a children's sleeping area. The furnishings on display, while not original to the Brouillet family, include many fine pieces in the French-Canadian Colonial style.

Notable Collections on Exhibit

Among the more notable items here are a *lit clos* (enclosed bed) decorated with carved galettes, a Breton motif; a set of tables and chairs done in the Canadian style called "Ile d'Orleans"; and a small trestle table and two chairs fashioned out of butternut tree trunks thought to have been made locally and owned by the Brouillets.

Additional Information

Located at the Old Vincennes State Historic Site is the Maurice Thompson Birthplace, a modest white frame house which was moved here from its original location in Fairfield, Indiana, when the Brookville Reservoir was built in 1967. Maurice Thompson wrote the 1900 novel *Alice of Old Vincennes*.

William Henry Harrison House– "Grouseland"

3 West Scott Street
Vincennes, IN 47591
(812) 882-2096

Contact: Francis Vigo Chapter of the Daughters of the American Revolution
Open: Jan.and Feb., daily 11 a.m.–4 p.m.; Mar.-Dec., daily 9 a.m.–5 p.m.; closed Thanksgiving, Christmas, New Year's Day
Admission: Adults $3.00; children (6-12) $1.00; special group rates available
Activities: Guided tours

Suggested Time to View House: 30–45 minutes
Description of Grounds: Yard with lawn
Best Season to View House: Spring-fall
Number of Yearly Visitors: 15,000
Year House Built: 1804
Style of Architecture: Federal, brick
Number of Rooms: 13
On-Site Parking: Yes **Wheelchair Access:** No

Description of House

In 1801 William Henry Harrison—a native Virginian who had married an Ohio woman and settled in North Bend near Cincinnati—had just begun serving twelve years as the first Governor of Indiana Territory and bought 300 acres of cleared land on the Wabash River where he built this house two years later in a grove of walnut trees. It was the first brick building in Vincennes and the Harrisons lived here until 1812, when Harrison became Commander-in-Chief of the Army of the Northwest. This soldier, politician, and patriot was elected to the Presidency of the United States in 1840; his campaign used the famous slogan "Tippecanoe and Tyler too," for it was at the Battle of Tippecanoe that Harrison had defeated Chief Tecumseh, virtually ending armed Indian resistance east of the Mississippi. Sadly, he died on April 4, 1841, only thirty-one days after his inauguration, leaving the office to his Vice-President John Tyler. Harrison's grandson, Benjamin Harrison, whose home in Indianapolis is also listed in this guide, was the twenty-third President of the United States.

This two-story Federal-style house features a full-height entry porch on the side, large twelve-over-twelve shuttered windows, and a covered passage in the rear leading to the "dependency." The local brick used to build "Grouseland" came from a 400-acre parcel of land bought just for that purpose and the stones used in the foundation were brought up from the river. Inside, we see some of the original flooring, clay-and-straw insulation laid between floors, and two original hand-carved mantels. The interiors have been restored to their appearance in the year 1812, the final year of Harrison's residency. The furnishings—some of which are original to the family—are done in a number of different styles, Hepplewhite, Chippendale, Queen Anne, and Sheraton.

Notable Collections on Exhibit

Seen in the house are two oil portraits of our ninth President, one painted by John Jarvis and one by Rembrandt Peale.

Additional Information

Outside of Harrison's birthplace—the plantation on the James River in Virginia called "Berkeley"—"Grouseland" is the only home in which he lived that still stands. It is listed on the National Register of Historic Places.

Wolcott House

500 North Range Street
Wolcott, IN 47995
(219) 279-2123

Contact: Anson Wolcott Historical Society
Open: By appointment only
Admission: Free; use of facilities by groups
is $15.00; summer festival Fourth of July
$.50 per person
Activities: Guided tours by appointment,
annual Christmas Open House
Suggested Time to View House: 90 minutes
Facilities on Premises: Museum
Description of Grounds: Park facilities
surround house
Best Season to View House: Spring-fall
Number of Yearly Visitors: 1,500
Year House Built: 1859
Number of Rooms: 11

Style of Architecture: Italianate
On-Site Parking: Yes **Wheelchair Access:** Yes

Description of House

In 1861, Anson Wolcott, a native of Lockport, New York, who had already taught school in Louisiana, practiced law in New York, and speculated in land, began to plat the town which bears his name on a 2,000-acre parcel of land he'd purchased three years earlier northwest of Tippecanoe County. After he managed to get a railroad station in his town—thus insuring its successful development—Wolcott built a grain elevator here and became active in agriculture as well as politics. He served briefly in the Civil War, then followed that service by working for both the state and Federal governments on behalf of Governor Morris. In 1868, Wolcott was elected to the Indiana State Senate as a Republican but broke from that party eight years later in an unsuccessful third-party run for governor. After his death, Anson Wolcott was followed in this house by three generations of his descendants. The family all claimed to be directly descended from one Oliver Wolcott, a delegate to the Continental Congress, signer of the Declaration of Independence, and general in the Connecticut State Militia during the Revolutionary War.

Construction on the Wolcott House began in 1859—some two years before the founding of the town—and was completed shortly after the end of the Civil War. The house originally consisted of two parlors, a library, dining room, kitchen, six bedrooms, and a bathroom. It also boasted of a full basement, two attic storage rooms, a wood storage room, and a large center tower which was used as an observatory. The interior features eight fireplaces and several pieces of furniture which belonged to the original residents.

Additional Information

The Wolcott House is listed on the National Register of Historic Places.

Iowa

1. Boone

Mamie Doud Eisenhower
Birthplace State Historic Site

2. Burr Oak

Masters Hotel

3. Cedar Falls

Victorian House Museum–
Barnum-Bryant-Dempster House
Wyth House

4. Cedar Rapids

Brucemore–The Sinclair Mansion
Seminole Valley Farm

5. **Clermont**
   Montauk

6. **Council Bluffs**
   Historic General Dodge House

7. **Des Moines**
   Hoyt Sherman Place
   *Terrace Hill–The Historic
   Governor's Mansion*

8. **Dubuque**
   Mathias Ham House Historic Site

9. **Elk Horn**
   Bedstemor's House

10. **Hawarden**
    Historical House

11. **Iowa City**
    Plum Grove

12. **Lamoni**
    Liberty Hall Historic Center

13. **Muscatine**
    Laura Musser Mansion

14. **Oskaloosa**
    Daniel Nelson Homestead

15. **Pella**
    Scholte House

16. **Washington**
    Jonathan Clark Conger House

17. **West Branch**
    *Herbert Hoover Birthplace
    Cottage*

Mamie Doud Eisenhower Birthplace State Historic Site

709 Carroll Street, P.O. Box 55
Boone, IA 50036
(515) 432-1896

Contact: Mamie Doud Eisenhower Birthplace Foundation, Inc.

Open: Apr., May, Tues.-Sun. 1–5 p.m.; June-Oct., daily 10 a.m.–5 p.m.; other times by appointment

Admission: Adults $2.50; children $.50

Activities: Guided tours, audiovisual presentations, special seasonal events

Suggested Time to View House: 45 minutes

Facilities on Premises: Gift shop, library, and museum areas

Description of Grounds: Restored landscape gardens, period 1890s

Best Season to View House: Summer

Number of Yearly Visitors: 8,000-12,000

Year House Built: c. 1880, remodeled c. 1940

Style of Architecture: Folk Victorian

Number of Rooms: 4

On-Site Parking: Yes **Wheelchair Access:** No

Description of House

Mamie Geneva Doud, First Lady of the United States from 1953 to 1961, was born here on November 14, 1896, to John Sheldon Doud and Elivera Carlson Doud. Carl Carlson, Mamie's grandfather, immigrated from Sweden and settled in Boone in 1868; from 1870 to 1903 he owned and operated a flourishing grain and flour mill in town. His daughter Elivera was born in Boone. The Douds, Royal and John Sheldon, formerly of Chicago, owned a meat-packing company here from 1890 to 1895. It was during those years that John courted Elivera and married her. In Boone, their daughters Eleanor and Mamie were born. After the business folded, the Douds moved, first to Cedar Rapids, then, in 1902, to Pueblo, Colorado. They would move once more, to Colorado Springs, before settling in Denver. In addition to Eleanor, Mamie had two other sisters, Eda and Mabel Frances—affectionately called Mike—who were both born in Cedar Rapids.

Mamie Doud met Lt. Dwight D. Eisenhower while vacationing in San Antonio in October of 1915. Apparently, she was as thoroughly charmed by this former Texan now hailing from Abilene, Kansas, as he was by her. They married the following July 1 at the Doud family home in Denver.

After the Doud family left Boone, the house went through many owners. Sometime in the 1940s, it was remodeled into three separate apartments and, in 1962, the First Baptist Church of Boone bought it and used it as a Sunday School. Having been established as a historical landmark,the house was moved from its original site at 718 Carroll Street to its present address. It now stands behind its period wrought-iron fence, a completely restored 1890s Victorian with a detached summer kitchen. The reproductions of the interior details are all authentic, including carpets patterned after those from the 1896 Sears Roebuck Catalogue. The documentation and research concerning the wall coverings is especially impressive.

Notable Collections on Exhibit

The furnishings in the bedroom and the parlor include many pieces from the Carlson home; among them, the bed in which Mamie was born, their dining room set, and an upright piano upon which the family Bible lies. The other rooms contain artifacts and utensils typical for the period. There is a painting here by Dwight Eisenhower, a chronology of the Doud family's story, a history of the restoration process and a number of personal items: an oil lamp brought from Sweden by Carl Carlson, a black-and-rose lace dress which belonged to Elivera and an Ansonia clock given as a wedding gift to Mamie's parents. A permanent exhibit shows the many awards given to Mamie in her lifetime as well as a collection of family photographs.

Additional Information

The restoration research for the Mamie Doud Birthplace was done by the William Wagner. This architect is also largely responsible for the accurate restoring of Terrace Hill in Des Moines and the Herbert Hoover Birthplace; both of those houses are included in this volume.

Masters Hotel

Route 52, twelve miles northwest of Decorah
P.O. Box 354
Burr Oak, IA 52131
(319) 735-5916

Contact: Laura Ingalls Wilder Parks
and Museum, Inc.
Open: May 1-Oct. 15, daily 9 a.m.–5 p.m.;
groups by appointment
Admission: Adults $2.00; kindergarten -
6th grade $.50; 7th-12th grade $1.00;
adult groups (10 or more) $1.50
Activities: Guided tours
Suggested Time to View House: 1 hour
Facilities on Premises: Restaurant
Description of Grounds: Picnic shelter
and play ground
Best Season to View House: Summer
Number of Yearly Visitors: 9,000
Year House Built: c. 1860
Number of Rooms: 11

Style of Architecture: National, frame
On-Site Parking: Yes **Wheelchair Access:** No

Description of House

Laura Ingalls Wilder, beloved author of the classic children's book *The Little House On The Prairie,* lived one year of her girlhood in Burr Oak at the Masters Hotel. This small town made quite an impression on young Laura—years later she would immortalize life there in her books *On The Banks Of Plum Creek* and *By The Shores Of Silver Lake.*

In 1876, her father, Charles Ingalls, had moved his family to Burr Oak in order for him to take the position of Manager of the Masters Hotel. Laura was nine. Unfortunately, the position proved a disappointment; the family left after one year and returned to Walnut Grove, Minnesota. Laura would ultimately settle in Mansfield, Missouri; her residence there is also included in this guide.

It is difficult to imagine the Masters Hotel a "hotel" at all since it now looks to be a quite ordinary, two-story clapboard hall-and-parlor house with side gables. In fact, by the early 1900s it was being used exclusively as a private residence. For the next sixty years its ownership passed through many hands until, showing the deleterious effect of age and neglect, it appeared to be no more than an old structure without a history or a future. Then, in 1973, a group of private citizens who'd discovered the fact of Laura's residence at the hotel, purchased it for $1,500 and began the hard work of restoring the frame structure to its 1876 appearance. Three years later, in 1976, the ribbons were cut on the Laura Ingalls Wilder Park and Museum. The furnishings which fill the Hotel are all from the mid- to late-19th century; they were donated after the restoration was complete.

Additional Information

The Masters Hotel is listed on National Register of Historic Places.

Victorian House Museum, Barnum-Bryant-Dempster House

303 Clay Street
Cedar Falls, IA 50613
(319) 266-5149

Contact: Cedar Falls Historical Society
Museum

Open: Year-round,Wed.-Sun. 2–4 p.m.

Admission: Donation box; adult charter
bus $2.00 per person; school groups free

Activities: Guided tour, slide shows

Suggested Time to View House:
45-60 minutes

Facilities on Premises: Book and gift shop,
research library

Description of Grounds: Landscaped yard
with shrubs

Best Season to View House: Spring

Year House Built: 1861

Number of Rooms: 12

Number of Yearly Visitors: 4,000

Style of Architecture: Italianate

On-Site Parking: No **Wheelchair Access:** No

Description of House

Cedar Falls was settled in 1845 by William Sturgis and E. D. Adams; this site on the Red Cedar River near Sturgis Falls was ideal for driving the mills which formed the basis for the town's growth. Scarcely 16 years later, in 1861, Azel Barnum, a local contractor, built the house at Clay and Third Streets where he was to live until 1874. The belvedere atop the Tuscan roof instantly became an important local landmark; there is speculation that it was used as a lookout against possible Indian attack because of the superb view of the river it afforded. Barnum also built the Civil War Soldiers' Orphans Home which was eventually to become the first building of the University of Northern Iowa campus. The house was purchased by William Bryant, who lived in it with his family until 1919. The last inhabitants, John and Myrna Dempster, lived here until 1966, when they sold the house to the Cedar Falls Historical Society.

The house that Barnum built is an especially fine example of the Italianate style with its long windows topped by arches, Tuscan roof with cupola and Ionic columns supporting the porch roofs. The cupola is still attached and open to the public. Constructed of brick, the exterior walls are 18 inches thick. The well-preserved interior has many original fixtures, including inside shutters with vertical louvers, a curved walnut banister, and numerous door-knobs. The parlor is preserved to appear exactly as it did in the 1890s. The house, which had been turned into apartments during the Dempster years, is undergoing a restoration. When done, it will appear as a private residence c.1890.

Notable Collections on Exhibit

The Barnum-Bryant-Dempster House is now the Cedar Falls Historical Society Museum. The collections on display consist of antique furniture and clothing, the latter including a number of gowns modeled on mannequins. There are also a research library, a picture file and numerous mementos about Cedar Falls and its early settlers.

Wyth House

303 Franklin Street
Cedar Falls, IA 50613
(319) 277-8817

Contact: Cedar Falls Historical Society
Open: Apr.-Dec., Sun. 2–4 p.m.; other times
by appointment
Admission: Donation box; adult tours $2.00
Activities: Guided tours
Suggested Time to View House:
45–60 minutes
Description of Grounds: Landscaped
flower gardens with benches
Best Season to View House: Spring
Year House Built: 1907
Number of Rooms: 10

Number of Yearly Visitors: 3,500
Style of Architecture: Prairie School
On-Site Parking: No **Wheelchair Access:** No

Description of House

The land on which the Wyth House sits was sold by the United States Government to William Sturgis in 1847. Sturgis was one of two men who settled Cedar Falls. Subsequent to the Sturgis purchase, the land went through several owners before being bought by F.W. Paugler. Paugler was the architect who designed and built this white frame house in 1907. In 1925, the house was purchased by George Wyth, one of the founders of the Viking Pump Company, currently Cedar Falls' largest private employer. When the Wyths moved in, they insulated the house against the harsh winters by adding a brick veneer. The family consisted of George, his wife, Alice, and their children, Dorothy, Russell and Robert; the last succeeded his father as president of the Viking Pump Company in 1944. Both were active in the life of Cedar Falls, but the father was especially so in establishing city parks and setting aside park land for future use. His memorial is the park between Cedar Falls and Waterloo which bears his name. Dorothy Wyth, whose primary residence was in New York where she pursued a career in music, stayed in the house during her visits to Cedar Falls in the years from 1955 to 1979. She bequeathed the house to the Historical Society in memory of her parents and established a fund for its restoration and upkeep; the landscaped flower garden was created at her request.

The exterior of the house is virtually unchanged from 1925 when the Wyths bought it—it remains a white frame structure with a brick veneer. The interior of the house has been decorated in the Art Deco style, much as it would have been during the early years of the Wyths. All of the furnishings are authentic, including a Stroud grand piano with its Duo-Arts player attachment, a Gilbert Rhode desk and the City of Paris torchere lamps in the living room. A forty-eight star flag is flown at the house, as it would have in 1925. The flag is a gift from the Daughters of the American Revolution.

Notable Collections on Exhibit

The third floor of the Wyth House is the home of the Viking Pump Company Museum. Here pump models, historic photographs and video presentations tell the story of the invention and development of the rotary pump, as well as the history of the Company George helped found in 1911.

Brucemore–The Sinclair Mansion

2160 Linden Drive Southeast
Cedar Rapids, IA 52403
(319) 362-7375

Contact: Brucemore, Inc., National Trust for Historic Preservation

Open: Feb.-Dec., Tues.-Sat. 10 a.m.–3 p.m.; additional summer and holiday hours

Admission: Adults $3.50; students $2.00; group and student group rates available

Activities: Guided tours, special seasonal programs including the June Arts Festival

Suggested Time to View House: 45–60 minutes

Facilities on Premises: Museum shop

Description of Grounds: 26 acre estate with formal gardens and orchards

Style of Architecture: Modified Victorian Queen Anne, masonry

Best Season to View House: Spring-fall

Number of Yearly Visitors: 30,000

Number of Rooms: 21

Year House Built: Started 1884, completed 1886
On-Site Parking: Yes **Wheelchair Access:** Yes

Description of House

This large Queen Anne-style mansion was built by Caroline Sinclair, the widow of pioneer industrialist T. M. Sinclair.She lived here until 1906 when it was purchased by the George Bruce Douglas family; Douglas was a founding partner in the Quaker Oats Company. The eldest Douglas daughter, Margaret, and her husband, Howard Hall, lived here from 1937 until his death. Mrs. Hall donated the estate to the National Trust for Historic Preservation in 1981.

This twenty-one-room mansion was designed by Cedar Rapids architects Josselyn & Taylor in 1884 and completed two years later. When the Douglas family took possession in 1906 substantive changes were made, including the relocation of the main entrance from the north to the south side where a conservatory was removed. The interior is interpreted to the period of the Douglas occupancy except for two rooms which are used for conferences. The Great Hall is paneled in butternut, the library in antiqued oak, and the dining room is done in a high-gloss white finish. Installed in the house is an impressive Skinner Pipe Organ—the console resides in the Great Hall while all 678 pipes can be seen on the third floor. Brucemore–The Sinclair Mansion is listed on the National Register of Historic Places. It sits amid twenty-six acres comprising an orchard, formal gardens, a pond and pool, and immense lawns.

Notable Collections on Exhibit

Brucemore features a porch done by the artist Grant Wood—of *American Gothic* fame—using a cement plaster process, two paintings done by Wood's contemporary Marvin Cone, and two basement rooms—the Tahitian Room and the Grizzly Bar—which serve as fine examples of 1930s casual entertaining quarters. A mural depicting scenes out of Wagner's Ring Cycle surrounds the Great Hall and a stairway leading to the second floor.

Seminole Valley Farm

1400 Seminole Valley Road Northeast
P.O. Box 605
Cedar Rapids, IA 52406
(319) 378-9240

Contact: Seminole Valley Farm, Inc.
Open: May–Oct., Sun. 1–4 p.m.; other times by appointment
Admission: Adults $1.00; children (under 12) free
Activities: Guided tours, slide presentations, special seasonal events including Autumn Apple Day
Suggested Time to View House: 1 hour

Description of Grounds: Working farm yard with several outbuildings
Best Season to View House: Spring-fall
Number of Yearly Visitors: 5,500
Year House Built: 1902
Style of Architecture: National, frame
Number of Rooms: 10
On-Site Parking: Yes **Wheelchair Access:** Yes

Description of House

If it may be said that the Farmhouse symbolized the twin American ideals of liberty and land ownership for successive waves of immigrants, then this house can be considered an embodiment of that symbol. Lafayette Franks, a Civil War veteran of Northern European stock, and his wife, Sarah, lived on this farm in the late nineteenth century. It was likely a simple log structure that the Franks inhabited; after all, their lives were little different from those of the pioneers who had settled here. By 1900, they were an anachronism. It was then, almost as if the new century demanded evidence of change, that the farm was bought by a city couple moving to the country in pursuit of a dream. Joseph and Frantiska Dostal, Czech immigrants, moved out to Cedar Rapids when he took the position of City Gardener. For his wife, Joseph replaced the log cabin with the structure which stands today: a salvaged Cedar Rapids hotel or tavern which he moved to the farm. Moving buildings from the business district to the northerly precincts of the city was not an uncommon practice at that time. The building that the Dostals took as their home is one of the few such structures still standing. The Dostals did not stay on the farm for long: in 1908 they sold the property to their distant relations, Joe and Marie Jasa. The Jasas took the farm into the modern era, ran it like a business, steadily made improvements, and finally expanded it to 330 acres. The family held the land until 1965, when it became a park.

The ten-room frame structure, more imposing than other local farmhouses, shows evidence that it had been moved by the Dostals to its present site: the windows have been shortened and the second story was apparently built out over the kitchen. Even so, it is a very appealing house. The furnishings include some pieces which belonged to the residents, but most have been collected from local area families seeking to preserve an accurate record of the common farm life of the era. The Seminole Valley Farm is listed on the National Register of Historic Places.

Notable Collections on Exhibit

The house contains a collection of women's handiwork, including a number of fine quilts. There is also an exhibit of farm tools and equipment; this collection of furnishings and artifacts is intended to render a portrait of the ordinary farm life of the time.

Montauk

Route 18 East, Box 372
Clermont, IA 52135
(319) 423-7173

Contact: State Historical Society of Iowa
Open: Memorial Day-Oct., daily
 Noon-5 p.m.
Admission: Adults $1.00; seniors and
 children (6-16) $.50
Activities: Guided tours
Suggested Time to View House: 1 hour
Description of Grounds: Sited on 46 acres
 with appointed front lawn
Best Season to View House: Spring and fall
Number of Yearly Visitors: 10,000
Year House Built: 1874
Style of Architecture: Italianate
Number of Rooms: 14

On-Site Parking: Yes **Wheelchair Access:** Yes

Description of House

William Larabee built his home on 46 acres of a hill rising two hundred feet above the town of Clermont; from the front lawn, one could look right down Main Street and see what everyone in town plainly knew: Mr. Larabee was easily Clermont's most important citizen and his exalted place in the town's affairs was nicely made manifest by his house and its site. Larabee, who lived for the eighty years between 1832 and 1912, was a farmer, land owner, banker, railroader, Iowa State Senator (1867-1885), Governor of Iowa (1886-1890), Chairman of the Iowa Board of Control (1898-1900) and President of the Iowa Commission to the Louisiana Purchase Exposition (1904). He was also chief benefactor to the town of six hundred his house overlooked; one still sees his gifts here: a school, a church and various bronze statues. He lived here with his wife, Anna, and their seven children from 1874 to 1912. Thereafter, the house remained in his children's hands until 1965.

The Italianate structure which so dominates the Clermont scene is executed in red brick and stone. Always intended as a family home, it has undergone hardly any change at all since its construction in 1874. Anna, the last of Larabee's daughters, who lived here until 1965, kept both the Larabee possessions intact and their traditions alive. All of the furnishings are from the original residents.

Notable Collections on Exhibit

The house contains many works of art: marble sculptures, numerous paintings, a collection of Renaissance Revival furniture, and other family holdings. Some of the paintings are by J. G. Brown and William Bradford; there is marble work by Pugi of Florence, Italy.

Additional Information

Montauk is listed on the National Register of Historic Places.

Historic General Dodge House

605 Third Street
Council Bluffs, IA 51503
(712) 322-2406

Contact: Historic General Dodge House, Inc.
Open: Tues.-Sat. 10 a.m.–5 p.m., Sun.
1–5 p.m.; closed Easter, Thanksgiving,
Christmas, month of January
Admission: Adults $3.00; children $1.50;
children (under 6) free
Activities: Guided tours, orientation video,
annual Holiday Open House
Suggested Time to View House: 1 hour
Facilities on Premises: Orientation center
with gift shop
Best Season to View House: Summer
Description of Grounds: Large yard with
carriage house, flower gardens and fountain
Number of Yearly Visitors: 20,000
Number of Rooms: 14

Style of Architecture: Transitional Italianate
style with Second Empire characteristics
Year House Built: 1869
On-Site Parking: Yes **Wheelchair Access:** No

Description of House

As the chief construction engineer for the Union Pacific Railway who helped complete America's first transcontinental rail line, General Grenville M. Dodge garnered a reputation as "the greatest railroad builder of all time." In addition to his railroad work, Dodge served with distinction as an officer during the Civil War and became an influential banker. He moved to Council Bluffs in 1853 and built this magnificent mansion overlooking the Missouri River valley in 1869.

The General Dodge House is a three-story brick mansion which combines elements of the Italianate and Second Empire styles. It features a slate mansard roof, bracketing, white trim, a partial wrap-around porch with rounded, fluted columns, both one- and two-story bay extensions, dormers, and hooded windows. Inside, one sees a wide variety of woods and wood finishes in the parquet floors, paneling, and molding. The floor plan is rather typical of mid-19th century upper-class homes; it consists of a dining room, two parlors, and a library on the first floor, the bedrooms on the second floor, and a third-floor ballroom. When it was built, it included the most modern conveniences: hot and cold running water, central heating, and closets. The furnishings are from the period between 1869 and 1920; some are original and all are appropriate to the period of the mansion's restoration. Furniture styles include Eastlake, Renaissance Revival, Rococo, Cottage, Empire, and Centennial. The General Dodge House is listed on the National Register of Historic Places. During the Christmas season, the house is decorated with fourteen Christmas trees trimmed with Victorian decorations.

Notable Collections on Exhibit

In addition to the furnishings mentioned above, the house has a collection of Victorian clothing, turn-of-the-century pressed glass, and Currier & Ives and Sadler prints.

Hoyt Sherman Place

1501 Woodland Avenue
Des Moines, IA 50309
(515) 243-0913

Contact: Des Moines Women's Club
Open: Mon.-Fri. 8 a.m.–4 p.m.; other times by appointment; closed all national holidays, week between Christmas and New Year's Day
Admission: $2.00 for guided tours; free browsing
Activities: Guided tours by appointment, slide presentations to groups
Suggested Time to View House: 1 hour

Facilities on Premises: Gift shop, art galleries and auditorium
Style of Architecture: Italianate with Victorian-style interiors
Description of Grounds: Sited on 5 acres
Best Season to View House: Year round
Year House Built: 1877
Number of Yearly Visitors: 40,000
Number of Rooms: 9
On-Site Parking: Yes **Wheelchair Access:** Yes

Description of House

In 1848, Hoyt Sherman came to Des Moines and promptly got admitted to the bar. He was twenty-two years old and confident of establishing himself in the young town. Hoyt had been born in Ohio where his father, and later his brother, served on the State Supreme Court. He was the youngest of eleven children, and one of three who would become famous. The other two were his brothers John, U. S. Senator, Secretary of the Treasury, and Secretary of State under Presidents Hayes and McKinley, and, of course, William Tecumseh, whose Civil War campaigns won international renown. Hoyt's fame rests on his authorship of the Sherman Antitrust Law. He, and his other brothers, James and Lampson, were amongst Des Moines' civic leaders for the entire second half of the nineteenth century. Hoyt married Sarah Moulton on Christmas Day of 1855. They had five children, built this house in 1877, and lived here until their deaths—Sarah's in 1893 and Hoyt's in 1904.

The original house had an entrance hall, parlor, library, dining room, Victorian bed and sitting room, and three other bedrooms, two of which were named for their occupants: the Helen Sherman room and the Deets room. The auditorium and the art galleries were added at later dates. One enters the hall through massive arched doors fashioned out of mahogany, cherry, walnut, maple, and pine. The staircase is solid walnut. Throughout the main floor, extensive runs of decorative stenciling have been carefully uncovered, thereby greatly adding to the impact of the overall design. The dining room furniture is original to the house and sits on a wonderful parquet floor with a border made of the same woods as the hallway doors.

Notable Collections on Exhibit

Located at the Hoyt Sherman Place is the Byers Collection. Major and Mrs. S. H. M. Byers collected many paintings and objets d'art during the Major's twenty-year stint with the U. S. Consular Service in Switzerland and Italy. The Byers couple, who had been close friends of the Sherman family, donated their collection to the Des Moines Women's Club in 1910 and the gallery in which it currently resides was completed in 1923.

Additional Information

The Hoyt Sherman Place is listed on the National Register of Historic Places. Another distinguished home in Des Moines is the Salisbury House— a twenty-one-room mansion built between 1924 and 1928 in the Tudor-Elizabethan style for the cosmetic manufacturer Carl Weeks and his wife, Edith. Both new and ancient materials from the United States and Great Britain were used in the construction of this magnificent house located at 4025 Tonawanda Drive.

Terrace Hill–The Historic Governor's Mansion

2300 Grand Avenue
Des Moines, IA 50312
(515) 281-3604

Contact: Terrace Hill Society
Open: Tues.-Sat. 10 a.m.–1:30 p.m.; closed
holidays, month of January
Admission: Adults $3.00; children (6-13)
$1.00; children (under 6) free
Activities: Guided tours, special quarterly
lectures
Suggested Time to View House: 45 minutes
Facilities on Premises: Visitor center, gift shop
Description of Grounds: Restored period
garden
Best Season to View House: Spring-fall
Number of Yearly Visitors: 30,000
Year House Built: Started 1865, completed
1869, remodeled 1883
Style of Architecture: Victorian Second
Empire
Number of Rooms: 12 open to the public
On-Site Parking: No
Wheelchair Access: Yes

Description of House

In 1869, Benjamin F. Allen built Terrace Hill at a cost of over $250,000. Less than ten years later, his fortune was lost in the bank failures of the '70s and he had to sell his mansion. The buyer was Frederick M. Hubbell, a Connecticut native who had come to Des Moines and made a fortune in real estate, railroads and insurance. At one time, Hubbell owned 90 percent of the shares in The Equitable Life Insurance Company of Iowa. Frederick and Frances Hubbell had three children; their daughter, Beulah, was married to the Swedish Count Carl Wachtmeister in the drawing room of Terrace Hill. The house remained in the family until 1971, when the Hubbell heirs gave the mansion to the State of Iowa for use as the governor's residence.

The three-story mansion, which once commanded an estate of over 30 acres, was designed by W. W. Boyington, builder of the Chicago Water Tower. The asymmetrical exterior features a full story side tower, paired and tripled combinations of hooded and rounded windows, a patterned roof, and heavy quoins. The elaborate gardens were designed by J. T. Elletson; set on the grounds is a swimming pool, one of the first ever seen in Iowa. The interiors were handled by the New York firm of Jacob Ziegeler, who had to work with fourteen-and-a-half-foot ceilings, twelve-foot doorways, and pocket doors weighing 400 pounds each. The stenciling in the main floor rooms and hallways has been restored to its original grandeur and sets off the other interior details: oak wainscoting, eight marble fireplaces accented with pier mirrors, hand-carved woodwork, and a grand staircase composed of various native inlaid woods. Along with all of the furnishings made specially for the house, there are also nine chairs and a settee designed by John Henry Belter, the Chippendale table and chairs in the formal dining room, and a Louis XVI side chair covered with an Aubusson tapestry. It is a most impressive house, inside and out.

Notable Collections on Exhibit

The collections at Terrace Hill include some remarkable items: a silver and crystal chandelier imported from Czechoslovakia containing more than 1,500 prisms, an oxblood Ming vase c. 1426-1435, a Lowestoft hand-painted porcelain vase c. 1880 and the original lamps on the newel posts of the grand staircase.

Additional Information

After Terrace Hill was opened as the Iowa governor's mansion, the first overnight guest was Mrs. Lillian Carter. Terrace Hill is listed on the National Register of Historic Places.

Mathias Ham House
Historic Site

2241 Lincoln Avenue, P.O. Box 305
Dubuque, IA 52004
(319) 557-9545

Contact: Dubuque County Historical Society
Open: Memorial Day–Oct., daily
10 a.m.–5 p.m.
Admission: Adults $3.00; children $1.50;
family $9.00; group rates available
Activities: Guided tours, exhibits, special
seasonal programs, historic dining
experiences
Suggested Time to View House: 45 minutes
Facilities on Premises: Gift and book shop
Description of Grounds: Located on a
Mississippi River bluff
Best Season to View House: Spring-fall
Number of Yearly Visitors: 30,000
Year House Built: Between 1855 and 1856
Style of Architecture: Italianate Villa with
Gothic Revival modifications
Number of Rooms: 29
On-Site Parking: Yes
Wheelchair Access: Yes

Description of House

Mathias Ham came to the Upper Mississippi Lead Mine District in 1826 just as the nation's first mining boom was getting under way; within ten years, he had become one of the region's most prominent operators, the owner of lead mines and smelting furnaces. In 1856, he hired the architect John Francis Rague—whose buildings included the Old Illinois State Capitol and the Iowa Capitol—to design and build a home of sufficient grandeur to signal his wealth and status. The monumental limestone villa Ham got is perhaps one of the finest homes in all of Iowa. He lived here until 1912 when the mansion was sold to the city of Dubuque.

This two-story Italianate-style mansion is built out of native limestone of various hues—much of the exterior stonework has been hand-dressed—and features a small entry porch with exotic supports. Other exterior details include: paired window treatments with flat lintels on both stories, wide eaves with paired brackets, angled dormers on the corners of the roof, and a center octagonal-shaped cupola. Inside, the restoration has faithfully reproduced the richness and beauty of the wood grains, decorative moldings, plaster cornices, medallions, and rosettes, and gilding. The Classical Revival-style American and European furnishings were shipped to Dubuque by steamboat from New Orleans and St. Louis. They have been donated by Dubuque-area residents whose ancestors were of the same social and economic status as the Hams and represent the height of Victorian opulence.

Notable Collections on Exhibit

In addition to the period furnishings, the mansion contains a costume collection including French-made dresses and accessories from the middle decades of the 19th century; numerous paintings by American and European artists dating from the 1830s to 1890; and many fine examples of the decorative arts, ranging from a carcel lamp to a 363-piece set of French porcelain.

Additional Information

The Mathias Ham House Historic Site is listed on the National Register of Historic Places. There is also a simple log cabin standing on the property dating from 1833; it is thought to be the oldest building in Iowa.

Bedstemor's House

2105 College Street, P.O. Box 178
Elk Horn, IA 51531
(712) 764-7001

Contact: Danish Immigrant Museum
Open: May-Sept., Mon.-Sat. 10 a.m.-4 p.m.,
Sun. 1-4 p.m.; closed Memorial Day,
Fourth of July, Labor Day
Admission: Adults $1.50; children $1.50;
special group rates
Activities: Guided tours, special exhibits
Suggested Time to View House: 45-60
minutes
Facilities on Premises: Front-porch swing
has been described as the "most relaxing
spot in town"
Description of Grounds: Corner lot
surrounded by picket fence
Best Season to View House: Late spring
Style of Architecture: Late Victorian Queen
Anne with Danish-style variations
Number of Yearly Visitors: 2,500
Year House Built: 1908
Number of Rooms: 7
On-Site Parking: No
Wheelchair Access: No

Description of House

In 1889 Jens Otto Christensen emigrated from Denmark to America and twenty years later built this house to impress a young woman he wanted to marry. Christensen—nicknamed "Prince Otto" by local residents because of his stiff posture and his tailored coat and derby hat—was turned down by the woman and vowed never to live in the house he had built for her. Instead, he moved into a room behind his dimestore and remained a bachelor for the rest of his days. He rented the house to a series of Danish immigrant families until 1933 when he gave it to the Salem Old Peoples' Home as payment for his care. After Christensen died in 1946, the home was bought by Meta Mortensen who lived here for the next thirty-five years. Mortensen was a true "bedstemor" (Danish for "grandmother").

This two-story frame house features a beautiful and complex roof-line (combining cross gables, a hipped roof, and a ridge line broken by a center chimney). There is a symmetrical double gable facade with a center dormer, clapboard siding with decorative bands of fish-scale and angle-cut shingles, and a small entry porch with turned posts and spindlework detailing. The roof ridge line of this porch is capped with a "cut-out" and the gables, dormer, and portico are all decorated with a "sunburst" design; this pattern is a motif common to the region. The interior of the house is interpreted to the years between 1910 and 1920 when it was inhabited by Danish immigrants and the original egg-and-dart moldings are visible throughout.

The interior details include linoleum floor coverings, fir floors, an angled upstairs hallway, and reproduction wallpaper similar to that originally found here. The Bedstemor's House has been furnished by area residents with items which had belonged to their grandmothers.

Notable Collections on Exhibit

The Bedstemor's House is a museum dedicated to preserving the heritage of the area's Danish immigrants for future generations; as such, it houses a wide array of objects related to the Danish-American experience.

Historical House

803 Avenue "H"
Hawarden, IA 51023
(712) 552-2233

Contact: Big Sioux River Valley Historical Society
Open: Daily, no regular hours; house undergoing restoration
Admission: Donations only
Activities: Guided tours by appointment, special activities for holidays, flower show, antique displays
Suggested Time to View House: 1 hour

Description of Grounds: House is surrounded by flowers and shrubs, some decorative trees
Best Season to View House: Spring-fall
Number of Yearly Visitors: 600-1,200
Year House Built: c. 1900
Style of Architecture: Early Victorian Queen Anne-Eastlake
Number of Rooms: 8

Description of House

Around the turn of the century, Proctor Maynard, a local businessman with a number of buildings to his credit, completed this fine Victorian house at 803 Avenue H. Ownership of the house went from the Proctors to the Slife family who donated the home to the Big Sioux River Valley Historical Society. In 1993, Earl Slife, Jr., son of the bank's founder, celebrated his 75th anniversary with the bank where he holds the title of Honorary Chairman. A number of other Hawarden families can claim involvement with this house; at one time, the author Ruth Suchow was a resident here and some remember that it was once used as a hospital. For some years the pretty house just off Main Street stood empty and suffered from neglect. Fortunately, it is now undergoing restoration, and already parts of it, like the floor and wood moldings, have been brought back to their original state.

The house was built largely from the fine brick manufactured at the kilns of the local Calliope brick yards. The structure was graced with an unusual steeple when originally completed; the steeple was later removed, then rebuilt to a new position on the roof. The house has an open stairway which leads one up to a large upstairs hall surrounded by windows; the effect of all the light thus let in is quite inviting. There are now four fully renovated original pieces of furniture on display—a bookcase, rocking chair, fainting couch, and table.

Notable Collections on Exhibit

The collection of familial objects includes: antique furniture, braided rugs, a Hoosier cabinet, light fixtures, a wedding suit made by a local tailor in 1911 and the wedding dress of a Slife daughter who married in 1917. There are some lovely quilts and two watercolors from the Maynard family. Perhaps the most touching piece is a cradle made by a local amateur wood carver in 1857.

Plum Grove

1030 Carroll Street
Iowa City, IA 52240
(319) 337-6846

Contact: Johnson County Historical Society
Open: Mid Apr.-Oct., Wed.-Sat. 1–5 p.m.,
Sun. 1–4 p.m.
Admission: Donations accepted
Activities: Guided tours
Suggested Time to View House: 30 minutes
Year House Built: 1844

Description of Grounds: 4 acre plot in the
midst of an urban setting
Best Season to View House: Year round
Style of Architecture: Rural Greek Revival
Number of Rooms: 7
On-Site Parking: Yes **Wheelchair Access:** No

Description of House

In 1838 President Martin Van Buren appointed Robert Lucas the first governor of the Territory of Iowa. Lucas—born in 1781 of Quaker ancestors who'd settled in Pennsylvania in 1679—had served as a state legislator in Ohio, an officer in General Hull's Detroit campaign during the War of 1812, and as Ohio's governor from 1832 to 1836. He was married twice; first to Elizabeth Brown, then, in 1816, to Friendly Sumner. At the end of his term as Territorial Governor in 1841 Lucas built this house on a small farm at the edge of Iowa City amid a thicket of plum trees; hence, the name "Plum Grove." Robert and Friendly Lucas had three children, a daughter and two sons; the family stayed on at Plum Grove for thirteen years after the Governor's death in 1853. The State of Iowa acquired the house and four acres in 1941 and completed its restoration five years later.

Plum Grove is a two-story brick house built in the popular Greek Revival style as adapted to a rustic setting. The floor plan consists of seven rooms connected to a kitchen in its separate south wing. Exterior details include walls built of the original soft red brick fired locally, six-over-six window treatments with shutters, a segmented transom light over the front door, and a small elliptical window in the front facade pediment. This latter feature is closer to the Adam, or Federal, style. The interior has been interpreted to the period of the Lucas residency; the furnishings, wallcoverings, and other details were acquired after much research by members of the National Society of Colonial Dames of America. These furnishings are all period pieces—some of which are original to the Lucas family—in a rather modest style which accurately reflects that family's taste.

Notable Collections on Exhibit

Among the items on display at the house are: an imposing portrait of Governor Lucas, a melodeon, a spindle bed, and a four-poster bed with acorn detailing carved into the top of each post.

Additional Information

Plum Grove is listed on the National Register of Historic Places.

Liberty Hall Historic Center

1300 West Main Street
Lamoni, IA 50140
(515) 784-6133

Contact: Restoration Trail Foundation
Open: Mon-Fri.10 a.m.–4 p.m.,
   Sat.10 a.m.–2 p.m.
Admission: Free
Activities: Group tours by appointment,
   school programs, antique seminars,
   special events including Victorian teas
Suggested Time to View House: 1 hour
Facilities on Premises: Gift shop
Description of Grounds: 12 acres with
   fishing pond and picnic area
Best Season to View House: Early
   spring-late fall
Style of Architecture: Folk Victorian,
   farmhouse
Number of Yearly Visitors: 8,000
Number of Rooms: 18

Year House Built: 1881
On-Site Parking: Yes **Wheelchair Access:** No

Description of House

Joseph Smith III, son of the founder of the Church of Jesus Christ of Latter-day Saints, came to Lamoni with his followers in 1881. Here he would establish the headquarters of the Reorganized Church of Jesus Christ of Latter-day Saints, which he had founded in 1860. Liberty Hall, the Smith home from 1881 to 1906, was the center of both his middle-class family life and his community activities. As such, it is a remarkably well-preserved evocation of the midwestern small town life common at the turn of the century.

Although Liberty Hall is a simple front-gabled Victorian farmhouse, a number of details provoke admiration: the trim on the front porch which shows off the Victorian flat jigsaw cut to such good effect, the oval topped and twelve pane windows, the beautiful plant conservatory, the five bedroom suites including built-in closets, and the three fireplaces. A number of the pieces on display belonged to the Smiths; many more are furnishings original to the period 1860 to 1900.

Notable Collections on Exhibit

The collection of textiles and quilts includes: an 1844 hand-loomed Lindsey-Woolsey, a Flower Basket Appliqué made in 1885, and a double-tucked log cabin made of 5,000 tiny pieces called "Light and Shadows." These are in addition to several silk and velvet crazy quilts.

Additional Information

Liberty Hall, which entered the National Register of Historic Places in 1984, is unique in that the entire house is accessible to the public—there are no off-limits areas—and physical interaction with the structure and its contents is encouraged.

Laura Musser Mansion

1314 Mulberry Avenue
Muscatine, IA 52761
(319) 263-8282

Contact: Muscatine Art Center

Open: Tues.-Fri. 11 a.m–5 p.m., Thurs. evening 7–9 p.m., Sat. and Sun. 1–5 p.m.; closed major holidays

Admission: Free

Activities: Guided tours with reservation, special music programs, public lectures, special seasonal programs

Suggested Time to View House: 1 hour

Facilities on Premises: Art reference library and music room

Description of Grounds: 1929 Japanese-style garden installed by original owners

Best Season to View House: Late spring and early fall

Number of Yearly Visitors: 10,000

Number of Rooms: 10

Style of Architecture: Edwardian style, four-over-four

Year House Built: 1908, addition 1920

On-Site Parking: Yes **Wheelchair Access:** Yes

Description of House

On November 23, 1877, Laura Musser was born in this city by the Mississippi to Peter and Tamson Musser. Twenty-six years later she married Edwin L. McColm, the owner of Muscatine's leading dry goods store. In 1908, McColm built this fine Edwardian mansion for his wife, and the couple moved in along with Laura's father. Laura Musser McColm died in 1964, at which time her stepdaughter and niece gave the property to the City of Muscatine to be used as a museum and art gallery dedicated to Laura's memory.

The mansion was designed and built by Muscatine architect Henry Zeidler in the Edwardian style; it is constructed of tan brick and features a decorative stone band with dentils, attached wooden porches, a center dormer with a splendid bonnet-top pediment, and a porte cochere. Inside, three of the four original fireplaces can be seen; other interior details include a summer sleeping porch converted into a meeting room, the oak-paneled 1920 music room containing an Estey Player Pipe Organ, stained glass windows, some of the original woodwork and light fixtures, and a copper sink in the butler's pantry. The house is filled with examples of mid-19th to early 20th-century decorative arts.

Notable Collections on Exhibit

The museum dedicated to Laura Musser McColm features oriental carpets, American Art pottery, paperweights, table service, and many fine pieces of furniture. The Fine Arts Collection includes American and European paintings, prints, drawing, and sculpture.

Daniel Nelson Homestead

Rural Route 1
Box 216, P.O. Box 578
Oskaloosa, IA 52577
(515) 672-2989

Contact: Mahaska County Historical
Society, Inc.
Open: May 12-Oct. 12, Tues.-Sat.
10 a.m.–4:30 p.m., Sun. 1–4:30 p.m.
Admission: Adults $2.00; students (5-16)
$1.00; children (under age 5 with an
adult) free
Activities: Guided tours
Suggested Time to View House: 1 hour
Facilities on Premises: Gift shop
Best Season to View House: Summer
Description of Grounds: 15 buildings and
a museum with woodland trail
Number of Yearly Visitors: 6,000
Number of Rooms: 5

Style of Architecture: National, brick
farmhouse with Georgian elements
Year House Built: 1853
On-Site Parking: Yes **Wheelchair Access:** Yes

Description of House

Daniel Nelson, pioneer farmer and early Iowa businessman, acquired the land for his farm from the government in 1844. When he sold a grist mill on the South Skunk River in 1852, he took the profits and began construction on the house which he had long promised his wife, Margaret. The home and the 310 acre farm upon which it sits was operated continuously by the Nelson family until 1958, when Daniel's grandchildren bequeathed it to the county historical society as a memorial to their forebears.

The limestone foundation for the house was laid in the fall of 1852 and building commenced the following spring. Bricks were made from native clay baked in a kiln just south of the house and the lumber came from timber found on the Nelson land. Woods used in the house included elm for the joists and timbers, walnut for the door jambs and stair railings, ash for the floors, and basswood for the doors and window casings. The kitchen fireplace mantel and cupboards were fashioned from butternut. The twelve-inch-thick interior walls were made of a mixture composed of limestone, sand and cattle hair. The exterior was given numerous coats of paint as waterproofing and the windows were real twelve-pane glass, not oiled paper, as was frequently the case in houses of that period. Around 1900, three porches and a front door with a pane of etched-glass were added to the brick house. Furnishings are all appropriate for the period, but few are original to the house. The Daniel Nelson Homestead is listed on the National Register of Historic Places.

Notable Collections on Exhibit

The objects on display are primarily the utensils, tools and artifacts commonly in use at a typical farmhouse of the era. In addition, there are portraits of Daniel Nelson and his wife, some unique dolls and two matching oak pieces in the east bedroom.

Scholte House

728-734 Washington Street
Pella, IA 50219
(515) 628-3684

Contact: Scholte House
Open: Mon.-Sat. 1–4 p.m.
Admission: Adults $2.50; students $1.00
Activities: Guided tours, group tours by appointment
Suggested Time to View House: 1 hour
Description of Grounds: Landscaped yard with beautiful tulip gardens part of the original Scholte garden

Best Season to View House: Spring-late fall
Number of Yearly Visitors: 6,000
Year House Built: 1847
Style of Architecture: Federal style with Dutch Colonial influences
Number of Rooms: 22, 9 open to the public
On-Site Parking: Yes **Wheelchair Access:** No

Description of House

The official seal of the City of Pella reads "In Deo Spes Nostra et Refugium" (In God is our hope and refuge) and the very word "Pella" means "refuge" in Dutch. The town was built on an 18,000 acre tract of land purchased for $1.25 an acre by a group of eight hundred Hollanders calling themselves The Association for Emigration to the United States of America. Led by Dominie Henrik Pieter Scholte, these immigrants left Holland in early 1847 and came to this beautiful site on a ridge between the Skunk and Des Moines Rivers in southern Iowa via Baltimore and St. Louis. Scholte was a natural leader whose foresight and organizational skills earned him the title, "father of Pella." He and his refined second wife, Mareah, were resolved to build as grand a home here in Pella as the one they had left behind in Europe. Toward the end of 1847, they moved into this twenty-two-room house with the three daughters from his first marriage and began a family of their own. The wife of their eldest son, Leonora Keables, lived here until 1978, when she and her family donated the house to the Pella Historical Society to be preserved as a monument to the Dutch settlers who had built the town.

The Scholte House is built on a foundation of cut stone, framed in rough oak and walnut timber. The floor plan consists of a large entrance hall with a wide stairway leading to a second floor drawing room and study, behind which lie Mareah's private sitting room, the master bedroom and other bedrooms, and the servants' quarters to the rear; downstairs, there is a reception room, library, dining room and kitchen. The wallpaper in the library was ordered from Paris and hung in 1850; the carpet came from Brussels and was laid in the same year. Among the few possessions the Scholtes brought with them on their transatlantic journey was a complete set of Delft china plates; today, only one of these plates is on view in the house. The rest came through the trip in fragments—these fragments were used to line a path which led from the family's temporary shelter to their permanent house.

Notable Collections on Exhibit

Many of the Old World furnishings on display were donated by the estate of John and Margaret Lautenbach—these pieces are primarily Italian and French dating from the 17th century. In addition to the furnishings, the house contains many wonderful items related to the founding of Pella; these include the iron chest in which the Dutch settlers brought their gold from Holland and the town's original plat done in pen-and-ink.

Additional Information

The Scholte House is listed on the National Register of Historic Places. In May, the Pella Historical Society sponsors an annual Tulip Time Festival, a celebration of Dutch crafts, customs, food, and music which includes a tour of the Scholte House and the Pella Historical Village; on view in the Village is the boyhood home of Wyatt Earp.

Jonathan Clark Conger House

903 East Washington Street
Washington, IA 52353
(319) 653-3125

Contact: Washington County Historical Society, Inc.

Open: June-Aug., daily and first two weekends in December 1–5 p.m.

Admission: Adults $1.50; children (under 12) $.50

Activities: Summer exhibits, annual Christmas Open House

Suggested Time to View House: 2 hours

Facilities on Premises: Gifts available

Description of Grounds: Original trees, rock gardens, flower gardens, restored herb garden and gazebo

Best Season to View House: Late spring and summer

Year House Built: 1847, additions 1855 and 1906

Number of Yearly Visitors: 1,000

Style of Architecture: Folk Victorian, brick

Number of Rooms: 14

On-Site Parking: Yes **Wheelchair Access:** Yes

Description of House

This fully restored Victorian house is named for Jonathan Conger, the owner of a bootmaking business and land investor who lived in it from 1855 to 1904. He purchased the house, and its 77 acre property, from Thomas Ritchey who built it in 1847. After Conger's death, Colonel C. J. and Clara Wilson bought the house and began extensive remodeling in 1906: a den was added, the dining room was entirely redone, and the exterior walls were cemented over. The Colonel was a lawyer who served on the governor's staff for over thirty years; he and his family lived here until 1936. The house remained closed until 1948, when it was used as a supper club, and then a nursing home.

The original exterior of the three-story structure was made of red brick against which green shutters smartly contrasted. Colonel Wilson's later coat of cement has been removed. Inside, the house has a number of details: an original walnut staircase and double front door, the Ritchey third floor which became a closet, a restored back staircase, and the oak woodwork and colonnades in the dining room. The period rooms contain both original and collected furnishings; the rosewood chairs and settee in the parlor belonged to Jane Conger and the walnut desk and rocker in a smaller bedroom belonged to Helen "Patsy" Wilson. Some of the china and glassware on display was once in use at the Columbia Hotel in Davenport, Iowa. The Conger and Wilson families received them as gifts.

Notable Collections on Exhibit

Eight of the house's fourteen rooms are given over to the period exhibits. In the other rooms, there are exhibits illustrating Washington County history, its Native American artifacts, Pioneer Kitchen utensils, locally manufactured items, and something of its medicine, military history, and cosmetology.

Additional Information

The Jonathan Clark Conger House is listed on the National Register of Historic Places.

Herbert Hoover Birthplace Cottage

Parkside Drive, P.O. Box 607
West Branch, IA 52358
(319) 643-2541

Contact: National Park Service, Herbert Hoover National Historic Site

Open: Daily 9 a.m.–5 p.m.; closed Thanksgiving, Christmas, New Year's Day

Admission: Adults (16-62) $1.00

Activities: Guided tours by appointment

Suggested Time to View House: 1 hour

Facilities on Premises: Bookstore

Description of Grounds: 186 acre park, including a 76 acre restored prairie with hiking trails

Best Season to View House: Early spring-early fall

Number of Yearly Visitors: 320,000

Year House Built: 1871

Number of Rooms: 2

Style of Architecture: National, cottage

On-Site Parking: Yes **Wheelchair Access:** Yes

Description of House

In this two-room, fourteen-by-twenty foot cottage Herbert Hoover, the thirty-first President of the United States, was born on August 10, 1874. The modest structure was built in 1871 by Jesse and Eli Hoover, Herbert's father and grandfather, near the blacksmith shop where Jesse worked. Young Herbert lived here with his parents and siblings until 1879. Five years later, he would be orphaned and sent to live with relatives in Oregon. His subsequent illustrious career suggests that his troubled early life provided the goad which drove him to excel. In 1895, he graduated from Stanford University and for the next thirty years traveled around the world as a mining engineer and consultant. After the First World War, he served under both Presidents Harding and Coolidge as Secretary of Commerce. In 1928, he followed them into the White House. The Crash of 1929, and its disastrous aftermath, insured that Hoover would be a one-term President. He did, however, remain active in public life, even chairing the historic Commission on the Organization of the Executive Branch of the Government in 1947 and 1953. Hoover died on October 20, 1964.

The little cottage derives its dignity entirely from the history of its famous son. It has been faithfully restored and contains as many of the furnishings and artifacts belonging to Jesse and Hulda Hoover as could be found and collected. There are books and furniture from The Schoolhouse and the replica of Jesse's blacksmith shop contains a number of authentic items.

Additional Information

The Herbert Hoover Birthplace Cottage is a National Historic Site administered by the National Park Service; it is also listed on the National Register of Historic Places.

Kansas

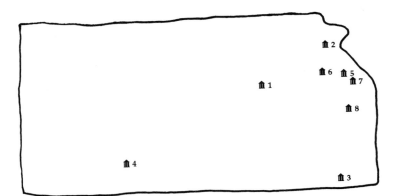

1. **Abilene**
   Eisenhower Family Home
   Historic Kirby House
   Lebold Vahsholtz Mansion
   Seelye Mansion

2. **Atchison**
   Amelia Earhart Birthplace
   Museum

3. **Coffeyville**
   W.P. Brown Mansion

4. **Dodge City**
   1878 Hardesty House
   Mueller-Schmidt House–
   "House of Stone"

5. **Kansas City**
   Grinter Place

6. **Leavenworth**
   Edward Carroll Mansion

7. **Olathe**
   Mahaffie House

8. **Osawatomie**
   John Brown-Adair Cabin

Eisenhower Family Home

South Buckeye and Fourth Streets
Abilene, KS 67410
(913) 263-4751

Contact: Dwight D. Eisenhower Library
and Museum

Open: Daily 9 a.m.–5 p.m.; closed
Thanksgiving, Christmas,
New Year's Day

Admission: Home-free; museum–
adults $1.50; seniors $1.00

Activities: Guided tours, orientation film

Suggested Time to View House: 30 minutes

Facilities on Premises: Museum, visitor
center and gift shop

Description of Grounds: Small yard with
shrubs and brick walk

Style of Architecture: Folk Victorian
farmhouse

Best Season to View House: Summer

Number of Yearly Visitors: 126,000

Number of Rooms: 9

Year House Built: 1887

On-Site Parking: Yes **Wheelchair Access:** Yes

Description of House

Dwight David Eisenhower, Supreme Commander of the Allied Expeditionary Forces of World War II and thirty-fourth President of the United States, was born in Denison, Texas, on October 14, 1890; one year later, the infant boy and his family moved to this house in Abilene. Here he grew up and went to school; in 1911 he entered the U. S. Military Academy at West Point and graduated four years later. The plain Victorian farmhouse continued to be the home of the Eisenhower family until 1946, when the President's mother died. The house was opened for public viewing the following year. The furnishings here are all original to the family and date from the 1880s to the early 1940s. These include a number of late Victorian pieces and a collection of quilts made Mrs. Eisenhower. The wood frame house stands on its original site.

Additional Information

The Eisenhower Family Home is listed on the National Register of Historic Places.

Historic Kirby House

205 Northeast Third Street
Abilene, KS 67410
(913) 263-7336

Contact: Tietjens, Hartenstein and Company
Open: Year-round, daily 11 a.m.–2 p.m.,
  5–9:30 p.m.
Admission: Free
Activities: Guided tours
Suggested Time to View House: 30 minutes
Facilities on Premises: Family restaurant
Description of Grounds: Landscaped yard
  surrounded by a white picket fence
Style of Architecture: Mix of late Italianate
  and early Victorian Queen Anne
Best Season to View House: Summer
Number of Yearly Visitors: 3,500
Number of Rooms: 15

Year House Built: 1885
On-Site Parking: Yes **Wheelchair Access:** Yes

Description of House

The success story of Thomas Kirby is the oft-repeated tale of the immigrant who comes to America and makes a fortune through a combination of hard work and good timing. He was born in Ireland in 1844, moved with his parents to Johnstown, Pennsylvania, at age four, and struck out on his own in 1872, when he moved to Abilene. Here he took the job of cashier at the Lebold-Fisher Bank where he remained for six years. In 1878, he founded his own bank in a building that still stands in downtown Abilene. In 1882, he was elected to the first of two consecutive terms as Dickinson County Treasurer. Three years later, he built this magnificent home on Grand Avenue (now Third Street). In subsequent years, Kirby lost an election for State Treasurer, built the Mount Saint Joseph's Academy, drew up the plans for the northern section of the city of Abilene, and invested in vast tracts of land. During the infamous Panic of 1893-1896, Kirby was forced to close his bank and retire to his lovely home with his wife. He died in 1905; nine years later, his widow sold the house to the Abilene Commercial Club, forerunner to the Chamber of Commerce. The structure underwent a number of changes over the years—the tower, front porch, and dormer windows were all removed, and a new porch with four full-height white pillars was added, as was a single-story dining hall on the north side. In the 1930s it was converted into an apartment building and remained so until 1986, when it was bought by Terry and Jerry Tietjens.

Today, the Kirby House is fully restored to its appearance in 1885; all of the later alterations have been erased. One now sees the exquisite mix of Italianate elements—the center tower and low-pitched dormer roof—and early Queen Anne-style elements—the beautiful gable detailing, especially in the extended triangular section and finials, and the spindlework, the lace-like brackets, and frieze which decorate the full-width asymmetrical porch. The restoration includes having the original color scheme in place: a shell-pink body with red and green trim. In the summer of 1987, the Kirby House opened as a family restaurant; it is open daily for lunch and dinner.

Leopold Vahsholtz Mansion

106 North Vine Street
Abilene, KS 67410
(913) 263-4356

Contact: Lebold Vahsholtz Mansion
Open: Daily by appointment only
Admission: Adults $5.00;
  children $2.00
Activities: Guided tours
Suggested Time to View House:
  90 minutes
Description of Grounds: ½ city block
Best Season to View House: Spring-fall
Number of Yearly Visitors: 2,000-3,000
Year House Built: 1880
Style of Architecture: Late Italianate
Number of Rooms: 23
On-Site Parking: Yes
Wheelchair Access: No

Description of House

The Leopold Vahsholtz residence—built in 1880 by one of the city's founding fathers—is the oldest home in Abilene, a large Italianate-style mansion which stands as a testimony to the financial success of its builder. Today the mansion has been completely restored to mint condition and members of the Vahsholtz family conduct unique reservation-only tours covering the architecture and history of their home.

The Vahsholtz mansion is a fine example of the Romantic Italianate style built of stone—it features an elaborate central tower capped with a wrought-iron finial, two full-width porches, and an impressive double portico. The interior is decorated in the high Victorian style; it includes a hand-painted ceiling, a fully restored child's playhouse in the attic, and numerous period pieces of furniture.

Additional Information

The house contains a wide array of decorative objects including: tapestries, fine china, wedding gowns, fans, hand-made quilts, cut and pressed glass pieces, and a collection of pearl-handled sterling silver flatware.

Seelye Mansion

1105 North Buckeye
Abilene, KS 67410
(913) 263-7336

Contact: Tietjens, Hartenstein and Company
Open: Year-round, Tues.-Sat. guided tours
10 a.m. and 2 p.m., Sun. 2 p.m. only
Admission: $5.00 per person
Activities: Guided tours, special tours by
appointment
Suggested Time to View House: 90 minutes
Description of Grounds: Small yard with
flower beds and trees
Style of Architecture: Eclectic Colonial
Revival, Georgian
Number of Yearly Visitors: 3,500
Year House Built: 1905
Best Season to View House: Summer

Number of Rooms: 25

On-Site Parking: Yes **Wheelchair Access:** No

Description of House

This superb Georgian-style Colonial Revival mansion was built by Dr. and Mrs. A. B. Seelye in 1905. Dr. Seelye had made his fortune in patent medicines—some of his better known curatives were called Wasa-Tusa, Ner-vena, and Fro-Zona.

The house was designed by a New York-based architect and has a floor plan which includes eleven bedrooms, a ballroom, a music room, a captain's walk, and a gazebo. The Grand Hall fireplace was designed by Tiffany's of New York and is executed in imported Venetian tiles; above the mantel is one of Thomas Edison's original electric light fixtures. Other interior details include a large oak staircase, hot-water radiators set under the leaded glass windows located in the front rooms, and a bowling alley purchased at the 1904 World's Fair.

Notable Collections on Exhibit

The Seelye Mansion contains many fine period furnishings and decorative art objects, including: a fourteen-leaved dining room table, a 1920 Steinway piano, a 1905 Edison Cylinder Phonograph, and collections of Haviland china and Croesus glassware.

Additional Information

The Seelye Mansion is listed on the National Register of Historic Places.

Amelia Earhart Birthplace Museum

223 North Terrace
Atchison, KS 66002
(913) 367-4217

Contact: Ninety Nines, Inc., International
Women Pilots Association

Open: May 1-Sept. 30, Mon.-Sat.
9 a.m.–4 p.m., Sun. 1–4 p.m.;
other times by appointment

Admission: Adults $2.00; children
(12 and under) $.50

Activities: Guided tours

Suggested Time to View House: 45 minutes

Facilities on Premises: Postcards,
ornaments and commemorative silver
coins are for sale to aid restoration fund

Description of Grounds: Scenic location
overlooking Missouri River Bluffs

Best Season to View House: Spring-fall

Number of Yearly Visitors: 4,000

Year House Built: 1860

Number of Rooms: 16, 9 open to the public

Style of Architecture: Gothic Revival

On-Site Parking: No **Wheelchair Access:** Yes

Description of House

America's most famous aviatrix, Amelia Earhart, was born in the upstairs bedroom of this house in Atchison on July 24, 1898, to Edwin and Amy Earhart. The house had been built by Amelia's grandfather, the Atchison lawyer Alfred Otis, in 1860. At the time, Atchison—the town that inspired Horace Greeley's famous "Go West" editorial—was a booming riverfront transportation hub. Here Amelia and her sister Muriel spent their childhood; when her mother died in 1912, the children got possession of the house. Seven years later, it was sold to Alfred C. Winsor—it is said that a portion of the proceeds from this sale enabled Amelia to purchase her first airplane. After Winsor, ownership of the house passed through several families before Dr. Eugene R. Bribach, a prominent Atchison physician, presented it as a gift to the Ninety-Nines—the International Women Pilots Association founded in 1929, whose first president was Amelia Earhart.

The house is a two-story frame structure built in Andrew Downing's Gothic Revival style; its characteristic features include: a steep pitched roof with a prominent center gable, a full-width front porch, and a front facade wall which extends into the gable without a break and is accented with a lancet-shaped, segmented window. The fenestration throughout bears notice, especially the large, double-sash arched windows in paired combinations. The front entry has an elaborate glazed door with segmented sidelights and a drip-mold decorative crown. However, there are some elements of the style missing: decorative vergeboards, porch trim, and finials. The house is currently undergoing a thorough restoration to its appearance at the turn of the century when Amelia lived here, but its reception room will be kept as a memorial to Dr. Bribach.

Notable Collections on Exhibit

The house contains several pieces of Amelia Earhart memorabilia, including two pieces of furniture that belonged to her, as well as numerous photographs, and her childhood swimsuit.

Additional Information

The Amelia Earhart Birthplace Museum is listed on the National Register of Historic Places. The memory of the famous pilot is held dear by her hometown: located in the city's former Santa Fe Railroad freight depot is the Atchison County Historical Society Museum, which houses a significant collection of artifacts related to her; the airport and high school stadium are named after her; and a large bronze statue of her made by David S. T. Jones stands overlooking the downtown mall. Just south of Atchison lies the International Forest of Friendship at Warnock Lake, a nature preserve developed in 1976 by the Ninety-Nines, Inc.

W.P. Brown Mansion

2019 Walnut Street
Coffeyville, KS 67337
(316) 251-0431

Contact: Coffeyville Historical Society
Open: Mar. 1-May 15 and Sept.16-Dec. 31, daily 1–5 p.m.; May 15-Sept. 15, daily 9 a.m.–5 p.m.
Admission: Adults $4.00; children (5-16) $2.50
Activities: Guided tours, annual ball
Suggested Time to View House: 1 hour
Facilities on Premises: Visitor center and gift shop

Number of Yearly Visitors: 15,000
Description of Grounds: Spacious lawn and formal gardens
Style of Architecture: Colonial Revival, Georgian
Year House Built: 1906
Number of Rooms: 16
Best Season to View House: Year round
On-Site Parking: Yes **Wheelchair Access:** No

Description of House

W. P. Brown came from Independence, Missouri, to Coffeyville—the once-named "Cow Town" founded by James Coffey on the Verdigris River—where he made a fortune owning natural gas and oil fields with side interests in lumberyards and a grain dealership. He built this house in 1906 and it remained in the family until his daughter, Mrs. Violet Brown Kohler, sold it to the Coffeyville Historical Society so that it might serve as a public museum.

This three-story mansion was designed by the architectural firm of Edward Wilder and Thomas Wight—both of whom studied with the renowned Stanford White—and built at a cost of $125,000. The floor plan consists of: the entry, great "hall" (or living room), parlor, music room, library, conservatory, dining room, billiard room, kitchen and maids' quarters on the main floor; five bedrooms and three full baths on the second floor; and a large ballroom on the third floor. The basement houses the butler's quarters, laundry, the natural gas heating system, walk-in icebox, and storage space. Each room features a distinctive fireplace and mahogany is used in the moldings throughout. Outside, the sheer weight of the house is seen in the twenty-inch-thick brick and concrete walls, the massive two-story portico with classical-style columns, and the full-width-and-height rear porch and balcony.

Many of the furnishings which belonged to the Browns are still in use here; most of these pieces were bought at Marshall Field's in Chicago or Sloan's in New York; the rest were purchased on European trips. The wallcoverings and floor treatments are original to the house.

Notable Collections on Exhibit

The Brown family collection includes china, crystal, silver, and vintage clothing.

Additional Information

The W. P. Brown Mansion is listed on the National Register of Historic Places.

1878 Hardesty House

Contact: Boot Hill Museum

Open: Memorial Day-Labor Day, daily 8 a.m.–7:30 p.m.; Labor Day to Memorial Day, Mon.-Sat. 9 a.m.–5 p.m., Sun. 1–5 p.m.; closed Thanksgiving, Christmas, New Year's Day

Admission: Summer, adults $5.50, seniors and children $5.00; winter, adults $4.50; seniors and children $4.00; group and family rates available

Activities: Guided tours, "living history" interpretation, annualVictorian Christmas Tea event

Facilities on Premises: Visitor center, gift and book shop, restaurant

Suggested Time to View House: 30 minutes

Description of Grounds: Large museum complex of restored and reconstructed historic buildings c. 1876. The grounds of the 1878 Hardesty House include a fenced yard with flower and herb gardens.

Best Season to View House: Summer

Number of Yearly Visitors: 110,000

Year House Built: 1878

Style of Architecture: Modified Queen Anne with Gothic Revival features

Number of Rooms: 8

On-Site Parking: Yes **Wheelchair Access:** Yes

Description of House

In the mostly inhospitable prairie of central Kansas, accessible to the "civilized" east only by railroad, the two-fisted settlement called Dodge City took root and attracted those hardy souls who sought their fortune in ranching. One such individual was Richard Hardesty who, after having made some money in the gold fields of Colorado and Montana, began cattle-ranching here on South Beaver Creek and moved into this home in December of 1880 with his wife, Margaret. They'd been married earlier that year in Leavenworth, Kansas, at the home of Fred Harvey, owner of the famous Harvey House chain of restaurants. Their only child, Sallie, was born in the house in 1883; Hardesty died in 1910 and his wife sold the house four years later to the D. W. Gilmore family.

It is believed that the Hardesty House was built from plans purchased through the mail drawn up by New York architect Richard Upjohn; these customizable mail-order homes afforded citizens of the Western frontier a measure of luxury which contrasted sharply with the typical Dodge City home which was made out of buffalo grass sod, pineboard, and tarpaper plaster, then whitewashed. The house was assembled in 1878 by Alonzo Webster and attests to his relative affluence. It is a one-and-a-half-story structure with a front-facing gable, Queen Anne-style bay windows, Gothic Revival-inspired lancet windows in the second level of the front facade, "gingerbread" vergeboard trim with cross-bracing and brackets, and a wrap-around porch since replaced.

The parlor is decorated in Bradbury & Bradbury's William Morris Kelmscott frieze in green with "Mangold" wallpaper and Morris's acanthus border on the ceiling; the music room features Bradbury & Bradbury's Eastlake Dado pattern in olive and burgundy; and the dining room is done in Scalamandres' rose pattern. All three rooms were decorated in the 1880s. The furnishings—most of which were acquired from Dodge City's Beeson family—are authentic to the period from 1875 to 1885; they include Eastlake and Renaissance Revival-style pieces.

Notable Collections on Exhibit

Among the many decorative objects on display are a collection of 19th-century paintings and prints, light fixtures, hand-painted ceramics, and a variety of cut and molded glassware.

Additional Information

To put the relative luxury of the Hardesty House into perspective, one should visit the typical sod house also on view in the Boot Hill Museum complex.

Mueller-Schmidt House, "House of Stone"

112 East Vine Street, P.O. Box 131
Dodge City, KS 67801
(316) 227-6791

Contact: Ford County Historical Society
Open: June-Sept., Mon.-Sat. 9 a.m.–6 p.m.,
Sun. 1 p.m.–5 p.m.; special tours anytime
Admission: Free
Activities: Guided tours
Suggested Time to View House: 30 minutes
Facilities on Premises: Small gift shop
Description of Grounds: Lawned yard
with plantings
Style of Architecture: Eclectic mix of
Italianate and Folk Victorian styles
Number of Rooms: 5
Year House Built: 1879, "modernized" 1949
Number of Yearly Visitors: 4,200

Best Season to View House: Spring-fall
On-Site Parking: Yes **Wheelchair Access:** No

Description of House

German immigrant John Mueller first established himself as a bootmaker in St. Louis; then, in 1879, he moved to Dodge City, bought up three cattle ranches, and built this house with his wife, Caroline. Once it was completed, cattle cars loaded with Mueller's stock were taken to Kansas City and came back to Dodge City filled with new furniture for the couple's home. The blizzard of '86 wiped out Mueller's cattle and a fire that same year destroyed his bootmaking shop: the two blows forced him to sell out and return to St. Louis. In 1890 Adam Schmidt bought the house and all of its furnishings. Here the blacksmith and his wife raised three children, Elma, Heinie, and Louis. Elma and Heinie—unlike Louis they never married—lived in the house all their lives; Heinie Schmidt was Dodge City's long-time postmaster and a well-known local author.

The two-story house that the Muellers built is the only stone house in all Dodge City; it features a center gable on the front facade, hooded windows, a partial single-story porch, double doors, side balconies, and decorative verge boards. The stone of which the walls are built was quarried less than twelve miles away. Inside, there is a fine hand-carved black walnut and maple banister. The house has undergone modernization—the kitchen is now inside and bathrooms have been added—and serves as a museum of and memorial to the pioneer mothers of Dodge City. Many of the furnishings on display are original to the Schmidts and Muellers; these include a walnut love seat and matching chairs, a china cabinet, and a black walnut bed and dresser. The Mueller-Schmidt House, "House of Stone" is listed on the National Register of Historic Places.

Notable Collections on Exhibit

In addition to the furnishings mentioned above, one may also view photographs of the two families and many homely artifacts which portray their lives. One bedroom is given over to an exhibit depicting many of Dodge City's early families.

Grinter Place

1420 South Seventy-eighth Street
Kansas City, KS 66111
(913) 299-0373

Contact: Kansas State Historical Society
Open: Year-round, Tues.-Sat.
10 a.m.–5 p.m., Sun. 1–5 p.m.;
closed holidays
Admission: Free
Activities: Guided tours, special seasonal
events including the Spring Quilt Show,
Summer Farmer's Market, and
September Applefest
Suggested Time to View House: 30 minutes
Best Season to View House: Year round
Description of Grounds: Picnic facilities
Style of Architecture: Georgian style with
Greek Revival characteristics
Year House Built: Between 1857 and 1859
Number of Rooms: 8

Number of Yearly Visitors: 21,000
On-Site Parking: Yes **Wheelchair Access:** Yes

Description of House

Native Kentuckian Moses Grinter (1809-1878) was an Indian trader and farmer who operated a ferry across the Missouri River used by U. S. Government troops moving between Forts Leavenworth and Scott on the Permanent Indian Frontier. Grinter owned a trading post in the area from 1855 to 1860 and built this house overlooking the Kansas River between the years 1857 and 1859; his wife, Annie Marshall Grinter—daughter of an Indian trader and a Delaware woman—raised ten children and lived here until her death in 1905. A Grinter daughter married the Rev. Henry Clay Kirby and their family lived in the house until 1950.

This simple two-story home is modeled on a rather typical Southern colonial home—a c. 1800 Rural Choiced structure found near Russellville, Kentucky. The exterior features brickwork in the American Bond pattern and a breezeway separating the body of the house from the kitchen. Inside, the very fine steam-curled walnut landing at the head of a curved stairway shows a master carpenter's hand. The house is furnished with pieces from the late 19th century.

Notable Collections on Exhibit

In addition to the more than 3,000 items on display—few of which belonged to the Grinters—the entrance hall houses a diorama of the Grinter farm.

Additional Information

The Grinter Place is listed on the National Register of Historic Places.

Edward Carroll Mansion

1128 Fifth Avenue
Leavenworth, KS 66048
(913) 682-7759

Contact: Leavenworth County Historical Society and Museum

Open: Mid Feb.-Dec. 25, Tues.-Sun. 1–4:30 p.m.

Admission: Adults $2.00; seniors $1.75; children $.50

Activities: Guided tours

Suggested Time to View House: 45–60 minutes

Facilities on Premises: Gift shop with books

Number of Yearly Visitors: 5,000-6,000

Description of Grounds: Large back yard with picnic tables

Style of Architecture: Eclectic mix of Italianate and Queen Anne-Eastlake

Best Season to View House: Late spring-early fall

Year House Built: 1858, with alterations and additions 1867, 1882-1883, 1930

Number of Rooms: 16

On-Site Parking: Yes **Wheelchair Access:** Yes

Description of House

The Edward Carroll Mansion started life as a modest two-story frame house which was expanded and given a brick, Italianate-style face in 1867 by its owner John McCullough Foster, a prosperous lumberman and contractor. Fifteen years later, Foster sold the property to Lucien Scott, the first president of the First National Bank of Leavenworth, and more remodeling took place: bays were added, the porch and roof treatments were altered, interior woodwork was done, and indoor plumbing and gas lighting were installed.

In 1888, the year before his death, Scott sold the mansion to one of Leavenworth's leading citizens, Edward Carroll. Carroll, who had settled in Leavenworth before the Civil War and helped establish the bank of which Scott was president, served in numerous local and state governmental positions and ran a wholesale grocery business in town. In 1890, he too became an officer of the First National Bank, finally achieving the presidency of that institution in 1914. His descendants lived here until 1965, when his last surviving child donated the house and its contents to the Leavenworth County Historical Society.

This two-story red brick structure—the rear wall encases the older four-room frame house—stands on a stone foundation and features a truncated hipped roof, eight rooms, and two single-story porches built onto the eastern and southern elevations. In 1882, an impressive, heavily-carved, Eastlake-inspired wooden porch with balusters and modillions replaced the earlier porches; second-story porches were built on the bays and single-story wooden porches featuring incised friezes were wrapped around three sides of the 1858 wing; in addition, the structure was finished with beautifully wrought modillioned entablature and dentils. This superb house is filled with locally-found furnishings dating from the same period as the major alterations.

Notable Collections on Exhibit

On display here is a wonderful collection of ladies' costumes; Sevres, Dresden, and early American porcelain; Steuben glass; antique silver; oriental carpets; and antique toys. One may also see "country store" and "barber shop" exhibits, and a rare luxury in the kitchen—a copper sink.

Additional Information

The Edward Carroll Mansion is listed on the National Register of Historic Places.

Mahaffie House

1100 Kansas City Road, P.O. Box 768
Olathe, KS 66061
(913) 782-6972

Contact: Mahaffie Farmstead and Stagecoach Stop Historic Site

Open: June-Aug., Wed.-Sat. guided tours at 10:30 a.m., 1:30 p.m., 2:30 p.m., 3:30 p.m., Sun. guided tours start at 12:30 p.m.; Sept.-May, Mon.-Fri. same hourly schedule; closed major holidays, month of January

Admission: Adults $2.50 + tax; children $1.50 + tax; group rate available with two-week notice

Suggested Time to View House: 45 minutes

Facilities on Premises: Gift and book shop

Activities: Guided tours, school trunk programs available

Description of Grounds: 20 acre farmstead with heirloom vegetable and herb gardens and orchard. The property consists of three historic buildings, the Mahaffie House, the Limestone Ice House, and the Wood Peg Barn

Year House Built: 1865, additions 1870, 1920 through 1940

Style of Architecture: Greek Revival, stone

Number of Rooms: 4

Best Season to View House: Late spring-fall

Number of Yearly Visitors: 15,000

On-Site Parking: Yes **Wheelchair Access:** No

Description of House

In 1857 James Beatty Mahaffie and his wife, Lucinda, came to the Kansas Territory from Indiana and purchased this farmstead on the Santa Fe Trail. Here they raised eight children and ran a stagecoach stop from 1863 to 1869; this station stop was the first place that westbound passengers could eat after leaving the terminus at Westport, Missouri. By 1865, Mahaffie was the largest landowner and livestock breeder in Johnson County. Then, in 1870, the railroad through Olathe was built and the stop closed down. The family stayed on here until 1886 when Mahaffie sold his holdings and moved into town.

The two-story structure is built of two-foot-thick brick-shaped limestone quarried on the site. The plan consists of four rooms—two pair flanking a center hall on each floor—which served as the Mahaffies' living quarters and a full basement containing the kitchen and travelers' dining area. The exterior is painted in three documented colors and features working shutters and a full-facade front porch. The interior has been done to interpret the period from 1860 to the late 1880s and includes authentically reproduced wallpaper in the style of William Morris and Charles Eastlake. There are no original furnishings in the house. The Mahaffie House is listed on the National Register of Historic Places. A cornerstone on the outside of the second story is marked "1865 JBM."

Notable Collections on Exhibit
Several of the Mahaffie family's possessions are on display: some pieces of cranberry glass, a large family "hair" wreath, three toiletry sets, and an 1850 sewing machine with its original instruction book.

John Brown-Adair Cabin

120 West Tenth Street, P.O. Box 275
Osawatomie, KS 66064
(913) 296-3251

Contact: Kansas State Historical Society

Open: Tues.-Sat. 10 a.m.–5 p.m.;
closed major holidays

Admission: Free

Activities: Special seasonal events
including the Spring Quilt Show,
Summer Arts and Crafts Fair, and
Holiday Open House

Suggested Time to View House: 30 minutes

Description of Grounds: 20 acre park with
picnic grounds

Best Season to View House: Spring and
summer

Year House Built: 1854

Style of Architecture: National, log cabin

Number of Yearly Visitors: 9,000

Number of Rooms: 3

On-Site Parking: Yes **Wheelchair Access:** No

Description of House

The fiery abolitionist John Brown stayed in this house on his several trips to Kansas in the years between 1855 and 1858. It was owned by his stepsister Florella and her husband, the Reverend Samuel I. Adair, abolitionists both, and may have been used as a station on the Underground Railroad. The cabin was built in 1854 by a squatter and bought by the Adairs when they came to Kansas from Ohio with the intention of establishing a mission for free-state settlers. They had to abandon their largely unsuccessful effort and Adair took a position as military chaplain at Forts Scott and Leavenworth. The cabin remained their home until Samuel died in 1898.

This one-and-a-half-story cabin has two rooms downstairs and a loft upstairs. It is an eighteen-foot by thirty-foot rectangular structure made out of white-washed logs and featuring a fieldstone hearth, plank flooring, and a woven rag rug up in the loft. In the front room, many pieces of original furniture are on view; they were brought from Ohio by the Adairs.

Notable Collections on Exhibit

Among the pieces on display is the melodeon played at John Brown's funeral.

Additional Information

The John Brown-Adair Cabin is listed on the National Register of Historic Places. When in Osawatomie, be sure to visit the Old Stone Church; this limestone structure is the site of Reverend Adair's Kansas mission.

Michigan

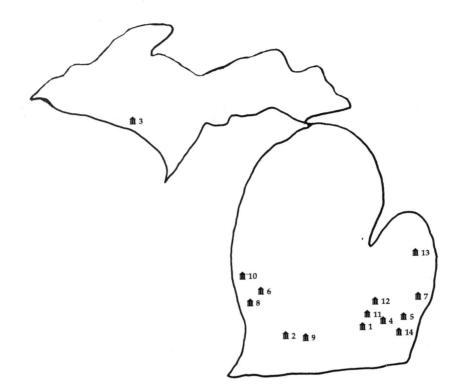

1. **Ann Arbor**
   Ticknor-Campbell House at Cobblestone Farm

2. **Battle Creek**
   Kimball House

3. **Caspian**
   Carrie Jacobs Bond House

4. **Dearborn**
   Henry Ford Estate, Fair Lane

5. **Detroit**
   Historic Moross House

6. **Grand Rapids**
   Voigt House Victorian Museum

7. **Grosse Pointe Shores**
   Edsel and Eleanor Ford House

8. **Holland**
   Cappon House Museum

9. **Marshall**
   Honolulu House

10. **Muskegon**
    Charles H. Hackley House at the
    Hackley and Hume Historic Site
    Thomas Hume House at the
    Hackley and Hume Historic Site

11. **Northville**
    Robert Yerkes House at
    Mill Race Historical Village

12. **Pontiac**
    Governor Moses Wisner Historic
    House and Grounds, Pine Grove

13. **Port Sanilac**
    Loop-Harrison House

14. **Wyandotte**
    Ford-MacNichol Home

Ticknor-Campbell House at Cobblestone Farm

2781 Packard Road
Ann Arbor, MI 48108
(313) 994-2928

Contact: City of Ann Arbor
Open: May-Oct., Thurs.-Sun. 1–4 p.m.;
   group tours by appointment
Admission: Adults $1.50; seniors and
   children (17 and under) $.75
Activities: Guided tours, children's
   programs, workshops, holiday events
Suggested Time to View House: 1 hour
Facilities on Premises: Gift shop
Description of Grounds: 4½ acre site with
   1837 log cabin and other outbuildings.
   Farm animals present during open season
Style of Architecture: Early Classical Revival
Best Season to View House: Summer and fall
Number of Rooms: 10

Year House Built: 1844
On-Site Parking: Yes **Wheelchair Access:** Yes

Description of House

Though Dr. Benajah Ticknor, U. S. Naval Surgeon, self-taught classical scholar, and inveterate diarist, made the decision to purchase land in the Territory of Michigan and settle here, it was his brother Herman who farmed the land successfully and became one of the region's leading citizens. For years, the doctor only lived here with his brother between naval assignments. In 1844, the house was greatly expanded to accommodate the family and farmhands. In 1854 Dr. Ticknor retired and settled on the farm for good. After his death in 1858, the superb library he had amassed was given to the University of Michigan. The journal he kept—which ran to seven volumes covering the years 1818 to 1852—is now housed in the Yale University Library.

Cobblestone Farm was purchased in 1881 by Scotch-born William Campbell, a former schoolteacher and Ypsilanti shopkeeper. Here he gained wide renown for his pure-bred Durham cattle and sustainable farming techniques. His descendants worked the farm until the end of World War Two when most of it was sold and subdivided for tract housing. Family members remained here until 1972; at that time, the City of Ann Arbor bought the house and remaining acreage.

This five bay, four-over-four cobblestone structure features a facade of herringbone-coursed stone, classical detailing, and a rear ell. This ell contains the kitchen with its fireplace and brick "beehive" oven, dining room, granary, milk room, wash house, privies, and wood-shed downstairs, and the hired hands' rooms upstairs. The early structural elements are clearly visible—hand-split laths, hand-hewn timbers, and hand-wrought nails. The interior woodwork was woodgrained and features rare built-in closets. The period furnishings date from the middle 1800s but are not original to the house. Cobblestone Farm was listed on the State and National Registers of Historic Places in 1972.

Notable Collections on Exhibit

In addition to the furniture on display, there is also a collection of 19th-century medical instruments.

Kimball House

196 Capital Avenue Northeast
Battle Creek, MI 49016
(616) 965-2613

Contact: Historical Society of Battle Creek
Open: Tues.-Fri. 12:30–4:30 p.m.
Admission: Adults $2.00; students $1.00
Activities: Group and school tours, craft classes, special events
Suggested Time to View House: 60–90 minutes
Facilities on Premises: Gift shop
Description of Grounds: Small city yard surrounded by wrought iron fence
Best Season to View House: Spring and summer
Number of Yearly Visitors: 17,500
Year House Built: 1886
Number of Rooms: 14

Style of Architecture: Eclectic Chateauesque
On-Site Parking: Yes **Wheelchair Access:** No

Description of House

This three-story mansion features a center tower, a full, two-story bay extension with a turret, and a smaller corbeled tower with a "candle-snuffer" roof. Noteworthy exterior details include: a combination hipped roof with a ridge line and rear cross-gabling, highly visible bracketing, decorative finials, paired window arrangements, an entry with multiple-paned, glazed doubled doors, and a small front porch with a pediment and column supports. Inside, there are parquet floors and a large collection of furnishings from the second half of the 19th century, some of which belonged to the original owners of the house.

Notable Collections on Exhibit

Of special interest is the display relating the story of Sojourner Truth, the famous ex-slave woman who traveled America speaking out for women's rights and against slavery. And, as befits a house in Battle Creek, there are also exhibits focusing on the cereal industry.

Additional Information

When driving between Battle Creek and Grand Rapids on M-37, one should plan to stop at the Historic Charlton Park Village and Museum in Hastings, founded by the late Irving Delos Charlton. Known for many years as Indian Landing, the three hundred acre county park is the site of more than fifteen relocated historic houses and commercial buildings dating from 1858 to present day. For more information, call (616) 945-3775.

Carrie Jacobs Bond House

Iron County Museum Park
P.O. Box 272
Caspian, MI 49915
(906) 265-3942

Contact: Iron County Historical and Museum Society

Open: May and Sept., Mon.-Sat. 10 a.m.–4 p.m., Sun. 1–4 p.m.; June and Aug., Mon.-Sat., 9 a.m.–5 p.m., Sun. 1–5 p.m.

Admission: Adults $2.50; children $1.00; family $6.50

Activities: Guided tours, slide presentation

Suggested Time to View House: 15 minutes

Facilities on Premises: Gift shop in museum

Best Season to View House: Summer

Year House Built: 1890

Number of Rooms: 7

Description of Grounds: 8 acre tract with 19 historic buildings

Number of Yearly Visitors: 18,000+

Style of Architecture: Eclectic Victorian

On-Site Parking: Yes **Wheelchair Access:** Yes

Description of House

The lyricist and composer of such popular tunes as "Perfect Day," "I Love You Truly," and "Just A-Wearying For You," Carrie Jacobs Bond once claimed that the happiest seven years of her life were spent in Iron River— four of them in this house, which has since been moved to Museum Park in nearby Caspian. She and her husband, Dr. Frank Bond, lived there from 1889 to 1895, the year of his untimely death. She then moved to Chicago to pursue her fifty-year-long career in music. The last visit the composer made to Iron County was in 1938; she died in California in 1946.

This modest—though well-built—balloon-frame Victorian house features clapboard siding, gables with octagonal patterned shingles, bay windows, and a wrap-around porch. Inside, the oak floors meet wide, painted pine baseboards and there is a fine open stairwell. The interior is interpreted to the period c. 1890-1912 to permit the use of electricity and is filled with many personal items and furnishings which belonged to Carrie Jacobs Bond, including a bed, desk, and chair donated by an area resident.

Notable Collections on Exhibit

The museum devoted to Carrie Jacobs Bond contains over two dozen of the nearly one-hundred-fifty photographs from the composer's estate, two hand-painted plates and a watercolor done by her, a painting of her birthplace in Jamesville, Wisconsin, two of her gowns, several sheet music covers she designed, and the Bible given to her by her son Fred Smith.

Additional Information

In 1979 the house was moved to its present location at the Museum Park, an outdoor museum and pioneer village consisting of nineteen historic buildings.

Henry Ford Estate, Fair Lane

4901 Evergreen Road
Dearborn, MI 48128
(313) 593-5590

Contact: Henry Ford Estate at the University of Michigan-Dearborn

Open: Year-round, Sun. 1–4:30 p.m.; Apr.-Dec., guided tours on the hour, Mon.-Sat. 10 a.m.–3 p.m.; Jan.-Mar. guided tour Mon.-Fri. 1:30 p.m.; closed Thanksgiving, Christmas

Admission: Adults $6.00; seniors and students $5.00; children (under 5) free

Activities: Guided tours and audiovisual presentation, Discovery Trail, Henry Ford Day : A Family Festival in June, special holiday events and luncheons

Suggested Time to View House: 2 hours

Facilities on Premises: Gift shop and book store

Description of Grounds: Rose garden, tea house, greenhouse and rustic outdoor trails located on 72 acres

Best Season to View House: Spring-fall

Number of Yearly Visitors: 100,000

Year House Built: 1914

Style of Architecture: Eclectic Period Revival with Tudor elements resembling a Scottish Baronial

Number of Rooms: 56

On-Site Parking: Yes **Wheelchair Access:** Yes

Description of House

Michigan native Henry Ford, the mighty industrialist whose name has become synonymous with the development of America's auto industry and "assembly-line" manufacturing, built this grand residence in 1914 and lived here until his death in 1947. His widow, Clara, lived on here for another three years; she was president of the National Woman's Farm and Garden Club. Over the years, Fair Lane received many notable guests, including: Charles Lindbergh, the Duke of Windsor, President Herbert Hoover, and two of Henry Ford's close friends, Thomas A. Edison and Harvey Firestone.

Fair Lane is a baronial mansion of epic proportions—the basic design is executed in the Prairie school with a mixture of Tudor elements and an imposing crenelated tower. The marvelous details here are far too numerous to list; to take only a few: in the mansion's original swimming pool room—now the Pool Restaurant—one still sees the original steam-heated benches and surfaces of rare green Swedish marble; in the entry to the Main Hall, one marvels at the exquisite stained glass windows and intricately carved wood railings; and, running underground from the six-level powerhouse to the main residence, is a three hundred foot tunnel jointly designed by Ford and Edison. There are eight different fireplace designs to be seen, each with one of Ford's favorite mottoes carved into it. One such reads: "Chop your own wood and it will warm you twice." The furnishings on display—both collected and original—are mainly in the Colonial Revival and Mission styles.

The superb grounds designed by Jens Jensen—one of America's finest examples of landscape art—consist of a meadow and cascade. Over ten thousand roses once grew in the garden; today it is used as an official birdbanding station of the U. S. Wildlife Service.

Notable Collections on Exhibit

The two-room miniature farmhouse complete with furniture (including scaled-down cast-iron stoves) that Ford had built for the 1924 Michigan State Fair was moved to Fair Lane to be used as a playhouse for his grandchildren.

Additional Information

Fair Lane—which is now located on the University of Michigan's Dearborn campus—has been designated a National Historic Landmark and is listed on the National Register of Historic Places.

Historic Moross House

1460 East Jefferson Avenue
Detroit, MI 48207
(313) 259-6363

Contact: Detroit Garden Center
Open: Year-round, Tues.-Thur.
9:30 a.m.–3:30 p.m.; special holiday
openings on weekends
Admission: Free; guided tour $.50 per person
Activities: Guided tours by appointment,
slide presentation
Suggested Time to View House: 30 minutes
Facilities on Premises: Garden center, gift
shop with books, horticultural library,
meeting room

Description of Grounds: Enclosed,walled
garden designed in the mid-1800s to
emulate colonial row house gardens
Best Season to View House: Spring-fall
Year House Built: c. 1843
Style of Architecture: Late Federal-style
brick row house with modified Greek
Revival elements
Number of Rooms: 13
On-Site Parking: Yes **Wheelchair Access:** No

Description of House

The Moross House is the oldest standing brick house in Detroit and one
of only five Federal-style row houses left in the city; it was built between
1843 and 1848 by Christopher Moross out of brick of his own manufacture
on land belonging to his father, Victor, an early French settler to the Detroit
area. Christopher and his wife, Emily, lived in another structure located
behind this house, which was rented out for needed additional income.

The first known resident of the Moross House was Freeman Norvell,
editor and part-owner of the Detroit Free Press and son of U. S. Senator John
Norvell, who lived here from 1872 to 1877. Subsequent owners include:
Colonel Samuel Mansfield of the Army Corps of Engineers, Millard T.
Conklin, the Rev. Alfred H. Barr, pastor of the Jefferson Avenue Presbyterian
Church, and Harold Fuller. From 1920 to 1969 the Beaver Realty Company
used the building as a real estate office.

Restoration began in 1971; it was Michigan's first preservation project
to be financed under the Federal Housing Act of 1966. The lovely garden,
which matches the period of the house, is maintained by the Detroit Garden
Center. The furnishings on display are from the Detroit Historical Museum.

Notable Collections on Exhibit

Among the many items on display here are: a Sheraton secretary, two
original Hitchcock chairs c. 1820s, an 18th-century jardiniere—the oldest
piece in the house—with inlaid tortoise shell and brass, a zither, two dome-
font whale-oil lamps, an astral lamp from H. N. Hooper Company of Boston,
two urns which belonged to Michigan's first territorial governor, Lewis
Cass, and a portrait of Alexander Macomb, the first graduate of West Point
and General-in-Chief of Detroit.

Additional Information

The Historic Moross House is listed on the National Register of Historic
Places.

Voigt House Victorian Museum

115 College Avenue Southeast
Grand Rapids, MI 49503
(616) 458-2422

Contact: Grand Rapids Public Museum
Open: Year-round, Tues. 11 a.m.–3 p.m.;
second and fourth Sunday 1–3 p.m.;
Sunday after Thanksgiving and all
Sundays in December 1–4 p.m.; other
times group tours by appointment
Admission: Adults $3.00; seniors $2.00;
children $2.00; preschoolers free
Activities: Guided tours, Victorian slide
show, seasonal exhibits
Suggested Time to View House: 1 hour
Facilities on Premises: Gift shop
Description of Grounds: ¼ acre in city.
Period annuals, perennials, shrubs, bird
houses enhance the property.
Best Season to View House: Spring-fall
Year House Built: 1895
Number of Rooms: 14

Number of Yearly Visitors: 6,000
Style of Architecture: Eclectic Chateauesque
On-Site Parking: No **Wheelchair Access:** No

Description of House

In 1875 the German immigrant Carl Gustav Adolf Voigt brought his young family to Grand Rapids from Michigan City, Indiana, and established himself as a successful merchant and miller. The Voigt mills—which operated until the 1950s—enabled the hitherto middle-class family to become one of Grand Rapids' wealthiest and most prominent. The youngest Voigt child, and last heir, died in 1971. Since then it has been owned and operated by the Public Museum of Grand Rapids as a example of the family's Victorian attitudes, aesthetics, and economic status as embodied in their home.

The grand residence that the Voigts built is based on the famous chateau at Chenonceaux, France; it was designed by the local architect W. G. Robinson. It is built out of Cleveland pressed-brick walls on a cut granite foundation with sandstone trim and a slate roof; the roof is a complex arrangement of hips and dormers, and features a superb corner turret. Inside, the materials used include: mahogany, quarter-sawn oak, cherry, and black ash. The furnishings are all original to the Voigts; pieces date from 1860 to 1920.

Notable Collections on Exhibit

The Voigt collection includes six hundred cubic feet of archives comprising family and business records, correspondence, photographs, and personal mementos; taken together, they present a very detailed portrait of a typical late 19th-century family.

Additional Information

The Voigt House Victorian Museum is located in the Heritage Hill Historic District of Grand Rapids. Also on the grounds is an original two-story carriage house with stables, living quarters for the groom, and a restored carriage.

Edsel and Eleanor Ford House

1100 Lake Shore Road
Grosse Pointe Shores, MI 48236
(313) 884-4222

Contact: Edsel and Eleanor Ford House

Open: Year-round, Wed.-Sun. guided tours on the hour from 1 p.m.–4 p.m.; Apr.-Dec. guided tours start at Noon

Admission: Adults $4.00; seniors $3.00; children $2.00

Activities: Guided tours, lecture and concert series, children's theater, art exhibitions

Suggested Time to View House: 2 hours

Best Season to View House: Spring-fall

Description of Grounds: Beautifully landscaped 87 acre garden on the shores of Lake St. Clair

Facilities on Premises: Gallery shop, activities center, tea room

Style of Architecture: Eclectic Period Revival, Tudor-English Cotswold

Number of Yearly Visitors: 35,000

Year House Built: Between 1926 and 1929

Number of Rooms: 60

On-Site Parking: Yes **Wheelchair Access:** No

Description of House

This wonderful Cotswold-inspired house was built for Edsel Ford, only son of Henry Ford, the world-famous car manufacturer. Edsel, who served as secretary, then president, of the Ford Motor Company, was married in 1916 to the former Eleanor Clay and the couple had four children: Henry II, Benson, Josephine, and William. The Fords used their enormous wealth to put together a world-class collection of art and antiques, and to practice philanthropy through the foundation which bears their name. One of the prime beneficiaries of the Fords' largess has been the Detroit Institute of the Arts.

The well-known architect Albert Kahn designed the Ford House after the architecture of the English Cotswolds in County Gloucestershire. The English elements are many and extend beyond the mere design; they include imported English stone in the roof, hand-plastered ceilings, leaded windows with stained glass medallions, wrought ironwork by Samuel Yellin, and cast-stone mullions and transoms. The exterior of the mansion is finished with Indiana sandstone. Even though the house is primarily furnished in antique French and English pieces, there are several outstanding Art Deco-style rooms designed by Walter Dorwin Teague.

The 87-acre grounds were designed in a naturalist plan by Jens Jensen, the prominent landscape architect also designed the grounds at Henry Ford's mansion, Fair Lane.

Notable Collections on Exhibit

The Edsel and Eleanor Ford House contains an important collection of French and English period furniture, silver, ceramics, historic textiles, and many fine works of art, including original paintings by Cézanne, Matisse, and Diego Rivera, as well as 18th-century portraits by Sir Joshua Reynolds and Sir Henry Raeburn. Also on view is a beguiling playhouse built in 1930 for the Fords' daughter Josephine and, in the Gate Lodge Garage, Eleanor's one-of-a-kind 1952 Lincoln Town Car.

Cappon House Museum

228 West Ninth Street and
Washington Boulevard
Holland, MI 49423
(616) 392-6740

Contact: Holland Historical Trust
Open: May-Oct. Thur.-Sat. 1–4 p.m.; special
open times in December; group tours by
appointment year round
Admission: Adults $2.00; children
(6-13) $1.00
Activities: Guided tours, Victorian teas in
December
Suggested Time to View House:
45–60 minutes
Description of Grounds: Small, fenced city
yard with plantings
Best Season to View House: Spring-fall
Number of Yearly Visitors: 5,000
Year House Built: Between 1873 and 1874
Number of Rooms: 9

Style of Architecture: Late Italianate
On-Site Parking: Yes **Wheelchair Access:** No

Description of House

Isaac Cappon was born in the Netherlands in 1830, emigrated to the United States, established the Cappon-Bertsh Tannery, and became the first mayor of Holland, Michigan, in 1867. Cappon was also instrumental in founding the town's Third Reformed Church. He had eleven children by his first wife, Catarina, and five by his second wife, Jocoba.

This late Italianate-style house features unusual heavy woodwork executed in ash and black walnut, and plasterwork—as seen in the medallions—on the first floor; upstairs, the woodwork is painted in a faux wood grain. The main hall is a fine example of late-19th-century decoration; the parlor features a cast-iron chimney piece with a marbled painting c. 1893. The kitchen, service area, and all of the porches were altered in the 1920s. Most of the furnishings belonged to the original residents and are placed to reflect a probate inventory done in 1902.

Notable Collections on Exhibit

Among the items on display are: steel engravings of literary and patriotic subjects c. 1870s, three landscape paintings, a large collection of the family's toys, and a large closetful of vintage clothing.

Additional Information

The Cappon House Museum is listed on the National Register of Historic Places.

Honolulu House

107 North Kalamazoo Street, P.O. Box 68
Marshall, MI 49068
(616) 781-8544

Contact: Marshall Historical Society
Open: May 1-Oct. 31, daily Noon–5 p.m.;
Nov. 1-Apr. 30, Sat. and Sun. Noon–5 p.m.
Admission: Adults $3.00; seniors and
students $1.50; guided school groups free;
groups of 6 or more reduced rates
Activities: Guided tours, annual Historic
Home Tour and Parade
Suggested Time to View House:
30–45 minutes
Best Season to View House: Spring-fall

Facilities on Premises: Related publications
and souvenirs for sale
Description of Grounds: Landscaped yard
with herb, rose and perennial gardens
Number of Yearly Visitors: 3,000
Year House Built: 1860, remodeled 1885
Style of Architecture: Eclectic mix of Gothic
Revival, and Italianate with Polynesian
influences
Number of Rooms: 10
On-Site Parking: Yes **Wheelchair Access:** No

Description of House

In 1857 Abner Pratt, a native New Yorker who'd come to Marshall,
established a successful law practice, and served as Chief Justice of the
Michigan Supreme Court, was appointed U. S. Consul to the Sandwich
Islands. He and his wife were forced to return to Marshall for health reasons
in 1859 and here they built a house to resemble the Executive Mansion in
Honolulu. Mrs. Pratt died in 1861 and the Judge two years later; the house
was sold to Charles Cameron who lived here until 1883, when it was
purchased by Mayor Martin V. Wagner. Wagner, who had made a fortune in
various mail-order schemes and owned a stable of fine race horses, completely redecorated and altered the house—some of its appearance today
reflects this remodeling. Subsequent owners were the George Bullard family
and Harold C. Brooks; Brooks was dedicated to preservation and educating
his fellow citizens' historical sense. He maintained the property until it was
acquired by the Marshall Historical Society.

The Honolulu house has been largely restored to its appearance in 1883; it is said to have been built by the prominent Marshall carpenter William L. Buck out of local sandstone, faced with vertical board and battens. Exterior features include: a nine-bay full-width porch with a centered tower and flared roof line, a raised veranda and observation platform with elaborate brackets and grouped open-design supports, and a pointed arch at the main entry. The structure stands five feet off the ground on a cut stone foundation. Inside, one sees the tropical-inspired fifteen-foot ceilings, ten-foot-tall doors, and long open galleries. The walls were painted with South Pacific scenes. The floor plan consists of a dining room, kitchen, and servants' quarters downstairs; and a central hall containing a spiral staircase, flanked by two formal rooms on the main floor. The extensive restoration reflects the 1885 color scheme and painstakingly recreates all of the original moldings, details, floor coverings, and five faux finish fireplaces.

Notable Collections on Exhibit
In addition to the many pieces of period furniture on display, one of which—the mahogany Empire-style sofa—belonged to Judge Pratt, there is a one-of-a-kind chandelier c. 1880 presented to Mayor Wagner by the citizens of Marshall as a token of their appreciation.

Additional Information
Honolulu House is listed on the National Register of Historic Places. It is only one of many fine buildings which lie in Historic Marshall, the largest National Landmark Historic District in the United States classified small urban (650+ buildings). Several streets in this district have no 20th-century buildings and virtually every style of residential architecture from 1835 on is represented. It is an especially fine repository of restored Victorian houses.

Charles H. Hackley House at the Hackley and Hume Historic Site

484 West Webster Avenue
Muskegon, MI 49440
(616) 722-7578

Contact: Muskegon County Museum
Open: May-Sept.,Wed., Sat. and Sun. 1–4 p.m.
Admission: Adults $2.00
Activities: Guided tours of both homes and barn
Suggested Time to View House: 1 hour
Facilities on Premises: Gift counter
Best Season to View House: Spring-fall

Description of Grounds: Complex of three buildings with minimum landscaping: the Charles H. Hackley House, the Thomas Hume House and Carriage House
Number of Yearly Visitors: 6,000
Year House Built: Started 1887 completed 1888
Style of Architecture: Victorian Queen Anne style with Exotic Moorish influence
Number of Rooms: 12 open to the public
On-Site Parking: No **Wheelchair Access:** No

Description of House

In its heyday Muskegon was known as the "Lumber Queen of the World"; it was here that Charles H. Hackley (1837-1905) and his partner, Thomas Hume, owned and operated the Hackley and Hume Lumber Mill, one of the largest such mills in all of western Michigan. When the lumber industry collapsed, the two were instrumental in attracting new businesses to the city, thereby insuring its continued reputation as an industrial powerhouse.

This three-story wood house—designed by Grand Rapids architect David S. Hopkins—features a porte cochere topped with a modified onion dome, bands of exterior trim setting off each floor, a second-story recessed porch and adjacent window with horseshoe arches, and a full three-story tower located on the opposite facade. The house is currently undergoing restoration; the exterior will be painted in its thirteen original colors and the interior will be returned to its appearance c. 1891 incorporating existing details: several mantels and stained glass windows made in Chicago, elaborate interior woodwork hand-carved by Kelly Brothers & Company, and foyer floors made of French encaustic tiles. Twelve of the rooms will once again show their beautiful stencil work.

The furnishings are a combination of original and donated pieces; the original pieces include a Steinway upright piano and a Swiss music box.

Additional Information

The Hackley and Hume Historic Site is listed on the National Register of Historic Places. Along with its two neighbors, the Thomas Hume House and the Carriage House—both also designed by David S. Hopkins, the Hackley House is in the midst of a six-year restoration project. The Thomas Hume House is also listed in this guide.

Thomas Hume House at the Hackley and Hume Historic Site

484 West Webster Avenue
Muskegon, MI 49440
(616) 722-7578

Contact: Muskegon County Museum
Open: May-Sept., Wed., Sat. and Sun. 1–4 p.m.
Admission: Adults $2.00
Activities: Guided tours of both homes and barn
Suggested Time to View House: 1 hour
Facilities on Premises: Gift counter
Best Season to View House: Spring-fall

Description of Grounds: Complex of three buildings with minimum landscaping: the Charles H. Hackley House, the Thomas Hume House and the Carriage House
Number of Yearly Visitors: 6,000
Year House Built: Started 1887, completed 1888
Style of Architecture: Victorian Queen Anne with Norman influences
Number of Rooms: 15 open to the public
On-Site Parking: No **Wheelchair Access:** No

Description of House

Thomas Hume was the business partner of Muskegon lumber baron, Charles Hackley, whose house is listed above. Hume and Hackley made their fortunes by operating one of the largest lumber mills in Michigan; when that industry fell onto hard times, the two were responsible for bringing new industries to Muskegon, thus assuring the town's survival. Three generations of the Hume family lived in this house; at one time, it was used as a daycare center.

The Hume House was designed by Michigan architect David Hopkins in the popular Queen Anne style; unlike the Hackley House, it lacks some of the exotic Moorish touches, featuring Eastlake-style spindlework instead. The asymmetrical exterior has been beautifully restored to its original appearance, showing fourteen different colored paints (burgundy and dark green predominate), a hipped roof with lower cross gables, several wide overhangs, and a dominant rounded tower on the front facade abutting the main porched entrance. This tower is capped with a "candle snuffer" shingled roof and each level has its own set of windows. The varied shingle patterns and textures in the decorative bands and gable detailing is far more exaggerated in this house than in the Hackley House. Unfortunately, the interior has not yet been restored.

Additional Information

In addition to this house, and the Hackley House listed above, there is a fine Carriage House at the Hackley and Hume Historic Site. The Carriage House—designed by the same architect—shows an eclectic mix of elements seen in both houses; it is a T-shaped structure with a cross-gabled roof and two cantilevered towers on the front facade, each matching the one found on its closest neighboring house. The site—which is listed on the National Register of Historic Places—is undergoing a six-year restoration.

Robert Yerkes House at Mill Race Historical Village

535 East Base Line Road
and Griswold Street
P.O. Box 71
Northville, MI 48167
(313) 348-1845

Contact: Northville Historical Society

Open: June–Oct., Sun. 2–5 p.m.

Admission: Donations accepted

Activities: Self-guided tours

Suggested Time to View House: House-30 minutes, village-3 hours

Description of Grounds: "Living history" museum and grounds consisting of the New School Church, the Cady Inn, the Hunter House, the Wash Oak School, the Yerkes House, the Cottage House, and the Hirsch Blacksmith Shop. Original site of local grist mill.

Best Season to View House: Late spring-fall

Year House Built: 1868

Number of Rooms: 9

Style of Architecture: Gothic Revival

On-Site Parking: Yes **Wheelchair Access:** No

Description of House

In 1868 William Yerkes—practicing lawyer, judge, and village president—built this house on the south side of Cady Street between Church and Center Streets in the little town of Northville. Here he lived with his wife, Sarah. The house has since been moved to the Mill Race Historical Village.

The house Yerkes built is a fine example of a typical asymmetrical Gothic Revival-style home. Some of its characteristic elements include the point-arched windows showing wood cut-outs above, and the ornately-trussed decorative gable trim featuring the cross-bracing common to such homes built after 1860. The entryway, parlor, and dining room furnishings are from the National and Michigan Quester organizations; the other pieces are donations to the Historical Society or direct purchases made by that group. Taken together, they reflect the Victorian taste of the home's occupants well.

Additional Information

The Robert Yerkes House at Mill Race Historical Village is listed on the National Register of Historic Places.

Governor Moses Wisner Historic House and Grounds, Pine Grove

405 Oakland Avenue
Pontiac, MI 48342
(313) 338-6732

Contact: Oakland County Pioneer and
Historical Society

Open: Mon.-Fri. 9 a.m.–4 p.m.

Admission: Adults $3.00; seniors and
children $1.50

Activities: Guided tours, audiovisual
presentations, special seasonal events
including annual Ice Cream Social, and
Victorian Christmas Open House

Suggested Time to View House: 45 minutes

Facilities on Premises: Farm museum

Description of Grounds: 4½ acres which
includes a one-room schoolhouse,
carriage house, flower and herb garden

Best Season to View House: Spring,
summer and winter

Year House Built: Rear portion 1845, front
portion between 1848 and 1855

Number of Yearly Visitors: 4,000

Number of Rooms: 12

Style of Architecture: Greek Revival, brick

On-Site Parking: Yes **Wheelchair Access:** No

Description of House

Moses Wisner was elected Governor of Michigan in 1858 and, from 1859 to 1861, he used this house as his official residence and office. In 1844 Wisner—then a young lawyer—had bought 150 acres on the outskirts of Pontiac along the Saginaw Trail; here he and his wife, Angeolia, established a "gentleman's farm" and built the Greek Revival-style house and several outbuildings. Members of the Wisner family lived here until 1945; at that time, his granddaughter, Florence Wisner Clark, sold the house and the farm's remaining acreage to the Oakland County Pioneer and Veterans Historical Foundation.

The Wisner farm includes the Greek Revival-style house with its gable front and wing, an orchard barn, carriage house, extensive flower and vegetable gardens, and a stand of native pine and spruce trees. The house features a wrap-around porch in the rear with full-length, round and unfluted columns, and a less-than-full-height entry porch on the front facade with columns matching those in the rear. The window sashes are in an eight-pane arrangement instead of the far more common six-pane glazing typically found in Greek Revival structures. Many of the mansion's furnishings were donated by Florence Wisner Clark; the parlor and bedroom are filled with period Victorian pieces.

Additional Information

Pine Grove is listed on the National Register of Historic Places.

Loop-Harrison House

228 South Ridge Street, P.O. Box 158
Port Sanilac, MI 48469
(313) 622-9946

Contact: Sanilac County Historical Society
Open: Mid-June-Labor Day, Tues.-Sun.
1–4 p.m.; group tours by appointment
Admission: Fee
Activities: Guided tours, special programs
Suggested Time to View House:
60–90 minutes
Style of Architecture: Victorian Second
Empire

Description of Grounds: 7 acres with three
outbuildings including the Village of
Banner log cabin, the Pioneer Barn and
the Dairy Museum
Best Season to View House: Summer
Number of Yearly Visitors: 2,200
Year House Built: Between 1872 and 1875
Number of Rooms: 20
On-Site Parking: Yes **Wheelchair Access:** No

Description of House

Before settling in the small Lake Huron village of Port Sanilac, adventurous Joseph Loop traveled from the Midwest to California—mainly on horseback—then down to South America and up through Louisiana and the Mississippi River Valley back to Wisconsin and Michigan. Loop had garnered some medical experience by assisting a practicing physician; after returning to Michigan and marrying Jane Gardner of Novi, he enrolled in the College of Medicine and Surgery at the University of Michigan. There he earned his M. D. in the school's fifth graduating class and became the area's first physician. In the early 1870s, he and his wife built this, their third Port Sanilac house. After his death in 1903, possession of the house went to his daughter, Ada Estelle Loop Harrison, and her minister husband. Mrs. Harrison died in 1925 and her son Stanley made this his home. Stanley Gardner Harrison, a Great Lakes ship captain, died in 1977.

This three-story Second Empire-style house features a characteristic high mansard roof, dormers, and two decorated chimneys. Other exterior details include: six entrances, four three-window bays, Palladian windows at the front entrance, and an attached wood shed. The specifications for the house were drafted by Dr. Loop to include a doctor's office with full-standing bookcases meant to house his large medical library. His wife, Jane, kept a herb garden here; many of the medicinal plants were used by the doctor to prepare prescriptions for his patients.

The furnishings are mostly Victorian pieces original to the Loop-Harrison family; they were donated by Captain Stanley G. Harrison in 1964.

Notable Collections on Exhibit

Among the many items on display are: a collection of maritime artifacts and instruments from Stanley's early sailing days and various Lake Huron shipwrecks; medical instruments and medicines used by Dr. Loop; a collection of Carnival and Depression Glass; a Steinway piano c. 1856; and an assortment of mastodon and mammoth bones found in Sanilac County.

Additional Information

The Loop-Harrison House has been placed on the National Register of Historic Places.

Ford-MacNichol Home

2610 Biddle Avenue at Vinewood
Wyandotte, MI 48192
(313) 246-4520

Contact: Wyandotte Cultural and Historical Commission

Open: Mon.-Fri. Noon–4 p.m., first Sunday of each month except July and August 2–5 p.m.

Admission: Adults $1.00; seniors and students $.50

Activities: Group and school tours by appointment, special seasonal events including Heritage Days, Christmas celebrations, and candlelight tours

Suggested Time to View House: 45–60 minutes

Facilities on Premises: Gift shop

Best Season to View House: Spring-fall

Number of Rooms: 29

Style of Architecture: Victorian Queen Anne-Eastlake

Description of Grounds: Small yard

Year House Built: 1896

On-Site Parking: Yes **Wheelchair Access:** Yes

Description of House

Dr. George and Mrs. Laura Ford MacNichol built this house in 1896; Mrs. MacNichol was the daughter of Captain John Ford, the founder of the Michigan Alkali Company (today's BASF Corporation). Her husband, who graduated medical school but never practiced, became a prominent figure at Michigan Alkali and one of Wyandotte's leading citizens. The couple lived here for some seven years, then moved to Toledo, Ohio. The Drennan family owned the house for the next sixty years, until it was sold in 1967 to Yvonne Latta, an active member of the Wyandotte Historical Society. Ten years later it was purchased by the city with the help of the Society.

The house is a very fine example of the Queen Anne style, with its turret, projecting gables, wrap-around porch, and elaborate trim. The Eastlake spindlework is especially impressive: the banister on the veranda has five hundred spindles alone! Other exterior details include: a conical roof atop the turret, the "sunburst" pattern at the southeast corner of the porch, curved plate-glass windows in the turret and beveled leaded-glass windows elsewhere, and Doric columns on the veranda. The interior features sliding oak doors, original wallpaper in both the first and second floor hallways, six fireplaces, original carpet in the parlor, a mosaic tile floor and rich oak paneling in the vestibule, many original light fixtures, and a golden oak staircase. The entire home is filled with period furnishings which reflect the late Victorian taste common to Wyandotte's wealthier citizens at the turn of the century. The Ford-MacNichol Home is listed on the National Register of Historic Places.

Notable Collections on Exhibit

Most of the collections here are related to the early history of Wyandotte and include items relating the histories of Michigan Alkali, the local shipbuilding industry, Bishop Furs, the Wyandotte Toy Factory, and the local Native American peoples.

Minnesota

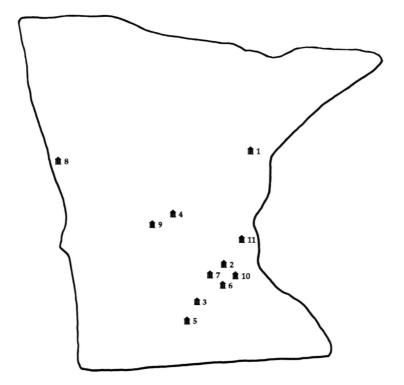

1. **Duluth**
   Glensheen

2. **Falcon Heights**
   Gibbs Farmstead Museum

3. **Le Sueur**
   W.W. Mayo House

4. **Little Falls**
   Charles A. Lindbergh House

5. **Mankato**
   Rensselaer D.Hubbard House

6. **Mendota**
   Faribault House Museum
   Henry Hastings Sibley House

7. **Minneapolis**
   Turnblad Mansion

8. **Moorhead**
   Comstock Historic House

9. **Sauk Centre**
   Boyhood Home of Sinclair Lewis

10. **St. Paul**
    Alexander Ramsey House
    James J. Hill House

11. **Taylors Falls**
    W.H.C. Folsom House

Glensheen

Contact: University of Minnesota
Open: Summer, daily except Wed.
9 a.m.–4 p.m.; winter, weekdays except
Wed. 1–2 p.m., Sat. and Sun. 1–3 p.m.;
closed major holidays
Admission: Adults $6.00; seniors and
children (6-11) $3.00; children
(under 5) free
Activities: Guided tours, audio visual
presentations, special seasonal events
Suggested Time to View House: 2 hours
Facilities on Premises: Museum shop,
tea room
Best Season to View House: Summer
Description of Grounds: 22 acre historic
lakefront estate with formal gardens
Number of Yearly Visitors: 100,000
Number of Rooms: 39

Style of Architecture: Eclectic Period
Revival, Tudor Jacobean
Year House Built: 1908
On-Site Parking: Yes **Wheelchair Access:** Yes

Description of House

This 39-room period revival mansion—sited on twenty-two acres of lakefront property—is a fitting testament to the business acumen of Chester Congdon. A successful lawyer and businessman, he made his fortune in Minnesota's iron ore mining industry and out-of-state ventures like the the Yashima Valley Water Project in Washington State. Congdon also served in the Minnesota Legislature.

Glensheen is a three-story, reinforced concrete structure with a brick facade. The house—surrounded by formal gardens and outbuildings—was modeled after a Tudor Jacobean-style English manor; it features parapeted gables and a two-story bay entry with an arched door jamb and projecting door hood. Although the style recalls England's architectural heritage, Glensheen was built with the latest technology in mind: central heating, vacuum and humidification systems, and an intercom system.

While the public areas were executed in a traditional manner, the family chambers were designed in the style of the American Arts and Crafts Movement with emphasis placed on Art Nouveau. Many patterned fabrics inspired by the work of William Morris were used extensively throughout the bedrooms. All of the furniture on view belonged to the Congdon family, including antique pieces in the Jacobean, Georgian, and Sheraton styles, as well as many well-crafted examples of the more modern American Eastlake style.

Notable Collections on Exhibit

Several fine American Impressionist paintings and Arts and Crafts-style ceramics are on display throughout the house.

Gibbs Farmstead Museum

2097 West Larpenteur Avenue
Falcon Heights, MN 55113
(612) 646-8629

Contact: Ramsey County Historical Society

Open: May 1-Oct. 31, Tues.-Fri. 10 a.m.-4 p.m.;
June-Aug., Sat. and Sun. Noon-4 p.m.

Admission: Adults $2.50; seniors $2.00;
children $1.00; group rates (15 or more)
available

Activities: Guided tours, audiovisual
introduction, special Sunday programs,
festivals, October evening storytelling

Suggested Time to View House: 2 hours

Facilities on Premises: Admissions
building and gift shop

Description of Grounds: Site is surrounded
by gardens; outbuildings include two
barns and a one-room schoolhouse

Best Season to View House: Summer-fall

Year House Built: 1854, additions 1867 and
1873

Number of Rooms: 9

Number of Yearly Visitors: 15,000

Style of Architecture: National, prairie
farmhouse

On-Site Parking: Yes **Wheelchair Access:** Yes

Description of House

The town of Falcon Heights now lies at the edge of the Minneapolis-St. Paul city limits, but in the first half of the 19th century this site—which served as a "camp-over" for the Dakota Sioux—lay on the extreme western frontier of America. As a child and young woman growing up on a Sioux mission near Minneapolis, Jane Gibbs learned the ways and the language of the native peoples; when she married one of the area's original settlers, Herman Gibbs, they established their farmstead not far from where she grew up. In 1849, Jane and Herman Gibbs built their first home here—a simple log and sod house—and proceeded to farm the land and raise a family. In later years, the market-garden operation included a nursery managed by their sons. The Gibbs family and their descendants remained active in farming and community affairs into the 1940s.

Although the original sod house is gone, the two-story frame farmhouse built by the Gibbses in 1854 is still intact. This second house with its wrap-around porch and numerous additions reflects the family's increasing good fortune. Originally a one-room structure with a sleeping loft, it was expanded in 1867 to include a parlor, a downstairs office, and several upstairs bedrooms. In 1873, an attached summer kitchen and additional sleeping space for hired farm hands was built. The Gibbs house has been restored to the period of 1890 to 1910, and contains several original family pieces. The Gibbs Farmstead Museum, which provides a unique opportunity to view the daily life of an early Minnesota settler, has been placed on the National Register of Historic Places.

Notable Collections on Exhibit

Besides the farmhouse, the site includes several barns containing authentic farm and garden equipment used by the Gibbs family.

W.W. Mayo House

118 North Main Street
Le Sueur, MN 56058
(612) 665-3250

Contact: Mayo House Interpretive Society

Open: June-Aug., Tues.-Fri. Noon–4:30 p.m.; mid May, Sept.-mid-Oct., Sat., Sun. and holidays Noon–4:30 p.m.

Admission: Adults $1.50; children (6-16) $.50; school tour program $1.00 each

Activities: Guided tours by costumed history interpreters, orientation program, exhibits, special seasonal events including Pierre Le Sueur Day, and "Christmas in 1860"

Suggested Time to View House: 1 hour

Number of Yearly Visitors: 2,500

Best Season to View House: Spring and summer

Facilities on Premises: Mayoview history center and gift shop

Description of Grounds: Adjacent to Louise Park with herb gardens at W.W. Mayo House

Year House Built: 1859 with several additions

Style of Architecture: Gothic Revival

Number of Rooms: 7

On-Site Parking: Yes **Wheelchair Access:** Yes

Description of House

William Worrall Mayo—the founder of the Mayo Clinic and father of Charles and William Mayo—was born in the English village of Eccles in 1819. After studying medicine in Manchester, Glasgow, and London, Mayo left for the United States in 1845 where he obtained a position as a pharmacist at Bellevue Hospital in New York City. Although awarded medical degrees in the early 1850s from Indiana Medical College and the University of Missouri, Mayo operated a tailoring business in Indiana, owned a farm and ferry service near Cronan's Precinct, and served as justice of the peace and published a weekly newspaper in Le Sueur. During the Civil War he served as examining surgeon for the state draft board in Rochester. Mayo and his family moved to this town in 1864; here he began a successful medical practice and, twenty years later, established his world-renowned clinic.

Mayo and his brother James built this charming two-story Gothic Revival-style cottage in 1859. The exterior features an unusual center-gable, full-height entry with a graceful flared roof line accentuated with elaborate bracket work.

Originally, this entry was defined by simple Classical-style pilasters and a decorative frieze. Although most of the windows are of a simple encasement design, the window in the center gable is segmented and lancet-shaped to complement the steep roof peak. The door panels also mirror this theme.

Notable Collections on Exhibit

The house has been restored to the 1860 period with simple interior furnishings indicative of the life of a frontier physician; pieces include: a Gothic Revival-style secretary bookcase said to be built by Dr. W.W. Mayo, several folding "ladies" chairs belonging to Louise Mayo, and her portrait painted by her daughter Phoebe.

Additional Information

In 1884, Carson and Elizabeth Cosgrove acquired the Mayo House. Although the Cosgrove family lived in the house for only nine years, the house remained in their possession until 1920. Carson Cosgrove was one of the founders of the Minnesota Valley Canning Company, later known as the Green Giant Company. The house is listed on the National Register of Historic Places.

Charles A. Lindbergh House

1200 Lindbergh Drive South
Little Falls, MN 56345
(612) 632-3154

Contact: Minnesota Historical Society

Open: May-Labor Day, Mon.-Sat.
10 a.m.–5 p.m., Sun. Noon–5 p.m.;
Labor Day-Oct., Sat. 10 a.m.–4 p.m.,
Sun. Noon–4 p.m.

Admission: Adults $3.00; students and
children $1.00

Activities: Guided tours, audiovisual
programs, special events

Suggested Time to View House: 30 minutes

Facilities on Premises: History center with
museum, theater and store

Description of Grounds: 17 wooded acres
located bordered by the Charles A.
Lindbergh State Park

Number of Rooms: 11, 7 open to the
public

Best Season to View House: Summer

Year House Built: 1906

Style of Architecture: Modified Craftsman,
bungaloid style

Number of Yearly Visitors: 25,000

On-Site Parking: Yes **Wheelchair Access:** Yes

Description of House

When Charles Augustus Lindbergh was born in 1902, little did his parents dream that twenty-five years later their son would win worldwide fame by flying non-stop from New York to Paris in his plane, the "Spirit of St. Louis." Lindbergh grew up in this simple frame bungalow on the west bank of the Mississippi River and lived here with his parents until 1920. It has been restored and interpreted to the period of 1907 to 1917—the period his father served as an United States Representative.

The two-story house was built in 1906 soon after the Lindberghs' original, larger home was destroyed by fire in 1905. It is typical of the area, with an exterior of gray clapboard with white trim, a red tar paper roof, and an interior of gray plaster walls and hardwood floors. The Lindbergh family lived a rather modest life: there is a conspicuous absence of electric lamps and telephones, wood stoves provided the heat, and water was pumped from a well into the house. All of the furnishings and household items belonged to the family including a Knabe piano, a Singer sewing machine, and a set of dishes hand-painted by Mrs. Lindbergh. Lindbergh's boyhood collectibles and toys can be seen throughout the house. The Charles A. Lindbergh House is listed on the National Register of Historic Places.

Notable Collections on Exhibit

The Charles A. Lindbergh History Center contains original parts from the "Jenny," Lindbergh's first plane, purchased in 1923, and the "Spirit of St. Louis."

Rensselaer D. Hubbard House

606 South Broad Street
Mankato, MN 56001
(507) 345-5566

Contact: Blue Earth County
Historical Society
Open: Summer, Sun.-Thur. 1–5 p.m.;
winter, Sat. and Sun. 1–5 p.m
Admission: Adults $2.50; seniors and
students $1.50; family $8.00
Activities: Guided tours
Suggested Time to View House:
30–60 minutes
Facilities on Premises: Gift shop
Description of Grounds: Victorian garden
Best Season to View House: Summer
Year House Built: 1871, additions c.1890
and 1912, remodeled 1905
Style of Architecture: Victorian Second
Empire, masonry
Number of Rooms: 15

On-Site Parking: No **Wheelchair Access:** No

Description of House

Rensselaer D. Hubbard—local businessman and entrepreneur—was born in the winter of 1837 in Ostego County, New York. By 1854, he'd made his way to California and secured work as a farm hand in Sacramento. During the succeeding sixteen years, Hubbard managed a grocery business in Sacramento, returned to New York State and raised tobacco, married his first wife, and traveled to Minnesota. In the small town of Mankato, Hubbard settled with his family and worked in the wheat business; soon he and two associates owned and managed their own company, the Mankato Linseed Oil Company. In 1879 Hubbard established himself as president of yet another business venture, the Mankato Milling Company—a company whose name he would change no less than three times.

From the moment the stone foundation was laid, the residence of Rensselaer D. Hubbard was the subject of curiosity and praise. In the spring of 1871, the *Mankato Weekly Record* commented, "Mr. Hubbard is progressing very well with his residence, and will have, when completed, one of the finest residences in town." Later in the same year, the *Mankato Weekly Union* reported, "Mr. R.D. Hubbard...is about completing one of the most commodious and rather the handsomest house in Mankato." And so, in late 1871, this three-story Second Empire-style house located on South Board Street was finished...for the time being. The house featured a three-color patterned slate roof, windows with stained glass transoms, and interior woodwork of oak, cherry, and mahogany. Over the next three decades, Hubbard improved, added onto, and completely remodeled his home. However, Hubbard did not see the completion of his 1905 remodeling: he died while on a business trip to Chicago. The Rensselaer D. Hubbard House is listed on the National Register of Historic Places.

Faribault House Museum

55 D Street
Mendota, MN 55150
(612) 452-1596

Contact: Sibley House Association and the Minnesota Society of the Daughters of the American Revolution

Open: May-Oct., Tues.-Sat. 10 a.m.–5 p.m., Sun. Noon–5 p.m.

Admission: Adults $3.00; seniors $1.00; children (6-16) $1.00; (under 6) free

Activities: Guided tours, special programs, guest speakers

Suggested Time to View House: 60–90 minutes

Number of Yearly Visitors: 6,000

Description of Grounds: Grounds consists of two historic houses: the Faribault House Museum and the Henry Hastings Sibley House

Facilities on Premises: Gift shop

Best Season to View House: Summer

Year House Built: Started 1836, completed 1840

Style of Architecture: Georgian

Number of Rooms: 12

On-Site Parking: Yes **Wheelchair Access:** No

Description of House

Jean Baptiste Faribault was born in the wilds of Quebec in 1775, and as a young man traveled throughout the Great Lakes area as a fur trader before settling in the land where the Minnesota and Mississippi Rivers meet. Here Faribault married Palagie Hanse, half Dakota Sioux and half French. The couple had eight children and the family remained in the house until 1847, the year of Palagie Hanse Faribault's death. At that time, Jean Baptiste moved further south and settled in an area that one day would bear his name—Faribault, Minnesota. He died there in the summer of 1860.

The two-story Georgian-style limestone house replaced an earlier log dwelling built in 1826. The twelve-room house took over four years to complete; after Jean Baptiste abandoned it in 1847, it served as a hotel, private residence, and warehouse. Although efforts were made by Faribault's grandson, George Faribault, to reclaim the former family residence, it was not until 1935 that a successful attempt was made to restore the house, by the Minnesota Highway Department. Using site drawings made by the Historic American Buildings Survey Project, the Department returned the Faribault House to its appearance of the 1840s. Soon thereafter, the house was exchanged for land owned by the Minnesota Society of the Daughters of the American Revolution. It is now under the direction of the Sibley House Association, which also maintains the Henry Hastings Sibley House.

Notable Collections on Exhibit

The Faribault House currently serves as a museum of Native American objects, period textiles, and costumes ranging from 1776 to 1900. It also houses an extensive photograph collection of Native American peoples, mostly from the Minnesota region.

Additional Information

Historic Fort Snelling is sited on a bluff at the convergence of the Minnesota and Mississippi Rivers, not far from the Sibley and Faribault Houses. The Fort is the oldest landmark in the Minneapolis-St. Paul area.

Henry Hastings Sibley House

**Willow Street
Mendota, MN 55150
(612) 452-1596**

Contact: Sibley House Association and the Minnesota Chapter of the Daughters of the American Revolution

Open: May-Oct., Tues.-Sat. 10 a.m.–5 p.m., Sun. Noon–5 p.m.

Admission: Adults $3.00; seniors $1.00; children (6-16) $1.00; (under 6) free

Activities: Guided tours, special programs, guest speakers

Suggested Time to View House: 60–90 minutes

Facilities on Premises: Gift shop

Description of Grounds: Grounds consists of two historic houses: the Faribault House Museum and the Henry Hastings Sibley House

Best Season to View House: Summer

Year House Built: 1835, addition 1843

Number of Rooms: 14

Number of Yearly Visitors: 6,000

Style of Architecture: Modified Federal

On-Site Parking: Yes **Wheelchair Access:** No

Description of House

Henry Hastings Sibley—fur trader and first governor of Minnesota—was born in 1811 near Fort Detroit. He moved to the settlement of Mendota in 1835 and began building this modest two-story, end-gabled stone farmhouse, completing it in 1836. After his marriage to Miss Sarah Jane Steele in 1843, he added several rooms to both the first and second floors: a dining room, kitchen, office, and two bedrooms. Henry Hastings Sibley was a confidant of Minnesota's two other founding fathers, Jean Baptiste Faribault and Alexander Ramsey. Despite the political differences between these three men, they remained lifelong and steadfast friends.

Just four years after the Minnesota Territory was admitted as the thirty-second state, Henry and Sarah Sibley moved to St. Paul in 1862. After their departure, the Sibley farmhouse, like the Faribault House mentioned above, served various purposes over the next forty-eight years, functioning as a school, artist's studio, warehouse, and transient lodging before it too was abandoned. Sadly, during this period much of the interior was destroyed. Finally, in 1910, the Parish of St. Peter gave the house to the St. Paul Chapter of the Daughters of the American Revolution; to their credit, the Sibley House was restored.

Additional Information

The Henry Hastings Sibley House is the oldest private residence in the state of Minnesota and is listed on the National Register of Historic Places.

Turnblad Mansion

2600 Park Avenue
Minneapolis, MN 55407
(612) 871-4907

Contact: American Swedish Institute
Open: Year-round, Tues.-Sat. Noon–4 p.m.,
Sun. 1–5 p.m., Wed. Noon–8 p.m.;
closed national holidays
Admission: Adults $3.00; seniors and
students $2.00
Activities: Guided tours, movies, musical
groups, special seasonal events including a
mid-summer celebration, and St. Lucia Day
Suggested Time to View House: 2–3 hours

Facilities on Premises: Gift shop, bookstore,
coffee area
Description of Grounds: City block
Best Season to View House: Summer-fall
Number of Yearly Visitors: 40,000
Year House Built: Started 1904, completed 1908
Style of Architecture: Eclectic Chateauesque
Number of Rooms: 33
On-Site Parking: Yes **Wheelchair Access:** Yes

Description of House

Driven from Sweden by famine, Swan Johan Turnblad and his family emigrated to southern Minnesota in 1868. At the age of eighteen, he traveled to Minneapolis and apprenticed to the printing trade. After establishing his own printing operation, he became the owner of the *Svenska Amerikanska Posten*, a weekly Swedish-language newspaper with a circulation of over 40,000, one of the largest in the country. Committed to advancing the culture of the Swedish-American community, Turnblad founded the American Swedish Institute in Minneapolis and, in 1929, donated his beautiful Chateauesque-style mansion and collection of Swedish fine arts and crafts to this cultural institution.

This majestic gray limestone Turnblad Mansion is a unique example of the Chateauesque style, a style which gained popularity among affluent immigrants at the turn of the century. The exterior of the mansion is distinguished by high parapeted gables, several circular turrets capped with steep conical-shaped roofs, and classical-inspired ornamentation. It boasts of no less than thirty-three rooms, of which the dining room—paneled with oak and bleached mahogany inlay—is the most elaborate. Its massive fireplace is made out of imported Swedish marble with a mantelpiece depicting a scene from Swedish folklore. In addition to this fireplace, the mansion contains eleven stoves hand-crafted with Swedish tiles. In fact, the Turnblad Mansion contains the largest collection of Swedish-style stoves outside of Sweden itself.

Notable Collections on Exhibit

On exhibit is the American Swedish Institute's collection of Swedish contemporary glass and its collection of Swedish immigrant artifacts.

Additional Information

The Turnblad Mansion is listed on the National Register of Historic Places.

Comstock Historic House

506 Eighth Street South
Moorhead, MN 56560
(218) 233-0848

Contact: Comstock Historic House

Open: Memorial Day-Labor Day, Sat. and Sun. 1–4:30 p.m.; other times by appointment only

Admission: Adults $3.00; students $1.50; student groups $.50 each

Activities: Guided tours by appointment, special seasonal events including the July Strawberry and Craft Festival, Christmas Candlelight tours

Suggested Time to View House: 45 minutes

Description of Grounds: Simple, unadorned yard

Best Season to View House: Year round

Number of Yearly Visitors: 3,000

Year House Built: 1882

Style of Architecture: Victorian Queen Anne

Number of Rooms: 11

On-Site Parking: Yes **Wheelchair Access:** Yes

Description of House

The Comstock Historic House was the childhood home of Ada Louise Comstock, who became the first full-time president of Radcliffe College in 1923 and remained in that position until 1943. Ada Louise Comstock is considered by many to be one of the outstanding woman educators of her time. The house was built in 1882 by her parents, Solomon and Sarah Balls Comstock. It contains many original family possessions including furniture dating from the late 1880s.

Additional Information

The house is listed on the National Register of Historic Places.

Boyhood Home of Sinclair Lewis

810 Sinclair Lewis Avenue
Sauk Centre, MN 56378
(612) 352-5201

Contact: Sinclair Lewis Foundation

Open: Memorial Day weekend-Labor Day, Mon.-Sat. 9 a.m.–4:30 p.m., Sun. 10:30 a.m.–5 p.m.; weekends in September by appointment only

Admission: Adults $2.50; seniors $2.00; students (11-15) $2.00; children (6-10) $1.50; (under 6) free

Activities: Guided tours, video presentations, large groups by appointment

Suggested Time to View House: 45 minutes

Facilities on Premises: Gift shop and bookstore

Description of Grounds: Lawn and picnic grounds

Best Season to View House: Spring-fall

Number of Yearly Visitors: 2,400

Year House Built: 1887

Style of Architecture: Eclectic Victorian

Number of Rooms: 11

On-Site Parking: Yes **Wheelchair Access:** No

Description of House

Harry Sinclair Lewis, the American novelist whose novels *Main Street* (1920), *Arrowsmith* (1925), and *Elmer Gantry* (1927) won international acclaim culminating in the 1930 Nobel Prize for Literature, was born in Sauk Centre, Minnesota, in 1885. Known as "Red" Lewis during his boyhood because of his shock of red hair and freckles, Lewis, with his brothers, grew up in this modest Victorian-style house located just across the street from the family's original home where the boys had all been born. He lived here until graduating from the local high school in 1902. After attending Yale University, Lewis drifted from state to state and job to job while constantly writing, always making time to return to Sauk Centre, visit his father, Dr. Edwin Lewis, who died in 1926. Although Lewis the writer—who died in 1951—was critical of "small town" life, he insisted on being buried here in his relatively small hometown.

The Boyhood Home was purchased by the Sinclair Lewis Foundation in 1962. The house was restored to its appearance c. 1900 with the approval of the Minnesota Historical Society: it was painted its original color, the wallpaper was scraped off until only the first layer was left, and the kitchen was refurbished with an open ceiling. Many of the family's personal belongings still remain in the house; notably, household items including an English Blue china set, a white "Mayflower" sugar bowl, and a silver teapot. In addition, there are also several family photographs including one of the author's mother, Emma Kermont, and Dr. Edwin Lewis's diploma from Rush Medical College.

Additional Information

The Boyhood Home of Sinclair Lewis is listed on the National Register of Historic Places. It has also been designated as a National Historic Landmark, a State Historic Site, and was a recipient of the Award of Merit from the American Association for State and Local History.

Alexander Ramsey House

265 South Exchange Street
St. Paul, MN 55102
(612) 296-8760

Contact: Minnesota Historical Society
Open: Apr.-Dec., Tues.-Sat. 10 a.m.–4 p.m.;
extended holiday hours in December
Admission: Adults $3.00; children (6-15)
$1.00; (under 5) free
Activities: Guided tours, special events
Suggested Time to View House: 1 hour
Facilities on Premises: Museum shop
Best Season to View House: Spring

Description of Grounds: Small yard
surrounded by ornate wrought iron
fence. Reconstructed carriage house.
Style of Architecture: Victorian Second
Empire, masonry
Number of Yearly Visitors: 25,000
Year House Built: 1872
Number of Rooms: 15, 10 open to the public
On-Site Parking: Yes **Wheelchair Access:** Yes

Description of House

During their lifetimes, Alexander and Anna Ramsey played important roles in local and state development. Alexander Ramsey—the first Territorial Governor of Minnesota—had a political career which spanned thirty years. He served as Minnesota Governor and United State Senator and was appointed Secretary of War under President Rutherford B. Hayes. Anna Ramsey was a respected community leader active in many social and cultural affairs. Although the couple had three children—two sons and a daughter—only the daughter, Marion Ramsey Furness, reached maturity, and married. It was her progeny who bequeathed the house to the Minnesota Historical Society in 1964.

The Alexander Ramsey House is one of the finest domestic examples of the Second Empire style in the Midwest. Based on the centered wing box plan, the limestone three-story house features many characteristic details: Italianate-inspired hooded windows and dormers, a flared mansard roofline with cresting, patterned chimneys, one-story bay windows, and a full-facade, one-story porch ornately embellished with incised supports, railing, and balustrade. The interiors are enhanced by hand-grained, black walnut woodwork.

Notable Collections on Exhibit

Over 10,000 original artifacts are on display and include furniture, china and crystal. It is thought many of these pieces were purchased from Stewart's Department Store in New York City, and shipped by rail to Minnesota.

Additional Information

On special occasions, the smell of fresh-baked pastries, breads, and other foods permeates the rooms of the Alexander Ramsey House. The recipes come from the receipt book of Anna Ramsey, and are prepared by staff members in the restored 19th-century kitchen. The Alexander Ramsey House is listed on the National Register of Historic Places.

James J. Hill House

240 Summit Avenue
St. Paul, MN 55102
(612) 296-9396

Contact: Minnesota Historical Society
Open: Wed.-Sat. 10 a.m.–3:30 p.m.
Admission: Adults and seniors $3.00; children (6-15) $1.00; (under 5) free
Activities: Guided tours, video introductory, exhibits, concerts, special seasonal events including dramatized holiday tours
Suggested Time to View House: 90 minutes
Facilities on Premises: Book shop

Description of Grounds: Partially restored grounds
Best Season to View House: Spring-fall
Number of Yearly Visitors: 45,000
Year House Built: 1891
Style of Architecture: Richardsonian Romanesque
Number of Rooms: 45
On-Site Parking: Yes **Wheelchair Access:** Yes

Description of House

Railroad magnate and principal owner of the Great Northern Railroad, Canadian-born James J. Hill (1838-1916) built this spectacular Romanesque Revival mansion in 1891. The 32,000 square foot structure was designed by the Boston architectural firm of Peabody, Stearns & Furber at a initial cost of $522,000. When the house was completed with furnishings, interior decoration, and exterior landscaping, the cost was well over $900,000. At the time, it was reputed to be the largest and most expensive private residence in the state of Minnesota.

Hill was a very opinionated man, in his work and writings as well as in his taste. He supervised the entire construction process, often dismissing competent architects and skilled craftsman from the project; one such artisan was Louis Comfort Tiffany whose work did not conform to Hill's demands. Even so, it is a wonderful house, in which the finest of interior embellishments—Lincrusta wallcovering, stained glass windows, and gold leaf ceilings—are coupled with the most modern domestic technology—gas and electric light fixtures and indoor plumbing. In addition to the fully restored public and private rooms, the house features a skylit art gallery.The James J. Hill House is listed on the National Register of Historic Places.

Notable Collections on Exhibit

Originally the house was decorated with hand-carved oak and mahogany furniture, but little of this collection remains. The pieces on display include a twenty-five-foot mahogany dining room table, several occasional tables and chairs, a rug chest, and a pipe organ.

Additional Information

James J. Hill was the author of a book entitled *Highways of Progress*, in which he proposed to the farmers of the Northwest the notion that they should use "scientific" principles to develop their lands.

W.H.C. Folsom House

120 Government Road, P.O. Box 147
Taylors Falls, MN 55084
(612) 465-3125

Contact: Taylors Falls Historical Society
Open: Memorial Day-mid Oct., daily
1–4:30 p.m.
Admission: Adults $3.00; children (6-15)
$1.00; group rates available
Activities: Guided tours
Suggested Time to View House: 45 minutes
Style of Architecture: Modified Greek
Revival with Federal-style galleries

Best Season to View House: Spring-fall
Description of Grounds: Large yard with
house overlooking the village of Taylors
Falls and located in the historic Angel
Hill District
Number of Yearly Visitors: 5,000
Year House Built: 1855, remodeled 1930s
Number of Rooms: 11
On-Site Parking: No **Wheelchair Access:** No

Description of House

Maine native William Henry Carman Folsom (1817-1900) was an early
settler to the St. Croix River Valley. At the age of nineteen, Folsom came to
this area of Minnesota—then part of the Wisconsin Territory—which was
already inhabited by many uprooted New Englanders. Folsom tried his
hand at clerking, farming, and trading until finally, in 1845, he became
involved in the burgeoning Northwest lumber industry. In Osceola and later
in Stillwater, Folsom joined a small group of men who started the successful
St. Croix Boom Company; here logs were prepared for distribution to the
numerous mills located downstream. The company provided Folsom's
wealth, and the springboard for his future political career, first as deputy
postmaster and treasurer of St. Croix County, then delegate to the 1857
Constitutional Convention, state representative, and state senator. In his
later years, Folsom wrote of his pioneer days in a work entitled Fifty Years
in the Northwest.

Folsom fashioned the exterior of his two-story frame house in a varia-
tion of Federal and Greek Revival styles, reminiscent of traditional New
England structures. It features a full facade gallery porch and six-over-six
shuttered windows. The interior was modeled after French Colonial-style

rooms Folsom had seen during his many business trips in the lower Mississippi River region with the main rooms of the first and second floor opening onto the same gallery. During the 1930s remodeling, the summer kitchen was replaced by a sun parlor, and the double cupboard between the kitchen and dining room was removed.

In 1968, the house was sold intact by Folsom's grandson Stanley to the State of Minnesota. Restored in 1970, many of the rooms contain original family furniture and photographs, vintage clothing—including a Civil War uniform, and many books. The twin parlors contain a rosewood grand piano and several pieces of furniture in the American Empire and Louis XV Revival styles.

Additional Information

The W.H.C. Folsom House is located in a State and National Historic District known as "Angel Hill," which is listed on the National Register of Historic Places.

Missouri

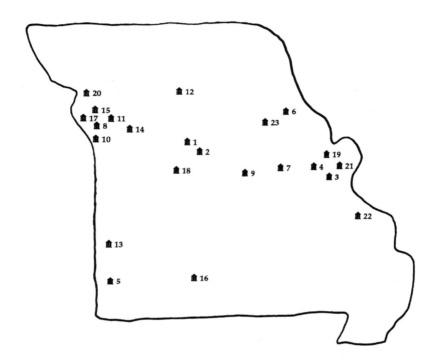

1. **Arrow Rock**
   Arrow Rock Tavern
   George Caleb Bingham House

2. **Boonville**
   Hain House

3. **Crestwood**
   Thomas Sappington House

4. **Defiance**
   Historic Daniel Boone House

5. **Diamond**
   Moses Carver House

6. **Hannibal**
   Garth Woodside Mansion
   *Mark Twain Boyhood Home
   and Museum*
   Rockcliffe Mansion

7. **Hermann**
   Pommer-Gentner House
   Strehly House and Winery

8. **Independence**
   *1859 Jail-Marshal's Home
   and Museum*
   Bingham-Waggoner Estate
   *Harry S Truman National
   Historic Site*
   Vaile Mansion–DeWitt Museum

9. **Jefferson City**
   B. Gratz Brown House

10. **Kansas City**
    John Wornall House Museum
    *Thomas Hart Benton Home
    and Studio State Historic Site*

11. **Kearney**
    Claybrook Plantation Home
    Jesse James Farm and Museum

12. **Laclede**
    *General John J. Pershing
    Boyhood Home*

13. **Lamar**
    *Harry S Truman Birthplace
    State Historic Site*

14. **Lexington**
    Anderson House

15. **Liberty**
    Lightburne Hall

16. **Mansfield**
    *Home in the Ozarks, Laura
    Ingalls Wilder-Rose Wilder
    Lane Museum and Home*

17. **Platte City**
    Krause Mansion

18. **Sedalia**
    Bothwell Lodge

19. **St. Charles**
    *First Missouri State Capital
    State Historic Site*

20. **St. Joseph**
    Jesse James Home

21. **St. Louis**
    Campbell House Museum
    Chatillon-DeMenil Mansion
    Eugene Field House
    *Grant's Farm and Cabin–
    "Hardscrabble"*
    *Samuel Cupples House and
    McNamee Gallery*
    Tower Grove House

22. **Ste. Genevieve**
    Felix Valle House
    Maison Guibourd–Valle

23. **Stoutsville**
    *Mark Twain Birthplace State
    Historic Site*

Arrow Rock Tavern

Main Street off Route 41, P.O. Box 1
Arrow Rock, MO 65320
(816) 837-3330

Contact: Missouri Department of Natural Resources, Arrow Rock State Historical Site
Open: June-Aug., daily 10 a.m.–4:30 p.m.; Oct.-May, daily 1–4:30 p.m.
Admission: Rates are under review
Activities: Guided tours, costumed historic demonstrations, audiovisual presentations, antique and crafts festivals
Suggested Time to View House: 45 minutes

Facilities on Premises: Visitor center
Description of Grounds: 150 acre state park area with camping and picnic facilities
Best Season to View House: Late spring-fall
Number of Yearly Visitors: 90,000
Year House Built: 1834
Style of Architecture: Federal
Number of Rooms: 12
On-Site Parking: Yes **Wheelchair Access:** Yes

Description of House

In 1819 Joseph Huston, a native Philadelphian who had already spent some years in Virginia, moved out to Missouri and settled at this site on the Missouri River just south of the "Arrow Rock." He became a justice of the peace, county court judge of Saline County, and county commissioner; in 1829 he helped select the site for the development of the river town called Arrow Rock. The location on the Missouri was a strategic one for expeditions heading west—it is reported that the famous William Becknell Expedition of 1821 stopped near Huston's place—who needed to stop for water. In the 1830s, Huston took advantage of the traffic and converted his brick home into a tavern for trail-weary pioneers. The Arrow Rock Tavern kept growing; sometime around 1840 he added a general store and ballroom to the structure and, in the following decade, a dining room and overnight guest rooms as well. Today, a modern addition to the rear of the tavern serves as a restaurant.

Huston sold his interest in the tavern in 1858 but kept his hand in the general store until his death in 1865. He was remembered as one of Arrow Rock's leading citizens. The two-story house which became a tavern still shows some original flooring, fireplaces, and stenciling in the ballroom. In 1923 the Arrow Rock Tavern was the first building set aside for historic preservation in the state of Missouri largely due to work done by the Daughters of the American Revolution.

Notable Collections on Exhibit

The general store is furnished with museum-quality reproductions of original items and the tavern contains the fine Daughters of the American Revolution Collection of period antiques.

Additional Information

Arrow Rock, a significant stop on the Santa Fe Trail, has been designated a National Historic Landmark. The Arrow Rock Tavern, which is listed on the National Register of Historic Places, forms the centerpiece of the Arrow Rock State Park, the oldest historic site in Missouri. Also open at the site is the Saline County Courthouse, a one-story log structure built with some Greek Revival elements. Though tradition has it that this building served as the courthouse when Arrow Rock was the county seat, and it is furnished to represent a 19th-century courthouse, it is now thought that a different log building served that function.

George Caleb Bingham House

First and High Streets
in Arrow Rock State Park
Arrow Rock, MO 65320
(816) 837-3330

Contact: Arrow Rock State Historical Site

Open: June-Aug., daily 10 a.m.–4:30 p.m.;
Oct.-May, daily 1–4:30 p.m.

Admission: Rates under review

Activities: Guided tours, costumed historic
demonstrations, audiovisual
presentations

Suggested Time to View House: 15 minutes

Facilities on Premises: Visitor center

Description of Grounds: 150-acre state
park area. Vegetable garden featuring
19th-century varieties adjacent to house.

Best Season to View House: Late spring-fall

Number of Yearly Visitors: 90,000

Year House Built: 1837

Number of Rooms: 3

Style of Architecture: Federal

On-Site Parking: Yes **Wheelchair Access:** No

Description of House

George Caleb Bingham, the artist whose genre paintings depicting frontier life in Missouri garnered world-wide acclaim, was born in Virginia in 1811, moved with his family to Missouri when he was eight years old, and spent his formative years on a farm in Arrow Rock before apprenticing as a cabinet-maker in nearby Boonville. He built this house in 1837 and lived here until 1845; after then, his mother stayed on and Bingham returned intermittently from his travels. His fame was such that the town board—of which he was member—noted his absences in their minutes. The artist moved, first to Independence, then to Kansas City, where he died in 1879. Bingham's reputation remains undiminished and paintings like "Fur Traders Descending the Missouri," "Shooting for the Beef," "The Jolly Flatboatman," and "The Election Series: The Verdict of the People" are considered an indispensable piece of America's cultural heritage.

This simple one-story brick house is built in the Federal style with an ell which contains the kitchen. Under the kitchen, which has been completely restored into a working demonstration room, is a root cellar; the ell is attached to the house by a breezeway. The furnishings have been collected to reflect the period of the artist's residency, 1837 to 1845; among them, only his easel is thought to have been original. The George Caleb Bingham House is part of the Arrow Rock State Historical Site and is listed on the National Register of Historic Places.

Notable Collections on Exhibit

At the Visitors' Center three original Bingham portraits are on display: Dr. John Sappington (1834), Mrs. Jane Sappington (1834), and Mr. James Piper (1874).

Hain House

412 Fourth Street, P.O. Box 1776
Boonville, MO 65233
(816) 882-7977

Contact: Friends of Historic Boonville

Open: Open by appointment only; closed
Jan. 1-Apr. 1

Admission: Donations welcome

Activities: Guided tours by appointment,
special programs, concerts

Suggested Time to View House: 1 hour

Description of Grounds: Hain Memorial
Garden planted with flowers, vines and
herbs. Restored in 1982.

Best Season to View House: Late
spring-early fall

Number of Yearly Visitors: 1,000

Year House Built: 1838

Number of Rooms: 6

Style of Architecture: National, log cabin

On-Site Parking: Yes **Wheelchair Access:** Yes

Description of House

Like so many Europeans of his time, George Hain heard about the un-limited opportunity available to all people in America and decided to make his own future here. The Swiss-born blacksmith and horticulturist emigrated in 1836 and came to settle in Boonville by July of that year. He purchased property at the corner of Fourth and Chestnut Streets, married another Swiss immigrant, Sophia Aull, built this house, and started a family. The Hain family would live here for the next 140 years. When George died in 1877 he left everything to his wife with the stipulation that she not remarry. When she did remarry, the will was carried out and the couple's son, George John Hain, was able to purchase the home for $1,500. The younger Hain was a successful merchant who ran the well-known Boonville establishment, "The People's Store." He and his wife raised five children and lived here until their deaths in 1927 and 1935, respec-tively; after 1935, the house was occupied by two of their daughters, Alice and Agnes. When Agnes died in 1981, the house was sold to the Crosby Kemper Foundation of Kansas City who donated it to the Friends of Historic Boonville.

The Hain House began as a simple two-room log house covered in clap-boards with a roof of cedar shakes to which several additions were made over the years; these additional rooms form a long ell off the original cabin. Interest-ingly, each of these rooms opens out onto a porch which runs the full length of the ell. The original structure features a front door showing the "Christian" design, in which the panels are meant to represent a Cross above an open Bible, six-over-six fenestration, and a loft reached by a boxed stair. The few furnish-ings on display in the house are authentic to the period of 1855 to 1860.

Additional Information

The Hain House, which is a fine example of a typical pioneer home in central Missouri, is operated by the Friends of Historic Boonville who also oversee another splendid property, the Old Cooper County Jail, the Sheriff's Residence, and the Hanging Barn at 614 East Morgan Street.

Thomas Sappington House

1015 South Sappington Road
Crestwood, MO 63126
(314) 957-4785

Contact: Sappington House Foundation
Open: Tues.-Fri. 11 a.m.–3 p.m., Sat. Noon–3 p.m.; closed New Year's Eve and Day, Good Friday, Memorial Day, Fourth of July, Thanksgiving Eve and Day, Christmas Eve and Day
Admission: Adults $1.00; children (6-11) $.50; seniors and scouts with reservation free
Activities: Guided tours, audiovisual presentations
Suggested Time to View House: 15-60 minutes
Facilities on Premises: Gift shop, library, tea room
Number of Yearly Visitors: 2,500
Year House Built: 1808
Number of Rooms: 5

Description of Grounds: 2.2 acres of grounds including a pond
Best Season to View House: Early spring-fall
Style of Architecture: Federal, brick
On-Site Parking: Yes **Wheelchair Access:** No

Description of House

In 1804, the Sappingtons, Kinkeads, and forty other families came to Missouri from Kentucky; four years later one of John Sappington's sons, Thomas, and Mary Kinkead were married and moved into this splendid Federal-style brick house. Theirs was the first wedding ever recorded in St. Louis County. Thomas Sappington served as a Lieutenant in the U. S. Army during the War of 1812. He died in 1860.

The house was built on a 200-acre parcel of land given to Thomas by his father and the structure itself is thought to have been built from plans brought from Maryland by the Sappingtons because of the rarity of the design in Missouri. The house was built of locally-fired brick by slave labor in the year of the Sappingtons' wedding; it is believed to be the oldest house in St. Louis County. The wood frame is joined by pegs instead of nails and the hearthstones and mantels exhibit their original carvings. The house has been fully restored to appear as it did in 1808; the colors have been matched to scrapings of the originals. The living room contains a fine 18th-century Adam fireplace with double columns. The collected furnishings are all period antiques common to region.

Notable Collections on Exhibit

Among the many items on display are collections of Staffordshire and Rockingham china pieces, samplers, silhouettes, theorem painting, silk embroidery, pistol-handle flatware, and pewter trays.

Additional Information

The Thomas Sappington House is listed on the National Register of Historic Places.

Historic Daniel Boone House

1868 Highway F
Defiance, MO 63341
(314) 987-2221

Contact: Historic Daniel Boone Home and Boonesfield Village, Inc.

Open: Mid Mar.-mid Dec., daily 9 a.m.–6 p.m.; mid Dec.-mid Mar., Sat. and Sun. 11 a.m.–4 p.m.

Admission: Adults $5.00; children (4-11) $2.50

Activities: Guided tours, special seasonal events including the annual Christmas Candlelight Tour

Suggested Time to View House: 45 minutes

Facilities on Premises: Gift shop located in the village

Description of Grounds: Historic village of Boonesfield in the Femme Osage Valley with several restored homes and tradesman buildings including the Daniel Boone House, the 1832 Log School House, the 1830 Chapel and Merchant's Home

Best Season to View House: Year round

Year House Built: Started 1803, completed 1810

Style of Architecture: Georgian

Number of Rooms: 8

On-Site Parking: Yes **Wheelchair Access:** No

Description of House

Perhaps no one epitomizes America's relentless surge west as much as the near-legendary figure of Daniel Boone (1735-1820), the restless trailblazer who always seemed to be searching for a little "elbow room." In his early days, Boone lived with his brother-in-law in the wilds of Kentucky, led a party of settlers through the Cumberland Gap in 1767, fought the Shawnees at Boonesboro and escaped capture by that tribe twice, then served in the state militia, legislature, and as a judge. In 1788, he foolishly lost a land grant in western Virginia because he had failed to record his holdings correctly. In 1798, Boone moved west again, this time to Missouri, where he had received another land grant. Here he renewed his frontier life of hunting and trapping.

On this site in the Femme Osage Valley, Boone built a fine four-story Georgian-style house which he modeled after his Pennsylvania birthplace, which itself was patterned on the ancestral Boone residence in Devon, England. The blue limestone structure features twelve-over-eight-pane windows, double-end chimneys, a full-width, two-story back porch and balcony added later, and ten fireplaces. The walls are two and a half to three and a half feet thick. The dining room and drawing room both show hand-hewn beamed ceilings; other interior details include five fireplace mantels made of black walnut carved by Boone himself, and some of the original stenciling and wallpaper. Several of the Windsor-style furnishings are original, including the large four-poster bed in which Boone died and his personal writing desk.

Notable Collections on Exhibit

Among the items on display are a family collection of early 19th-century coins, powder horns, Mrs. Boone's butter churn and sewing basket, and a portrait of Daniel Boone done by Chester Harding in 1819.

Additional Information

On the property stands an old elm called the Judgment Tree; it is said that Daniel Boone, acting as a syndic for the Spanish Government, held "court" under this tree for the purpose of settling disputes between settlers and native peoples. His home is listed on the National Register of Historic Places.

Moses Carver House

Contact: George Washington Carver
National Monument

Open: Apr.-Oct., daily 8:30 a.m.–4:30 p.m.;
closed Christmas

Admission: Adults $2.00

Activities: Guided tour starts at 2 p.m.
daily with introductory video

Suggested Time to View House: 30 minutes

Facilities on Premises: Visitor center and
bookstore

Description of Grounds: 210 acre park and
restored prairie with original cabin site,
family cemetery, and the Moses Carver
house

Best Season to View House: Year round

Year House Built: 1881

Number of Rooms: 3, 2 open to the public

Number of Yearly Visitors: 50,000

Style of Architecture: National

On-Site Parking: Yes **Wheelchair Access:** No

Description of House

George Washington Carver (1861?-1943), the famous African-American botanist, agricultural chemist, and educator, was born into slavery on the Moses Carver Farm. After his mother was kidnapped by Confederate soldiers during the Civil War—never to be seen again—the infant George (who was also kidnapped but safely returned) and his older brother, Jim, were raised by their former owners, Moses and Susan Carver. In 1894, he received his degree in agricultural science from Iowa State University and later returned to that institution as a teacher. Two years later, he was invited by Booker T. Washington to become the director of the agricultural program at Alabama's Tuskegee Institute; he would remain there for the rest of his life. Both Washington, the great educator, and Carver, the peerless scientist, became real-life heroes to generations of African-Americans; among the latter's many contributions to American farming are his development of the uses and cultivation of soybeans and—most famously—peanuts. George Washington Carver died in 1943; he is buried next to Booker T. Washington at Tuskegee.

This hall-and-parlor two-story frame house has a porch with simple turned supports, a shed roof, side gables, a rear kitchen extension with its own small porch. It is all of two rooms wide and one room deep. The windows are four-over-four arrangements with double sashes and the chimney is placed at the side gable. The house was relocated to its present site in 1916. The George Washington Carver National Monument is listed on the National Register of Historic Places.

Notable Collections on Exhibit

The house currently features exhibits relating its architectural history and the Carver family genealogy.

Garth Woodside Mansion

Rural Route 1, P.O. Box 304
Hannibal, MO 63401
(314) 221-2789

Contact: Garth Woodside Mansion
Open: Daily 11:30 a.m.–3 p.m.; closed
  Thanksgiving, Christmas, New Year's Day
Admission: Group rates $2.75 per person;
  open for groups of 10 or more
Activities: Guided tours, annual Victorian
  Christmas
Suggested Time to View House: 45 minutes
Facilities on Premises: Gift shop

Description of Grounds: 39 acres of gardens
  and woodlands
Best Season to View House: Spring-fall
Number of Yearly Visitors: 3,000
Year House Built: 1871
Style of Architecture: Victorian Second
  Empire, towered
Number of Rooms: 20
On-Site Parking: Yes **Wheelchair Access:** No

Description of House

John C. Garth—successful broker, manufacturer, and banker—grew up in Hannibal with Mark Twain and the two remained lifelong friends; it is said that Garth formed the basis for one of Twain's most famous fictional characters, Tom Sawyer. After Garth graduated college, he married Helen Kercheval, a childhood sweetheart and another schoolmate of Twain's. The couple had two children, moved to New York for nine years, and returned to their hometown for good in 1871. Here Garth pursued a multitude of business opportunities. After his death in 1899, Mrs. Garth was elected to the board of the Farmers and Merchants Bank, which her husband had helped to found, thus making her the first woman bank director in Hannibal.

This three-story Second Empire-style mansion was originally intended to be a summer residence for the Garths. It features a splendid three-story flying staircase, partial wrap-around porch with incised trim, hooded dormer windows, and a slate roof showing a pattern of alternating octagonal and straight-edge tile bands. The house has been painted to reflect its appearance in the 1880s: three different shades of green on the body and a brownish red on the sashes. The whole restoration has been carried out superbly; in fact, the Garth Woodside Mansion was awarded the National Trust for Historic Preservation's "Great American Homes" Award in 1992, given for an outstanding residential rehabilitation. Several of the furnishings on display—including a seven-piece Eastlake parlor set and a Renaissance Revival-style walnut bed—are original to the Garth family; the rest are period pieces collected by the mansion's present owners.

Notable Collections on Exhibit

Among the items on display is a library of hundreds of volumes which belonged to Garth and a collection of vintage clothing, Victorian paper valentines, perfume bottles, fans, and hatpins.

Additional Information

The Garth Woodside Mansion now serves as a bed-and-breakfast establishment owned and operated by Irv and Diane Feinberg. The award-winning restoration was done by River City Restoration which also restored the Lincoln Home in Springfield, Illinois.

Mark Twain Boyhood Home and Museum

206 Hill Street
Hannibal, MO 63401
(314) 221-9010

Contact: Mark Twain Home Foundation

Open: Memorial Day–Labor Day, daily 8 a.m.–6 p.m.; Sept. and Oct., Apr. and May, daily 8 a.m.–5 p.m.; Nov., Dec., Mar., daily 9 a.m.–4 p.m.; Jan. and Feb., daily 10 a.m.–4 p.m.

Admission: Adults $4.00; children (6-12) $2.00; group rates available

Activities: Self-guided tours, introductory slide program, displays of Twain's life in Hannibal

Suggested Time to View House: 1 hour

Facilities on Premises: Visitor center, museum and gift shop

Description of Grounds: Garden area

Best Season to View House: Late spring-fall

Number of Yearly Visitors: 130,000

Year House Built: 1843

Style of Architecture: Federal

Number of Rooms: 7

On-Site Parking: Yes **Wheelchair Access:** Yes

Description of House

If it can be said that one measure of a writer's greatness is his ability to evoke a place—real or imaginary—so strongly that the reader feels as though he has actually been there, then we must conclude that Mark Twain is a great writer indeed; for who has not felt themselves a visitor to Hannibal, Missouri, the "white town drowsing in the sunshine" on the banks of "the great Mississippi, the majestic, the magnificent Mississippi, rolling its mile-wide tide along, shining in the sun; the dense forest away on the other side," after having read *The Adventures of Tom Sawyer*, or *Life on the Mississippi*, or, most famously, *Adventures of Huckleberry Finn*?

This simple two-story Federal-style house was where Mark Twain, born Samuel Langhorne Clemens, spent his boyhood years. His family moved here in 1839 from Florida, Missouri, when he was four years old, and his father practiced law and served as justice of the peace in an office across the street. While living here, young Sam began his apprenticeship as a printer at a local newspaper and absorbed the life and stories lived on the mighty river which ran past the town just two blocks from his home. His father, who was pretty much a failure at all he undertook, died of pneumonia in 1847 and his mother took over ownership of the house. Sam lived here until 1853, when he left to work as a printer in St. Louis.

The house is covered in white clapboards and has been restored to its appearance in the years between 1847 and 1853; it features side gables with a rear extension, double-hung six-over-six windows, and interior walls of painted plaster. None of the period furnishings on display belonged to the Clemens family.

Additional Information

Adjacent to the Mark Twain Boyhood Home is the Mark Twain Museum where one may view several first editions of his books, one of his trademark white suits, and fifteen Norman Rockwell paintings used to illustrate various editions of *The Adventures of Tom Sawyer* and *Adventures of Huckleberry Finn*. The Home is listed on the National Register of Historic Places.

Rockcliffe Mansion

1000 Bird Street
Hannibal, MO 63401
(314) 221-4140

Contact: Rockcliffe Mansion
Open: Jan., Feb., Dec., daily
  11:30 a.m.–3:30 p.m.; Mar.-Nov., daily
  9:30 a.m.–5:00 p.m.
Admission: Adults $4.00; children (6-11)
  $1.50; groups (20 or more) $3.50 each
Activities: Guided tours
Suggested Time to View House: 45 minutes
Facilities on Premises: Gift shop

Style of Architecture: Eclectic Neoclassical
Best Season to View House: Year round
Description of Grounds: Large landscaped
  yard
Year House Built: Started in 1898, completed
  1900
Number of Rooms: 30
On-Site Parking: Yes **Wheelchair Access:** No

Description of House

Rockcliffe, once touted as "The Finest Home in Missouri," was built at the turn of the century by Hannibal lumber tycoon, John J. Cruikshank. As a boy, Cruikshank had emigrated to America from Scotland with his parents; his father first took a position as harbormaster on the Mississippi in Galena, Illinois, then moved the family to Alton, Illinois, where he started a lumber business. After a third and final move to Hannibal, the business flourished under the leadership of son John and soon became one of the largest in Missouri. The Cruikshanks moved into their mansion in 1900 and lived here until 1924, the year that John J. died. His wife closed the house and moved in with one of her daughters. For the next four decades, the house stood empty and decay set in—it got to be known as the neighborhood "haunted house"—before three prominent Hannibal families made it their project to restore the mansion to its former glory. It is reported that famous author and Hannibal native Mark Twain spoke from the steps of the mansion's Grand Staircase on a visit to his hometown in 1902.

This three-story frame house with its double-brick walls was designed and built by the St. Louis architectural firm of Barnett, Haynes & Barnett, whose other buildings included the Governor's Mansion in Jefferson City. It originally stood on a rocky promontory overlooking both the river and Cruikshank's lumber works before being moved 350 feet by mule team to its present site. Having been saved from neglect and vandalism, the interior of the house now shows itself a luxurious mixture of Art Nouveau and Neoclassical-style decorative elements. Many of the pieces on display were imported from Europe, and several were rescued by the Cruikshank daughters who donated them to be shown here again. Other details—like the French gilt wallpaper, red flocked velvet wallcovering, and laminated doors—were uncovered during the restoration process and found to be intact.

Notable Collections on Exhibit

The former ballroom at Rockcliffe is now a gallery featuring a splendid collection of vintage clothing, quilts, bedspreads, and beaded handbags. There are also numerous family heirlooms, including Mrs. Cruikshank's bed of carved walnut, a large platform rocker, the family silver, and Haviland china.

Additional Information

Rockcliffe Mansion is listed on the National Register of Historic Places.

Pommer-Gentner House

109 West Second Street
Hermann, MO 65041
(314) 486-2200

Contact: Deutschheim State Historical Site
Open: Summer, daily 10 a.m.–3:30.p.m.;
winter, daily 10 a.m.–3 p.m.; closed
New Year's Day, Easter, Thanksgiving,
Christmas
Admission: Adults $1.25; children $.75;
groups (10 or more) $1.00
Activities: Guided tours, exhibits featuring
Missouri-German peasant arts and crafts
Suggested Time to View House: 1 hour
Facilities on Premises: Museum shop with
books and gift items and research library
Best Season to View House: Spring
Description of Grounds: Period German
gardens with many heritage plantings
Number of Yearly Visitors: 12,000
Number of Rooms: 8

Style of Architecture: High German
Neoclassical
Year House Built: 1840
On-Site Parking: No **Wheelchair Access:** No

Description of House

This town on the Missouri River began life as the Hermann Colony, one of seven immigrant settlement societies established in Missouri in the third decade of the 19th century. Hermann Colony, founded by the German Settlement Society of Philadelphia, was perhaps the best planned and most systematically organized of these communities. It flourished as a self-sufficient economic and cultural settlement established as a joint stock company comprising town lots and 40 acre farms. The builders of this house, the Pommer family, owned a furniture shop on the premises.

The eight-room house built by Caroline Pommer in 1840 is a fine example of high-style German *Klassisismus* (neoclassicism) which differs from the more commonly encountered Greek Revival style in its lack of ornamentation and the severity of its line. Many middle-class German settlers of the early to mid-19th century built their homes in the Klassisismus style. The house provides an authentic glimpse into the lives of the German immigrants who came to Missouri; the furnishings reflect owners who were well-educated and more affluent than the norm. The pieces—both imported and locally manufactured—are primarily done in the Biedermeier style.

Notable Collections on Exhibit

Among the items on display are Chinese export and European porcelain pieces, a collection of hand-thrown pottery done by local German immigrants, and a 19th-century rare book collection.

Additional Information

The Pommer-Gentner House is the centerpiece of the Deutschheim State Historic Site, a museum dedicated to exhibiting the works and traditions of German immigrants throughout Missouri. School and group tours are encouraged, and German-speaking guides are available by prior arrangement.

Strehly House and Winery

109 West Second Street
Hermann, MO 65041
(314) 486-2200

Contact: Deutschheim State Historical Site

Open: Summer, daily 10 a.m.–3:30 p.m.; winter, daily 10 a.m.–3.p.m.; closed New Year's Day, Easter, Thanksgiving, Christmas

Admission: Adults $1.25; children $.75; groups (10 or more) $1.00

Activities: Guided tours

Suggested Time to View House: 1 hour

Facilities on Premises: Museum shop with books, toys and gift items

Description of Grounds: Two period German gardens with heritage plants and 1850s wine grapes

Best Season to View House: Spring

Year House Built: Between 1842 and 1869

Number of Rooms: 6

Number of Yearly Visitors: 12,000

Style of Architecture: German Vernacular

On-Site Parking: No **Wheelchair Access:** No

Description of House

The first German-language newspaper published in the German Settlement Society of Philadelphia's Hermann Colony was published here in the Strehly House in 1843. The newspaper—published by Eduard Muehl and Carl Procopius Strehly—was noted for its strong opposition to slavery. Between 1843 and 1855, these two men also published numerous books and a second newspaper out of the house. After that, Strehly built a winery on his property adjacent to the house and also operated a tavern here. The cultivation of grapes and production of wine became a significant industry in 19th-century Missouri. Carl Strehly's house remained in his family until 1964.

The Strehly House was built in stages over the years from 1842 to 1869; construction was done in a combination of timber, stone, and brick in the German vernacular style. The house is a fine example of the many such brick structures built throughout the Midwest by German immigrants during the 19th century. Many of the furnishings in the house belonged to the original residents and reflect the quality of their lives convincingly. Seen throughout the house are the colors common to all of Missouri's German immigrants.

Notable Collections on Exhibit

Behind the Strehly House is a vineyard in which one can see wine grapes originally planted in the 1850s. Inside the house, there are extensive collections of fabrics, little-seen ephemera, and peasant arts and crafts on view; the whole is intended to give an comprehensive view of the folk customs practiced by German immigrants throughout Missouri.

Additional Information

The Strehly House and Winery is also part of the Deutschheim State Historical Site, a living museum dedicated to preserving the folkways of Missouri's 19th-century German immigrants.

1859 Jail–Marshal's Home and Museum

217 North Main Street
Independence, MO 64050
(816) 252-1892

Contact: Jackson County Historical Society
Open: Tues.-Sat. 10 a.m.–5 p.m.; Sun.
1–4 p.m.; closed month of January
Admission: Adults $2.50; seniors $1.75;
children (under 12) $.50
Activities: Guided tours, rotating exhibits,
spring "living history" schoolhouse
Suggested Time to View House: 30 minutes
Facilities on Premises: Museum
Description of Grounds: One room
schoolhouse adjacent to the courtyard
gardens
Best Season to View House: Late
spring-late fall
Number of Yearly Visitors: 11,000
Year House Built: 1859
Number of Rooms: 6

Style of Architecture: Federal
On-Site Parking: No **Wheelchair Access:** No

Description of House

On Main Street in downtown Independence stands the 1859 Jail Museum which encompasses four structures: the Jail itself—made famous when Frank James was incarcerated here, the marshal's home, an annex which has been turned into a museum building, and a furnished one-room schoolhouse. The home, which was occupied by many marshals and jailers during the years that the jail was in use, also housed a federal marshal during the Civil War, when Union troops were garrisoned in Independence. The Jackson County Historical Society restored the four buildings and opened them to the public in 1959. The authenticity of the restoration was made possible by the discovery of six pages of original plans and specifications in an Independence bank.

The Marshall's Home is a two-story brick structure in the Federal style fully furnished with period pieces. The twelve-cell jail, with its thick limestone walls, features a cell furnished the way it might have been when Frank James was kept here.

Notable Collections on Exhibit

Items on display in the museum include several of George Caleb Bingham's paintings, a desk which belonged to Henry Clay, a collection of various weapons confiscated from prisoners kept in the jail, and a rotating exhibit of military uniforms of different eras.

Bingham-Waggoner Estate

313 West Pacific, P.O. Box 1163
Independence, MO 64051
(816) 461-3491

Contact: Bingham-Waggoner Historical Society

Open: Apr.-Oct., Mon.-Sat. 10 a.m.–4 p.m., Sun. 1–4 p.m.; special Thanksgiving-New Year's Eve hours

Admission: Adults $3.00; seniors $2.50; children $1.00

Activities: Guided tours, special exhibits, special seasonal events including annual trail ride breakfast and summer antique and craft fair

Suggested Time to View House: 45 minutes

Facilities on Premises: Gift shop, prescheduled group tour accommodations

Description of Grounds: 20 acre estate with five outbuildings and many walnut trees

Best Season to View House: Spring and fall

Number of Yearly Visitors: 15,000

Year House Built: 1855, remodeled 1895 and 1900

Style of Architecture: Italianate Villa

Number of Rooms: 26

On-Site Parking: Yes **Wheelchair Access:** No

Description of House

In 1864 the famous Missouri artist George Caleb Bingham purchased this house and its 19 acres from John Lewis, an Independence pioneer, and lived here until 1870. At the time Bingham was deeply moved by the carnage and displacement caused by the Civil War in western Missouri—two battles would have been visible from his property—and made his great and controversial painting "Martial Law" in protest against the Federal Government's Order Number Eleven which made refugees of thousands of border residents. This painting, now more familiarly known as "Order Number Eleven," was painted in a studio located on this estate. In 1866, native Pennsylvanians Peter and William Waggoner bought an established flour mill across the street from the Bingham estate; thirteen years later, the family purchased the estate itself. The mansion served as the Waggoner home until the death of Harry Waggoner in 1976.

This three-story, twenty-six-room Italianate-style mansion began life as a relatively simple six-room house in 1855. In 1895, and again in 1900, the house underwent major remodeling under the supervision of Kansas City architects Root & Seimans and interior decorator Henry Ohaus. The house as it now stands reflects all of the changes and additions made in those years. The first floor comprises a parlor, large L-shaped entry, music room, library, dining room with mahogany woodwork, and large kitchen with a butler's pantry. The second floor consists of seven bedrooms, a sewing room, bath, and large central hall, and the third floor contains the servants' quarters and a "tank" room. The tank controlled the water supply for the entire mansion. Most of the light fixtures—both gas and electric—are original to the house. Outside, details include twelve gabled dormers in the Federal style, a large cupola atop a low-pitched hipped roof, extended and bracketed eaves, a wrap-around porch with segmented posts, and a small covered balcony on the second story. Most of the furnishings on display were purchased around the turn of the century by the Waggoners and show a broad range of styles.

Notable Collections on Exhibit
Two original Bingham portraits hang in the mansion.

Additional Information
The Bingham-Waggoner Estate is listed on the National Register of Historic Places. The George Caleb Bingham House in Arrow Rock, which the artist occupied in his early years, is also listed in this guide.

Harry S Truman National Historic Site

Contact: National Park Service

Open: Memorial Day-Labor Day, daily 8:30 a.m.–5 p.m.; Labor Day-Memorial Day, Tues.-Sun. 8:30 a.m.–5 p.m.

Admission: Adults $2.00

Activities: Guided tours, audiovisual presentations

Suggested Time to View House: 15 minutes

Facilities on Premises: Visitor center located on North Main Street, bookstore

Description of Grounds: Grounds are not accessible to the general public

Best Season to View House: Late spring-fall

Number of Yearly Visitors: 60,000 -70,000

Year House Built: 1867, remodeled 1885

Number of Rooms: 14

**219 North Delaware Street
Independence, MO 64050
(816) 254-2720**

Style of Architecture: Victorian Queen Anne

On-Site Parking: Yes **Wheelchair Access:** Yes

Description of House

When Harry S Truman, thirty-third President of the United States, married his sweetheart, Bess, in 1919, the couple moved into this house; it was built in 1867 by Bess Truman's grandfather, George Porterfield Gates. Gates was a partner with the Waggoner brothers in the Waggoner & Gates Milling Company, a successful flour milling concern in Independence. The Trumans lived here for the rest of their lives—during Harry's term as President it became known as "The Summer White House." After the widowed Bess Truman died in 1982, the home became the Harry S Truman Historic Site.

This asymmetrical two-and-a-half-story Victorian Queen Anne house features a very distinctive flared roof line, a partial-width wrap-around porch with "lace" bracketing, exaggerated bracketing under the eaves, highly ornamented vergeboards, and elongated double-sash windows with stained glass sidelights. All of the furnishings in the house are original.

Additional Information

The Harry S Truman National Historic Site is listed on the National Register of Historic Places. In nearby Grandview, Missouri, one can visit the Truman Farm Home, the farmhouse where Harry S Truman grew up. That home is located at 12121 Blue Ridge Extension and the phone number is (816) 795-8200, ext. 260.

Vaile Mansion-DeWitt Museum

1500 North Liberty Street
Independence, MO 64050
(816) 833-0040

Contact: City of Independence and the
Vaile Victorian Society

Open: Apr. 1-Oct. 31, daily
10 a.m.–4:30 p.m.; between
Thanksgiving and Christmas,
Sun. Noon–4:30 p.m.

Admission: Adults $2.50, children
(under 12) $.50; group rates available

Activities: Guided tours, annual June
Strawberry Festival

Suggested Time to View House: 1 hour

Facilities on Premises: Gift shop

Description of Grounds: Full city block
with park-like grounds

Style of Architecture: Eclectic High
Victorian Queen Anne and Second Empire

Best Season to View House: Summer

Number of Yearly Visitors: 6,000

Number of Rooms: 30

Year House Built: 1881

On-Site Parking: Yes **Wheelchair Access:** No

Description of House

Native Vermonter Harvey Merrick Vaile came west to Missouri where
he set up the Star Route Mail Service, a private carrier under contract to the
Federal Government which specialized in delivering mail to far-flung communities on the Western frontier. The mail service was only one of many
businesses that the entrepreneur operated—others included real estate
speculation and cattle-raising—in addition to his involvement with local
and national politics. Local residents Roger and Mary Mildred DeWitt
acquired the house in the 1960s; in 1983, Mrs. DeWitt left the home to the
citizens of Independence.

This large and heavily ornamented three-story mansion, designed by its
owner, Harvey Vaile, working with architect Captain A. B. Cross, was so
impressive that the local press dubbed it the "Maison D'Or." The exterior
features a multi-colored tile mansard roof with cresting and finials, open
gable ornaments, exaggerated decorative brackets, patterned masonry
chimneys, and very elaborate Queen Anne-style trim throughout. The interior is no less impressive; here one sees multiple wall and ceiling frescoes,
trim featuring woodgraining, grotesques and other decorative elements,
and a huge wine cellar. The property boasts a lake, landscaped arbors,
fountains, and a green house.

Additional Information

The Vaile Mansion-DeWitt Museum is listed on the National Register of
Historic Places.

B. Gratz Brown House

109 Madison Street
Jefferson City, MO 65101
(314) 635-1850

Contact: Cole County Historical Society
Open: Tues. 10:30 a.m.–3:30 p.m., Wed.-Sat.
Noon–3:30 p.m.
Admission: Adults $1.00; students $.50;
children (under 5) free
Activities: Guided tours
Suggested Time to View House: 45 minutes
Facilities on Premises: Postcards and local
history books for sale
Description of Grounds: Courtyard garden
Best Season to View House: Late
spring-early winter
Style of Architecture: Federal-style row
house with early Victorian decorative
elements
Number of Yearly Visitors: 4,000
Number of Rooms: 5

Year House Built: c.1871
On-Site Parking: No **Wheelchair Access:** No

Description of House

High on the bluffs which overlook the Missouri River in Jefferson City,
across from the present Executive Mansion, stands the B. Gratz Brown
House. Built around 1870 by a former governor of Missouri, B. Gratz Brown,
the home served as the official residence for Missouri's governors until the
present residence was completed.

The Brown House is built in the Federal style with the addition of some
Victorian elements—a decorative hood over the entrance and iron hand
rails. The spacious rooms are filled with numerous objects related to the
early history of Cole County and the State of Missouri; some of these objects
date to the days when the area was merely a part of the Louisiana Territory.

Among the many period furnishings on view here is a collection of
pieces which came from the Thomas Lawson Prince Mansion, an early
Independence home demolished in 1905 to make way for the Missouri State
Supreme Court building. The furnishings reflect the mid-Victorian period
and are done in rosewood and mahogany.

Notable Collections on Exhibit

Among the items found here is a superb collection of Inaugural Ball
Gowns that belonged to Missouri's former First Ladies—only a few of which
are on display at any given time—and a four hundred piece assortment of
wine, liquor, and cordial glasses.

John Wornall House Museum

146 West Sixty-first Street Terrace
Kansas City, MO 64113
(816) 444-1858

Contact: Jackson County Historical Society
Open: Tues.-Sat. 10 a.m.–4 p.m., Sun.
1–4 p.m.; closed major holidays and
private functions
Admission: Adults $2.50; seniors $2.00;
children $1.00
Activities: Guided tours, adult and children
workshops, speaker's bureau, music series,
special seasonal events including spring
garden activities, Civil War encampments,
and October kitchen program

Suggested Time to View House: 1 hour
Facilities on Premises: Gift shop
Description of Grounds: Formal herb garden
Best Season to View House: Spring-fall
Number of Yearly Visitors: 5,000
Year House Built: 1858
Style of Architecture: Greek Revival-style
farmhouse
Number of Rooms: 8
On-Site Parking: Yes **Wheelchair Access:** Yes

Description of House

Sometime in the early 1840s John Bristol Wornall migrated from Kentucky to Missouri with his parents and brother and the family settled in the Westport area. Here they cultivated grain and raised livestock which they sold to pioneers traveling west on the Santa Fe Trail. In 1849, disaster befell the family: John's mother and brother died, and his father returned to Kentucky, leaving him the farm. In 1852, after just less than a year of marriage, Wornall's first wife, Matilda, died. Two years later, he married Eliza Shalcross Johnson, daughter of the Reverend Thomas Johnson who founded the Shawnee Methodist Indian Mission and Manual Labor School. After living for some years in his father-in-law's house, Wornall built this brick house in 1858; from that time it was continuously occupied by descendants of Wornall until 1964. In that year, the Jackson County Historical Society restored the house to its appearance in the years 1830 to 1845. The John Wornall House, which originally stood on a 500 acre property, is now surrounded by one of Kansas City's residential neighborhoods.

This two-story brick farmhouse is built in the Greek Revival style and features a gable front and a centered full-height entry porch with simple squared Doric columns and two extending side wings. During the Civil War, the home was used a a field hospital and headquarters for both sides engaged in the 1864 Battle of Westport. Upstairs, and accessible only from the outside, are the "Strangers' Rooms"—rooms originally used by itinerant workers which now house a gift shop and office. The house is a fine museum interpreted to the period 1830 to 1865 which depicts the lives of those prosperous farm families who came to Missouri from the south.

Notable Collections on Exhibit

Among the many items on display is a restored Steinway piano and a collection of Bingham engravings.

Additional Information

The John Wornall House Museum is listed on the National Register of Historic Places.

Thomas Hart Benton Home and Studio State Historic Site

3616 Belleview
Kansas City, MO 64111
(816) 931-5722

Contact: Missouri Department of Natural Resources

Open: Year-round, Mon.-Sat. 10 a.m.–4 p.m.; summer, Sun. Noon–5 p.m.; winter, Sun. 11 a.m.–4 p.m.; closed New Year's Day, Easter, Thanksgiving, Christmas

Admission: Adults $1.25; children (6-12) $.75; under 6 free

Activities: Guided tours for groups

Suggested Time to View House: 30 minutes

Description of Grounds: Yard with carriage house-studio

Best Season to View House: Year round

Number of Yearly Visitors: 8,000

Year House Built: 1903

Style of Architecture: Eclectic Period Revival

Number of Rooms: 24

On-Site Parking: No **Wheelchair Access:** Yes

Description of House

When Thomas Hart Benton moved into this house in 1939, he was already one of America's best known Regionalist painters whose muscular depictions of the American scene and the myth of the West grew out of a loud chauvinism explicitly rejecting "European" modernism. Today he is perhaps best known for the murals he painted in New York City in the 'thirties. Benton, a native Missourian born in Neosho in 1889, was named for his grand-uncle—and Missouri's first U. S. Senator—Thomas Hart "Old Bullion" Benton. When young Thomas's father, Maecenas Benton, went to Congress in 1897, the boy took art lessons at the Corcoran Gallery in Washington, D. C. Later, he attended the Art Institute of Chicago, studied overseas, and served in the U. S. Navy as a draftsman during World War I. After the war, Benton moved to New York, married Rita Piacenza, taught at the Chelsea Neighborhood Association and painted many of his more well-known works. In 1935, the Bentons moved to Missouri; he became an instructor at the Kansas City Art Institute and won a commission to do a large mural in the State Capitol. His home on Belleview became one of Kansas City's principal meeting places for its intellectual and political elite. Thomas Hart Benton died in January 1975.

The house that Thomas Hart Benton moved into is a two-story late Victorian-style built just after the turn of the century. The home, and the adjoining carriage house which had been turned into a studio, is a repository of Benton memorabilia, personal effects, and furnishings. Much of the house appears just as it did when the artist and his wife were in residence here.

Notable Collections on Exhibit

In addition to the original Benton belongings on display, some of his artwork—on loan—may also be seen here.

Additional Information

The Thomas Hart Benton Home and Studio State Historic Site is listed on the National Register of Historic Places.

Claybrook Plantation Home

21011 Jesse James Farm Road
Kearney, MO 64060
(816) 635-6065

Contact: Clay County Department of
Historic Sites

Open: May, Sat. and Sun. 9 a.m.–4 p.m.;
Memorial Day-Labor Day, daily
9 a.m.–4 p.m.

Admission: Adults $2.00; seniors $1.80;
children $1.00

Activities: Guided tours, special events
including "Springtime and Christmas at
Claybrook" and "A Day in Rural
Missouri"

Suggested Time to View House: 30 minutes

Facilities on Premises: Visitor center,
museum store

Best Season to View House: Spring-fall

Description of Grounds: Long gravel
driveway lines with trees. Original barn.

Number of Yearly Visitors: 30,000

Number of Rooms: 8

Style of Architecture: Federal with Greek
Revival variations

Year House Built: 1858

On-Site Parking: Yes **Wheelchair Access:** Yes

Description of House

George E. Claybrook, who had come to Missouri from Virginia, bought
313 acres of land from Ashley Peters for $5,000 with the intention of estab-
lishing a plantation much like the ones he remembered from back home. He
planted corn, flax, wheat, tobacco, and hemp; in 1858, he built this plantation
home out of timber sawn at his own mill located just a half mile away.
Unfortunately, Claybrook lost his property in 1865 because of unpaid taxes.
The plantation turned over quickly and was purchased by Robert Chancelor
who lived here from 1866 to 1900. In that year, it was acquired by Henry
Barr—Barr was married to the daughter of Jesse James, Mary. The James
farm lay just across the street from the Claybrook Plantation. The Barrs lived
here for twenty-one years; they were followed by a series of owners until
Mrs. Eileen Riley—the last owner of Claybrook—donated the property to
Clay County in 1976.

This fully restored two-story Federal-style plantation home is framed in
oak and fastened using pegs; the only purchased materials used in its
construction are the glass for the windows, the paint, and the hardware.
Exterior details include gable-end chimneys, six-over-six-pane windows,
and an entry door with a segmented transom and sidelights. The floor plan
comprises a parlor, family room, dining room, and kitchen downstairs, and
the bedrooms upstairs; there is a "pass-through" between the dining room
and kitchen. Because the second floor had no functioning fireplaces, the
family slept downstairs in the family room during the cold winters. With
one exception, the furnishings are all donated antiques appropriate to the
period of the 1860s; the exception is an oak jelly cabinet. The Claybrook
Plantation Home is listed on the National Register of Historic Places.

Jesse James Farm and Museum

21216 Jesse James Farm Road
Kearney, MO 64060
(816) 792-7691

Contact: Clay County Department of Historic Sites

Open: May–Sept., daily 9 a.m.–4 p.m.; Oct.-Apr., Mon-Fri. 9 a.m.–4 p.m., Sat. and Sun. Noon–4 p.m.

Admission: Adults $3.00; seniors $2.75; children (6-12) $1.00

Activities: Guided tours, audiovisual presentation, exhibits, James family gravesite

Suggested Time to View House: 90 minutes

Facilities on Premises: Museum store

Description of Grounds: 40 acre farm with river running through the property

Best Season to View House: Year round

Number of Yearly Visitors: 30,000

Year House Built: 1822, additions 1893 and 1937

Style of Architecture: Folk, log cabin with Victorian-style extension

Number of Rooms: 5

On-Site Parking: Yes **Wheelchair Access:** Yes

Description of House

There a few figures in all of American history who have achieved the legendary status of Jesse James—subject of countless books, movies, television shows, and songs—and, to a lesser extent, his brothers in the infamous James Gang. To visit this farm where the boys grew up is to dispel some of that legend and perhaps see them as real flesh-and-blood human beings. Here one views the homely artifacts that belonged to the family, hears the story of their parents, the Reverend James and his wife, Zerelda, who moved here from Kentucky, and learns of Jesse's role as a Confederate guerrilla during the Civil War. For fifteen years after that war, James and his armed bandits robbed banks and trains throughout the American West before he was shot and killed by one of his own men in 1882 (at the Jesse James Home in St. Joseph which is also listed in this guide). Members of the family remained on here until 1959.

The original section of the James farmhouse is a two-room log cabin with back-to-back chimneys; the north side of this structure shows some deterioration. The addition to the cabin is done in the Victorian-Eastlake style, is painted white, and features a small entry porch. These two pieces of the house were rather loosely joined, forming a "T." In the cabin, one sees rough logs chinked with mortar, a shed extension with a "shed" roof line, and a central "saddlebag" chimney; while the Victorian piece features clapboard siding and a hipped roof. The house also has a built-in bedroom closet—a rarity at the time. The house is fully restored to the period when Jesse lived here and all of the furnishings are original.

Notable Collections on Exhibit

In addition to the James family's furnishings—including a washstand belonging to Zerelda and a table and chairs brought from Kentucky—the museum contains the world's largest collection of James memorabilia.

Additional Information

The Jesse James Farm and Museum is listed on the National Register of Historic Places. While in the area, it is worth visiting the Jesse James Bank Museum, the site of the first successful peacetime bank robbery carried out in broad daylight in United States history. The Bank Museum is located at 103 North Water Street in Liberty, Missouri; Liberty is just a few miles south of Kearney on I-35. Ironically, the James-Younger Gang was never convicted of this robbery although they were commonly thought to be the culprits.

General John J. Pershing Boyhood Home

1000 Pershing Drive, P.O. Box 141
Laclede, MO 64651
(816) 963-2525

Contact: Missouri Department of Natural Resources

Open: Mon.-Sat. 8 a.m.–4 p.m., Sun. Noon–5 p.m.; closed New Year's Day, Easter, Thanksgiving, Christmas

Admission: Adults $1.25; children $.75; groups half-price

Activities: Guided tours, annual "Pershing Days" in September

Suggested Time to View House: 30–45 minutes

Facilities on Premises: Book store, souvenirs available

Description of Grounds: Half a city block with several outbuildings including the Prairie Mound School

Best Season to View House: Summer

Number of Yearly Visitors: 7,000 - 10,000

Year House Built: c.1857

Style of Architecture: Rural Gothic Revival

Number of Rooms: 9

On-Site Parking: Yes

Wheelchair Access: Yes

Description of House

One of America's greatest soldiers, General John J. Pershing, was born near Laclede on September 13, 1860, in a small section house on what is now called Burlington Road. When he was six years old, the Pershings moved into this larger house and the young man lived here until his acceptance into the U. S. Military Academy at West Point. His father owned the general store in town and also served as postmaster and captain of the home guard. John attended the Kirksville School, got a degree, and taught for a time at the Prairie Mound School before applying to West Point in 1881. His subsequent career spanned the globe, from the northern Great Plains to the Battle of San Juan Hill, from the Philippines and Japan to the Mexican border, and, finally, to Europe during World War I. For his role in that conflict, Pershing was named General of the Armies by a special act of Congress. In addition to his military exploits, Pershing won the Pulitzer Prize for his memoirs, *My Experiences in the World War*. The General also lived through a horrible personal tragedy: while stationed at The Presidio in San Francisco, his wife and three daughters were killed in a fire.

This rural interpretation of the Gothic Revival is an asymmetrical, L-shaped nine-room house framed in wood featuring a small front porch and ornamental gable trim in the form of vergeboards without cross-bracing. The structure was well-preserved when purchased in 1952 and given to the State of Missouri. A complete restoration done then—dedicated to the general's memory and to his troops when he was Commander-in-Chief of the American Expeditionary Force—returned the house to its appearance in the 1870s. The furnishings are all appropriate to the period, though only a handful are original.

Notable Collections on Exhibit

A number of items belonging to General Pershing are on display, including his sword and school desk.

Additional Information

The General John J. Pershing Boyhood Home is both a National Historic Landmark and listed on the National Register of Historic Places. When visiting the house, a short side trip can be made to see the Locust Creek Covered Bridge State Historic Site. This bridge is one of only four remaining in Missouri.

Harry S Truman Birthplace State Historic Site

1009 Truman Street
Lamar, MO 64759
(417) 682-2279

Contact: Department of Natural Resources
Open: Daily; closed New Year's Day, Easter, Thanksgiving and Christmas
Admission: Free
Activities: Guided tours, tour buses
Suggested Time to View House: 45–60 minutes
Facilities on Premises: Gift shop
Description of Grounds: Garden and flowers
Best Season to View House: Spring-fall
Number of Yearly Visitors: 28,000
Year House Built: c.1880
Number of Rooms: 6

Style of Architecture: Folk Victorian
On-Site Parking: Yes **Wheelchair Access:** No

Description of House

This simple Victorian house was nearly new when the Trumans purchased it in 1882. Two years later, on May 8, 1884, Harry S Truman was born here; on that day, his father, John Anderson Truman, planted an Austrian Pine tree on the property—and the tree still stands. Before the house was bought by the United Auto Workers in 1957 and restored as a monument to President Truman, it was owned for years by the Earp family, second cousins to Wyatt Earp, the famous lawman.

The property includes a smokehouse and a hand-dug well as well as the above-mentioned tree. The house itself features a large bay window in the parlor. The home is decorated in an early Victorian motif and all of the furnishings on display date from the period from 1840 to 1880.

Notable Collections on Exhibit

Hanging in the house is a portrait of the President done by Margaret Miller and several Truman family photographs, including a baby picture of Harry, his mother, Martha Ellen Young Truman, and his grandparents, Anderson Shippe Truman and Mary Jane Holmes Truman.

Additional Information

The Harry S Truman Birthplace State Historic Site is listed on the National Register of Historic Places.

Anderson House

North Thirteenth Street
Lexington, MO 64067
(816) 259-4654

Contact: Battle of Lexington State Historic
Site
Open: Year-round, daily
Admission: Adults $1.25; children (6-11)
$.75; groups (ages 12 and over) $.50;
groups (ages 6-11) $.25 each
Activities: Guided tours, slide show
Suggested Time to View House:
45–60 minutes
Facilities on Premises: Visitor center and
gift shop
Description of Grounds: Battlefield
Best Season to View House: Spring-fall
Number of Yearly Visitors: 30,000
Year House Built: 1853
Number of Rooms: 8

Style of Architecture: Greek Revival
On-Site Parking: Yes **Wheelchair Access:** Yes

Description of House

One rarely thinks of Missouri as the site of a Civil War battlefield, yet
here in 1861 Union and Confederate troops clashed and suffered casualties.
During that battle, both sides used this house as a field hospital. It was built
in 1853 by local rope-manufacturer Colonel Oliver Anderson. Anderson
went bankrupt before the war and his house was put up for auction—at
which it was purchased by his son-in-law Thomas Akers. After the war, it
was bought by Lexington attorney Tilton Davis who lived here until 1916.

The Anderson House is a two-story symmetrical structure built in the
Greek Revival style. It features four rooms on the first floor and four
upstairs, two pair flanking a central hall on each floor. The furnishings on
display are authentic 19th century pieces, some of which belonged to the
Davis family. These include a Rococo Revival-style bedroom set which dates
from the 1850s.

Additional Information

The Anderson House is part of the Battle of Lexington State Historic Site;
the house is listed on the National Register of Historic Places.

Lightburne Hall

301 North Water Street
Liberty, MO 64068
(816) 781-5567

Contact: Lightburne Hall
Open: Daily 10 a.m.–7 p.m.; closed Thanksgiving and Christmas Day
Admission: Adults $3.00; children (over 12) $1.00; not recommended for children under 12
Activities: Guided tours; special seasonal candlelight tours
Suggested Time to View House: 1 hour

Description of Grounds: Large front lawn with various fruit trees and flower gardens
Best Season to View House: Early spring and fall
Number of Yearly Visitors: 2,000
Year House Built: Between 1845 and 1852
Style of Architecture: Early Classical Revival
Number of Rooms: 26
On-Site Parking: Yes **Wheelchair Access:** Yes

Description of House

Major Alvan Lightburne came to Missouri from Kentucky and settled in Clay County where he grew hemp on his plantation and manufactured rope. Lightburne and his wife, Ellen Sutton Lightburne, began construction on their residence in 1845 and completed it some seven years later. It was one of the grandest homes in the county. Lightburne served as mayor of Liberty and provided financial support for the founding of William Jewell College. After the Lightburnes died, the house was converted into apartments and then a fraternity house. In 1971, the house was rescued from demolition—it had lain vacant for years and fallen into ruin—by a group of local concerned citizens and historians.

Lightburne Hall is an impressive two-story brick structure built in the Early Classical Revival style by slaves; it contains twenty-six rooms and is thought to be one of Missouri's largest plantation homes still standing. The exterior of the L-shaped house features double porticoes on the south facade supported by four thirty-five-foot-tall Doric columns holding a massive pediment. Inside, each of the rooms has label-style woodwork done in virgin pine decorated in a different color. The scale of the rooms is immense—twenty-by-twenty-foot squares with twelve-foot ceilings containing double hung windows seven feet tall. It took over thirty-five yards of fabric to curtain and drape a single window! The original tongue-and-groove flooring was overlaid with oak boards in 1913. Though none of the furnishings belonged to the original owners, all of the pieces date from the 1820s to the 1870s and comprise a wide range of styles: Early Empire, Louis XV, and Gothic, Rococo, and Renaissance Revival.

Notable Collections on Exhibit

Lightburne Hall houses a rare collection of early 19th-century kerosene banquet lamps; in addition, the four flags of the Confederacy are on display, as are two first editions of *Gone With The Wind* and a copy of the life-size portrait of Scarlett O'Hara painted by Helen Carlton in 1939 which presently hangs in the Margaret Mitchell School in Atlanta.

Additional Information

Lightburne Hall is at the center of Liberty's Lightburne Historic District, established in 1985.

Home in the Ozarks, Laura Ingalls Wilder–Rose Wilder Lane Museum and Home

1 mile east of town
on U.S. Business 60
P.O. Box 24
Mansfield, MO 65704
(417) 924-3626

Contact: Laura Ingalls Wilder Home Association

Open: Apr. 1-Nov. 15, Mon.-Sat.
10 a.m.–4 p.m., Sun. 1:30.–4 p.m.

Admission: Adults $3.00; seniors and students $2.00; children (under 12) $1.00

Activities: Guided tours, enhancement lectures

Suggested Time to View House: 20 minutes

Facilities on Premises: Museum, bookstore and gift shop

Best Season to View House: Early fall

Description of Grounds: 4 acres with benches

Number of Yearly Visitors: 37,000

Number of Rooms: 10, 7 open to the public

Year House Built: First room in 1895, last room in 1913

Style of Architecture: National, farmhouse

On-Site Parking: Yes **Wheelchair Access:** Yes

Description of House

On a low rise which drops off into a ravine, framed by the lovely hills of the Ozarks, sits the wood frame house built by Laura Ingalls Wilder and her husband, Almanzo, when they moved to Mansfield from their farm in the Dakotas. The Wilders had one daughter, Rose, who convinced her mother to write down her reminiscences of life on the prairie as a child and young woman. These writings—based on her early experience—gained wide popularity and soon became one of the best-known and most-beloved series of children's books written in America, including titles like *Little House On The Prairie* and *By The Shores of Silver Lake*. Laura Ingalls Wilder died here in 1957.

This modest farmhouse was built by the Wilders out of timber harvested on their forty-acre farm, Rocky Ridge. The foundation was laid using rocks collected on the property in 1895 when the first room—a simple box structure—was built. A year later another room and attic were added; four second-story bedrooms followed and, finally, in 1913, a bath house. Most of the furnishings date from the late 1920s and were left in the house after Laura's death. Her kitchen features a wood stove, low baking cabinet, and a pass-through leading to the dining room. The upstairs is reached by climbing a small ladder. The living room is especially comfortable: three large windows that frame a corner sitting area, the ceiling showing exposed oak beams, and a fireplace made out of three native boulders all mirror the warmth of the home's former occupants. The Home in the Ozarks is listed on the National Register of Historic Places.

Notable Collections on Exhibit

The house is a wonderful small museum dedicated to the life and works of Laura Ingalls Wilder and her daughter, Rose; on view are many of their personal belongings, as well as five original hand-written manuscripts of the "Little House" books, family pictures, and Pa's fiddle.

Krause Mansion

Third and Ferrel Streets, P.O. Box 103
Platte City, MO 64079
(816) 431-3599

Contact: Platte County Historical Society, Inc.
Open: Apr.-Oct., Tues.-Sat. Noon–4 p.m.;
groups by appointment only
Admission: Adults $1.00; students to
grade 12 $.50
Activities: Volunteer docent tours, Victorian
Christmas Tours
Suggested Time to View House: 1 hour
Facilities on Premises: County archives and
genealogical library

Description of Grounds: Small city yard
with plantings
Best Season to View House: Late spring-late
fall
Number of Yearly Visitors: 5,000
Year House Built: 1882
Style of Architecture: Victorian Second
Empire
Number of Rooms: 12
On-Site Parking: Yes **Wheelchair Access:** No

Description of House

This small-scale replica of the Missouri Governor's Mansion in Jefferson City was built in 1882 by Frederick Krause, a native Prussian and prominent Platte County businessman who'd become friends with Governor Silas Woodson of St. Joseph. Krause served as the Missouri Ambassador to the World's Fair held in his homeland. In 1917, the house was sold to two-term Platte County Sheriff Thomas Perry and shortly thereafter his daughter turned the structure into a rooming house. In 1973 Mr. and Mrs. Charles Beals bought the house and converted it into a wood-working and ceramics shop. Four years later, the Platte County Historical Society and the Platte Purchase Chapter of the Daughters of the American Revolution bought the property with funds bequeathed to them for that purpose by Mr. Ben Ferrel.

This three-story brick house is built in the Victorian Second Empire style and features the typical mansard roof and ornate grillwork common to that style. The owner, Frederick Krause, owned and operated a brick-making plant and the lower level excavations show bricks fired from native clay. These brick walls were painted Venetian red—except for the west face which was never painted and has no windows—and the two porches were painted turquoise and gray. Inside, the house features a heavy wood-on-wood

German motif and the kitchen has a rare tongue-and-groove wood ceiling. Since its completion, the house has only seen three substantive alterations: the front entry is now a single glass door instead of two narrow wooden doors, the west bedrooms have had an archway cut between them, and a doorway was added between the kitchen and pantry giving access to the back porch. All of the furnishings on display are turn-of-the-century pieces donated by Platte County families.

Notable Collections on Exhibit

Three local families donated large collections of furniture including a five-piece parlor set and organ. There is an Interurban train exhibit downstairs and the lower level houses the County Archives Room and Platte County Genealogical Library Room.

Additional Information

The Krause Mansion was added to the National Register of Historic Places in 1977 and its restoration was completed in 1991.

Bothwell Lodge

Eight miles north of Sedalia on
U.S. Highway 65 and Route 4, P.O. Box 38B
Sedalia, MO 65301
(816) 827-0510

Contact: Bothwell State Park
Open: Mon.-Sat. 10 a.m.–4 p.m.,
  Sun. Noon–5 p.m.
Admission: Adults $1.25, children $.75
Activities: Guided tours, audiovisual
  presentations, special programs
Suggested Time to View House:
  30–45 minutes
Description of Grounds: Picnic area and
  hiking trail

Best Season to View House: Spring-fall
Number of Yearly Visitors: 49,000
Year House Built: 1897, additions in 1913,
  1922, 1928
Style of Architecture: Eclectic late
  Richardsonian Romanesque, stone
  "castle"
Number of Rooms: 38
On-Site Parking: Yes **Wheelchair Access:** Yes

Description of House

John Homer Bothwell—Sedalia lawyer, circuit judge, State Representative (1888-1923), and owner of the Sedalia National Bank—built this "castle" on a spectacular 120-foot bluff overlooking the Muddy Creek Valley some eight miles north of town. Bothwell went on to found the West St. Louis Water and Lighting Company and practice philanthropy by funding the Bothwell Memorial Hospital and building a school near this lodge.

This massive stone "get-away" lodge was built by Bothwell in four stages: the east wing, a relatively small structure begun in 1897 which included a living room, dining room, and three bedrooms; the west wing with its large and elaborate library; an addition onto this west wing done in 1922; and, finally, the addition of a large music room. Most of the lodge is really quite simple with unadorned plaster walls and wood floors, just three sets of French doors, and several other doors featuring beveled glass panes. When building the west wing, Bothwell tapped into a cave which he then used to provide ventilation for the whole house. The furnishings are mostly original pieces done in the American Arts & Crafts style; there are also many Persian and Oriental-style carpets, as well as three brass beds, and an overstuffed couch and chair made by the Pullman Company.

Additional Information

The Bothwell Lodge is located in the state park of the same name, on Highway 65 just north of Sedalia. Sedalia is a lovely town containing many superb examples of Victorian Queen Anne-style domestic architecture; it justly deserves the nickname, "The Queen City of the Prairie."

First Missouri State Capital State Historic Site

200 South Main Street
St. Charles, MO 63301
(314) 946-9282

Contact: Missouri Department of Natural Resources

Open: Year-round, daily; closed New Year's Day, Easter, Thanksgiving, Christmas

Admission: Adults (12 and up) $1.25; children (5 and over) $.75; group rates available

Activities: Guided tours, audiovisual presentations, graphic displays

Suggested Time to View House: 45–60 minutes

Description of Grounds: Old log cabin in the backyard with picnic tables

Best Season to View House: Spring, early summer and fall

Style of Architecture: Federal, brick row house

Number of Yearly Visitors: 35,000

Year House Built: Between 1818 and 1819

Number of Rooms: 9

On-Site Parking: No **Wheelchair Access:** No

Description of House

For five years and four months between 1820 and 1826, before Missouri's government moved to the new capitol in Jefferson City, this Federal-style row house in St. Charles served as the state's first capitol. At the time the building was jointly owned by Charles and Rulaff Peck—the upper floor of their section of the house served as meeting rooms for the Senate and the House of Representatives—and Chauncey Shepard. The second floor of Shepard's section housed the Governor's office and a committee room. The Peck brothers lived downstairs and ran a hardware-dry goods store in half of the building; Shepard lived in the other half of the first floor and is believed to have been a carpenter.

This brick house was built around 1818 and is furnished to reflect its appearance in the years when it served as Missouri's capitol. On display are many pieces in the Federal style, featuring both the American and European types, Hepplewhite and Sheraton. In addition, the house contains Empire-style pieces, Windsor chairs, and some simple country furniture.

Notable Collections on Exhibit

In the restored hardware store downstairs is a large collection of antique implements, tools, and other items typically offered for sale in such an establishment.

Additional Information

The First Missouri State Capitol State Historic Site is listed on the National Register of Historic Places.

Jesse James Home

Twelfth and Penn Streets
St. Joseph, MO 64502
(816) 232-8206

Contact: Pony Express Historical
Association, Inc.

Open: Daily 10 a.m.–4 p.m.; June–
Aug.10 a.m.–5 p.m.; Nov., Sat. and
Sun. only 1 p.m.–5 p.m.

Admission: Adults $1.00; students
(under 18) $.50

Activities: Audio tape

Suggested Time to View House: 20 minutes

Facilities on Premises: Gift shop

Description of Grounds: A gazebo, a
Victorian outhouse and graveyard

Best Season to View House: Summer- fall

Number of Yearly Visitors: 22,000

Year House Built: 1878

Number of Rooms: 4

Style of Architecture: National, frame

On-Site Parking: Yes **Wheelchair Access:** No

Description of House

Jesse James, and his older brother Frank, are perhaps America's best-known outlaws. Their fifteen-year crime spree, which followed on the heels of the Civil War, ended in this house when Robert Ford, a member of the James Gang, killed Jesse hoping to collect the $10,000 reward that had been put on his head by Missouri Governor T. T. Crittenden. The killing took place on April 3, 1882. Jesse, his wife, and their two children had only moved into the house the previous Christmas Eve—under the name of Howard.

Since the murder, the house has been moved several times: it originally stood on a high hill overlooking the Patee House, the hotel where Jesse's widow, children, and mother-in-law lived for a spell after his murder; it was moved to the belt highway in 1939 as a tourist attraction; and, finally, in 1977, it was purchased by Mr. and Mrs. Robert Keatley for the Pony Express Historical Association who returned it to its original site. The simple wood-frame house is noted for the famous bullet hole in the living room—today much enlarged by thousands of inquisitive fingers—and a spot on the wood floor where one of the house's owners once spilled chicken blood, then tore up the slats into splinters and sold them as souvenirs. The furnishings on display are all authentic period pieces and include some items which belonged to the Jameses.

Additional Information

The Jesse James Home is located adjacent to the Patee House Museum—then called the World's Hotel—a four-story, block-square hotel built in 1858 which served as headquarters for the Pony Express. The Patee House Museum has been designated a National Historic Landmark. The Jesse James Home is listed on the National Register of Historic Places. For a detailed look at the life of the James Gang, one should visit the James Farm and Museum in nearby Kearney (also listed in this guide).

Campbell House Museum

1508 Locust Street
St. Louis, MO 63103
(314) 421-0325

Contact: Campbell House Museum
Open: Tues.-Sat. 10 a.m.4 p.m., Sun.
Noon–5 p.m.; open months January and
February by appointment only; closed
national holidays
Admission: Adults $3.00; children
(under 12) $1.00; groups (25 or more)
$1.50; school groups free
Activities: Guided tours, teas with Mrs.
Campbell with advance reservations
Suggested Time to View House:
45–60 minutes
Facilities on Premises: Gift shop
Description of Grounds: Victorian gazebo
and garden, carriage house with original
family carriages
Best Season to View House: Spring and
summer
Number of Yearly Visitors: 5,000
Number of Rooms: 12

Style of Architecture: Greek Revival-style
town house
Year House Built: 1851
On-Site Parking: Yes **Wheelchair Access:** No

Description of House

Of the once-elegant St. Louis address Lucas Place, there is nothing left save this magnificent house built in 1851 by Robert Campbell. Campbell was an Irish immigrant who made his fortune in fur trading after commanding a brigade in the struggle against the Blackfeet Indians. With his money, he moved to St. Louis in the 1830s and became a highly-respected merchant and banker. During the Mexican War, he recruited four regiments of Missouri volunteers to serve under General Stephen Watts Kearney and earned the title "Colonel." In 1841, Campbell married native North Carolinian Virginia Kyle; the couple had thirteen children but only three survived to adulthood. As leading members of St. Louis' elite, the Campbells entertained many notable guests including the President and Mrs. Ulysses Grant, Jesuit Father De Smet, and Native American chieftains. Robert Campbell died in 1879 and his wife two years later; the last surviving child, Hazlett, lived here until his death in 1932.

The Campbells' Greek Revival-style townhouse was built in 1851 and has undergone virtually no major alterations since then; the furnishings— including a wonderful collection of Philadelphia Rosewood Rococo—date from the period between 1850 and 1880 and most of the pieces belonged to the family.

Additional Information

The Campbell House Museum is listed on the National Register of Historic Places.

Chatillon-DeMenil Mansion

3352 DeMenil Place
St. Louis, MO 63118
(314) 771-5828

Contact: DeMenil Mansion Board of Directors

Open: Wed.-Sat. 10 a.m.–4 p.m.; closed Christmas and New Year's Day

Admission: Adults $3.00; children $.50; group rate (20 or more) $1.50

Activities: Guided tour, video introductory presentation

Suggested Time to View House: 1 hour

Facilities on Premises: Museum gift shop and restaurant

Description of Grounds: Flower gardens enclosed by wrought-iron fence

Best Season to View House: Summer

Number of Yearly Visitors: 5,000

Year House Built: 1848, remodeled 1863

Style of Architecture: Greek Revival

Number of Rooms: 7

On-Site Parking: Yes **Wheelchair Access:** No

Description of House

Embodied in the personal histories of the occupants of the Chatillon-De-Menil Mansion is the history of St. Louis itself—the fur trading center established by Pierre Laclède Liguest which has grown into one of America's great cities. The mansion is built around a four-room brick farmhouse erected in 1848 by Henri Chatillon on a twenty-one-acre lot owned by his second wife, Odile, a wealthy widow and cousin. Chatillon's first wife had been Bear Robe, the daughter of Oglala Sioux Chief Bull Bear; she died in 1846 while Chatillon was out west acting as a scout for Francis Parkman, the famous American historian in whose book, *The Oregon Trail*, the French-Canadian hunter and trapper appears. In 1856, the Chatillons sold the house to banker Eugene Miltenberger and Dr. Nicholas N. DeMenil; within five years, Miltenberger had sold his share to the doctor who then rebuilt the entire house into the fine Greek Revival structure we see today. DeMenil was married to Emilie Sophie Chouteau, great granddaughter of Mme. Marie Thérèse Bourgeois Chouteau, the first white woman to settle in St. Louis and common-law wife to Pierre Laclède. The house stayed in the DeMenil family until 1929 when it became the residence of the family caretakers. It was later owned by Lee Hess, who used the house to store artifacts intended to be put on display in the Hess Museum, before being saved for demolition by the Landmarks Association of St. Louis and Union Electric.

The painted brick exterior of this fine two-story Greek Revival-style house features a gable front with fluted Ionic columns, second floor balconies accented with wrought-iron railings, pilasters highlighting the wings, dentils under the cornice molding, and six-over-six windows with flat lintels. Inside, one sees the original parquet floor in the hallway and superbly restored hand-painted stenciling around the cornices and chandelier in the drawing room. The split window frames on the second floor allow access to the balconies. Many of the furnishings have been donated by the DeMenil and Chouteau families—including a full bedroom set, "what-not" shelf, rosewood piano, Sheraton banquet table c. 1830, and a Rococo Revival-style rosewood settee c. 1855 attributed to Alexander Roux.

Notable Collections on Exhibit

In addition to the furnishings listed above, the house contains a "modesty" bootjack c. 1850, a silver-plated tea service manufactured by Reed & Barton, a "fainting couch" or Adelaide, a sterling silver epergne made by London silversmith Thomas Pitts in 1790, and two oil portraits painted in 1837 by George Caleb Bingham.

Additional Information

The Chatillon-DeMenil Mansion is listed on the National Register of Historic Places.

Eugene Field House

634 South Broadway
St. Louis, MO 63102
(314) 421-4689

Contact: Eugene Field House Foundation
Open: Wed.-Sat. 10 a.m.–4 p.m.,
Sun. Noon–4 p.m.
Admission: Adults $2.00; children
(under 12) $.50
Activities: Guided tours, special topic tours
with prior notice
Suggested Time to View House:
45–90 minutes
Facilities on Premises: Gift shop
Description of Grounds: City block
Best Season to View House: Spring and
summer
Style of Architecture: Romantic Greek
Revival-style row house
Number of Yearly Visitors: 15,000
Year House Built: 1845
Number of Rooms: 6

On-Site Parking: Yes **Wheelchair Access:** No

Description of House

It was in this St. Louis row house—one of the very earliest rental dwellings in the city—that Eugene Field, the well-known children's poet ("Wynken, Blynken, and Nod") and literary columnist, was born on September 3, 1850, to Roswell Martin Field and Frances Marie Redd. He was the second of six children and one of only two to have survived beyond infancy. Field, who married Julia Comstock in 1873 and had eight children of his own, moved to Chicago where he wrote his "personal" column and published verse. He died in that city in 1895.

Eugene Field's father, Roswell, was the lawyer who defended Dred Scott, the slave and household servant of St. Louis' Dr. John Emerson who sued for his freedom after being taken by his master to Illinois in 1834. It was argued that Scott's four years on free soil entitled him to full U. S. citizenship and freedom. The rejection of Scott's claims by the United States Supreme Court is frequently cited as one of the signal precursors to an inevitable Civil War.

Notable Collections on Exhibit

Among the many homely items on display is a collection of Julia's clothing and the bed in which Eugene Field died. In addition, there is a first-rate collection of antique dolls and toys dating from the 1830s on.

Additional Information

The Eugene Field House is listed on the National Register of Historic Places. The tour offered here which focuses on the Dred Scott Case and the history of St. Louis up to the Civil War is especially rewarding.

Grant's Farm and Cabin— "Hardscrabble"

10501 Gravois Road
St. Louis, MO 63123
(314) 843-1700

Contact: Anheuser-Busch, Inc.

Open: Apr.-May and Sept.-Oct., Thurs.-Sun.
9 a.m.–3 p.m.; May-Sept., Tues.-Sun.
9 a.m.–3 p.m.

Admission: Free

Activities: Guided tours of grounds
including exterior viewing of cabin

Facilities on Premises: Gift Shop and
Bavernhof Courtyard concession stand

Description of Grounds: 281 acre home and
game preserve of famous brewery family
including land from the former Grant farm

Best Season to View House: Early fall

Number of Yearly Visitors: 512,000

Year House Built: 1855

Style of Architecture: National-folk,
Southern-style log cabin

Number of Rooms: 4

On-Site Parking: Yes   **Wheelchair Access:** Yes

Description of House

In 1843 Lt. Ulysses S. Grant, recently graduated from West Point, came to St. Louis to serve with the Fourth U. S. Infantry. Grant's roommate at the Academy had been Frederick Tracy Dent, the son of wealthy St. Louis planter Colonel Frederick Dent; when Grant arrived in town, he looked up the Dents and presented himself to the family. One who particularly caught his eye—and who, for her part, seemed genuinely happy to be caught—was the Colonel's petite daughter, Julia. The two fell in love and, despite some prickliness in the matter of acquiring the Colonel's blessing, were married in the Dent family's St. Louis townhouse in 1848.

Some six years later, Grant left the Army—where his prospects seemed rather shallow—and began to farm an 80-acre parcel of land given to Julia by her father. In 1855, he decided to build a house of his own on the land; Grant himself cut, shaped, and notched the logs, split the shingles, and hauled the stones which would form the foundation. Then he invited his neighbors over for a cabin-raising. Once the foundation and frame were complete, he laid the floors, built the stairs, and finished the shingle roof. Carpenters were only brought in to frame out the windows and door, and make the window sashes. Calling their rough home "Hardscrabble," the Grants lived here until Julia's mother died and they moved in with her father. They owned the farm and cabin until 1884 when their financial situation forced them to sell the property to its mortgage holder, William H. Vanderbilt of New York. The house passed through the hands of several owners until it was bought by Adolphus Busch, founder of Anheuser-Busch, Inc., following its exhibition at the 1904 World's Fair held in St. Louis.

"Hardscrabble" is an unusual two-story, double-pen log cabin with a center entry, two chimneys at either end, and a hipped roof. Grant's hand-hewn logs are very heavily chinked. Today, most of the original rotting timber has been replaced by wood taken from a 19th-century barn. Anheuser-Busch has done a complete restoration of the property, including the erection of outbuildings and a kitchen garden to reflect the appearance of the farm in the mid-1850s when it was occupied by the Grants.

Samuel Cupples House and McNamee Gallery

University Mall and
3673 West Pine Boulevard
St. Louis, MO 63103
(314) 658-3025

Contact: Samuel Cupples House Foundation
Open: Tues.-Fri. Noon–4 p.m., Sun. 2–4 p.m.; closed all legal holidays
Admission: Adults $2.00; seniors and children (over 12) $1.00
Activities: Guided group tours by reservation
Suggested Time to View House: 1 hour
Facilities on Premises: House museum, art gallery

Description of Grounds: Small landscaped gardens surrounding house
Best Season to View House: Year round
Number of Yearly Visitors: 6,000
Year House Built: 1889
Style of Architecture: Victorian Richardsonian Romanesque
Number of Rooms: 42
On-Site Parking: Yes **Wheelchair Access:** No

Description of House

Samuel Cupples came from Pennsylvania to Missouri by way of Cincinnati; as a young man he worked at a wood products company in that city and was sent to establish a branch of the operation in St. Louis. Upon arriving in the burgeoning riverfront town, Cupples realized that he could make a fortune in the business by striking out on his own. Within a few years, his business had grown from a single warehouse to a complex of twenty-two warehouses known as Cupples Station located near the St. Louis railroad terminus; part of this complex survives to this day. Cupples practiced philanthropy on a grand scale, endowing hospitals, schools, and orphanages—his bequest of the entire Cupples Station to Washington University still forms a significant part of that school's endowment.

In 1889, Cupples hired the well-known local architect Thomas Annan to build as fine a house as money could buy. Annan designed this massive three-story mansion to be built out of stone in the Romanesque style pioneered by the great Boston architect Henry Hobson Richardson. It took two years and the staggering sum of $500,000 to build. The exterior is constructed of native pink granite and purple Long Mead sandstone from Colorado cut by craftsmen brought over from England expressly for that purpose and features two rounded towers with conical roofs flanking the main facade. The interior features exquisite woodwork throughout, twenty working fireplaces—many of which are decorated with intricate wrought-iron grillwork, and nine stained glass windows designed by Louis Comfort Tiffany. At the time of its completion the house was filled with furniture designed by Annan but now only one roomful of his pieces remain; the rest are purchased period antiques.

Notable Collections on Exhibit

Each room is decorated to reflect a different period: for example, the dining room is done in the French Empire style and includes pieces signed by Jacob de Smalter. Other styles on display include: Louis XV, Louis XVI Rococo and Empire, English Queen Anne, German Biedermeier, American Federal, Sheraton, and Victorian. In addition to these wonderful displays, there is a glass collection of over five hundred pieces, and a fine assemblage of small decorative objects rendered in jade, ivory, and rare woods.

Additional Information

The Samuel Cupples House and McNamee Gallery is listed on the National Register of Historic Places. When in St. Louis, one can view another building designed by Thomas Annan, the restored Dollar Building on Washington Avenue.

Tower Grove House

2101 Tower Grove, P.O. Box 299
St. Louis, MO 63166
(314) 577-5100

Contact: Missouri Botanical Garden
Open: Daily, 10 a.m.–4 p.m.; closed Thanksgiving, Christmas, month of January
Admission: Adults $2.00; children $.50; under 6 free; group rates available
Activities: Guided tours, special garden events
Suggested Time to View House: 30–45 minutes

Facilities on Premises: Tea Room by reservation only; Botanical Garden includes gift shop, restaurant, gardening center
Description of Grounds: Well maintained botanical gardens
Best Season to View House: Year round
Number of Yearly Visitors: 17,500
Year House Built: 1849
Style of Architecture: Italianate
Number of Rooms: 13
On-Site Parking: Yes **Wheelchair Access:** No

Description of House

Henry Shaw was born in Sheffield, England, in 1800, attended the Mill Hill School where he showed great talent in mathematics, visited London's Kew Gardens, and left school to travel with his father to Canada at the age of eighteen. He then traveled on alone to New Orleans to study the cotton business before heading up the Mississippi to St. Louis. Here Shaw sought to make his fortune in hardware; he took $3,000 given to him by an uncle and turned it into a vast personal fortune which enabled him to retire by age forty. In 1851, he moved into this "country house" and soon began work on the project which would engage him for the rest of his life—the development of the world-class Missouri Botanical Garden, often referred to as "Shaw's Garden." After his death in 1889, the house was used by successive Directors of the Garden, then turned into classrooms and dormitories for University of Washington School of Botany students. It was restored as house museum in 1953.

Shaw's Tower Grove House is a two-story brick structure done in the Italianate style and covered in white stucco. The characteristic feature of the house is the exaggerated central tower which gives it its name; it is presumed that this tower has its origins in English manor design, where the tower provides a vantage point from which the owner may survey all his property. Other exterior details include a small second-floor balcony with an elaborate wrought-iron railing, six-over-six-pane windows, and two pairs of full-height pilasters flanking the tower bay on the facade.The original east wing was replaced by a larger structure after Shaw's death to give the Garden's Director more living space. Rooms of note are the January Room (winter sleeping quarters), double parlors, Henry Shaw's fully restored bedroom, and the dining room. All of the rooms feature matching wallpaper and carpeting in popular Victorian designs. The house is furnished in period antiques.

Notable Collections on Exhibit

In addition to some splendid pieces of furniture, the house also contains a collection of rare "poesy holders," ranging from the quite plain to some set with semi-precious stones. A few of these holders have snap-out tripods and can be stood up when not being carried.

Additional Information

The Tower Grove House sits in the middle of the Missouri Botanical Garden, one of the great gardens in the world featuring an English maze, Japanese garden, Herbarium, and internationally renowned Library. The Garden is listed on the National Register of Historic Places.

Felix Valle House

198 Merchant Street, P.O. Box 89
Ste. Genevieve, MO 63670
(314) 883-7102

Contact: Felix Valle House State Historic Site

Open: Mon.-Sat. 10 a.m.–4 p.m., Sun. Noon–5 p.m.; closed New Year's Day, Easter, Thanksgiving and Christmas

Admission: Adults $2.50; children (6-12) $1.25; groups of 15 or more, $1.00 and $.50 respectively

Activities: Guided tours, special seasonal events

Suggested Time to View House: 45 minutes

Facilities on Premises: Book store

Description of Grounds: Fenced town lot with garden and several old boxwood bushes

Best Season to View House: Spring-fall

Number of Yearly Visitors: 14,000

Year House Built: 1818

Style of Architecture: Federal, stone

Number of Rooms: 8

On-Site Parking: No **Wheelchair Access:** No

Description of House

In 1808 the Philipson brothers traveled from Philadelphia to the Louisiana Territory and established a mercantile business in St. Louis. When Ste. Genevieve, the first permanent settlement in Missouri located some sixty miles south of St. Louis on the Mississippi, expanded its port facilities, one of the brothers, Jacob, established a trading firm there and built this house. In 1824, he sold his house to Jean Baptiste Valle, the town's commandant. Valle was descended from French-Canadians who had come to the Mississippi valley in the early 18th century; he had an interest in the Valle Mines and a partnership in Menard and Valle, a company which controlled most of the Indian trade in Missouri and Arkansas. Jean Baptiste's fourth son, Felix, took possession of the house and lived here with his wife, Odile, until he died in 1877. Felix was a prominent Ste. Genevieve businessman with interests in mining, the American Iron Mountain Company, and the Laclede Iron Works of St. Louis. Odile, a devout Catholic who lived here until 1894, is remembered as an active churchgoer.

This one-and-a-half-story limestone structure is an early example of a "mixed-use" building wherein a family residence is combined with a commercial space used to conduct a mercantile business. Thus the house features two front doors and double chimneys, one each for the home and one for the business. The Federal-style house has twelve-over-twelve windows on the lower level under the six-over-six-pane windows seen in the upper half-story. This type of house was a rarity in Ste. Genevieve, where most of the structures were built in the French or Spanish Colonial styles. The furnishings on display are in the American empire style of the period from 1820 to 1850; some of the pieces belonged to the Valle family.

Notable Collections on Exhibit

Hanging in the house are original portraits of Jean Baptiste Valle and his wife, Marie Jeanne Barbeau.

Additional Information

Ste. Genevieve is the oldest permanent white settlement in Missouri and it contains many fine historic structures. In addition to the Felix Valle House and the Maison Guibourd-Valle listed below, one should not miss the Vital Beauvais House, the Bolduc House, and the Amoureaux House (lost in the Flood of 1993) which present a fascinating portrait of the lives of the French and German immigrants who founded and built the town.

Maison Guibourd-Valle

Fourth and Merchant Streets
Ste. Genevieve, MO 63670
(314) 883-7102

Contact: Foundation for the Restoration of Ste. Genevieve

Open: May-Aug., daily 10 a.m.–4:30 p.m.; Apr., Sept., Oct. Noon–4 p.m.; Mar.- Nov. Sat. and Sun. Noon–4 p.m.; closed months of January and February

Admission: Adults $2.00; students $1.00; groups of 20 or more, $1.00 each

Activities: Guided tours, special seasonal events, annual Garden Dinner Theater

Suggested Time to View House: 30 minutes

Facilities on Premises: Gift shop

Description of Grounds: Large formal gardens enclosed by a brick wall

Best Season to View House: Summer

Number of Yearly Visitors: 3,000

Year House Built: c. 1785

Style of Architecture: Rural French Colonial

Number of Rooms: 5

On-Site Parking: No **Wheelchair Access:** No

Description of House

Though this house was built around 1785, the first recorded owner was Jacques Guibourd, about whom little is known except that he is thought to have died prior to 1844, the year that two of his sons returned to France. A third son, Eugene, remained in Ste. Genevieve and married Marie Therese St. Gemme. The couple had eight children, one of whom, Victorine, lived here until her death in 1903. In 1931, the house was purchased and restored by Jules Felix Valle; it was one of the first homes in historic Ste. Genevieve to be restored.

The house is a fine example of the rural French Colonial style; it is a one-and-a-half-story building featuring vertical log construction, a Norman-style truss roof, dual-pitched and hipped, and a raised front porch that opens directly onto the street. The furnishings are a combination of period pieces in the Louis XIV, XV, and XVI styles shown beside several oriental pieces belonging to Mr. and Mrs. Jules Valle.

Additional Information

The Maison Guibourd-Valle is listed on the National Register of Historic Places.

Mark Twain Birthplace State Historic Site

South of Florida on Route 107
P.O. Box 54
Stoutsville, MO 65283
(314) 565-3449

Contact: Missouri Department of Natural Resources

Open: Mon.-Sat. 10 a.m.–4 p.m., Sun. Noon–5 p.m.; New Year's Day, Easter, Thanksgiving, Christmas

Admission: Adults $2.00; children $1.25; group rates for student visitors

Activities: Guided tours with a reservation, audiovisual presentations

Suggested Time to View House: 45–60 minutes

Description of Grounds: Natural wooded area overlooking the Clarence Canon Dam with various recreational facilities

Best Season to View House: Fall

Facilities on Premises: Museum and souvenir counter

Style of Architecture: National-folk, oak frame

Number of Yearly Visitors: 25,000

Year House Built: 1835

Number of Rooms: 2

On-Site Parking: Yes **Wheelchair Access:** Yes

Description of House

In this simple frame structure in Florida, Missouri—some thirty miles west of Hannibal and the mighty Mississippi—Samuel Langhorne Clemens was born on November 30, 1835. When the Clemens family rented the two-room house it was one of the only frame houses in the settlement—all of the others were log dwellings; the family stayed here until 1839, then moved to Hannibal. Sam Clemens would, of course, become Mark Twain, the great American author and humorist, and the humble cabin is now preserved as a memorial to the life that inspired his work.

The cabin is framed in wood covered in clapboards; all of the lumber is native oak cut at a local mill. Despite its rustic simplicity, it features double-hung six-over-six-pane windows and a segmented light over the transom. None of the furniture in the house belonged to the Clemens family; that was first taken by them to their next residence in Hannibal, then auctioned off to raise money when the family went into bankruptcy. Nonetheless, all of the collected pieces are true to the region, period, and the family's economic and social status.

Notable Collections on Exhibit

The Mark Twain Birthplace State Historic Site is a modern museum featuring two distinct exhibits: the first is the cabin and its contents which depict the homely lives of the Clemens and Quarles families; the second is a gallery containing many artifacts pertaining to the adult Mark Twain, including manuscripts, furniture from his Hartford, Connecticut, home, and a reproduction of a Mississippi steamboat pilot's wheel.

Additional Information

The Mark Twain Birthplace State Historic Site is listed on the National Register of Historic Places. If viewed in conjunction with the author's boyhood home in Hannibal (which is also listed in this guide), perhaps one can see the genesis of many of his greatest writings.

Nebraska

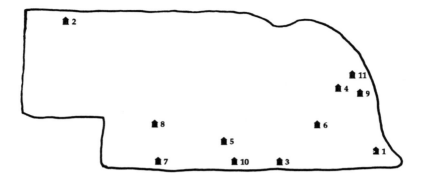

1. **Brownville**
   Carson House

2. **Chadron**
   Bordeaux Trading Post and Home

3. **Fairbury**
   Smith House

4. **Fremont**
   Theron Nye House–
   Louis E. May Museum

5. **Kearney**
   Frank House

6. **Lincoln**
   Home of William Jennings
   Bryan, "Fairview"
   Kennard House, Nebraska
   Statehood Memorial

7. **McCook**
   George W. Norris

8. **North Platte**
   Buffalo Bill Ranch House

9. **Omaha**
   General Crook House Museum

10. **Red Cloud**
    Willa Cather Childhood Home

11. **Tekamah**
    E.C. Houston House

Carson House

Contact: Brownville Historical Society
Open: June-Aug., daily 1–5 p.m.; May and Sept., Sat. and Sun. 1–5 p.m.
Admission: Adults $1.00; children $.50
Activities: Guided tours, special events including flea markets and a fall festival
Suggested Time to View House: 1 hour
Description of Grounds: Small yard and carriage house

Best Season to View House: Late spring-early fall
Number of Yearly Visitors: 1,500
Year House Built: 1860, additions 1861 and 1880
Style of Architecture: Italianate
Number of Rooms: 11
On-Site Parking: Yes **Wheelchair Access:** No

Description of House

The Carson House was built in 1860 for Richard Brown, eponymous founder of Brownville, who added a wing to it in 1861, then sold it three years later to John L. Carson. Carson was one of the leading bankers in southeastern Nebraska—founder of the Carson National Bank in nearby Auburn—and a leading citizen of this small town on the Missouri River. Although the Carson family left Brownville in 1882, they did not sell the house; instead, they maintained it for their use when visiting the town. The house was left to the Brownville Historical Society by John Carson's daughter Rose, who died in 1966. Much of its unique historic value is due to the fact that Rose Carson's will stipulated that the contents of the house were not to be altered or replaced. The Society has complied with her wishes; thus, one sees the original furnishings, floor coverings, drapes, dishes and kitchen equipment, and wallpaper on view.

The original one-story, four-room house built in 1860 for Richard Brown quickly proved too small for him; thus, one year later he added a two-story frame wing. Then, in 1880, the Carsons added a second wing, bringing the house to its present appearance.

Additional Information

The Carson House is listed on the National Register of Historic Places.

Bordeaux Trading Post and Home

East of Chadron on U.S. Highway 20
and HC 74, Box 18
Chadron, NE 69337
(308) 432-3843

Contact: Museum of the Fur Trade
Open: June–Sept., daily 8 a.m.–5 p.m.; other times by appointment
Admission: Adults $1.50
Activities: Self-guided tour with pamphlet
Suggested Time to View House: 60 minutes
Facilities on Premises: Gift shop and bookstore

Description of Grounds: Natural plains environment with Plains Indian garden a part of the Museum of the Fur Trade
Best Season to View House: Summer
Number of Yearly Visitors: 50,000
Year House Built: 1833
Style of Architecture: Folk, log with sod roof
Number of Rooms: 2
On-Site Parking: Yes **Wheelchair Access:** Yes

Description of House

The Bordeaux Trading Post—located on a scenic creek of the same name near the old Fort Pierre-Fort Laramie Trail—was owned and operated by the American Fur Company until 1849; at that time, it became an independent trading post and "wintering house" for the Brule Sioux operated by James Bordeaux. Bordeaux was a trader from St. Charles, Missouri; he ran the post until 1872 when it was occupied by Francis Boucher, son-in-law of the great Chief Spotted Tail of the Brule Sioux. When a squad of U. S. Calvary confiscated illegal ammunition here in the summer of 1876, Boucher abandoned the post. In 1955, the trading post was completely reconstructed on its original foundation with the assistance of descendants of both James Bordeaux and Francis Boucher.

The Bordeaux Trading Post is a rude structure dug into the side of a hill, built of large pine logs chinked with clay, and covered with a sod roof. Its fifteen-foot by twenty-seven-foot interior is divided into two rooms and interpreted to the period between 1840 and 1870. Furnishings include a wooden table, a bunk bed fashioned out of poles, trading blankets, and a buffalo robe.

Adjacent to the trading post—following tradition—lies a garden full of nearly extinct native crops such as: "Mandan tobacco," several varieties of midget corn, early beans, pumpkins, and squash. These crops reflect the common agriculture of the Sioux, Mandan, Hidatsa, and Omaha peoples.

Notable Collections on Exhibit

In addition to the furnishings, the trading post houses a collection of items which would have been offered for barter or sale to the native people as well as the area's pioneer settlers.

Additional Information

The Bordeaux Trading Post and Home is listed on the National Register of Historic Places. It is part of the Museum of the Fur Trade, which sits on the north edge of the Nebraska National Forest and Chadron State Park.

Smith House

Route 1
Fairbury, NE 68352
(402) 729-3000

Contact: Jefferson County Historical Society
Open: June-Aug., Sun. 2–4 p.m.
Admission: Free
Activities: Guided tours
Suggested Time to View House: 15 minutes
Description of Grounds: 2 acre tract
Best Season to View House: Summer
Number of Yearly Visitors: 200
Year House Built: c.1876, addition 1883
Style of Architecture: National, limestone
Number of Rooms: 8
On-Site Parking: Yes **Wheelchair Access:** No

Description of House

Woral C. Smith—nicknamed "Limekiln" for his profession—was born in Clinton County, New York, in 1841, learned the trade of burning lime from his father, Alonzo, then moved with his family to Wisconsin in 1860. During the Civil War, Woral volunteered for service with the Illinois Cavalry and was wounded in action. In 1865 he married native Pennsylvanian Phebe Anne Foreman in Osage County, Iowa; the couple's two sons were born there. Finally, in 1868, the family—including Alonzo—moved to this farm in Jefferson County and here Woral Smith built his kiln in 1874. The St. Joseph and Denver City Railroad ran a siding to the kiln and began shipping Smith's limestone products far and wide. In 1876, he built this house out of materials fired in his own kiln. He lived here with his two sons—both of whom helped in the business along with the hired hands—until his death in 1906. By that time, the limestone industry had declined, the kiln was shut down, and the family was relying on farming for its sustenance.

The original two-story limestone structure was built in two parts: the first part was the two-story structure facing the railroad tracks built in 1876; the addition of 1883 consisted of a two-story rear wing. The house features unusual retaining walls, two "patios" located on either side of the main structure, small four-over-four windows, piped-in spring water, and a ridge line just below the second story which clearly shows that there was once a partial wrap-around porch here. Old photographs confirm that the porch had Victorian spindlework and incised brackets. The furnishings—all from the same period as the house—include two wooden beds, one iron bed, and a cane-bottomed straight chair.

Notable Collections on Exhibit

There is an informative exhibit here relating the history of the lime-burning industry and Jefferson County's numerous historical sites.

Additional Information

The Smith House is listed on the National Register of Historic Places.

Theron Nye House– Louis E. May Museum

1643 North Nye Avenue
Fremont, NE 68025
(402) 721-4515

Contact: Dodge County Historical Society
Open: Mar.-Dec., Tues.-Sat. 1–5 p.m.; closed Thanksgiving, Christmas
Admission: Adults $2.00; children (13-18) $.50; children (12 and under) free
Activities: Guided tours, exhibits,special seasonal events including the October Homesteader's Fair, and Victorian Christmas
Suggested Time to View House: 1 hour
Facilities on Premises: Gift shop, bookstore, research library

Description of Grounds: Half a block of formal landscaped Victorian gardens with gazebo
Best Season to View House: Summer
Number of Yearly Visitors: 4,000-5,000
Year House Built: 1874, addition 1885, remodeled 1901 and 1910
Style of Architecture: Obscured Italianate style combined with Eclectic Colonial Revival and Neoclassical
Number of Rooms: 30
On-Site Parking: Yes **Wheelchair Access:** Yes

Description of House

Theron Nye came to Fremont one year after the town's founding in 1857 and quickly established himself in a number of enterprises: grain, lumber, and coal. It was in grain that he found his fortune: ultimately Nye, who served as Fremont's first mayor, became president of the Nye, Schneider and Fowler Company, the owners and operators of over two hundred grain elevators throughout the Midwest. He built this splendid mansion in 1874; it was inherited by his son Ray in 1901, then given to the Midland College Western Theological Seminary twenty years later. It was used as a dormitory and classrooms for the school until 1967. The house now serves as the Dodge County Historical Society's museum through funds given by the Louis E. May Trust.

The mansion is built of red brick with wood trim painted white and features a massive full-facade entry porch with six fluted Ionic columns answered in the rear by a row of Ionic pilasters. The first floor fenestration—rectangular windows with pediments and brackets—recalls the Italianate style; on the front facade the windows are arranged in multiple groupings. Inside details include two sun rooms—one each on the first and second floors, heavily-carved oak and mahogany paneling on the staircase and walls, several superb carved mantels, art glass windows, and elaborate tile work in the master bath. Each of the rooms is interpreted to a different decade in the life of the house; for example, there are the 1870s Parlor, 1880s Sitting Room, 1890s Kitchen, and the 1880s Bedroom. The furnishings are appropriate to the periods of the rooms; most of the pieces are in the Victorian-Eastlake, Louis XIV, and Colonial Revival styles.

Notable Collections on Exhibit

The collections here focus on the history of Fremont and Dodge Counties.

Additional Information

The Theron Nye House-Louis E. May Museum is listed on the National Register of Historic Places.

Frank House

2010 West Twenty-fourth Street
Kearney, NE 68847
(308) 234-8282

Contact: University of Nebraska at Kearney
Open: June-Aug., daily 1–5 p.m.; other times for group tours by appointment only
Admission: $2.00 per person
Activities: Guided tours, special seasonal programs
Suggested Time to View House: 30 minutes
Description of Grounds: On-going restoration

Best Season to View House: Spring and fall
Number of Yearly Visitors: 2,500
Year House Built: 1889
Style of Architecture: Eclectic mix of Richardsonian Romanesque and Shingle Style
Number of Rooms: 42, only first floor rooms are open to the public
On-Site Parking: Yes **Wheelchair Access:** Yes

Description of House

George Washington Frank was a banker in Iowa who came to Nebraska and started the Frank Improvement Company, a contracting firm responsible for building and maintaining canals, electric street railways, and an area power plant. He commissioned his architect son, G. W. Frank, Jr., to build this imposing mansion so he could entertain Eastern businessmen and convince them to invest in his town. Ultimately, Frank's enterprises went bankrupt and he was forced to sell the mansion to Dr. and Mrs. O. Grothan, who used it as a clinic. At one point, it even served as the staff residence for the Tuberculosis Hospital.

G. W. Frank, Jr., designed his father's house in the Shingle style of Henry Hobson Richardson and built it out of sandstone quarried in Wyoming. The Romanesque interior of this three-story house features six of its nine original fireplaces, oak paneling and woodwork, a stained glass window from the studio of Louis Comfort Tiffany, pocket doors on the first floor, elaborate stenciling, and beveled window glass. It also boasts some very modern conveniences: two bathrooms, steam heat, built-in closets, and electrical wiring. All of the period furnishings have been donated; pieces include a

19th-century French Provincial bedroom suite, Chippendale chairs, and an Early American dining room set.

Restoration of the Frank House was begun in 1974—many of the interior elements have been returned to their former glory—and still proceeds. Soon the porte cochere and veranda will be ready for viewing.

Notable Collections on Exhibit

There are many fine examples of decorative art on display in the home, including: Sheffield, Rogers, and Reed silver plate appointments, Chinese embroideries, a hand-blown Venetian glass chandelier, and a Meissen candelabra.

Additional Information

The Frank House is listed on the National Register of Historic Places. In nearby Minden, located twelve miles south of Exit 279 off Route 80, is the Harold Warp Pioneer Village. Built by Harold Warp, the son of Nebraska homesteaders, the village consists of several buildings which contain historic artifacts dating to the 1830s. In addition to these buildings—the 1889 Baldwin & Lowell Depot, the 1869 Elm Creek Indian Fort, and the original Pony Express station are especially worthy—the largest single collection of antique automobiles in the United States may also be seen here.

Home of William Jennings Bryan– "Fairview"

4900 Summer Street
Lincoln, NE 58606
(402) 483-3721

Contact: Bryan Memorial Hospital
Foundation
Open: House is undergoing restoration; call
for information
Description of Grounds: City lot
Best Season to View House: Spring and
early fall
Year House Built: 1903
Style of Architecture: Late Victorian Queen
Anne with elements of several early
revival styles
Number of Rooms: 25

Description of House

The veteran Nebraska politician and populist William Jennings Bryan (1860-1925) was called "The Great Commoner" and "the Boy Orator of the Platte." He ran for President of the United States three times—in 1896, 1900, and 1908—and failed three times, but he did serve as Secretary of State under President Woodrow Wilson from 1913 to 1915. Bryan's long and fruitful public career ended rather ignominiously at the infamous Scopes trial in which he was pitted against defense attorney Clarence Darrow.

"Fairview" is an asymmetrical, three-story Queen Anne-style house with a partial wrap-around porch and dominating off-center tower. The original floor plan had the family's living quarters and Bryan's study on the lower level; a large reception area, front parlor, and William Bryan, Jr.'s bedroom and bath on the main floor; and the rest of the family's bedrooms upstairs. When the restoration of "Fairview" is complete, the lower level will serve as a museum and interpretive center, the main floor will appear as it did during the years of Bryan's occupancy, and the upstairs will serve as The Center for Advanced Nursing Practice. All of the finishes will accurately reflect the appearance of the house when it was built. The Bryan Memorial Hospital is working closely with the Nebraska State Historical Society to insure that the restoration is historically accurate.

Kennard House– Nebraska Statehood Memorial

1627 H Street
Lincoln, NE 68501
(402) 471-4764

Contact: Nebraska State Historical Society

Open: Year-round, Tues.-Sat.
9 a.m.–4:30 p.m., Sun. 1:30–5:00 p.m.;
closed Veteran's Day, Thanksgiving,
Christmas, New Year's Day

Admission: Adults $1.00; children (under
18) free; groups of 20 or more $.50 each

Activities: Guided tours

Suggested Time to View House:
30–45 minutes

Description of Grounds: Present corner lot
with shrubs and trees surrounded by
white picket fence

Best Season to View House: Summer

Number of Yearly Visitors: 7,000

Year House Built: 1869

Style of Architecture: Italianate

Number of Rooms: 8

On-Site Parking: No

Wheelchair Access: No

Description of House

When this superb example of those Italianate-style homes which were popular during the pioneer days of early Nebraska—one of only three such structures still standing in all of Lincoln—was threatened with demolition in 1965, the state legislature, realizing the importance of the property, voted to designate the house as the "Nebraska State Memorial." It was then restored and refurnished by the Nebraska State Historical Society. In addition to being the home of Thomas Perkins Kennard, Nebraska's first Secretary of State, the house also represents the struggle to name Lincoln the state capital—it was literally built in defiance of those who opposed such an action.

Kennard, a native Ohioan who moved to Nebraska with his brother Levi in 1858, was a successful Lincoln lawyer and businessman who became deeply involved in the politics of the territory and, later, the newly admitted state, serving as Secretary of State and state legislator. In 1869, the year of capital controversy, he commissioned Chicago architect John Keyes Winchell to design and build this house, one of only three to make up the fledgling city of Lincoln. Winchell also designed the Governor David Butler House and the John Gillespie House in Lincoln, as well as the Lincoln State Asylum.

Kennard married Livia Emily Templeton of Indiana and the couple had three children. When Mrs. Kennard died in 1887, the family moved out of the house but remained in the neighborhood. Mr. Kennard died in 1920 in a house on the corner of H and 17th Streets. Before being taken over by the state, the Kennard House was a boarding house, a fraternity house, and a single-family home. Even though the restoration is still in progress—the goal is to return the mansion to its earliest appearance and there have been many remodelings over the years—the great beauty of its lines is clearly in evidence.

Notable Collections on Exhibit

In addition to the 1870s furnishings on display, many pieces of which came from the original Governor's Mansion, there is also a flatware collection from the Kennard and Pound families, and a set of wooden cups which belonged to Robert W. Furnas, Nebraska's second governor.

Additional Information

The Kennard House is listed on the National Register of Historic Places.

George W. Norris

706 Norris Avenue
McCook, NE 69001
(308) 345-5293

Contact: Nebraska State Historical Society
Open: Year-round, Wed.-Sat. 10 a.m.–Noon, Tues. and Sun. 1:30–5 p.m.
Admission: Adults $1.00; children $.25
Activities: Guided tours, special seasonal events, on-going period quilt exhibition
Suggested Time to View House: 30 minutes
Facilities on Premises: Gift shop located across the street in park
Best Season to View House: Summer
Description of Grounds: Small town yard with plantings
Number of Yearly Visitors: 3,000
Number of Rooms: 8

Style of Architecture: Early Eclectic Period Revival, Tudor half-timbered
Year House Built: 1886, remodeled 1931
On-Site Parking: Yes **Wheelchair Access:** No

Description of House

George W. Norris, who served in the U. S. House of Representatives (1902-1912) and Senate (1912-1942), is best known as one of the organizers of the Tennessee Valley Authority and as a key figure in the establishment of the Rural Electrification Administration, the 20th Amendment to the Constitution, and Nebraska's Unicameral Legislature. His biography is featured in John F. Kennedy's book, *Profiles in Courage.*

This two-story gray stucco house set amid an impressive stand of American elms was built in 1886 and purchased by Norris in 1899. Norris gave the house a thorough remodeling in 1931; at that time, the entry and oak staircase, the sun room, and the fireplace were all added to the front of the house. He also rearranged the rooms on the second floor so each of the three bedrooms would have its own bathroom, a rarity back then. Most of the interior walls are covered in an ivory striped moiré wallpaper common for the era; interior details include white wooden cornices upstairs, hardwood floors covered with fourteen Oriental rugs, and plywood paneling with oak trim in the sun room.

When the Norris family gave the house to Nebraska in 1968, all of the original furnishings came with it; these include some antiques, mostly from the period 1910 to 1940.

Notable Collections on Exhibit

The house contains Oriental rugs, Royal Worchester and Limoges china, and memorabilia from Norris's many years in Washington, D.C.

Additional Information

The George W. Norris House is listed on the National Register of Historic Places. One block south of the Norris House is the only house in Nebraska to have been designed by Frank Lloyd Wright. It was built in 1906 and remains a private residence.

Buffalo Bill Ranch House

Routes 1 and 97 North, P.O. Box 229
North Platte, NE 69101
(308) 535-8035

Contact: Buffalo Bill Ranch State Historical Park

Open: Apr.-Memorial Day and Labor Day-Nov., Mon.-Sat. 9 a.m.–5 p.m., Sun. 1–5 p.m.; Memorial Day to Labor Day, daily 10 a.m.–8 p.m.

Admission: $2.50 per car

Activities: Hourly movie with original film clippings of Buffalo Bill Cody and his Wild West Show

Suggested Time to View House: 1 hour

Best Season to View House: Summer

Number of Yearly Visitors: 36,000

Facilities on Premises: Gift shop and bookstore, trail rides and cookouts, special seasonal programs

Description of Grounds: 25 acre state park containing William Cody's Victorian home, barn and several outbuildings. Buffalo graze nearby.

Year House Built: 1886, remodeled 1909

Style of Architecture: Eclectic mix of late Italianate, Victorian Queen Anne and Second Empire styles

Number of Rooms: 18

On-Site Parking: Yes **Wheelchair Access:** No

Description of House

In 1886, at the height of his success as America's Wild West showman, the "last of the great scouts," Colonel W. F. "Buffalo Bill" Cody, contracted Patrick Walsh to build a grand house with large porches here, on a 4,000-acre ranch in North Platte called "Scout's Rest." Bill, who had already packed many lifetimes of experience into his forty years, would live for twenty-five years on his beloved ranch when not touring the world with his Wild West Exposition. In 1911, foolish financial ventures brought him near ruin and he was forced to sell off large portions of his land to William "Pawnee Bill" Lillie, one of his partners in the show. In 1913, the Codys moved to Wyoming; and, in 1917, Buffalo Bill died in Denver.

The house that Walsh built for Cody—designed by Cody's sister, Julia Goodman—was a two-story, nine-room structure with a third-story lookout and extended two-story bay. Cody insisted that the house contain a parlor, a bedroom with an adjoining bathroom, and over-sized porches—he said that there was "nothing finer than a large porch"—decorated with elaborate Eastlake spindlework. In 1909, it was given an addition of nine more rooms, electricity, indoor plumbing, and a furnace. The wallpaper currently seen in the dining room is a reproduction of the original which depicts scenes from the Wild West Exposition. Most of the furnishings on display are in the Victorian Eastlake style; several of them belonged to the Codys.

Notable Collections on Exhibit

Displayed in the ranch house are many photographs, paintings, and other memorabilia of Buffalo Bill and his Wild West Exposition.

General Crook House Museum

Thirtieth and Fort Streets at
Metro Community College
Omaha, NE 68111
(402) 455-9990

Contact: Historical Society of Douglas County

Open: Year-round, Mon.-Fri. 10 a.m.–4 p.m., Sun. 1–4 p.m.; closed Sat. and major holidays; other times by appointment

Admission: Adults $3.50; children $1.50; groups rates available through reservation

Activities: Docent and self-guiding tours, audiovisual introduction, "living history" demonstrations and special seasonal events

Suggested Time to View House: 45–60 minutes

Facilities on Premises: Museum shop, library/archives center

Description of Grounds: 1880s restored Victorian home and gardens located at Historic Fort Omaha

Best Season to View House: Spring-fall

Number of Yearly Visitors: 12,000

Year House Built: 1878

Style of Architecture: Italianate

Number of Rooms: 11

On-Site Parking: Yes **Wheelchair Access:** Yes

Description of House

General George Crook, who gained fame during the Civil War as one of Phil Sheridan's corps commanders in the Shenandoah Valley campaign, later became one of the U. S. Army's premier Indian fighters. He twice commanded the Department of the Platte, fought the Sioux, led an expedition against the Chiricahua Apache, persuaded Geronimo to surrender, won a promotion to the rank of major general, and ended his career as commander of the Division of Missouri. Crook, who was considered by his Native American adversaries an honorable man who understood them, died in 1890.

This elegant house—now fully restored—was built in 1878 to serve as the residence for the commander of the Department of the Platte. Originally called Quarters One, it became known as the Crook House shortly after the General and his wife moved in. Here, in November 1879, the couple hosted former President and Mrs. Grant—their furnishings had not yet arrived, so all of the furniture, china, and silver had to be borrowed from area residents—and the following year, they entertained President and Mrs. Rutherford B. Hayes.

The Crook House is a two-story Italianate-style brick structure—it is one of the only examples of this style of architecture in Omaha—and features bay windows, paired and tripled window treatments, and a full-width front porch with intricate incised brackets. Inside, there are high-ceilinged rooms, elaborately-patterned wallpaper, the original oak and walnut flooring, and wide moldings. The house was designed around the reception room; the need to entertain large parties was perhaps the most important consideration in laying out the floor plan. Most of the furnishings here are Eastlake-style pieces dating from the 1880s.

Notable Collections on Exhibit

General Crook was an avid sportsman and taxidermist who also collected birds' nests and butterflies—collections on display here attest to all of these passions. Also on display are paintings by John Ross Key, the official painter of the Trans-Mississippi Exposition (1898).

Additional Information

The General Crook House Museum is listed on the National Register of Historic Places. The trial of Ponca Chief Standing Bear took place at Fort Omaha—as reported by John C. Neihardt, Nebraska's Poet Laureate, the decision was a landmark in that it declared "that the Indian was legally a Person and therefore had the same rights under the law as a white man."

Willa Cather Childhood Home

245 Cedar Street
on the corner of Third Street
Red Cloud, NE 68970
(402) 746-3285

Contact: Willa Cather House and Historical Center

Open: May 1-Sept. 30, Mon.-Fri. 8 a.m.–Noon, 1–5 p.m., Sat. and Sun. 1–5 p.m.; closed Monday rest of the year, Thanksgiving, Christmas, New Year's Day

Admission: Adults $1.00; children with an adult free

Activities: Guided tours, annual Christmas Open House

Suggested Time to View House: 20 minutes

Facilities on Premises: Books for sale at Farmers' and Merchants' Bank

Description of Grounds: Picket fence surrounding yard

Best Season to View House: Summer

Number of Yearly Visitors: 5,000-6,000

Year House Built: c. 1879

Style of Architecture: Rural Greek Revival

Number of Rooms: 6 plus attic

On-Site Parking: Yes **Wheelchair Access:** No

Description of House

Virginia-born Willa Cather, the Pulitzer Prize-winning author whose novels and stories of America's great western plains are considered by many the truest and most moving depictions we have of the effect of that landscape on its inhabitants, moved with her parents to Nebraska and lived in this house in Red Cloud from 1884 to 1890. She left Red Cloud when she was seventeen years old. Her parents, Charles and Mary Virginia Cather, lived on here until 1904, when they moved to a house at Sixth and Seward Streets. Her days here formed her as a writer—Red Cloud figures in six of Cather's novels—whose novels *O Pioneers, My Antonia,* and *Death Comes for the Archbishop* would win her worldwide fame.

The house is a modest one-and-a-half-story Greek Revival-style structure with a gabled roof, upright frame, and north wing. The front facade features three bays asymmetrically placed and a Victorian porch. Inside, one sees Cather's attic bedroom exactly as it appeared when she lived here—even the wallpaper is original—and other details which are described in her books: slanted parlor doors, high ceilings, Grandma Book's bedroom, and several pieces of furniture that belonged to the family.

Notable Collections on Exhibit

In addition to the furnishings mentioned above, one may also see Willa Cather's collection of shells and rocks and the Bible in which she altered her birthdate.

Additional Information

The Willa Cather Historical Center is a branch museum of the Nebraska State Historical Society. The other five branches are: Farmers' and Merchants' Bank Headquarters, Burlington Depot, Grace Episcopal Church, St. Juliana Falconieri Roman Catholic Church, and Pavelka Farmhouse. All are listed on the National Register of Historic Places; the houses have also been designated National Historic Landmarks.

E.C. Houston House

319 North Thirteenth Street
Tekamah, NE 68061
(402) 374-1505

Contact: Burt County Museum, Inc.
Open: Year-round, Tues., Thur. and Sat.
1–5 p.m.
Admission: Free, contributions encouraged
Activities: Guided tours, special events
during Memorial Day, the Fourth of July,
Labor Day weekend and the month of
December
Suggested Time to View House: 1 hour
Facilities on Premises: Gift shop with small
book store
Description of Grounds: Nice landscaping
with gazebo and one room country
school
Best Season to View House: Spring-fall
Number of Yearly Visitors: 4,000-5,000
Year House Built: 1904
Number of Rooms: 14

Style of Architecture: Eclectic Neoclassical
On-Site Parking: Yes **Wheelchair Access:** Yes

Description of House

This fine house was built in 1904 for E. C. Houston, the founder and owner of the Houston Lumber Company in Tekamah and nearby Herman. He also served as the vice president of the First National Bank for over twenty years. Two other families lived here before the Burt County Museum purchased it in 1985 for $65,000.

Although the massed geometry of the house suggests the Victorian Queen Anne style, the detailing—porch supports, trim, door and window treatments, cornices, and railings—is strictly in the Neoclassical Revival. Some of the features include: leaded-glass windows, a full wrap-around porch, a large bay window sitting area, and a characteristic third-floor ballroom. Each of the rooms currently reflects a different period in the life of the house, but the museum is drawing plans to redecorate within the next few years.

Notable Collections on Exhibit

Many fascinating objects are on display, including: a sugar bowl that came to America on the Mayflower, a painting of the Last Supper c. 1700, an example of the first portable typewriter (1893), a magic lantern c. 1880, a charcoal iron used in the late 19th century, and a dentist's chair and cabinet c. 1900.

Additional Information

The E. C. Houston House is listed on the National Register of Historic Places.

North Dakota

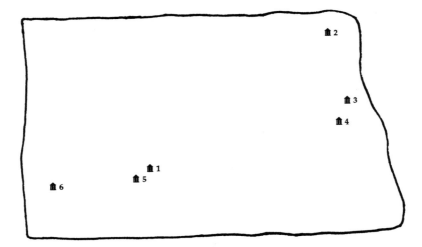

1. **Bismarck**
   Former Governors' Mansion

2. **Cavalier**
   Gunlogson Homestead and Arboretum

3. **Grand Forks**
   Thomas D. Campbell House

4. **Hatton**
   Eielson-Osking House

5. **Mandan**
   Custer Home at Fort Abraham Lincoln State Park

6. **Medora**
   Theodore Roosevelt's Maltese Cross Cabin

Former Governors' Mansion

320 Avenue "B" East
Bismarck, ND 58505
(701) 224-2666

Contact: State Historical Society of North Dakota

Open: May 16-Sept. 15, Wed.-Sun 1–5 p.m.; other times by appointment

Admission: Donation

Activities: Guided tours, audiovisual presentations, seasonal programs including annual lawn party

Suggested Time to View House: 45–90 minutes

Best Season to View House: Late summer

Facilities on Premises: Related material on history and restoration of mansion for sale

Description of Grounds: ½ acre corner lot located in city residential area with lawn, flower beds, scrubs and large shade trees. Carriage house.

Number of Yearly Visitors: 3,000

Year House Built: 1884

Style of Architecture: Victorian Stick Style

Number of Rooms: 12

On-Site Parking: No **Wheelchair Access:** No

Description of House

On hills overlooking the Missouri River lies the state capital of Bismarck, North Dakota. Once the land of ancient peoples, this Dakota territory was the object of exploration by Lewis and Clark, and later by the Northern Pacific Railroad. Named after the First Chancellor of the German Empire, Prince Otto von Bismarck, the town itself was established in the early 1870s as a labor camp for railroad workers. It soon became a hub of commerce whose merchants sold supplies, services, and transportation to those who sought their fortune in Black Hills gold. By the time North Dakota became a state in 1883, Bismarck had become the center of government.

The Former Governor's Mansion was originally owned by Bismarck businessman, Asa O. Fisher; it was built in 1884 for his wife and daughter. This example of the unique Stick Style—an architectural style which combines the best of the "picturesque" Gothic Revival and the Queen Anne—features a steep, multi-gable roof, a partial front-facade porch and a second-level recessed porch, overhanging eaves, and a two-story side bay extension. Perhaps the most unusual characteristic of this house is the highly decorative detailing most notably seen in the patterned shingling, the exaggerated horizontal and vertical section bands, the segmented porch supports, and the repetition of the flower-and stem motif found in the trusswork, the front entry pediment, and the front porch wood foundation.

The house was purchased by the state in 1893 for the sum of $5,000 and subsequently used as the governor's residence until 1960. From 1960 until 1975, the mansion served as office space for the State Health Department. Finally in 1975, the State Historical Society assumed control of the house, and a complete restoration began. The Former Governor's Mansion was restored to its appearance of the 1893 period with the removal of a window c. 1908 and a two-story screened porch c. 1919. Interior rooms were restored to various periods with the aid of documentation. The mansion is listed on the National Register of Historic Places.

Notable Collections on Exhibit

For those visitors interested in historic preservation, there are exhibits showing the many paint and wallpaper layers, as well as the original wall construction techniques used in the house.

Additional Information

Not far from the Bismarck-Mandan area, and located near Stanton are two important prehistoric sites—the Knife River Indian Villages National Historic Site and the Fort Clark State Historic Site. The former is comprised of three villages—Hidatsa, Awatixa, and Xi'e Awatixa—all of which offer interpretive tours, and exhibits on the history and culture of the Mandan and other Dakotan tribes.

Gunlogson Homestead and Arboretum

Icelandic State Park off
U.S. Highway 81 West
Cavalier, ND 58220
(701) 265-4561

Contact: North Dakota Parks and
Recreation Department

Open: Mid May-Labor Day, daily 1–5 p.m.

Admission: $3.00 per car

Activities: Guided tours, annual Heritage
Day Festival

Suggested Time to View House: 30 minutes

Facilities on Premises: Pioneer Heritage
Center with gift shop and book store

Description of Grounds: Turn-of-the-
century homestead located in a nature
preserve setting with several outbuildings
including a barn, and a granary

Best Season to View House: Late spring
and early summer

Number of Yearly Visitors: 10,000

Year House Built: Started 1882, completed
1890, addition 1921

Style of Architecture: National,
Icelandic-style frame

Number of Rooms: 6

On-Site Parking: Yes **Wheelchair Access:** Yes

Description of House

From their native land of Iceland, Eggert and Rennveig Gunnlaugsson
came to North America—first to Canada, then to the Dakota Territory—in
1876. The couple farmed a plot of land near Husey for a spell but failed
crops, near-starvation, and the death of their infant son forced them to flee
their home. By 1880, they settled on a 160-acre plot on the banks of the
Tongue River; they called their new homestead, "Tunguá." Here the
Gunnlaugssons (now Gunlogson) prospered despite the loss of two other
children. They raised cows, sheep, hogs, and chickens, and were able to
afford a team of horses. Five of their children survived to adulthood. Loa,
a daughter born in 1890, lived most of her life at the homestead spending
only the harsh winter months in town. Her skill as a carpenter can be seen
in the construction of the summer kitchen and some of its furniture.

The Gunnlaugsson family's first home was a log cabin built to meet their
immediate needs. Two years later, Eggert constructed a multi-story wood frame
house with an attached kitchen—one of the first such houses in the territory.
The house was painted white with gray trim, and featured such "luxuries" as
glass pane windows, decorative wood shingles, and two doors! It was inhabited by two generations and still contains all of their furnishings and items
brought from Iceland, such as the family Bible, a ship's clock, and several bone
spoons and sugar cutters. The period of interpretation spans from 1883 to 1983.

Additional Information

The Pioneer Heritage Center is dedicated to all pioneers who settled in
North Dakota.

Thomas D. Campbell House

2405 South Belmont Road
P.O. Box 5096
Grand Forks, ND 58201
(701) 775-2216

Contact: Grand Forks County Historical
  Society
Open: May-Sept., daily 1–5 p.m.
Admission: Adults $3.00; seniors $2.50;
  children $1.50
Activities: Guided tours, annual Ice Cream
  Social
Suggested Time to View House: 1 hour
Facilities on Premises: Gift shop
Description of Grounds: Complex includes
  five buildings-the Campbell House and
  Carriage House, the Myra Museum, the
  1870 Log Cabin Post Office and the 1907
  One Room School House
Best Season to View House: Late spring
  and summer
Number of Yearly Visitors: 2,000
Number of Rooms: 7

Style of Architecture: Original-log cabin,
  addition-Folk Victorian farmhouse
Year House Built: 1879, addition 1900
On-Site Parking: Yes **Wheelchair Access:** Yes

Description of House

General Thomas Campbell, Jr., was born to Thomas and Almira Campbell, a couple of modest means, in the frontier town of Grand Forks. Imbued with the enterprising spirit seen in his pioneer parents, Campbell went on to purchase over 95,000 acres of land in the Red River Valley of Montana; he converted the prairie to wheat fields and operated a large cattle ranch in New Mexico. Known as "The Wheat King of America," Campbell was often called upon by international agencies for advice on farming operations. In the 1930s and 1940s, he became a consultant to both the Soviet and British governments, and authored the book *Russia–Market or Menace*. He died in 1966.

This simple Folk Victorian structure was constructed in two stages. The original log cabin was built by the senior Campbell in 1879; the wood frame addition was built by a later tenant in 1900, at which time the log cabin was covered with white clapboard. The final result was a gable-front-and-wing-design building with a full-width front porch and variegated design verge-boards. The Campbell House has been restored to its appearance of the late 1800s and early 1900s. American vernacular-style furniture, family photographs, and children's toys and clothing are on display throughout the house.

Additional Information

The Campbell House has been restored and dedicated to the memory of Almira Campbell and to all pioneer women; it is listed on the National Register of Historic Places.

Eielson-Osking House

**405 Eighth Street
Hatton, ND 58240
(701) 543-3726**

Contact: Hatton Eielson Museum and
Historical Association

Open: Sun. 1–4:30 p.m.; other times
(summer) by appointment

Activities: Guided tours

Best Season to View House: Summer

Year House Built: 1900

Number of Rooms: 11

Admission: Adults $1.50;
children $.50

Description of Grounds: Landscaped yard

Number of Yearly Visitors: 3,000

Style of Architecture: Victorian Queen Anne

On-Site Parking: Yes **Wheelchair Access:** No

Description of House

Carl Ben Eielson—famed World War I aviator and Arctic explorer—was the son of Ole Eielson. The elder Eielson started his career as a clerk in the employ of local merchants and town founders M.F. Hegge and his brother-in-law, T.E. Nelson; but, by 1908, Ole Eielson became successful in his own right, establishing a town bank with assets over $25,000 and going on to surpass the fortunes of his previous employers. So much so that Eielson was able to purchase the fancy "grand" house of T.E. Nelson that same year. This elegant Queen Anne-style house—six upstairs bedrooms and five downstairs rooms—was the right size for the the Eielson family of eight children. After the death of Mrs. Eielson in 1911, the large brood was raised by the elder daughter, Elma Eielson Osking, who dedicated her life to the care of her siblings and her own three children. Upon the death of Ole Eielson in 1931, Elma inherited the family house. When the house was finally sold, it was with the stipulation that the first floor would remain "just like Elma had it," and the second floor would serve as exhibit area for local history displays. The Eielson-Osking House has never been altered, and is listed on the National Register of Historic Places.

Notable Collections on Exhibit

Among the many family souvenirs, the library contains the personal items, historical photographs, and books of Carl Ben Eielson. Of particular note is a photograph showing the young Eielson receiving the Harmon Trophy from President Herbert Hoover.

Custer Home at Fort Abraham Lincoln State Park

4 miles south of
Mandan on Route 1806
Mandan, ND 58554
(701) 663-9571

Contact: Fort Abraham Lincoln Foundation

Open: Year-round, daily 9 a.m.–9 p.m.

Admission: Custer Home tours, adults $4.00; children (K-12th grade) $2.50

Activities: Guided and "living history" tours, exhibits, special park programs including the Native American Cultural Celebration and Frontier Army Days, special seasonal events and concerts

Suggested Time to View House: Home-45 minutes, park sites-3 hours

Facilities on Premises: Museum/visitor center and trading post, various outdoor park recreational facilities

Number of Yearly Visitors: 39,000

Description of Grounds: 977 acre park and historic fort with several reconstructed buildings sited on Cavalry Square defined by the Commanding Officer's Quarters, the Commissary and Storehouse, the Central Barracks and the Granary

Best Season to View House: Spring and early fall

Year House Built: Original-1874, reconstructed-1987

Style of Architecture: Modified Greek Revival

Number of Rooms: 10

On-Site Parking: Yes **Wheelchair Access:** Yes

Description of House

In 1874, after a fire destroyed their original barracks home, George Armstrong Custer and his wife, Elizabeth, built this house at Fort Abraham Lincoln—the General was assigned to the fort as its first commanding officer—where the Missouri and Heart Rivers meet. The couple was able to modify the building plans to accommodate their entertaining and living needs. They didn't live here long—in 1876, Custer would ride from here to his destiny at the Little Big Horn. After the destruction of the Sioux and Cheyenne tribes by the U. S. Army, the fort fell into disuse and was abandoned in 1891.

The State of North Dakota took on the rebuilding of the Custer Home as its first officially sanctioned centennial project; the archaeological dig was begun in 1987 to determine the exact site of the house. Then, using available historic photographs, original hand-drawn building plans, and personal letters and diaries, the house was completely reconstructed to appear as it did during the two years that the Custers lived here.

The Custer Home is a two-story structure featuring a rear kitchen extension, twelve-foot ceilings, eight-foot, twelve-pane front facade windows, and end gables accented with paired patterned masonry chimneys. Other exterior features include: six-over-six window treatments on the other sides, wall dormers, a full-width step-up front porch, a main entry door with a full transom and segmented sidelight panels, and a single-story bay extension. The colors outside are white with maroon and gray trim.

The center hall floor plan consists of the study (the General's library), main bedroom, dressing room, parlor, dining room, and kitchen on the ground floor; and the servants' quarters, guest rooms, and billiards room upstairs. The walls are unpapered to reflect their original appearance and four red drapes hang in the windows of the east living room.

Notable Collections on Exhibit

The house has been furnished with a number of period pieces, some of which are reported to have been owned by the Custers. These pieces include: a lap desk, a turkey serving platter, and a five-piece bedroom set which came from one of the houses on Officer's Row.

Additional Information

The land which now comprises Fort Abraham Lincoln State Park was deeded to North Dakota in 1907 by Teddy Roosevelt and development of the park itself was started in 1934 by the Civilian Conservation Corps. Located within the park boundaries are the ruins of On-A-Slant—a Mandan tribal village dating to the middle of the 17th century, the Infantry Post Blockhouse, and a number of structures built by the CCC, including a museum. Complete information regarding the Custer Home can be gotten by contacting the Fort Abraham Lincoln Foundation at 311 East Broadway in nearby Bismarck (701) 258-0203.

Theodore Roosevelt's Maltese Cross Cabin

Off Route I-94, north of Medora
Medora, ND 58645
(701) 623-4466

Contact: U.S. Department of the Interior, Theodore Roosevelt National Park
Open: Daily 8 a.m.–4:40 p.m.
Admission: $4.00 per car; $2.00 per person bus/motorcycle
Activities: Mid June–mid September guided tours
Suggested Time to View House: 20 minutes
Facilities on Premises: Visitor center-museum with auditorium and bookstore

Description of Grounds: Working ranch located in the Theodore Roosevelt National Park near the town of Medora
Best Season to View House: Spring–early fall
Number of Yearly Visitors: 470,000
Year House Built: Between 1883 and 1884
Style of Architecture: National, log cabin
Number of Rooms: 3
On-Site Parking: Yes **Wheelchair Access:** Yes

Description of House

In 1883, eighteen years before being sworn in as the 26th President of the United States, Theodore Roosevelt made his first trip to the Little Missouri Badlands to hunt bison. He fell for this rugged country and purchased the Chimney Butte Ranch seven miles south of Medora. It came to be called the Maltese Cross after its brand. That spring, Roosevelt returned to his ranch and occupied his newly built cabin; the following year, he moved to the nearby the Elkhorn Ranch. After the severe winter of 1886-1887, he rarely spent time in the Dakotas and, in 1898, sold off both properties.

After Roosevelt became President, North Dakota bought the cabin from Jack Snyder, a local cowboy, and exhibited it at numerous fairs and expositions. After the State Fair of 1906, it was placed on the grounds of the capitol in Bismarck. In 1959, the National Park Service acquired the cabin, moved it to its present location, and restored it to its original appearance—even reconstructing a steep-pitched roof which had been replaced by Snyder. It is the only remaining structure on either of Roosevelt's two ranches which stood at the time of his residence.

Sylvane Ferris and Bill Merrifield built the cabin out of ponderosa pine they found stranded on the riverbanks—the logs were probably cut and sawn upstream for use as railroad ties. The cabin's features include: two doors, a cellar, several glass-paned windows, mortar chinking, and the steep shingle roof which afforded an extra half-story for storage and sleeping. All of the furnishings date to the 1880s and some of them belonged to Teddy Roosevelt: his writing desk (between 1884 and 1885, he completed *Hunting Trips of a Ranchman* here), the rocking chair in the living room, and a wicker-lined trunk.

Additional Information

Another noted Badlands historic site is the Chateau de Mores, a twenty-six room frame house built by the Marquis de Mores and his wife, Medora von Hoffman. The French-born de Mores came here in 1883 and developed and the area's largest cattle ranch and meat packing plant. The disastrous winter of 1886 decimated his herds and forced him to leave. The Chateau de Mores is listed on the National Register of Historic Places. For information call (701) 623-9571.

Ohio

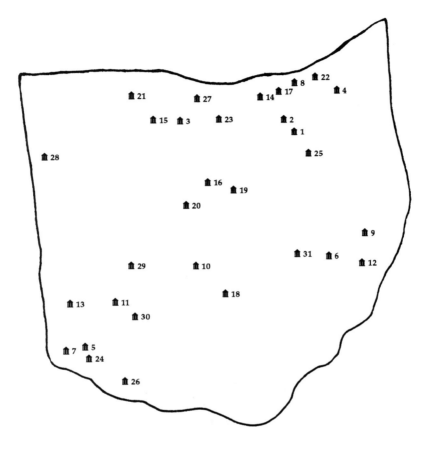

1. Akron
   Hower House

2. Bath
   Hale House at Hale Farm and Village

3. Bellevue
   John Wright Mansion

4. Burton
   Hickok Brick House at Century Village

5. Camp Dennison
   Christian Waldschmidt House and Gate House

6. **Carrollton**
   Daniel McCook House Museum

7. **Cincinnati**
   Cary Cottage
   Harriet Beecher Stowe House
   Taft Boyhood Home

8. **Cleveland**
   Bingham-Hanna Mansion
   Hay-McKinney Mansion

9. **Columbiana**
   Log House Museum

10. **Columbus**
    Kelton House Museum and Garden
    Thurber House

11. **Dayton**
    Daniel Arnold House at Carriage Hill Farm

12. **East Liverpool**
    Cassius Clark Thompson House

13. **Eaton**
    Lewisburg Log House
    Sayler-Swartsel House

14. **Elyria**
    Arthur R. Garford House and Hickories Museum

15. **Fremont**
    Rutherford B. Hayes Home– "Spiegel Grove"

16. **Galion**
    Brownella Cottage

17. **Lakewood**
    Oldest Stone House

18. **Lancaster**
    Sherman House Museum

19. **Lucas**
    Louis Bromfield's Big House

20. **Marion**
    President Warren G. Harding Home

21. **Maumee**
    Gilbert Flanigan Saltbox Farmhouse
    Wolcott House

22. **Mentor**
    James A. Garfield National Historic Site, "Lawnfield"

23. **Milan**
    Galpin House
    Sayles House
    Thomas A. Edison Birthplace

24. **Milford**
    Promont

25. **North Canton**
    Hoover House

26. **Point Pleasant**
    U.S. Grant's Birthplace

27. **Sandusky**
    Oran Follett Museum

28. **Van Wert**
    "House of Seven Oaks"

29. **West Liberty**
    Mac-A-Cheek Castle
    Mac-O-Chee Castle

30. **Wilmington**
    Rombach Place

31. **Zoar**
    Number One House–The "King's Palace" at Zoar Village

Hower House

60 Fir Hill
Akron, OH 44325
(216) 972-6909

Contact: University of Akron
Open: Feb.-Dec., Wed.-Sat. Noon–3:30 p.m.,
Sun. 1–4 p.m.; closed major holidays,
month of January
Admission: Adults $4.00; seniors $3.50;
students $2.00; children (under 6) free
Activities: Guided tours, special exhibits,
special seasonal events including Ice
Cream Socials, and "Victorian Holiday"
Suggested Time to View House: 1 hour
Facilities on Premises: Gift shop
Description of Grounds: Original 2½ acre
plot with seasonal plantings and trees
Best Season to View House: Summer
Number of Yearly Visitors: 9,500
Year House Built: 1871
Style of Architecture: Late Italianate and
Second Empire
Number of Rooms: 28
On-Site Parking: Yes
Wheelchair Access: No

Description of House

In 1871 John Henry Hower, who made his fortune in manufacturing and cereals, built this exquisite Second Empire mansion. After his wife, Susan, died in 1896, John Henry remarried and the house fell to his son, Milton Otis Hower, and Milton's wife Blanche. The younger Hower was a successful businessman who ran the family gear manufacturing plant and sat on the boards of several noted Akron-based businesses. Both he and his father died in 1916. The house was occupied by immediate family until 1973, when Grace Hower Crawford—Milton's daughter—died. It is now owned by the University of Akron.

The Hower House was designed by Akron architect Jacob Snyder, who numbered many of that city's prosperous elite among his clients. It is the last remnant of Akron's long-forgotten "Gold Coast," a neighborhood of stunning wealth which saw its heyday in the first decades of the 20th century—when Akron had more millionaires than any other comparably-sized town in America. The asymmetrical design is Second Empire with certain details—most prominently the window arrangement—in the Italianate style. The exterior elements include: sixteen-inch-thick walls made of red-brick manufactured in Pittsburgh, a high slate mansard roof, elaborate ornamental stonework around the main windows, a marvelous two-story tower reaching up from the third floor and capped by delicate wrought-iron cresting, three porches, and six chimneys. Inside, the three floors—each 3,000 square feet in area—are laid out with the public rooms downstairs, the bedrooms on the second floor, and a fifty-eight-foot long ballroom on the top floor. On the main floor, this plan features a large octagonal center hall from which the main rooms radiate out, themselves smaller octagons. The opulence of the interior decoration is everywhere visible; from the French crystal chandeliers to the black walnut woodwork, from the Egyptian telephone room to the ornate plaster ceiling medallions. The furnishings are original to the Hower family and come in a riot of styles; they collected both antique and contemporary pieces from around the world.

Notable Collections on Exhibit

The assortment of objects collected by John and Susan Hower and their descendants on display includes: travel trunks, exotic ethnic clothing, a 1905 Chickering piano, Sèvres urns, vintage family accessories, and hand-cut, three-layered stenciled rose glass.

Additional Information

The Hower House is listed on the National Register of Historic Places.

Hale House at Hale Farm and Village

2686 Oak Hill Road, P.O. Box 296
Bath, OH 44210
(216) 666-3711

Contact: Western Reserve Historical Society
Open: May 30-Nov. 1, Wed.-Sat.
  10 a.m.–5 p.m., Sun. Noon–5 p.m.
Admission: Adults $6.50; seniors $5.50;
  children (6-12) $4.00
Activities: Video orientation, 19th-century
  craft demonstrations, educational
  programs, special monthly events
  including Maple Sugaring, Music and
  Harvest Festival, the Herb Fair
Suggested Time to View House: 2½ hours

Facilities on Premises: Museum shop,
  restaurants
Description of Grounds: "Living history"
  museum with numerous outbuildings
Best Season to View House: Fall
Number of Yearly Visitors: 100,000
Year House Built: c.1830
Style of Architecture: Federal, brick
Number of Rooms: 10
On-Site Parking: Yes **Wheelchair Access:** No

Description of House

Once upon a time, Ohio was merely a part of Connecticut; that's not the first line of a fairy tale but the amazing and sometimes brutal story of the land rush which began with Columbus landing in the New World. In the 17th century, King Charles II granted a tract of land to the colony of Connecticut approximately fifty miles across and three thousand miles long, extending from the Atlantic to the Pacific. Connecticut sold much of the land for forty cents an acre to meet its Revolutionary War reparation payments. Then, after the war, some of it was bought back from the Native Americans for $500 in cash, two beef cattle, and 199 gallons of whiskey. This parcel, called the Western Reserve, was settled by squatters, hunters, trappers, and ordinary New Englanders looking for opportunity.

One such individual was Jonathan Hale, who arrived in the Western Reserve in 1810 and built a small log cabin on 500 acres of prime land. He had made a good choice: the Cuyahoga Valley exploded in importance during the second decade of the 19th century when the Erie Canal was opened. Hale rapidly grew prosperous and built this magnificent three-story, Federal-style brick home sometime around 1830. Beautiful decorative molding and brick work, and a traditional shuttered window treatment of twelve-over-twelve panes (ground and first levels), and twelve-over-eight panes (upper level) clearly set this house apart as an outstanding example of the style.

The present day Hale Farm and Village is an open air museum which depicts life in a typical small village in the early 19th-century Western Reserve. The property includes the original Jonathan Hale Homestead, which has been extensively restored and contains many items belonging to the Hale family, three barns—one for sheep, one for the carriage, and one for everything else on the farm, a sugar house, and a number of other buildings. In 1956, the Jonathan Hale Homestead was deeded to the Western Reserve Historical Society by Miss Clara Belle Ritchie, the great-granddaughter of Jonathan Hale.

Additional Information

Hale House is listed on the National Register of Historic Places. East of Oak Hill Road is the Western Reserve Village, a reconstructed early 19th-centruy town; the village features the Federal-style Saltbox House c. 1830, the Goldsmith House c. 1832, and the Greek Revival-style Jagger House c. 1845.

John Wright Mansion

5487 Route 113, P.O. Box 342
Bellevue, OH 44811
(419) 483-4949

Contact: Historic Lyme Village Association
Open: Apr. and Sept., Sun. 1–5 p.m.;
June-Aug., Tues.-Sun. 1–5 p.m.
Admission: Adults $2.50; seniors $2.25;
students $1.25
Activities: Guided tours, visual
presentations, special seasonal programs
Suggested Time to View House:
60–90 minutes
Facilities on Premises: Gift shop,
genealogical and historical research library

Description of Grounds: Spacious, tree
covered yard with front wrought iron
fence and west pond
Best Season to View House: Early spring-fall
Style of Architecture: Victorian Second
Empire, brick
Number of Yearly Visitors: 7,500
Year House Built: 1882
Number of Rooms: 16
On-Site Parking: Yes **Wheelchair Access:** Yes

Description of House

John Wright came to Ohio from England in 1842 at the age of nineteen. By the time he started work on his dream house fifty years later, he owned 2400 acres of land, a grist mill, a blacksmith shop, a harness shop, and a carriage house. His property also included the barns and stables which housed the Percherons—Belgian work horses—that Wright bred and sold and the garden which provided much of the family's food. Besides running his farm and sundry businesses, he and his wife, Betsy Ford, raised eight children.

Wright died in 1908 and his youngest daughter, Damaris, inherited the property; Damaris had been born to Wright's second wife, Fanny, in 1895, when he was seventy-two years old. After Damaris, ownership of the property passed through a number of hands. Robert and Louise Ferres owned the house from 1972 until 1978 and made extensive renovations; the Historic Lyme Village Association bought the mansion and completed the work that the Ferreses had begun.

The Victorian mansion has a center tower with projecting two-story side bays and the straight roof of the cupola is patterned in gray and red tiles; elaborate cornice and bracket work can be seen on the roof, the porch, and the secondary entrances. The tower affords marvelous views of the Lake Erie Islands. The materials used in building the house—clay brick, oak, and walnut—all came from Wright's property.

Inside the house, the newel post at the base of the main stairway once held a brass lamp. The house had a number of fireplaces, but it also had a central heating system with hot steam radiators. The west dining room entrance has been restored with doors found in the carriage house attic. The second floor has seven bedrooms, three of which were, at one time, a music room, a toy room, and a school room, and the entire third floor was a ballroom.

Additional Information

The John Wright Mansion is listed on the National Register of Historic Places. Other historic buildings at this site include the Seymour House Museum, the Annie Brown Log Cabin, the Bribricher Centennial Barn, and the Cooper General Store.

Hickox Brick House at Century Village

14653 East Park Street
Burton, OH 44021
(216) 834-4012

Contact: Geauga County Historical Society
Open: May 1-Oct. 31, Tues.-Sat.
10:30 a.m.–3 p.m., Sun. 1–3 p.m.;
other times by appointment
Admission: Fee $3.00
Activities: Guided tours, weekend
special events
Suggested Time to View House: 2 hours
total village
Facilities on Premises: Gift shop
Description of Grounds: Village grounds
comprised of numerous historic
buildings celebrating the early history of
the Western Reserve
Best Season to View House: Spring-fall
Number of Yearly Visitors: 50,000
Year House Built: 1838
Number of Rooms: 1

Style of Architecture: Federal
On-Site Parking: Yes **Wheelchair Access:** No

Description of House

The Hickox Brick House is part of Century Village, the Geauga County Historical Society's recreation of a small town of the mid-1800s. The house was built in 1838 by Eleazer Hickox; his wife, Stella, was the daughter of Thomas Umberfield, one of Burton's early settlers, who came here in 1798. The addition at the east of the house is part of Thomas Umberfield's first home, and it shows the furnishings and construction of a typical early pioneer one-room house.

Inside the house are many artifacts on display, including a unique 9,000 piece toy soldier collection. Congresswoman Frances P. Bolton acquired and presented this house to the Historical Society in 1941.

Additional Information

Century Village contains several historic structures; another house worth a visit here is the Broughton House.

Christian Waldschmidt House and Gate House

7567 Glendale Milford Road
Camp Dennison, OH 45111
(513) 231-0612

Contact: Ohio Society Daughters of the American Revolution

Open: May–Oct., Sun. 1–5 p.m.; other times by appointment

Admission: Donations welcome

Activities: Guided tours by costumed docents

Suggested Time to View House: 45 minutes

Facilities on Premises: Souvenir notecards and postcards for sale

Description of Grounds: Period landscaped yard with grape arbors and herb garden

Best Season to View House: Spring-early fall

Style of Architecture: Federal, fieldstone and mortar

Number of Yearly Visitors: 1,200

Year House Built: 1804

Number of Rooms: 8

On-Site Parking: No **Wheelchair Access:** No

Description of House

Native Pennsylvanian Christian Waldschmidt served as a private in the Continental Army during the Revolutionary War. In 1794 he bought 1140 acres along the Little Miami River in southwestern Ohio. Here he led a group of German Pietists in establishing the community of New Germany. Waldschmidt operated a gristmill and a distillery; in 1811, he started up a paper mill as well. During the Civil War the area around New Germany was used as an induction and training center for green Union troops and Waldschmidt's house served as headquarters for General Joshua Bates.

The two-and-a-half-story, Federal-style stone house has a single-story ell and gable roof. It features two recessed doorways in the front; the right entrance led to Waldschmidt's general store, the left entrance led to the living quarters, and between them is an entrance to the tavern in the basement. Other exterior details include: twelve-over-twelve-pane windows hung in a wood sash, flat arch lintels, and four light transoms above each of the doors. The fully restored interior is painted in Federal-style colors—off-white walls and Williamsburg blue trim. The parlor mantel was carved by Daniel Boone's cousin. The tavern room downstairs—which was completely restored during the Bicentennial Year—was frequented by travelers who came to Waldschmidt's to buy supplies at the general store above it. Also on the property is the Gate House, a two-story stone structure built by Waldschmidt for his daughter upon her marriage. This unrestored house is one of the earliest stone houses still standing in Ohio. Since the Civil War it has been known as the Camp Dennison Guard House. The furnishings are all authentic period pieces interpreting the American frontier prior to 1831.

Notable Collections on Exhibit

Among the items on display are: a framed "crazy" quilt made by two sisters who represented the last of the Waldschmidt family to occupy the house; a collection of early lamps and candle-holders; early German Kass with lemonwood inlay; paintings of the original inhabitants; and a fine assortment of pewter mugs given by various chapters of the Daughters of the American Revolution in Ohio.

Additional Information

The Waldschmidt-Camp Dennison District is listed on the National Register of Historic Places. Nearby is the local cemetery where family member—and other early residents of New Germany—are buried.

Daniel McCook House Museum

Public Square, P.O. Box 174
Carrollton, OH 44615
(216) 627-3345

Contact: Carroll County Historical Society
Open: Memorial Day through second
weekend of Oct., Fri. and Sat.
9 a.m.–5 p.m.; Sun. 1–5 p.m.
Admission: Adults $2.00; seniors $1.50;
children $.50
Activities: Guided tours, special displays,
special seasonal events including
Candlelight Tours, and Christmas Open
House

Suggested Time to View House: 1 hour
Facilities on Premises: Gift shop
Description of Grounds: Terraced back yard
enclosed with white picket fence
Best Season to View House: Summer
Number of Yearly Visitors: 2,500
Year House Built: 1837
Style of Architecture: Federal, brick
Number of Rooms: 9
On-Site Parking: No **Wheelchair Access:** Yes

Description of House

Daniel McCook and his brother John came from Pennsylvania to Ohio
in 1826 with their father; Daniel settled in Carrollton and John some twenty
miles away in Steubenville. Daniel became a lawyer and served as the first
Clerk of Carroll County while John practiced medicine and became active
in his church and town politics. Daniel built this house in 1837 and four of
his nine sons were born here. Those nine sons, and Dr. John McCook's five
sons, and Daniel himself—by then a major in the U. S. Army—won wide
renown during the Civil War as "The Fighting McCooks." Sadly, the reputation came at a high cost: Major Daniel McCook and two of his sons were
killed during that bloody conflict. Even so, many of the other "Fighting
McCooks" went on to illustrious careers in the law, government, and the
church. The house itself became Butler's General Store in the late 1860s and
served in that capacity until 1941.

The two-story, L-shaped house was built at the same time as Carroll
County's first courthouse—out of the same locally-fired red brick laid on a
gray brick foundation. It features a stone patio, second floor sleeping porch,
six-over-six-pane windows, an elliptical fanlight over the front door with
sidelights, and double-casement windows segmented by pilasters on the
second story. Inside, only the kitchen is interpreted to the Federal style; the
rest of the rooms are Victorian. One room has been turned into a museum

dedicated to the Civil War exploits of the "Fighting McCooks." The downstairs rooms—especially the parlor—contain furnishings which belonged to the McCooks, whereas the upstairs rooms are primarily given over to exhibits of Carroll County history.

Notable Collections on Exhibit

The McCook House Museum Civil War collection features such items as the family's uniforms and weapons; there are also paintings of the family members.

Additional Information

The McCook House Museum is listed on the National Register of Historic Places. In nearby New Philadelphia one may visit the Schoenbrunn Village State Memorial. Schoenbrunn Village was founded in 1772 by David Zeisberger as a Moravian mission to the Delaware Indians; it now features seventeen reconstructed log structures typical of the late 18th century and a museum relating the history of the missionaries, their converts, and the settlement of this part of Ohio. The Ohio Historical Society directs a living history program in the village; for information and tour reservations, call (216) 339-3636.

Cary Cottage

7000 Hamilton Avenue
Cincinnati, OH 45231
(513) 522-3860

Contact: Cary Cottage Group
Open: First Sunday of each month
1–4 p.m.; group tours Mon.-Fri. by
appointment
Admission: Free
Activities: Guided tours, special events
and exhibits as announced
Suggested Time to View House: 1 hour
Facilities on Premises: Small gift shop
Best Season to View House: Spring-late fall
Description of Grounds: Small yard with
gazebo
Number of Yearly Visitors: 400
Number of Rooms: 6

Style of Architecture: Modified Federal-style
white brick farmhouse
Year House Built: 1832
On-Site Parking: Yes **Wheelchair Access:** No

Description of House

Cary Cottage was the family home of poets Alice and Phoebe. The Carys were descendants of Sir Thomas Cary, a cousin of Queen Elizabeth, by way of an earlier Cary relation, John Cary, who had settled in Plymouth, Massachusetts, in 1630. Christopher Cary emigrated to Ohio in 1802 to claim a land grant and his son, Robert, purchased a parcel of land near the settlement on the Hamilton Road. Robert served in the War of 1812 and, with wife Elizabeth Jessup, raised nine children. Daughters Alice and Phoebe were born in 1820 and 1824, respectively. The sisters were encouraged by Horace Greeley to "go East" and, in 1850, they moved to New York to find their fortunes.

The Cary Cottage was built in 1832 overlooking the original homestead, a modest frame house constructed in 1814. The Cottage, a two-story white brick farmhouse, features unusual side porch pillars made of brick fired on the site. Five fireplaces, the floors, the narrow winding stairway, the stone terrace, and a deep well are all original and intact. Passages from *Clovernook, or Recollections of Our Home in the West* by Alice Cary and the sisters' poems were consulted when the Cottage was restored and furnished to its 1880s appearance. The Cottage now serves as the home for the papers which document the Cary family history, as well as the literary work of the two sisters.

A small room near the parlor is dedicated to Florence Trader and her sister, Georgia, who founded the Clovernook Home and School for the Blind at Cary Cottage in 1903. Ten years later, a separate structure called the Trader House was built next to the Cottage as a permanent residence for the blind. The Cary Cottage is listed on the National Register of Historic Places.

Notable Collections on Exhibit

Paintings of Alice and Phoebe Cary by G.P. A. Healy and a portrait of Anna Lewis Cary, stepmother to the two poets, signed "Kellogg," can be found here, along with a small ladderback chair which belonged to Phoebe and inscribed with the letters "PC."

Harriet Beecher Stowe House

2950 Gilbert Avenue
Cincinnati, OH 45206
(513) 632-5120

Contact: Harriet Beecher Stowe House
Open: Tues., Wed.,Thurs. 10 a.m.–4 p.m.
Admission: Donations accepted
Activities: Guided tours, exhibits and
concert series
Suggested Time to View House: 15 minutes
Facilities on Premises: Gift shop
Description of Grounds: Sited on a small
grassy knoll surrounded by a stone wall
bordering a park
Best Season to View House: Summer
Number of Yearly Visitors: 1,800
Year House Built: 1832
Number of Rooms: 15

Style of Architecture: Georgian
On-Site Parking: Yes **Wheelchair Access:** No

Description of House

One of the most famous novels in American history, *Uncle Tom's Cabin*, was written by Harriet Beecher Stowe and published in 1852, twenty years after she moved to the frontier town of Cincinnati from Connecticut and heard the stories of runaway slaves from her friends who helped run the Underground Railroad. Her father, the eminent preacher Lyman Beecher, had taken a position as president of the Lane Theological Seminary and pastor of Cincinnati's Second Presbyterian Church. During her years here, Harriet taught school, co-wrote a textbook with her older sister Catherine, and began to publish short stories; when visiting the home of a student across the Ohio River in Kentucky she experienced slavery first-hand. There is no question that this was a defining period in her life and writings—she got married to Calvin Stowe here, had her first children, and published her first stories. Restoration of the Stowe House began in 1977 and has been fully completed.

The house is a simple two-story structure which features a gabled roof, a single chimney at each end, a three-part front facade, and six-over-six window arrangements. It was originally built with a two-story veranda in the rear and had an interior floor plan which had a pair of rooms flanking a large central hall, but over the years alterations have been made. These additions include: a bay window, a front porch in the Late Classical Revival style, and a large wing at the rear. Inside, there are multiple fireplaces, a large central staircase, walls painted white, and a dining room and hallway decorated with maroon-and-white patterned wallpaper. All of the furnishings on display have been donated and collected to reflect the years when Stowe lived here. The Harriet Beecher Stowe House is listed on the National Register of Historic Places.

Notable Collections on Exhibit

Two of the items on display are worthy of special attention: a Gothic Revival-style carved-back chair presented to Major Henry W. Jones by Lt. Gen. Ulysses S. Grant, and a bookcase from the office of Lyman Beecher at the Lane Theological Seminary.

Taft Boyhood Home

2038 Auburn Avenue
Cincinnati, OH 45219
(513) 684-3262

Contact: William Howard Taft National Historic Site

Open: Daily, 10 a.m.–4 p.m.; closed Thanksgiving, Christmas, New Year's Day

Admission: Free

Activities: Guided tours, exhibits, group tours and educational with reservations, annual holiday decoration event

Suggested Time to View House: 1 hour

Facilities on Premises: Gift shop

Description of Grounds: ½ acre site in urban area. Landscape reflects that of the Taft home in 1868.

Best Season to View House: Year round

Number of Yearly Visitors: 10,000

Year House Built: 1841, remodeled 1851

Style of Architecture: Greek Revival, brick

Number of Rooms: 5 restored, 5 exhibit

On-Site Parking: Yes **Wheelchair Access:** Yes

Description of House

William Howard Taft—the only American to have served both as President of the United States and Chief Justice of the Supreme Court—was born in this house on September 15, 1857, to Alphonso and Louise Torrey Taft. Alphonso was a lawyer and judge who served as Secretary of War under President Grant; his wife was an educator and musician. William attended Yale and the Cincinnati Law School, took a job as a law reporter for local newspapers, and began his career in public service as an assistant county prosecutor. He was elected to the Presidency in 1908, running as a Republican against Democrat William Jennings Bryan, but lost four years later when the Republican vote was split by Teddy Roosevelt's Progressive Party. Taft was appointed to the Supreme Court in 1921 and remained on the bench until 1930, the year of his death. The Tafts sold the house in 1899; thirty-nine years later, it was saved from destruction by the William Howard Taft Memorial Association.

The Taft Birthplace is square two-story house built in the Greek Revival style which features a small entry porch with a decorative parapet, a widow's walk, a lower level carriage entrance, and shuttered windows in three-over-three arrangements above the more traditional six-over-six. The home was one of the first built in Cincinnati's Mt. Auburn neighborhood; it has been restored to its appearance in the years when Taft was growing up here. Much of this restoration was accomplished by consulting letters that Louise wrote to her family back in Massachusetts and many of the mid-Victorian furnishings—original or purchased—were made in Cincinnati.

Notable Collections on Exhibit
Among the items on display are: a William Sontag painting, brocatelle draperies, Wooten desk, a collection of 120 prints in a three volume set of North American Indian Tribes, and William Howard Taft's campaign memorabilia.

Additional Information
When in Cincinnati one should also plan a visit to the Taft Museum at 316 Pike Street. The Museum is the former home of William Howard Taft's brother, Charles Phelps Taft, and features a collection of European and American paintings, Chinese porcelains, and decorative arts.

Bingham-Hanna Mansion

10825 East Boulevard
Cleveland, OH 44106
(216) 721-5722

Contact: Western Reserve Historical
Society
Open: Year-round, Tues.-Sat.
10 a.m.–5 p.m., Sun. Noon–5 p.m.
Activities: Guided tours, audiovisual
presentations, special programming
Facilities on Premises: Gift shop
Description of Grounds: Formal Italian
gardens
Number of Yearly Visitors: 60,000
Number of Rooms: 35

Admission: Adults $4.00; seniors and
students $2.00
Suggested Time to View House:
60 minutes
Best Season to View House: Spring-fall
Style of Architecture: Eclectic Italian
Renaissance Revival
Year House Built: 1919
On-Site Parking: Yes **Wheelchair Access:** No

Description of House

The splendor of the Bingham-Hanna Mansion is a result of a fortuitous match between Harry Bingham, his wife, Harriette Gowen Bingham, and Mrs. Leonard Colton Hanna, widow of Leonard C. Hanna. The Binghams built one of the great mansions of Cleveland—perhaps in all of America— and Mrs. Hanna bought the mansion in 1920 and filled it with great art treasures, priceless Renaissance furniture, and her own expansive spirit.

It took several years to build this mansion; construction began in 1916 under the hand of the New York architectural firm Walker and Gillette. When World War I broke out, construction stopped and Harry Bingham left to serve in the U. S. Army in France, where he became captain of the 131st Field Artillery. Though the house was finally completed in 1919, the Binghams never lived here. Instead, they moved to New York, where Bingham took the position of President of the First National Bank.

The Bingham-Hanna Mansion was built in a style that combined the details of a Florentine palace with the setting of a northern Italian country villa. This thirty-five-room house features a unique morning room of Pompeian design, with marble walls and mosaic tiles, and thick walnut doors which perfectly complete the illusion of antiquity.

Leonard Hanna, the only son of Coralie Walker Hanna and Leonard Colton Hanna, exchanged this house for the Western Reserve Historical Society building at Euclid Avenue and East 107th Street in 1940, and the Mansion is now owned by the Society. The Bingham-Hanna Mansion is listed on the National Register of Historic Places. The Hay-McKinney Mansion is located next door.

Notable Collections on Exhibit

There is an extensive collection of American furniture and decorative art pieces from the mid-18th century to the 1920s, including glassware, silverware, paintings, ceramics, costumes, and domestic implements.

Hay-McKinney Mansion

10825 East Boulevard
Cleveland, OH 44106
(216) 721-5722

Contact: Western Reserve Historical Society
Open: Tues.-Sat. 10 a.m.–5 p.m., Sun. Noon–5 p.m.
Admission: Adults $4.00; seniors and students $2.00
Activities: Guided tours, audiovisual presentations, special programs
Suggested Time to View House: 1 hour
Facilities on Premises: Gift shop

Style of Architecture: Eclectic Italian Renaissance Revival
Description of Grounds: Formal gardens
Best Season to View House: Spring-fall
Number of Yearly Visitors: 60,000
Year House Built: 1911
Number of Rooms: 32
On-Site Parking: Yes **Wheelchair Access:** No

Description of House

The Hay-McKinney Mansion is an Italian Renaissance-style house built by Mrs. John Hay, born Clara Louise Stone. The mansion was joined to the above-mentioned Bingham-Hanna Mansion when the Norton Central Addition was built in 1959; they now form the core of the Western Reserve Historical Society complex.

Clara Hay had lived in the Hay-Adams House in Washington, D. C., with her husband, who was then Secretary of State. After John's death in 1905, she moved to Cleveland to be with her sister, Flora. The sisters were daughters of Amasa Stone, who brought Western Reserve College (forerunner of Case Western Reserve University) to Cleveland. Clara's home was designed by Abram Garfield, son of the U. S. President, but Mrs. Hay was intimately involved in every detail of the building.

The three-story masonry structure shows both Venetian and Florentine influences; behind the luxurious formal gardens, one finds a unique courtyard. When the home was completed in 1911, the magazine *Town Topics* reported that it was "in every way the equal of any of the magnificent residences in this country."

Unfortunately, Flora died during construction of the house and Clara decided not to move in. When she died in 1914, the house fell to her three children, who sold it to the McKinney family. Price McKinney, who had made his fortune in railroads, mining, and steel, was known as a generous and modest man who shunned the spotlight. He and his second wife, Lucy Dwyer, furnished the house with the art and antiques which they'd bought in Europe. McKinney died in 1926; his widow lived on here until 1938, when she gave the home to the Society.

Notable Collections on Exhibit

This house shares the same collections as the previously-mentioned Bingham-Hanna Mansion.

Additional Information

The Hay-McKinney Mansion—like its sister the Bingham-Hanna Mansion listed above—was placed on the National Register of Historic Places in 1976.

Log House Museum

10 East Park Avenue
Columbiana, OH 44408
(216) 482-3822

Contact: Historical Society of Columbiana-Fairfield Township

Open: Memorial Day through mid Sept., Sat. and Sun. 2–4 p.m.

Admission: Free

Activities: Guided tours

Suggested Time to View House: 45 minutes

Description of Grounds: Located on town square

Best Season to View House: Summer

Number of Yearly Visitors: 2,000

Year House Built: c. 1820

Style of Architecture: Folk, log house

Number of Rooms: 4

On-Site Parking: Yes **Wheelchair Access:** Yes

Description of House

The Log House was built in the 1820s on a land grant signed by President James Madison, and its history mirrors that of those who settled in Columbiana. Having seen ownership change hands more than ten times in 150 years, today the house is used by the Columbiana-Fairfield Township as a museum, and as a model of what life was like in 19th-century Ohio.

Displays are changed periodically and include quilts and coverlets of the 1800s, the General Ephraim Holloway collection of letters, pictures, uniforms, and field accessories from the Civil War, dolls, vintage clothing, and red clay Keister pottery which was manufactured in Columbiana in the early 19th century. The two-story log house has a side porch and its original tin ceiling.

Kelton House Museum and Garden

586 East Town Street
Columbus, OH 43215
(614) 464-2022

Contact: Junior League of Columbus, Inc.
Open: Every Sunday 1–4 p.m.; first three Sundays of December, 1–5 p.m.
Admission: Adults $1.50; seniors and students $1.00; $2.50 in December
Activities: Guided tours, luncheons, adult and children programming, April "Civil War" Month with special tours and exhibits
Suggested Time to View House: 1 hour
Facilities on Premises: Museum shop
Description of Grounds: Small but lovely Victorian garden in back of house
Best Season to View House: Spring and summer
Number of Yearly Visitors: 5,000
Year House Built: 1852
Number of Rooms: 6

Style of Architecture: Greek Revival, brick
On-Site Parking: Yes **Wheelchair Access:** Yes

Description of House

Kelton House was home to one of Columbus's upper middle class merchant families, and it stayed in the family for more than more than 120 years; during the Civil War, it served as a stop on the Underground Railroad.

Fernando and Sophia Kelton, originally from Vermont, built this house in 1852 and raised seven children here. As in many Ohio families of the mid-19th century, they had a son who fought and died in the Civil War. A younger son, Edwin, took possession of the house upon his parents' death; it was his daughter, Grace, who lived here until 1975 and left the house to the Columbus Foundation, which founded the Junior League of Columbus, Inc., in order to operate the Kelton House as a museum.

A unique feature of the house is the fact that the large staircase in the front hall cuts the sight lines of the front window in half—this is because the entire exterior was built before the interior was even designed! In addition to the oddly placed staircase, the floor plan includes front and back parlors, a ladies' parlor, a formal dining room, and two bedrooms; all of these rooms are furnished with Victorian pieces. Eighty percent of the collection belonged to the original owners.

Notable Collections on Exhibit

Two charming collections can be found on display: music boxes, some of which are still in working condition; and a collection of English country cottages hand-crafted in porcelain, originally used as censers.

Thurber House

77 Jefferson Avenue
Columbus, OH 43215
(614) 464-1032

Contact: Thurber House
Open: Daily Noon–4 p.m.; closed all major holidays
Admission: Free. Sunday tour rates, adults $2.00; seniors and students $1.50; children (under 12) free; guided group tour rates available
Activities: Guided tours, literary picnics, special seasonal events including October "Ghost Tour," and Annual James Thurber Birthday Celebration
Suggested Time to View House: 30–60 minutes
Facilities on Premises: Thurber Center and Book Store
Best Season to View House: Year round
Year House Built: 1873
Number of Rooms: 8

Description of Grounds: Landscaped grounds and house facing Jefferson Park
Number of Yearly Visitors: 3,000
Style of Architecture: Victorian Queen Anne
On-Site Parking: Yes **Wheelchair Access:** Yes

Description of House

James Thurber—humorist, author, cartoonist, and playwright—lived in this house with his parents, two brothers, and numerous dogs during his college years. It figured prominently in his work as the house where the ghost got in, the bed fell, and the electricity leaked! Today Thurber is perhaps best known for his work in the *New Yorker* magazine and his participation in the legendary literary round-table conducted at New York's Algonquin Hotel. After the Thurbers left, the house served as a boarding house and public school.

This two-story Victorian Queen Anne-style features a brick exterior with wood trim, beveled glass windows, a cross-gabled roof done in octagonal-shaped tiles, simple two-sash windows upstairs, an arched front window encased in patterned masonry with a stained-glass fanlight, and a small entry porch with elaborate spindlework and an incised frieze. Using a photograph taken in 1910 as a reference the house underwent a complete restoration; it is now interpreted to the years around 1910 when Thurber and his family lived here. The furnishings mix Mission-style oak pieces added to the earlier Victorian pieces; of these, only two actually belonged to the Thurbers.

Notable Collections on Exhibit

The house contains a large collection of Thurber memorabilia: thirty-one first editions, original drawings and manuscripts, his typewriter, the Tony Award he won, and the hoods he wore at honorary doctorate ceremonies.

Additional Information

The Thurber House is listed on the National Register of Historic Places. In addition to being a museum, the house also serves as a living memorial to the great American humorist; it is an active writers' center featuring literary picnics in the summer and an author's series in the fall and winter.

Daniel Arnold House at Carriage Hill Farm

**7860 Shull Road of Route 201
Dayton, OH 45424
(513) 879-0461**

Contact: Carriage Hill Farm-Park District

Open: Mon.-Fri. 10 a.m.–5 p.m., Sat.-Sun. 1–5 p.m.; closed Christmas, New Year's Day

Admission: Free

Activities: Self-guided tours, "living history" demonstrations, interactive exhibits, seasonal farm programs

Suggested Time to View House: 30 minutes

Facilities on Premises: Visitor center, country store, picnic shelters, hiking and horse trails

Description of Grounds: 1,000 acre reserve with restored and reconstructed historic house and farm outbuildings

Best Season to View House: Year round

Year House Built: 1830, rear addition 1878

Number of Rooms: 10, 5 open to the public

Number of Yearly Visitors: 100,000

Style of Architecture: Federal

On-Site Parking: Yes **Wheelchair Access:** Yes

Description of House

In 1830 Daniel and Catherine Arnold—and sixteen members of her family—came from Virginia's Shenandoah Valley to the banks of Dry Run off Ohio's Mad River. Here they built and operated a sawmill and began developing a farm. The Arnolds were a very religious German-Baptist family who lived in a log cabin on the farmstead for six years before moving into their farmhouse. The house, like all of the farm's outbuildings, was constructed by members of the family. The property was acquired by the Dayton-Montgomery County Park District in 1968; it has been preserved as a living museum depicting the life and culture of a late 19th-century Ohio farm family.

The Arnold House was built in 1836 as a two-story, three-ranked Federal-style brick house—the walls were three bricks thick—featuring a small green entry porch and double chimneys located at the side gabled ends. The green on the porch matches that on the shutters; all of the windows are shuttered, the six-over-six arrangements upstairs and the nine-over-six arrangements on the ground floor. This original part of the house had five rooms; in 1878, when Daniel's son Henry took over as head of the household, a large addition at the rear of the house was built. The interiors are very plain and sparsely furnished as befits the family's religious beliefs. The interior details include: painted walls, walnut wainscotting throughout, hand-woven rugs, and bare windows.

Additional Information

The 1,000 acre farmstead is listed on the National Register of Historic Places. In addition to the house, there is a blacksmith shop, engine and wood shop, icehouse, smokehouse, summer kitchen, barn, poultry house, carriage shed, sawmill, and sorghum evaporator—all built by the Arnolds. Two other historic properties of note in Dayton are the Dunbar House at Summit Avenue and Third Street, and the Patterson Homestead near the University of Dayton.

Cassius Clark Thompson House

305 Walnut Street
P.O. Box 476
East Liverpool, OH 43920
(216) 386-6026

Contact: East Liverpool Historical Society
Open: By appointment only
Admission: $2.00 per person
Activities: Guided tours, historical lectures, slide shows, special seasonal events including Victorian Christmas tours, and annual Victorian theme dinner
Suggested Time to View House: 2 hours
Description of Grounds: Small city yard on sloping knoll with various shrubs and trees
Best Season to View House: Spring-late fall
Number of Yearly Visitors: 600
Year House Built: 1876
Style of Architecture: Italianate
Number of Rooms: 16
On-Site Parking: Yes
Wheelchair Access: No

Description of House

The eponymous founder of the C. C. Thompson Pottery Company established the firm in 1867 and built this house in 1876; appropriately enough, it now features a large collection of local Thompson pottery. When C. C. died in 1905, his son Odle took over the pottery factory and also moved into the house. He lived here until 1972, and his widow bequeathed the home to the East Liverpool Historical Society in 1979.

The house, which has hardly been altered at all during its nearly 120-year-old history, is a striking two-story Italianate-style home with a large center tower featuring rather ornate wrought-iron finial work.

Additional Information

The Cassius Clark Thompson House is listed on the National Register of Historic Places.

Lewisburg Log House

7693 Swartsel Road
Eaton, OH 45320
(513) 787-4256

Contact: Preble County Historical Society, Inc.
Open: May–Dec., first Sunday of the month 1–5 p.m.; other times by appointment
Admission: Free
Activities: School and group tours
Suggested Time to View House: 1 hour
Facilities on Premises: General store, bank barn and educational building, exhibit hall

Description of Grounds: Farmstead includes 140 acres with creeks, grasslands and woods
Best Season to View House: Spring-fall
Number of Yearly Visitors: 10,000
Year House Built: 1813
Style of Architecture: Folk, log house steep notched design
Number of Rooms: 2
On-Site Parking: Yes **Wheelchair Access:** Yes

Description of House

Henry Horn, a founder of Lewisburg and a blacksmith by trade, was the first recorded occupant of the Lewisburg Log House. Built in 1813, this two-story log house is of a steep notched design, one of several types predominant in the years 1800 to 1825. When the house was moved to its current site, evidence was uncovered that early architectural changes had been made—apparently the work of two different carpenters. The Preble County Historical Society purchased the cabin from the Town of Lewisburg in 1975 for $1.00; they saved it from being torn down to make way for a parking lot.

The furnishings are pre-1840 and many belonged to the original residents, including the Horn family cradle, a double betty lamp, a pair of hog-scraper candlesticks, and a bedspread made before 1850.

Additional Information

Other buildings in the Preble County Historical Farm Center include the Phillips-Swartsel House, the Bank Barn and Educational Building, and the Exhibit Hall. There are extensive nature trails and a herb garden.

Sayler-Swartsel House

7693 Swartsel Road
Eaton, OH 45320
(513) 787-4256

Contact: Preble County Historical
Society, Inc.

Open: May-Dec., first Sunday of the month
1–5 p.m.; other times by appointment

Admission: Free

Activities: School and group tours,
environmental studies, historical
programs and adult workshops, special
seasonal events.

Suggested Time to View House: 1 hour

Description of Grounds: Farmstead
includes 140 acres with creeks,
grasslands and woods

Best Season to View House: Spring-fall

Facilities on Premises: General store, bank
barn and educational center, exhibit hall

Number of Yearly Visitors: 10,000

Number of Rooms: 10

Style of Architecture: Eclectic mix of Greek
and Gothic Revival styles

Year House Built: c. 1860

On-Site Parking: Yes **Wheelchair Access:** Yes

Description of House

This house, built by Sebastian and Eliza Kitson Sayler around 1860, had been in the Sayler-Swartsel family for more than 130 years before the last owner, Sara Swartsel, donated the house to the Preble County Historical Society in 1971. During that time, there were numerous additions and alterations made to the house; even so, the structure, a combination of Greek and Gothic Revival architecture, has retained much of its original character.

The Sayler-Swartsel House is part of the Preble County Historical Farm Center, which also includes the Lewisburg Log House, the Phillips-Swartsel House, and the Bank Barn and Educational Building.

Notable Collections on Exhibit

Items on display include: the St. Clair Columbian Cabinet, hand-carved by Preble County women out of the buckeye tree felled at Fort St. Clair, shown at the 1893 World's Fair; a piano purchased in New York c. 1828; a grandfather clock built in 1812; and a 1903 Model A Ford, a gift from Ohio's oldest Ford dealer. This car is one of only eighty-two currently in existence.

Arthur R. Garford House and Hickories Museum

**509 Washington Avenue
near Ohio Street
Elyria, OH 44035
(216) 322-3341**

Contact: Lorain County Historical Society
Open: Mar.-Dec., Mon.-Fri., Sun. 1–4 p.m.;
groups by appointment; closed holidays
Admission: Adults $2.00; children (5-18) $.50
Activities: Guided tours, lectures,
workshops, rotating exhibits, special
programs and fund raisers
Suggested Time to View House:
45–60 minutes
Facilities on Premises: Small gift shop
Description of Grounds: 1½ acre lawn area
Best Season to View House: Year round
Number of Yearly Visitors: 2,500
Year House Built: Started 1894, completed 1895
Number of Rooms: 20, 6 open to the public

Style of Architecture: Victorian Shingle Style
On-Site Parking: No **Wheelchair Access:** No

Description of House

This three-story home of the leading industrialist, civic leader, and philanthropist Arthur Lovett Garford is as original and imposing as its owner. Garford, who designed and manufactured everything from the first comfortable bicycle seat to the Garford automobile (built with the Studebakers of Indiana) was more than a businessman. A lifelong friend of Teddy Roosevelt, who gave him a moose head—now ensconced in an upstairs hallway—as a symbol of the Bull Moose Party, Garford was active in politics, banking, publishing, and even in developing his community's water supply; he was instrumental in building one of the first water purification and filtration plants in Ohio.

His home reflected his diverse interests and tastes. "The Hickories," designed by well-known Cleveland architect Arthur N. Oviatt, displays an eclectic mix of architectural styles, from Romanesque to Craftsman, and was called a "model" home of the 1890s. The 5,000 square feet interior includes twenty rooms, six fireplaces, sixteen built-in window seats, eight carved scrolls, and sixty elaborately carved wood faces—images of Lucifer and various mythological creatures grotesquely perched above each doorway and window.

Many of the rooms are bathed in light, with their large windows and facing mirrors; in some, Tiffany stained-glass panels even add color. The formal reception room has its original brocade curtains and two black walnut cupboards once belonging to Herman Ely, founder of Elyria. The living room has its original ceiling light fixture, a combination of electric bulbs and gas jets covered in cream-colored onyx shields.

The house was built with running water and central heat, and one bathroom imitates a Roman bath. On the third floor is the party room where the Garfords entertained on a grand scale. The Arthur C. Garford House and Hickories Museum is listed on the National Register of Historic Places.

Rutherford B. Hayes Home– "Spiegel Grove"

1337 Hayes Avenue
Fremont, OH 43420
(419) 332-2081

Contact: Rutherford B. Hayes Presidential
Center and the Ohio Historical Society

Open: Mon.-Sat. 9 a.m.–5 p.m., Sun. and
holidays Noon–5 p.m.; June-Aug. Wed.
9 a.m.–9 p.m; closed Thanksgiving,
Christmas, New Year's Day

Admission: Adults $4.00; seniors $3.25;
children (6-12) $2.00; combination fee for
house and museum

Activities: Guided tours

Suggested Time to View House: 45 minutes

Facilities on Premises: Museum shop,
library and research facilities

Description of Grounds: 25 acre wooded
estate with trails and exotic flora

Best Season to View House: Spring and fall

Number of Yearly Visitors: 45,000

Year House Built: 1859, additions 1880 and
1889

Style of Architecture: Modified Italianate,
brick

Number of Rooms: 33

On-Site Parking: Yes **Wheelchair Access:** No

Description of House

Rutherford B. Hayes (1822-1893), nineteenth President of the United
States, moved into this fine Italianate house in 1873 with his wife, Lucy Webb
Hayes. Hayes was between his second and third terms as Governor of Ohio.
The house had been built in the years 1859 to 1863 by his uncle, Sardis Birchard,
a prominent local businessman. It was given the name Spiegel ("mirror" in
German) Grove because of the sparkling pools of water on the property. He
was elected President in 1876 and served one term in that office, until 1881;
after the four years in Washington, D. C., he and his wife were delighted to
return to their estate in Fremont. Here at Spiegel Grove they lived out their
days and died. The couple is buried on a wooded knoll just off the
Sandusky-Scioto Trail, an old Indian trail which winds through the estate.
Descendants of the President lived here until 1966 when the house was
opened to the public as part of the Rutherford B. Hayes Presidential Center.

The large three-story house is a modified Italianate-style structure featuring unusual double front gables, a veranda, and a combined cupola (lantern) and conservatory. The porch, which is now screened in, has elaborate bracketing and dentil frieze work. On the second floor, the windows are narrow and have flat lintels; above them on the top floor, the small arch-shaped windows are hooded and segmented. Inside, the house features fifteen fireplaces, a bay window off one of the rear bedrooms, a five-landing staircase executed in four different woods, and a plaster ceiling medallion in a sunburst design chosen by Rutherford B. Hayes himself. The parlor, master bedroom, Sardis Birchard bedroom, Fanny Hayes bedroom, and dining room are preserved in their original state and contain the original furniture; the remaining rooms in the house feature pieces belonging to subsequent generations of the Hayes family or collected pieces.

Notable Collections on Exhibit

A number of pieces related to the Hayes Presidency are on display here: the White House china, a lacquered cabinet given to Hayes by the Emperor of Japan, a sideboard originally owned by James Madison, several Lincoln relics, and mementos of the Centennial Exposition.

Additional Information

The Rutherford B. Hayes Home-Spiegel Grove is listed on the National Register of Historic Places.

Brownella Cottage

132 South Union Street
Galion, OH 44833
(419) 486-1026

Contact: Galion Historical Society, Inc.
Open: May-Oct., Sun. 2–5 p.m.
Admission: Adults $1.50; students $.50
Activities: Guided tours, audiovisual presentations, special programs at Christmas
Suggested Time to View House: 1 hour

Description of Grounds: Quarter city block with small yard
Best Season to View House: Spring-fall
Number of Yearly Visitors: 500
Year House Built: 1887
Style of Architecture: Victorian
Number of Rooms: 12
On-Site Parking: Yes **Wheelchair Access:** Yes

Description of House

The only resident of the Brownella Cottage was Bishop Montgomery Brown, a famous figure in the Episcopal Church of the late 19th and early 20th centuries. Bishop Brown was a prolific writer known for his Communist leanings, which led to his being defrocked after a widely publicized heresy trial held in Cleveland in 1924.

Built as a wedding present for Ella Bradford Brown, the Bishop's wife, the house occupies a full quarter of a city block. There is a small area between the attic and the roof where the Bishop watched the stars—he was also an astronomy teacher at the local high school. Unique features of the house include circular steam heat radiators and a glass-covered walkway between the house and an adjacent building.

Furnishings are mostly original to the home and include antique and rare porcelains, clocks, furniture, books, and personal items that belonged to the Bishop and his wife. There are also a foot-pedal house organ and a grand music box. The carriage house on the grounds has been converted into a local historical museum which is open to the public.

Additional Information

Brownella Cottage is listed on the National Register of Historic Places.

Oldest Stone House

14710 Lake Avenue
Lakewood, OH 44107
(216) 221-7343

Contact: Lakewood Historical Society
Open: Feb.-Nov., Sun.and Wed. 2–5 p.m.
Admission: Free
Activities: Guided tours, slide presentations, Ohio Heritage program for school children
Suggested Time to View House: 30–40 minutes
Facilities on Premises: Gift shop
Description of Grounds: Herb garden behind house
Best Season to View House: Summer
Number of Yearly Visitors: 3,000
Year House Built: 1838
Number of Rooms: 5

Style of Architecture: Greek Revival
On-Site Parking: Yes **Wheelchair Access:** No

Description of House

John Honam was a weaver in Scotland before emigrating to the United States and settling on a farm in Lakewood—then called Rockport Township—in 1838. Although it isn't known whether he continued to work as a weaver, there is a special place in the Oldest Stone House for a loom, spinning wheels, and a yarn winder.

The one-and-a-half-story sandstone house features a kitchen, parlor, and bedroom on the first floor and two bedrooms on the second floor. Antique furnishings from the period of the Honam family's residence, 1838 to 1870, are represented in the house.

The Oldest Stone House was one of many built in this area in the first half of the 19th century, but is the only one still standing. It was on the verge of being demolished when arrangements were made to have it moved to Lakewood Park, where it has been restored and now houses the community's museum.

Additional Information

The Oldest Stone House is listed on the National Register of Historic Places.

Sherman House Museum

137 East Main Street
Lancaster, OH 43130
(614) 687-5891

Contact: Fairfield Heritage Association

Open: Apr.-Dec., Tues.-Sat. 1–4 p.m.; open other times by appointment; closed major holidays

Admission: Adults $2.00; students $1.00; group rates available

Activities: Guided tours

Suggested Time to View House: 45–60 minutes

Facilities on Premises: Some gifts and books for sale

Description of Grounds: Small garden with herb beds

Best Season to View House: Spring-fall

Number of Yearly Visitors: 7,500

Year House Built: 1811, additions 1816 and 1870

Style of Architecture: Original frame house Federal style with added Italianate style brick front

Number of Rooms: 9

On-Site Parking: No **Wheelchair Access:** Yes

Description of House

In 1820 William Tecumseh Sherman, the U. S. Army General whose notorious Atlanta Campaign in the Civil War saved the Union and is studied to this day as one of the most efficient military actions in modern history, was born in this house in New Lancaster (the town is now simply called Lancaster) and named Tecumseh ("Shooting Star") after the Shawnee chieftain who had fallen at the Battle of the Thames in 1813. He was one of eleven children born to Charles and Mary Sherman; Charles was a Connecticut-born lawyer who moved to Ohio and started a practice here in 1810, then moved his family out to be with him the following year.

Charles died of fever in 1829 and his widow, Mary, could not afford to raise the family; therefore the children were placed in various area homes. Tecumseh—considered the brightest of the children—was taken in by the Ewings. At the Ewings', he was baptized and given the name William. The father, Thomas Ewing, was a successful attorney who served in the United States Senate from 1831 to 1837. William Tecumseh entered West Point in 1836, married Ewing's daughter Ellen in 1850, practiced law, speculated in real estate and superintended the State Seminary of Learning and Military Academy in Alexandria, Louisiana. Then the War broke out and history was made. Sherman's siblings—most notably his brother John—were active and successful in state and national politics.

The 1811 and 1816 sections of this Federal-style house have been fully restored to their original appearance using documentary evidence of their wallcoverings, paint colors, and carpeting. The 1870 addition houses a Civil War Museum and is done in the later Victorian style. This two-story brick addition to the original frame house features large segmented and arched windows, ornately framed, double doors, and a full-width porch with decorative supports and railings. The furnishings reflect the two eras represented—Federal-style Hepplewhite and Sheraton pieces in the older section and Victorian-style pieces in the addition.

Notable Collections on Exhibit

In addition to the Civil War memorabilia on display, there is also a collection of family artifacts and possessions, including two framed silk on silk needlework pieces done by Mary Hoyt Sherman, William Tecumseh's mother.

Additional Information

The Sherman House, the Thomas Ewing Mansion, and the fully restored 1832 Georgian Museum are all located in Lancaster's Historic District. This district is listed on the National Register of Historic Places.

Louis Bromfield's Big House

4050 Bromfield Road
Lucas, OH 44843
(419) 892-2784

Contact: Malabar Farm State Park

Open: Apr.-Oct., daily 10 a.m.–5 p.m.;
Nov.-Mar., Tues.-Sat. 10 a.m.–5 p.m.;
closed Mondays and major holidays

Admission: Adults $3.00; seniors $2.70;
children $1.00

Activities: Guided tours of house, wagon
tours of farm, special seasonal events
including Ohio Heritage Days

Suggested Time to View House:
45–60 minutes

Best Season to View House: Spring and fall

Facilities on Premises: Gift shop and book
store, restaurant, youth hostel

Description of Grounds: 914 acre working
farm and preserved woodlands located
near state park

Number of Yearly Visitors: 180,000

Year House Built: 1936

Style of Architecture: Eclectic Colonial
Revival with regional influences

Number of Rooms: 32

On-Site Parking: Yes **Wheelchair Access:** Yes

Description of House

In 1939 the writer, agriculturalist and native Ohioan Louis Bromfield followed in his conservationist grandfather's footsteps and put together a working farm out of four neglected parcels of land located a few miles southeast of Mansfield, where he'd been born in 1896. He named the property Malabar Farm after the Malabar Coast of southwest India—the setting of his novel *The Rains Came*—and practiced a sustainable, grass-based agriculture he called "horse-sense farming," claiming it as an educational tool for any who wished to farm using Nature's template. Bromfield supported his farm and family by selling the movie rights to his popular fiction and writing film scripts; in 1927 he'd won the Pulitzer Prize for his novel *Early Autumn* but by the early 1950s his reputation was on the wane. After his death in 1956, the farm was mired in disrepair and debt; two volunteer groups—the Friends of the Land and the Louis Bromfield Malabar Farm Foundation—continued Bromfield's struggle to promote sustainable farming by preserving his noble experiment, and today the farm is one of Ohio's state parks, awaiting its return to prominence in American agriculture.

As impressive as Bromfield's agricultural ideology is the Big House he designed and built with architect Louis Lamoreux; the two deployed the many and varied architectural styles found in northeastern Ohio to create a home which began as a simple small farmhouse and is intended to appear as though it had been added to over the years. Interior details include a magnificent floating double staircase in the main hall, French-made custom wallpapers, an impressive fireplace in the living room surrounded by a huge mirrored wall decorated at the top with forty-eight gilt stars and a golden eagle, solid walnut doors and oak floors, and a superbly idiosyncratic twenty-eight-drawer library desk that Bromfield found to be unusably tall upon its completion. Most of the furnishings in the house are French-style. (Bromfield had served in France during the First World War and lived subsequently lived there for some years.)

Notable Collections on Exhibit

Among the items on display are: several Walt Disney cartoon cells, a collection of Ming Dynasty porcelain, and two original Grandma Moses paintings.

Additional Information

Malabar Farm is listed on the National Register of Historic Places. Also located within the state park is the Malabar Inn, a restored stagecoach inn dating from 1820. The Inn is open from May 1 through October 31 and serves as a "home-style" restaurant.

President Warren G. Harding Home

380 Mount Vernon Avenue
Marion, OH 43302
(614) 297-2332

Contact: Ohio Historical Society
Open: Memorial Day-Labor Day, Wed.-Sat. 9:30 a.m.–5 p.m., Sun. Noon–5 p.m.; Sept. and Oct., Sat. and Sun. Noon–5 p.m.
Admission: Adults $2.50; seniors $2.00; children $1.00; groups rates available
Activities: Guided tours, historical reenactments
Suggested Time to View House: 1 hour
Facilities on Premises: Museum gift shop

Best Season to View House: Summer
Description of Grounds: Large yard with rose gardens and picnic facilities
Style of Architecture: Victorian Queen Anne with elements of Neoclassical style
Number of Yearly Visitors: 6,000
Year House Built: 1891
Number of Rooms: 10
On-Site Parking: Yes **Wheelchair Access:** Yes

Description of House

In 1920 Warren Gamaliel Harding defeated Democrat James Cox to become the twenty-ninth President of the United States—his famous "front-porch campaign" was conducted from the front porch of this house in Marion. The house was built in 1891 specifically for the Hardings—they were married in the house—with help from Mrs. Harding's father, one of the town's wealthiest Republicans. Unfortunately, Harding, the first of eight children born to Dr. George and Phoebe Harding in what is now Blooming Grove, Ohio, never finished his term. While his administration was embroiled in the notorious Teapot Dome scandal, he and his wife went on a transcontinental trip to Alaska during which Harding fell ill; he died in San Francisco on August 2, 1923, and his Vice-President, Calvin Coolidge, assumed the office of President. Mrs. Harding died a year later; both of them are buried at the Harding Memorial here in Marion.

This large cross-gabled, three-story home was built on Marion's main thoroughfare with a grand partial wrap-around porch done in the Neoclassical style—a fine place for a politician to conduct public business. The Queen Anne-style house features multiple Ionic columns, some in groups of three, scallop-design detailing on the front gable, and a dark green finish with white trim on the windows and porch. The interior is decorated in the High Victorian style as typified by the dark green and maroon drapery set against rust-colored flocked wallpaper in most of the downstairs rooms and the floral-patterned wallpaper in the bedrooms. All of the furnishings on display are original to the house; pieces include: a bird's-eye maple bedroom set, the state senator's desk in the library, brass beds in the bedrooms, and the small wood tables in the parlor.

Notable Collections on Exhibit

Many of the Hardings' personal possessions are on display, including Mrs. Harding's shoes, hats, and fans, a large collection of elephant figurines, marble statuary from Italy, and two paintings by Austin Knight.

Additional Information

The Warren G. Harding Home and Museum is listed on the National Register of Historic Places.

Gilbert-Flanigan Saltbox Farmhouse

1031 River Road
Maumee, OH 43537
(419) 893-9602

Contact: Maumee Valley Historical
Society-Wolcott House Museum
Complex

Open: Apr.-Dec.,Wed.-Sat. 1–4 p.m.; closed
major holidays

Admission: Adults $3.50; students $1.50

Activities: Walking tours of historic district,
exhibits

Facilities on Premises: Museum complex
with bookstore

Description of Grounds: 6 acre museum
complex with six restored historic
buildings located on riverfront including
the Wolcott House, the Gilbert-Flanigan
House, and the Noah Navarre Log House

Suggested Time to View House: 30 minutes

Best Season to View House: Early
spring-winter

Number of Rooms: 7

Year House Built: 1841

Style of Architecture: Greek Revival-style
farmhouse

On-Site Parking: Yes **Wheelchair Access:** No

Description of House

This house—built in 1841 by Jarvis Gilbert, a farmer and early resident
of Springfield Township—is a rare example of the Greek Revival-style Ohio
variant of the "saltbox" design which differs from the far more common
Georgian-style saltbox homes found throughout New England. The house
was later owned by the wealthy landowner Daniel Flanigan whose daughter
Minnie lived here until 1965.

Characteristic features of the design exemplified in the Flanigan house are:
matching chimneys on either gabled end, small three-over-three-pane windows set in barge board on the front facade above the typical six-over-six
arrangements, two entrances on that same facade, one leading into the parlor
and one into the family room, and the Greek Revival-style colors—yellow with
white trim. Inside, the floor plan consists of a fully furnished kitchen, parlor,
parlor-bedroom, and family room on the first floor and three bedrooms
upstairs. The interior has been interpreted to the period between 1841 and 1871;
furnishings include many Empire-style pieces and some early Victorian pieces.

Notable Collections on Exhibit

On view in the Flanigan House are several locally-crafted pieces: folk
paintings, a collection of farm implements, spinning wheels, a loom and
quilting frame, and a framed William H. Harrison political campaign banner.

Additional Information

The Gilbert-Flanigan Saltbox Farmhouse (and the Wolcott House listed
next in this guide) are only two of the many fine examples of American
architecture on view in the delightful and historic town of Maumee, Ohio,
located on the Maumee River just south of Toledo and Lake Erie.

Wolcott House

1031 River Road
Maumee, OH 43537
(419) 893-9602

Contact: Maumee Valley Historical Society-Wolcott House Museum Complex

Open: Apr.-Dec., Wed.-Sat. 1–4 p.m.; closed holidays

Admission: Adults $3.50; students $1.50

Activities: Guided tours, exhibits

Suggested Time to View House: 30 minutes

Facilities on Premises: Museum complex with bookstore

Description of Grounds: 6 acre museum complex with six restored historic buildings located on riverfront including the Wolcott House, the Gilbert-Flanigan House and the Noah Navarre Log House

Year House Built: 1835

Best Season to View House: Early spring-winter

Number of Rooms: 8 open to the public

Style of Architecture: Federal style with elements of Early Classical Revival

On-Site Parking: Yes **Wheelchair Access:** No

Description of House

James Wolcott, grandson of Connecticut Governor Oliver Wolcott, traveled from that New England state to Ohio and settled in Maumee where he became the city's mayor and sat on the city council. Wolcott was also a shipbuilder and trader who served as Lucas County judge. He took Mary Wells as his wife—she was the daughter of Captain William Wells, the noted Indian scout, and granddaughter of the great Miami Chief Little Turtle—and built this lovely house for her in 1835.

The Wolcott House is a two-story Federal-style structure exhibiting some elements of the Early Classical Revival. The exterior features a full-height columned porch, twelve-over-twelve-pane windows on the main floor and eight-over-four windows on the second floor, a front door with a glass transom and sidelights, fan-shaped ornamentation on the side gables, and an unusual cut-out pediment. The exterior and interior walls are painted white and the interior trim is done in Federal-style colors. Some of the furnishings belonged to the Wolcotts; these include Windsor-style chairs in the library and a Hepplewhite-style sideboard in the dining room.

Notable Collections on Exhibit

Items on display in the house include: an 18th-century grandfather clock, an English pianoforte, several pieces of Sandwich glass, a large doll and costume collection, a Currier & Ives print, and a collection of early embroidery samplers.

Additional Information

The Wolcott House is listed on the National Register of Historic Places.

James A. Garfield National Historic Site– "Lawnfield"

8095 Mentor Avenue
Mentor, OH 44060
(216) 255-8722

Contact: Western Reserve Historical Society
Open: Tues.-Sat. 10 a.m.–5 p.m.; Sun. Noon–5 p.m.
Admission: Adults $3.00; seniors $2.00; children $1.50; group rates available
Activities: Guided tours
Suggested Time to View House: 45–60 minutes
Facilities on Premises: Visitor center with gift shop

Description of Grounds: 7.8 acre tract with original outbuildings and plantings
Best Season to View House: Spring-fall
Number of Yearly Visitors: 10,000-13,000
Year House Built: 1832, additions c.1850, 1880, 1885
Style of Architecture: Modified Victorian Queen Anne
Number of Rooms: 30
On-Site Parking: Yes **Wheelchair Access:** No

Description of House

James A. Garfield, twentieth President of the United States was born in what is now Moreland Hills, Ohio, on November 19, 1831—it is said that he is the last President to have been born in a log cabin. His father died when he was only two and Garfield began working as a farm hand and muledriver on the Ohio Canal at an early age to supplement his widowed mother's income. Before entering national politics, Garfield had been a teacher, headmaster, lawyer, college principal, Ohio State Senator, and soldier during the Civil War—he was awarded the rank of general for his bravery at Chickamauga. He went to the U.S. House of Representatives as a Radical Republican in 1863. In 1880 he was elected to the Presidency; the following year, Garfield was victim of an assassin's bullet only four months after taking office: a disgruntled and unbalanced office-seeker named Charles Guiteau shot him in a Washington, D. C., railroad station. After lingering two months, Garfield died on September 19, 1881, at the age of forty-nine. The public outpouring of grief and rage after his shooting was such that his widow received over $400,000 in donations; this money was used by Mrs. Garfield to build a library as a memorial to her fallen husband. The Garfield

Memorial Library was the first Presidential Library built in America. Descendants of the President lived in the house until the 1930s.

Lawnfield—acquired by Garfield in 1876—was added to several times as the family grew; the original two-story wood frame structure now has an attic and a full wing built out of stone. Exterior details include an unusual hipped roof, decorative gable detailing, solid and cut-out design brackets, and a small columned side porch. The intent of the ongoing restoration is to interpret the interior to the period of the late 19th century; the next stages of this work include replacing the relatively recent wallcoverings and restoring the porch. The furnishings on display run the gamut of styles that one might find in a late Victorian home: Arts & Crafts Movement, Aesthetic, Egyptian, Colonial Rococo and Renaissance Revivals, and Eastlake. Approximately eighty percent of the pieces belonged to the Garfield family.

Notable Collections on Exhibit

Among the many family items on display is the trunk that Garfield used to carry his belongings while he was serving in the army, his favorite brown leather chair, and, perhaps most touching of all, the funeral wreath sent by Queen Victoria.

Additional Information

Lawnfield, the James A. Garfield Home, is a National Historic Site owned by the National Park Service and run by the Western Reserve Historical Society.

Galpin House

10 Edison Drive, P.O. Box 308
Milan, OH 44846
(419) 499-2968

Contact: Milan Historical Museum, Inc.

Open: Apr., May, Sept. and Oct.,Tues.-Sat.
1–5 p.m.; June, July and Aug., Tues.-Sat.
10 a.m.–5 p.m., Sun. 1–5 p.m.

Admission: Gift box admission; guided
tours $1.00 per person

Activities: Guided tours by appointment,
special seasonal events including
Holiday Open House

Suggested Time to View House: House-
30 minutes, historic district-2 hours

Facilities on Premises: Museum

Best Season to View House: Year round

Description of Grounds: City block with
grounds open to the public

Number of Yearly Visitors: 12,000

Number of Rooms: 11

Year House Built: 1846, right wing addition
1966

Style of Architecture: Greek Revival

On-Site Parking: Yes **Wheelchair Access:** No

Description of House

The Galpin House has two claims to fame: first, it was built by Dr.
Lehman Galpin, the attending physician at the birth of Thomas Alva Edison;
and, second, it features an amazing array of articles on display, from native
American artifacts to an extensive collection of contemporary glass. The
house is large—it had to be to house Galpin's collections—and sits on a
property which also includes a carriage shed, a blacksmith shop, and a
general store. In 1866, a wing was added to the original 1846 structure.

Notable Collections on Exhibit

On display here are over 350 dolls, 1,500 pieces of art glass, 80 mechani-
cal and still banks, numerous Civil War artifacts, clothing and textiles, shells,
large collections of boxes, fans, pewter, and miniature shoes, a "Little Red
Riding Hood" collection, and various pieces of Edison memorabilia. As if
that weren't enough, there's also a large collection of toothpick holders!

Sayles House

26 East Front Street, P.O. Box 308
Milan, OH 44846
(419) 499-2968

Contact: Milan Historical Museum, Inc.

Open: Apr., May, Sept.and Oct., Tues.-Sat. 1–5 p.m.; June, July and Aug., Tues.-Sat. 10 a.m.–5 p.m., Sun. 1–5 p.m.

Admission: Gift box admission

Activities: Guided tours by appointment, special seasonal events including Holiday Open House

Suggested Time to View House: House-30 minutes, historic district-2 hours

Description of Grounds: Benches available

Best Season to View House: Year round

Number of Yearly Visitors: 12,000

Year House Built: 1843

Style of Architecture: Greek Revival

Number of Rooms: 9

On-Site Parking: Yes **Wheelchair Access:** No

Description of House

Milan was a prosperous place in the 1840s when the three-mile-long Milan Canal linked the village with Lake Erie. The Sayles House was built in 1843, during those fat years, and its first occupant was Captain Kline, a shipmaster. Occupied continuously until the 1960s, when it was donated by the Sayles family to the Milan Historical Museum, the house now forms part of a seven building historic complex.

Guests enter the simple Greek Revival-style house through the side porch into the kitchen. The narrow back stairs and a front staircase both give access to the second floor. The up-ground cellar still has its original ceiling which is insulated with six inches of sawdust. The house also features the original locust floors. All of the furniture has been donated to the museum and is authentic to the period from 1800 to 1880. Pieces include a Hepplewhite chest c. 1790, a loveseat and matching chairs in the Louis XV style, and a Renaissance Revival-style breakfront c. 1830.

Notable Collections on Exhibit

A weaving room features quality quilts and spinning wheels made in Ohio and Pennsylvania. Also on display are a pencil-post bed, toy room, and horsehair parlor set.

Additional Information

Two other notable houses located in the complex are the 1830 Wadstrom House at 8 Edison Drive and the 1840 McClure House at 32 East Front Street. Both are also variations of Greek Revival architecture, the most popular style found in Ohio during the era of the Milan Canal.

Thomas A. Edison Birthplace

9 Edison Drive, P.O. Box 451
Milan, OH 44846
(419) 499-2135

Contact: Edison Birthplace Association, Inc.
Open: Feb.-May, Tues.-Sun 1–5 p.m.;
Memorial Day-Labor Day,
Mon.-Sat.10 a.m.–5 p.m., Sun. 1–5 p.m.;
Labor Day-Nov., Tues.-Sun 1–5 p.m.
Admission: Adults $3.00; children (6-12)
$1.50; group rates available
Activities: Guided tours
Suggested Time to View House: 1 hour
Facilities on Premises: Visitor center, gift
and book shop
Best Season to View House: Year round
Description of Grounds: Small front yard
with white picket fence
Number of Yearly Visitors: 14,000
Number of Rooms: 7 open to the public

Style of Architecture: Rural Greek
Revival-style cottage
Year House Built: 1841
On-Site Parking: Yes **Wheelchair Access:** No

Description of House

Thomas Alva Edison's family came to Milan, Ohio, by a circuitous—and violent—route. Edison's great-grandfather was a landowner and Loyalist during the American Revolution. He was under sentence of execution when powerful Whig friends helped him escape to Nova Scotia. There, Edison's grandfather served with the British during the War of 1812 and, in turn, his son—Edison's father—became involved in Canada's own version of our Revolution. Fortunately, he escaped and settled in Ohio. Thomas Edison was much too busy changing the world with his inventions to go out and fight losing battles like his forebears. These inventions included the phonograph and the incandescent light bulb; the exhibit room here has a model of each. There is also a model of the "Black Maria," the first motion picture studio ever built.

This three-story house, constructed in 1841 by Samuel and Nancy Elliott Edison, Thomas's parents, features a first floor sitting room just off the side door entrance; this room contains furniture belonging to Edison's uncle, and a mirror given to his oldest sister on the occasion of her wedding in 1849. Upstairs is the bedroom where Thomas was born in 1847; the bedspread has the year woven into its corner. Though many of the family's possessions were lost during their wanderings, two pieces of Nancy Edison's tea set and two spoons of "coin" silver can still be seen in the parlor. The pine and walnut furniture in the upper bedrooms, the spinning wheel, and the set of chairs in the parlor all belonged to Marion Edison Page.

The house was sold in 1854 by Edison's parents and the family did not return until 1894. Although the house was modernized by Page, electricity was not installed until 1923. Thomas, who had purchased the house in 1906, was shocked to find lamps and candles still used in his birthplace. It has been open to the public since 1947. The Thomas A. Edison Birthplace is listed on the National Register of Historic Places.

Promont

Contact: Milford Area Historical Society

Open: Year-round, Sun. 1:30–4:40 p.m.

Admission: Adults $2.00; children (6-12) $1.00

Activities: Special events including the Quilt Show, Doll and Toy Show, and Christmas Candlelight tours

Suggested Time to View House: 1 hour

Description of Grounds: Grounds are not open to the public

Best Season to View House: Summer

Year House Built: Started 1865, completed 1867

Style of Architecture: Italianate Villa

Number of Rooms: 8

On-Site Parking: Yes **Wheelchair Access:** No

Description of House

Promont was built by the Megrue family in the style of an Italian villa; construction was begun in 1865 and lasted until 1867, but the Megrues only lived in their house for one year. John M. Pattison, Ohio's forty-third governor, lived in the house with his family from 1879 to 1906. Then Henry Hodges, a wealthy tobacco farmer, moved in with his family and stayed until 1945. The last owner of the house, James Korgan, bequeathed Promont to the Milford Area Historical Society in 1983.

Promont's tower affords a panoramic view of Milford and is currently open to the public. Inside the house, fourteen foot ceilings, decorated with ornate medallions and moldings, set off rooms of dramatic spaciousness and light. Many of these rooms feature hand-carved Italian marble fireplaces. The main staircase is solid cherry and a beautiful stained glass window can be seen at the top of the stairs. A stairway leads from the basement to the third floor servants' quarters, where those who lived up there daily filled a water tank to be used by the family in the bathroom just below. Furnishings are authentic to the period of Governor Pattison's occupancy; pieces include a sofa and a china collection.

Notable Collections on Exhibit

Other furniture and artifacts were previously owned by the Gatch family, prominent local residents and founders of the Methodist Church here in 1797, and by John Kugler, an early Milford businessman. There are also paintings by noted Cincinnati-area artists.

Hoover House

2225 Easton Street Northwest
North Canton, OH 44720
(216) 499-0287

Contact: Hoover Historical Center
Open: Tues.-Sun. 1–5 p.m.; closed major
holidays; advanced reservations required
for groups
Admission: Free
Activities: Guided tours, audiovisual
presentations
Suggested Time to View House:
45–60 minutes
Best Season to View House: Spring-fall

Facilities on Premises: Hoover Research
Library
Description of Grounds: Herb gardens
Number of Yearly Visitors: 6,500
Year House Built: 1853, addition 1870
Style of Architecture: Modified
Italianate-style farmhouse
Number of Rooms: 8
On-Site Parking: Yes **Wheelchair Access:** Yes

Description of House

"It beats, as it sweeps, as it cleans." That was the 1920s slogan for the Hoover vacuum cleaner; by then, the Hoover had already acquired a good chunk of the vacuum cleaner market and was well on its way to becoming a household name. The man who started the company, William H. Hoover, was born and grew up in this restored Victorian-era farmhouse. Today, the building houses a collection of antique and early electric vacuum cleaners, as well as some very modern models.

His father, Daniel Hoover, came to Stark County in 1827 from Pennsylvania and apprenticed with a tanner at the age of sixteen. Eventually he started his own business and visitors can see some of his equipment in the fireplace room of the Hoover House.William joined his father in the tannery and purchased the business in 1871, subsequently expanding it to include horse collar and saddlery goods manufacturing. Although the tannery was successful, William had big dreams. He purchased a patent from the inventor of the suction sweeper and began manufacturing and selling the product under the name "The Electric Suction Sweeper." The rest is domestic history.

Hoover House is a two-story frame structure built in two stages: the rear portion in 1853, and the front in 1870. It features a hipped roof with asphalt shingles and an overhanging bracketed cornice. The woodwork, doors, window glass, and much of the hardware throughout the interior is original to the house. Though there are some pieces of Victorian furniture on display, the Hoover House is not furnished as a home. With its unique collection of domestic cleaning devices, it now serves as a museum that brings to life the history of an era and an industry. The Hoover House is listed on the National Register of Historic Places.

Notable Collections on Exhibit

In the upstairs gallery, there is a permanent collection of vacuum cleaners, including the "talking" Sensotronic Audio 500 Cleaner from France. In addition, there are changing exhibits and video presentations in the downstairs galleries. A research library is open to the public; it is a comprehensive resource for information on tanning, the vacuum cleaner industry, the Hoover Company, and the Hoover family.

U.S. Grant's Birthplace

U.S. Highway 52 and Route 232
Point Pleasant, OH 45153
(515) 753-7141

Contact: Land of Grant Tours
Open: Apr.-Oct., Wed.-Sat. 9:30 a.m.–Noon,
1–5 p.m., Sun. Noon–5 p.m.
Admission: Adults $1.00; seniors $.75;
children (6-12) $.50
Activities: Self-guided tours
Suggested Time to View House:
20–30 minutes
Best Season to View House: Spring and fall

Facilities on Premises: Grant-related
material for sale
Description of Grounds: Scenic view of the
Ohio River in park setting
Number of Yearly Visitors: 6,000
Year House Built: 1817
Style of Architecture: Folk, clapboard frame
Number of Rooms: 3
On-Site Parking: Yes **Wheelchair Access:** No

Description of House

Jesse Root Grant was a foreman at a tannery in the prosperous riverfront town of Point Pleasant; he and his family lived in a house which they rented from Lee Thompson. On April 27, 1822, the Grants had a son who they named Hiram Ulysses. This son would, of course, attend the U. S. Military Academy under the name Ulysses Simpson Grant, achieve worldwide fame as the General who won the Civil War for Lincoln, and serve as America's eighteenth President. When the child was only one, the Grants moved to nearby Georgetown, where Jesse started his own tannery. A few years later, Ulysses boarded with the Kirker family while attending school in Ripley. In 1845, some six years after their son graduated from West Point, the Grants moved to Bethel and Jesse became the town's first mayor in 1851. After U. S. Grant's death in 1877, the little Point Pleasant house was taken on a tour throughout the country.

The house in which the future President was born is a simple side-gabled, one-story frame structure measuring slightly less than twenty feet square. The layout consists of a kitchen with a large cooking fireplace, a living room, and a bedroom. Today the house is furnished with period pieces, some of which belonged to the Grant family. These include: a corner cupboard, boots, a chest with Jesse's initials ("JRG") carved into it, some articles of clothing, and pillows.

Notable Collections on Exhibit

On display here is Grant's personal travel box, which he used when President.

Additional Information

All of the sites associated with Ulysses S. Grant's youth can be found here in Southern Ohio's Clermont County: Point Pleasant, Georgetown, Ripley, and Bethel. In addition to the historic sites associated with Grant, one may also visit the Rankin Home in Ripley—a major stop on the Underground Railway.

Oran Follett Museum

404 Wayne and East Adams Streets
Sandusky, OH 44870
(419) 627-9608

Contact: Sandusky Library
Open: Memorial Day through Labor Day,
daily 1–4 p.m.; Labor Day through
December, Sun., Tues., Thurs. 1–4 p.m.;
closed Thanksgiving and Christmas
Admission: Donations welcome
Activities: Guided tours
Suggested Time to View House:
60–90 minutes
Facilities on Premises: Small gift shop and
reference library
Description of Grounds: Large lawn with
shrubs and trees
Best Season to View House: Summer
Year House Built: Started 1834,
completed 1837
Number of Yearly Visitors: 6,000
Number of Rooms: 14

Style of Architecture: Greek Revival
On-Site Parking: No **Wheelchair Access:** No

Description of House

Oran Follett started his career in newspaper publishing; he edited, published, and eventually owned newspapers in Batavia and Buffalo, New York. In 1823 he was elected to the New York State Legislature. Eleven years later, he moved his family to Sandusky, Ohio, where he became involved in real estate, banking, and railroads. He was named Superintendent of the Ohio Board of Public Works, a position in which he supervised the construction of many canals and roads. In later life, Follett fought slavery on the editorial pages of the influential *Ohio State Journal*, of which he was part owner. His wife, Eliza Ward Follett, was well known as a tireless worker on behalf of the poor and ill.

Follett started construction on this Greek Revival house in 1834; it was completed in 1837. Although it still contains some original furniture and personal items belonging to the Follett family, it is used primarily as a library and museum which displays memorabilia from Sandusky's early years.

Notable Collections on Exhibit

Displayed on the first floor are two paintings by Charles C. Curran, numerous old maps and pictures, pewter plates, and a weaving and spinning room with antique quilts. On the second floor is an exhibit relating the history of Johnson's Island Confederate War Prison and the Civil War.

Additional Information

The Oran Follett Museum is listed on the National Register of Historic Places.

"House of Seven Oaks"

602 North Washington Street
Van Wert, OH 45891
(419) 238-5297

Contact: Van Wert County Historical Society
Open: Year-round, Sun. 2–4 p.m.
Admission: Free
Activities: Guided tours, special seasonal events including Fourth of July Craft Fair, Christmas Dinner and Open House
Suggested Time to View House: 90 minutes
Facilities on Premises: Museum and annex
Description of Grounds: Front lawn
Best Season to View House: Summer
Number of Yearly Visitors: 4,000
Year House Built: 1898
Style of Architecture: Folk Victorian
Number of Rooms: 9

On-Site Parking: No **Wheelchair Access:** Yes

Description of House

The House of Seven Oaks was originally the residence of the John Clark family, who owned and operated the first cobbler shop in town. Descendants of the Clarks lived here until 1955, when William Fosnaught, a local attorney and school teacher, donated the house to the Van Wert Historical Society. Community members have donated thousands of artifacts to the museum, which is maintained as an example of a typical Victorian home or the era.

The limestone structure features a large front porch and curved front windows. A historic gazebo c. 1860s, originally sited on the grounds of the Van Wert County Courthouse, has been relocated to the front lawn of Seven Oaks and a one-room wooden schoolhouse is expected to be moved to the site as well.

Notable Collections on Exhibit

Paintings done by a local artist, Winifred Bonnewitz Ford, are on display here, as well as a collections of railroad memorabilia housed in a 1951 Penn Central caboose.

Mac-A-Cheek Castle

10051 Township Road 47, P.O. Box 507
West Liberty, OH 43357
(513) 465-2821

Contact: Piatt Castles
Open: Mar., Sat. and Sun. Noon–4 p.m.;
Apr., daily Noon–4 p.m.; May–Sept.,
daily 11 a.m.–5 p.m.; Oct., daily
Noon–4 p.m.
Admission: Adults $5.00; seniors and
students $4.00; children (6-12) $3.00;
children (under 6) free
Activities: Guided tours, adult and school
programming
Suggested Time to View House: 45 minutes
Description of Grounds: Gardens bordered
by extensive lawns in a rural setting
Best Season to View House: Late
Spring-fall
Number of Yearly Visitors: 20,000
Year House Built: Started 1864,
completed 1871
Number of Rooms: 32

Style of Architecture: Eclectic Norman-
French
On-Site Parking: Yes **Wheelchair Access:** Yes

Description of House

Mac-A-Cheek was built in the years 1864 to 1871 by Abram Piatt at the
place where the stream for which the castle is named joins the Mad River.
The castle walls are constructed of limestone; other materials include vir-
gin-cut walnut, oak, cherry, and other woods, all of which came from the
estate. The decorations were painted by Oliver Frey in 1881. The castle
features many original furnishings and other objects that belonged to the
Piatt family; these pieces range from 100 to 250 years old.

Notable Collections on Exhibit

In addition to the furnishings mentioned above, the Castle also houses
a rich collection of Native American artifacts and over 300 years worth of
family possessions, ranging from weapons to books.

Additional Information

The Mac-A-Cheek Castle is listed on the National Register of Historic
Places. It stands less than a mile from the similarly named Mac-O-Chee
Castle listed below.

Mac-O-Chee Castle

10051 Township Road 47, P.O. Box 507
West Liberty, OH 43357
(513) 465-2821

Contact: Piatt Castles
Open: Mar., Sat. and Sun. Noon–4 p.m.;
Apr., daily Noon–4 p.m.; May-Sept., daily
11 a.m.–5 p.m.; Oct., daily Noon–4 p.m.
Admission: Adults $5.00; seniors and
students $4.00; children (6-12) $3.00;
children (under 6) free
Activities: Guided tours, adult and school
programming
Suggested Time to View House: 45 minutes

Description of Grounds: Gardens bordered
by extensive lawns in a rural setting
Best Season to View House: Late Spring-fall
Number of Yearly Visitors: 20,000
Year House Built: Started 1864, completed
1881
Style of Architecture: Gothic frame with
Flemish Chateau-style addition
Number of Rooms: 37
On-Site Parking: Yes **Wheelchair Access:** Yes

Description of House

Viewing the Castle Mac-O-Chee on its magnificent site above the beautiful valley of which it has been said, "A man can better live and die here than
in any place I have ever seen," it is not impossible to imagine that one has
been transported to the Rhineland. The castle was built by Colonel Donn
Piatt, editor, diplomat, writer, and social critic.

Piatt married Louise Kirby, daughter of Timothy Kirby, a devoted Whig.
Colonel Piatt was an equally devoted Democrat, therefore Kirby strongly
opposed the union and the couple had to marry secretly. Soon after, Piatt
was appointed chargé d'affaires to the court of Louis Napoleon under the
Second Empire and Louise wrote a series of articles for the *Ladies' Home
Journal* about her life in Paris. Back in the United States during the Civil War,
Donn began building a Gothic-style home on his property for Louise but her
health deteriorated rapidly and never saw its completion. She was finally
reunited with her father just before her untimely death at the age of thirty-
eight. After the Civil War Piatt founded and edited *The Washington Capital*,

served as editor of *Belford's Magazine*, wrote poetry, and authored several volumes of fiction and non-fiction.

In 1879, the Colonel engaged his nephew, William McCoy Piatt, to design and build a castle to encase the earlier home built on the site; here he retired to write and farm. The Colonel had no surviving children and, after his death, his second wife, Ella, sold the castle. In the 1940s, a subsequent owner refurnished the Castle with objects collected from palaces and castles around the world. The Piatt family bought Mac-O-Chee again in 1956 and opened it for public viewing shortly thereafter. The extravagantly decorated limestone structure, with its two towers and slate roof, features original gaslight fixtures, plumbing, and parquet floors.

Notable Collections on Exhibit

The Castle contains an intriguing collection of European and Asian furnishings and objects, as well as special displays highlighting the life and careers of Donn, Louise, and Ella Piatt.

Additional Information

Less than a mile from Mac-O-Chee is the Mac-A-Cheek Castle, built by Donn Piatt's brother, Abram. That house is listed above. The Castle is listed on the National Register of Historic Places.

Rombach Place

149 East Locust Street, P.O. Box 529
Wilmington, OH 45177
(513) 382-4684

Contact: Clinton County Historical Society
Open: Mar.-Dec., Wed.-Fri. and the first
weekend of the month 1–4:30 p.m.
Admission: Donations welcome
Activities: Guided tours
Suggested Time to View House:
45–60 minutes
Facilities on Premises: Gift shop, art
gallery and genealogy library
Description of Grounds: Carriage house
and herb garden
Best Season to View House: Summer
Number of Yearly Visitors: 2,000-2,500
Year House Built: 1835, addition 1920
Number of Rooms: 20

Style of Architecture: Greek Revival
On-Site Parking: Yes **Wheelchair Access:** Yes

Description of House

Matthew Rombach bought this twenty-room Greek Revival-style home in 1855. A year later, James W. Denver married Louise Kathryn Rombach and their descendants lived here over the next four generations. Denver, a native Virginian who served as a Brigadier General during the Civil War, went on to become a successful businessman, Governor of Kansas, and Indian Commissioner. His family is still active in local businesses.

Originally there were eight rooms in the Rombach house, including the formal parlors, library, sitting room, and four bedrooms. Additions were made to the house in 1860 and again in the 1920s. The valance and mirrors are original to the house; most of the furnishings are collected period pieces.

Notable Collections on Exhibit

On display is a collection of Eli Harvey sculptures and paintings, as well as photographs by Carl Moon.

Additional Information

The Rombach Place is listed on the National Register of Historic Places.

Number One House—
The "King's Palace" at Zoar Village

Route 212, P.O. Box 404
Zoar, OH 44697
(216) 874-4336

Contact: Zoar Village State Memorial

Open: April-May, Sept.-Oct., Sat.
9:30 a.m.–5 p.m., Sun. Noon–5 p.m.;
May-Sept., Wed.-Sat. 9:30 a.m.–5 p.m.,
Sun.and holidays Noon–5 p.m.

Admission: Adults $3.00; seniors $2.40;
children (6-12) $1.00; children (under
age 5) free; group rates available

Activities: Guided tours, introductory
video, special events, craft
demonstrations, festivals

Suggested Time to View House: 90 minutes

Facilities on Premises: Gift shop

Description of Grounds: "Living history"
museum village with eight restored
buildings and formal gardens

Best Season to View House: Summer and
early fall

Number of Yearly Visitors: 18,000

Year House Built: 1835

Style of Architecture: Georgian

Number of Rooms: 18

On-Site Parking: Yes **Wheelchair Access:** No

Description of House

Fueled by the hope for freedom from religious persecution, some three hundred men, women, and children left southeastern Germany for the United States in 1817. They wished to worship according to their own lights; their way was one of simple communication with God, bereft of any ceremony, in a community of like-minded people. The Zoar community took their name from Lot's biblical town of refuge; the name translates as "a sanctuary from evil." They finally found their sanctuary here, on the banks of the Tuscaras River in Ohio.

The first homes the Zoar group built were simple log structures with shingle roofs. Though they had planned to enjoy private ownership of their land and homes, hard winters and scarce crops made communal life necessary. By 1834, the group had paid its debts and amassed a crop surplus. Their financial success did not help them overcome the death of the spiritual leader, Joseph Baumeler. Baumeler was a teacher, physician, business manager, architect, and pastor to the Separatists. When the railroad brought the outside world to its doorsteps, and with the rise of cheap mass-produced goods whose price they could not match, the community disbanded. Today the village remains a quiet, peaceful group of shops, private homes, gardens, and a museum—an oasis of simplicity and rural charm.

Number One House c. 1835 is a two-story Georgian-style structure originally planned as a home for the aged and infirm. Instead, it became the residence of Joseph Baumeler and two other trustee families. All of the food and provisions for the community were at one time stored in the cool cellar of this house. It features a recessed portico and stands as a good example of the distinctive German construction techniques which were rather uncommon then. Today visitors can see an introductory slide presentation on the Zoar community, as well as examples of their crafts.

Additional Information

Zoar Village is listed on the National Register of Historic Places.

Oklahoma

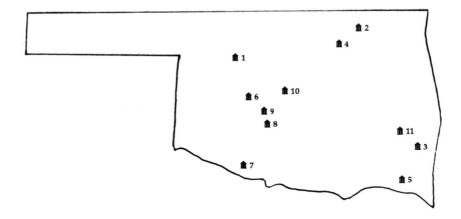

1. **Aline**
   Sod House Museum

2. **Bartlesville**
   Frank Phillips Home
   Woolaroc Lodge and Museum
   Complex

3. **Heavener**
   Peter Conser House

4. **Hominy**
   Drummond House

5. **Idabel**
   Barnes-Stevenson House

6. **Kingfisher**
   Seay Mansion, "Horizon Hill"

7. **Lawton**
   Mattie Beal Home

8. **Norman**
   Moore-Lindsey House

9. **Oklahoma City**
   Hefner Mansion
   Overholser Mansion

10. **Pawnee**
    Pawnee Bill Mansion

11. **Sallisaw**
    Sequoyah's Cabin

Sod House Museum

**4 miles north of Cleo Springs off Route 8
Aline, OK 73716
(405) 463-2441**

Contact: Oklahoma Historical Society
Open: Tues.-Fri. 9 a.m.–5 p.m., Sat. and
Sun. 2–5 p.m.; closed major holidays
Admission: Free
Activities: Guided tours, annual Pioneer
Christmas Program
Suggested Time to View House: 1 hour
Description of Grounds: Field with
horse-drawn equipment
Best Season to View House: Year round
Number of Yearly Visitors: 20,000
Year House Built: 1894
Style of Architecture: National, sod
Number of Rooms: 2

On-Site Parking: Yes **Wheelchair Access:** Yes

Description of House

This sod house is the only one built by a homesteader still standing in Oklahoma. Marshall McCully came to Aline in 1893, when the Cherokee Outlet was opened for settlement; in 1894, he and his family moved into this "soddy" and lived here until 1909. Then they moved into a new frame house and thereafter used the sod house for storage.

These sod houses—made out of buffalo grass sod cut into blocks—were meant to be temporary dwellings; their floors were originally dirt, but wooden planks began to be used around 1895. Alkali clay was used to plaster the interior walls and burlap flour sacks were sewn together to cover the ceiling, thus preventing dirt and debris from falling into the house.

The McCully's sod house has its original blackjack rafters and cedar pole supports. It is believed that the house survived because of the protection it got from the frame house to the west and a large elm tree just to the south. Most of the furnishings on display here came from other Oklahoma sod dwellings.

Notable Collections on Exhibit

Here one finds the homely artifacts of a typical homestead family: stoneware dishes, iron cookware, quilts, needlework pieces, and some toys; and, out in the yard, horse-drawn farm equipment

Additional Information

Sod House Museum is listed on the National Register of Historic Places.

Frank Phillips Home

1107 South Cherokee
Bartlesville, OK 74003
(918) 336-2491

Contact: Oklahoma Historical Society
Open: Year-round, Tues.-Fri. 9 a.m.–5 p.m.,
  Sat. and Sun. 2–5 p.m.; closed state
  holidays and all Tuesdays which follow
  Monday holidays
Admission: Free
Activities: Guided tours, special exhibits
Suggested Time to View House: 40 minutes
Description of Grounds: Original
  greenhouse, gardeners' shed and many
  plantings
Style of Architecture: Eclectic Neoclassical
  with Greek Revival characteristics
Best Season to View House: Spring-fall
Number of Yearly Visitors: 18,000
Number of Rooms: 26

Year House Built: 1909, remodeled 1930
On-Site Parking: Yes **Wheelchair Access:** Yes

Description of House

Frank Phillips dreamed of becoming a barber—by the time he was twenty, he owned virtually all of the barbershops in and around his hometown of Creston, Iowa—but married a banker's daughter and went into banking instead. When business took him to the Indian Territory, Phillips saw the enormous mineral potential in that unclaimed land. So he moved to Bartlesville in 1904 and, with his brother, L. E. Phillips, began to drill for oil. Their first three wells were "dusters," but with number four they struck black gold. Eventually, the brothers would organize the Phillips Petroleum Company; L. E. did the accounting and Frank arranged the financing. By the 1930s, their company was a leader in the industry.

Frank and his wife, Jane, built this magnificent twenty-six-room Greek Revival mansion in 1909. It was designed by Walton Everman to impress, from the full-height columned portico to the pink brick walls to the tiled roof. The opulence of the interior is perhaps best seen in the massive staircase fashioned out of Philippine mahogany, the brocaded walls, crystal chandeliers, and the decorative plaster embellishments on the ceilings.

In 1930-1931, the interior of the mansion underwent a thorough remodeling; it including enlarging the house and adding further refinements to the interior: imported wood trim and paneling, bathrooms, marble and damask wallcoverings, and even a barber's chair. The household furnishings seen here all belonged to the original Phillips family collection.

Additional Information

The Frank Phillips Home is listed on the National Register of Historic Places. Phillips's country retreat, "Woolaroc," which is also listed in this guide, is located approximately fourteen miles southwest of Bartlesville. It is now a lodge, museum, and wildlife preserve.

Woolaroc Lodge and Museum Complex

FP Ranch on Route 3
Bartlesville, OK 74003
(918) 336-0307

Contact: Frank Phillips Foundation, Inc.
Open: Tues.-Sat. 10 a.m–5 p.m.; special summer hours, daily 10 a.m.–8 p.m.; closed Thanksgiving, Christmas
Admission: Adults $4.00; seniors $3.00
Activities: Museum exhibits
Suggested Time to View House: 30 minutes
Facilities on Premises: Visitor center
Best Season to View House: Year round

Description of Grounds: Large ranch complex consisting of the Woolaroc Lodge, museum and guide center, wildlife preserve
Number of Yearly Visitors: 200,000
Year House Built: c.1925, repaired 1934
Style of Architecture: Elaborate "rustic" log cabin
Number of Rooms: 25
On-Site Parking: Yes **Wheelchair Access:** Yes

Description of House

Here in the Osage Hills, on a steep rock ledge that drops down to Clyde Lake, Frank Phillips built his country retreat, Woolaroc Lodge. The founder of the Phillips Petroleum Company first discovered the natural beauty of the area when he was drilling for oil on property leased from the Osage Indian tribe. In 1909, he built an impressive mansion in the town of Bartlesville (listed above) and, fifteen years later, began construction on this property.

The Lodge was planned to look like a log cabin, but the resemblance to an ordinary log cabin ends with the name. The first section built consisted of a kitchen and dining room—the dining room itself is a replica of the entire log cabin in which Phillips was born! A year later, the main section was built; it comprises the Great Hall and balcony, and nine bedrooms, each with its own bathroom. The rough log walls are chinked with cement and the floors are either hardwood or sandstone. In 1934, some of the logs in the north wall were replaced by concrete "logs" made to simulate wood; in 1959 to 1960, new pine logs and timbers were added, as well as steel supports.

Notable Collections on Exhibit

The most striking thing about the Lodge are the furnishings and objects it contains: a collection of animal heads and horns—once rated as one of the most complete in the world by Lloyd's of London—which includes many specimens culled from Phillips's own unsuccessful attempt to breed exotic animals here, four chandeliers in the Great Hall which used to hang in the Tap Room of New York's old Waldorf-Astoria Hotel before it was torn down (Phillips had been a partner in the hotel), Navajo Indian ritual rugs and blankets, a bark-covered piano, cow-horn chairs, ashtrays made from elk and buffalo hooves, and several fine paintings by the well-known western artists O. E. Berninghaus and Henry Balink. Of these unusual pieces, Phillips's own favorite is said to have been the Texas longhorn steer which sits on the balcony railing above the living room—when a button is pushed, its eyes light up, smoke billows out of its nose, and the voice of Will Rogers issues forth from its mouth!

Additional Information

Two miles from the Lodge (where visitors can see the Woolaroc monoplane which flew across the Pacific in 1927) is a Wildlife Preserve; also located on the grounds are the 1940s Trader's Camp, nature trail, and children's petting zoo.

Peter Conser House

Star Route and U.S. Highway 59
Heavener, OK 74937
(918) 653-2493

Contact: Oklahoma Historical Society
Open: Year-round, Tues.-Fri. 9 a.m.–5 p.m.,
Sat. and Sun. 2–5 p.m.; closed state
holidays
Admission: Free
Activities: Guided tours
Suggested Time to View House: 1 hour
Description of Grounds: Grass and shrub
yard. Family graveyard also on-site.
Best Season to View House: Spring and
summer
Number of Yearly Visitors: 7,000
Year House Built: 1894
Style of Architecture: National, frame
Number of Rooms: 8

On-Site Parking: Yes **Wheelchair Access:** No

Description of House

Peter Conser, born Peter Coinson, had a difficult childhood: his father, a trader of French descent, and his mother, a Native American of the Choctaw tribe, separated when he was young, and his mother died of smallpox soon thereafter. He worked as a farmhand in the south during the Civil War; when the war ended, he returned to Oklahoma and began farming. Through his own hard work and head for business, Conser became quite wealthy. He was made deputy sheriff in Sugar Loaf County and a captain of the Choctaw Lighthorse, the mounted police force that patrolled the Five Civilized Tribes. Later, he served as representative, then senator, to the Choctaw council. In addition, he ran a blacksmith shop, grist mill, saw mill, general store, and post office in town.

Conser married Amy Bacon, also a Choctaw, but she died after a brief period; he then married Martha Jane Smith, with whom he had eight children. In 1894, he built this two-story frame house for his family. Mrs. Lewis Barnes, a granddaughter of Peter Conser, donated the house to the Oklahoma Historical Society who have restored it to its original appearance during the Indian Territory period.

Additional Information

The Peter Conser House is listed on the National Register of Historic Places.

Drummond House

305 North Price Street
Hominy, OK 74035
(918) 885-2374

Contact: Oklahoma Historical Society
Open: Year-round, Tues.-Fri. 9 a.m.–5 p.m.,
Sat. and Sun. 2–5 p.m.; closed state
holidays
Admission: Free
Activities: Guided tours upon request,
audiovisual presentation
Suggested Time to View House:
30–45 minutes
Description of Grounds: Landscaped yard
Best Season to View House: Spring-fall
Number of Yearly Visitors: 3,000
Year House Built: 1905
Style of Architecture: Victorian Shingle
Style
Number of Rooms: 14

On-Site Parking: Yes **Wheelchair Access:** No

Description of House

Fred Drummond arrived in the United States from Scotland in 1884 and dreamt of becoming a rancher. He soon got a dose of reality when the Texas cattle venture he'd joined fell through. Though Drummond was forced to settle for a less glamorous job as a clerk for a mercantile company in St. Louis, his dreams persisted.

In 1886, he moved to the Osage Reservation in Pawhuska and became a government-licensed trader; four years later, he married Adeline Gentner. His dreams began to take on the aspect of reality when he was able to take his savings and buy out another trader in Hominy; soon he was on his way to expanding into ranching, banking, and real estate speculation, becoming a wealthy man in the process.

This three-story, fourteen-room house was completed in 1905 and fully reflects Drummond's hard-won financial success. It features a central squared tower, a second-floor balcony, and false dormers. The first story is built of native sandstone, while the upper floors are framed in wood and covered in shingles of alternating light and dark green. By the 'teens, the house had electricity, natural gas, and city water; this is the period that it has been restored to. It was deeded to the Oklahoma Historical Society in 1980, and is listed on the National Register of Historic Places.

Barnes-Stevenson House

302 Southwest Adams Street
Idabel, OK 74745
(405) 286-6314

Contact: McCurtain County Historical
Society
Open: May-Sept., Sun. 2–4 p.m.; other times
by appointment
Admission: Free
Activities: Guided tours
Suggested Time to View House: 30 minutes
Best Season to View House: Spring-fall

Description of Grounds: Simple grounds
with landscaping under development
Number of Yearly Visitors: 500
Year House Built: 1912
Style of Architecture: Late Victorian Queen
Anne, free classic style
Number of Rooms: 16
On-Site Parking: Yes **Wheelchair Access:** No

Description of House

The young lawyer Thomas Jefferson Barnes arrived in McCurtain County in 1902 with little to call his own; by 1907, the year that Oklahoma became a state, he'd become a judge and a leading figure in county government. Judge Barnes, whose income was derived largely from banking and real estate investments, decided to build a home for his family here in Idabel in 1912 and chose Jewell Hicks, a well-known Oklahoma architect, to design it.

The two-story structure has sixteen rooms, was built of the finest materials available (for example, the basement is concrete and brick), and incorporated into its design all of the latest conveniences: indoor plumbing, electric lights, and a coal-fired central heating system. The first floor wood-work is of quartered hand-finished oak and the parquet floors are made of white ash; most of the windows have leaded glass panes.

Judge Barnes died in 1950 and his wife twenty years later. Harold Stevenson, Jr., an artist, bought the house and helped raise the finances used to restore it. Today the fully restored house is owned by the McCurtain County Historical Society and is listed on the National Register of Historic Places.

Seay Mansion– "Horizon Hill"

Eleventh Street and Zellers Avenue
Kingfisher, OK 73750
(405) 375-5176

Contact: Chisholm Trail Museum, Inc.
Open: Tues.-Sat. 9 a.m.–5 p.m., Sun.
1–5 p.m.
Admission: Free
Activities: Guided tours, annual Christmas
Open House
Suggested Time to View House: 30 minutes
Facilities on Premises: Gift shop and book
store across street at museum
Description of Grounds: Landscaped yard
Best Season to View House: Spring-fall
Style of Architecture: Modified Victorian
Queen Anne, towered
Number of Yearly Visitors: 9,000
Number of Rooms: 10

Year House Built: 1892
On-Site Parking: Yes **Wheelchair Access:** Yes

Description of House

Even though Abraham Jefferson Seay's dream—that the town of Kingfisher would be named the capital of the Oklahoma Territory—was never realized, his contributions to the development of the state and the welfare of its people were memorable. Seay was born in Virginia in 1832 and moved to Missouri where he became a teacher, lawyer, judge, businessman, banker, and politician. During the Civil War, he served for four years in the Union Army.

After the war, he returned to civilian life and practiced law before being appointed Associate Justice of the first Supreme Court of the Oklahoma Territory; from that position his star rose steadily. His court was known as a "shotgun court" because of his blunt—but fair—judgments. Seay was definitely someone who could make things happen: he presided over the opening of the Cheyenne and Arapaho lands, improved conditions for blacks in the Territory, and proved to be a moving force in securing grants for educational institutions.

He built this three-story late Queen Anne-style mansion in 1892 on 15 acres just outside Kingfisher. It features a hipped roof, cross-gabling, and a tower. The interior still has its original woodwork, parquet flooring, and three-way fireplace decorated with imported Italian tiles.

Notable Collections on Exhibit

Pieces on display include: a collection of Haviland china, sterling silver, and pewter coffee and tea services. There is also an extensive array of Civil War memorabilia.

Additional Information

The Seay Mansion, "Horizon Hill," is listed on the National Register of Historic Places. Also located at the same address are two other historic homes which have been moved to this site: the Dalton Cabin (home of the infamous Dalton brothers) and the Cole Cabin, home to a territorial settler and his family.

Mattie Beal Home

1006 Southwest Fifth Street
at corner of Summit Street
Lawton, OK 73502
(405) 353-6884

Contact: Lawton Heritage Association

Open: Second Sundays 1:30–4 p.m.; special hours at Christmas and Lawton's Birthday; other times by appointment

Admission: Adults $1.00; children (under 12) $.50

Activities: Guided tours, special Christmas displays

Suggested Time to View House: 45 minutes

Facilities on Premises: Limited publications for sale

Description of Grounds: Fenced grounds

Style of Architecture: Eclectic Neoclassical with Italian and Greek Revival elements

Best Season to View House: Spring

Number of Yearly Visitors: 1,800

Number of Rooms: 13

Year House Built: 1908, remodeled 1923

On-Site Parking: Yes **Wheelchair Access:** No

Description of House

Mattie Beal was a feisty and brave twenty-two-year-old woman from Kansas who entered the Oklahoma Territory land lottery; on July 29, 1901, her name was selected and she became the owner of 160 acres of prime land here, in an area that would become the town of Lawton. Miss Beal found that her newly won position in Oklahoma society attracted suitors. She finally chose one out of the many proposals she'd received and wed Charles Payne; the couple had three children—Lahoma, Martha Helen, and Louisa.

Plans for their house were drawn up in 1907 and construction was completed around 1910. The design of the thirteen-room mansion shows a superb mix of Greek Revival and Italianate elements; most impressive are the semi-circular, full-height entrance portico, the Corinthian columns, and the dentiled cornices. Inside, stained glass windows depict scenes of the Wichita Mountains. Most of the furnishings are from the 1920s; some are original to the Paynes.

Notable Collections on Exhibit

A monthly open house is held here which affords local artists and craftspeople the opportunity to exhibit their works.

Additional Information

The Mattie Beal Home is listed on the National Register of Historic Places. It is available for luncheons, meetings, weddings, and receptions.

Moore-Lindsey House

508 North Peters Street, P.O. Box 260
Norman, OK 73070
(405) 321-0156

Contact: Cleveland County Historical
Museum

Open: Sat. 10 a.m.–5 p.m.; other times by
appointment

Admission: Donation

Activities: Guided tours, concerts, projects
for scouts

Suggested Time to View House:
45–60 minutes

Facilities on Premises: Some items for sale

Description of Grounds: Town yard with
shrubs and trees

Best Season to View House: Year round

Number of Yearly Visitors: 2,000

Year House Built: c.1900

Number of Rooms: 8

Style of Architecture: Victorian Queen Anne

On-Site Parking: Yes **Wheelchair Access:** Yes

Description of House

Oklahoma proved to be fertile ground for William Moore's talents to bear fruit—he and his wife, Agnes, moved to Norman from Missouri in the mid 1890s and, by 1908, he was listed in the city directory simply as "capitalist." His primary investments were in real estate; in 1899 his success in that field was recognized when he was named president of the Norman Building and Loan Association. That same year the Moores decided to build their Queen Anne-style home near the Norman city limits. This neighborhood became known as "Silk Stocking Row," and other affluent residents joined them in building here.

At a time when the average home built in Norman cost $400, the Moores spent over $5,000 on their dream house; it was considered the finest private residence in the town. It features an impressive two-story turret, wraparound porches, and art-glass windows. Eight rooms have been decorated and furnished to represent a typical turn-of-the-century residence of an upper middle class family in the Oklahoma Territory. Harry Lindsay—also an arrival from Missouri who was married to Agnes Moore's niece Daisy—bought the Moore house in 1908. Lindsay was president of the Norman Grain and Milling Company.

Additional Information

The Moore-Lindsay House is listed on the National Register of Historic Places.

Hefner Mansion

201 Northwest Fourteenth Street
Oklahoma City, OK 73103
(405) 235-4458

Contact: Oklahoma Heritage Assoc. Center
Open: Mon.-Sat. 9 a.m.–5 p.m.,
Sun. 1–5 p.m.
Admission: Adults $3.00; seniors free;
children $2.00
Activities: Guided tours
Suggested Time to View House:
45–60 minutes
Facilities on Premises: Galleries and
research library
Number of Yearly Visitors: 3,000
Description of Grounds: Formal flower
gardens with ornamentation
Year House Built: 1917
Number of Rooms: 17

Best Season to View House: Spring and
summer
Style of Architecture: Eclectic Neoclassical
On-Site Parking: Yes **Wheelchair Access:** Yes

Description of House

R. A. Hefner was a lawyer and oilman in Ardmore before becoming a judge and moving with his wife to Oklahoma City in 1926. The Hefners had been collectors and connoisseurs of fine art for many years before they purchased this mansion, which had been built in 1917. They filled it with museum-quality furnishings and art works from across the United States, as well as Europe and Asia, which they'd acquired on their various trips abroad. Hefner was elected Mayor of Oklahoma City in 1939; during his eight-year term in that position, this house was frequently used as the setting for formal events.

This richly detailed three-story Neoclassical-style brick mansion features a porte cochere entrance on the side, sun porches on both the first and second floors, a full-height entry porch, and seventeen rooms. Inside, some of the rooms have been given over to galleries: the Oklahoma Hall of Fame Gallery housing portraits in oil and bronze, as well as photographs of the state's notable citizens; the Oklahoma Heritage Galleria, housing rotating art exhibits; and the Shepherd Oklahoma Heritage Library with its ten thousand volumes about the state. The Hefner Memorial Chapel features a 17th-century Gobelin tapestry and a meditative attached garden. The first two floors of the Hefner Mansion have been restored with original furnishings from dating from 1927 to 1970.

Notable Collections on Exhibit

The Mansion is a monument to the good taste and substantial means of its occupants—it is filled with many exquisite decorative objects: crystal chandeliers imported from Bohemia, France, or Italy; Oriental rugs, both from Persia and China; a Japanese lacquered chest; a Louis-Philippe credenza with Sèvres porcelain insets; an early 18th-century oak cabinet; a massive rosewood canopy bed c. 1800 which had been shown at the 1904 World's Fair in St. Louis; extensive collections of silver; and—in the Meissen Room—a more-than-120-piece set of china in the rare Meissen "Onion" pattern. There are also paintings by W.A. Bouguereau, A. Schreyer, Martin Rico, L.A. Carolus, and J. Karliwan.

Overholser Mansion

405 Northwest Fifteenth Street
Oklahoma City, OK 73103
(405) 528-8485

Contact: Oklahoma Historical Society
Open: Year-round, Tues.-Fri. guided tours on the hour beginning at 10 a.m.; Sat. and Sun. beginning at 2 p.m.; last daily tour beginning at 4 p.m.; closed major holidays
Admission: Free
Activities: Guided tours only
Suggested Time to View House: 45 minutes
Description of Grounds: Large city lot at former "north end" of town
Style of Architecture: Late Victorian Queen Anne, patterned masonry
Best Season to View House: Spring and summer
Number of Yearly Visitors: 16,000
Number of Rooms: 13

Year House Built: 1903
On-Site Parking: No **Wheelchair Access:** No

Description of House

Henry Overholser moved to the Oklahoma Territory with his wife and son in 1889, shortly before the Great Oklahoma Run. Over the next two decades, as the Territory grew and ultimately became a state, he aided in its development and partook of its riches; he was instrumental in the building of Oklahoma City's Grand Avenue Hotel and Opera House and, perhaps more importantly, getting a railroad extension built to run from Tulsa through Oklahoma City.

Overholser and his wife, Emma, were divorced soon after they arrived in Oklahoma City and he married eighteen-year-old Anna Ione Murphy; the couple would have two children, one of whom reached maturity. In 1901, Overholser purchased land just north of Oklahoma City for the purpose of building a new home for his growing family and hired W. S. Matthews—a recent graduate of London's Kensington Academy—as architect and construction supervisor.

The thirteen-room mansion is designed in the French Chateauesque style; some of the decorative elements inside include: Brussels lace curtains, English carpets, and French stained-glass windows. The furnishings are predominantly in the Art Deco style, a rarity for the time.

Additional Information

The Overholser Mansion is listed on the National Register of Historic Places.

Pawnee Bill Mansion

Route 64 west of Pawnee, P.O. Box 493
Pawnee, OK 74058
(918) 762-2513

Contact: Oklahoma Tourism and Recreation Department
Open: Oct.-Mar., Wed.-Sat. 9 a.m.–5 p.m., Sun. 1–5 p.m.; Apr.-Sept., also open Tues. 9 a.m.–5 p.m.
Admission: Free
Activities: Guided tours, special presentations upon request
Suggested Time to View House: 60–90 minutes
Facilities on Premises: Nature trails, observation tower, picnic shelter

Description of Grounds: Built on historic Blue Hawk Peak. Grounds include several recreational facilities such as picnic shelters, play areas and nature trails.
Best Season to View House: Spring-fall
Number of Yearly Visitors: 140,000
Year House Built: 1908
Style of Architecture: Eclectic Craftsman and Mission styles
Number of Rooms: 14
On-Site Parking: Yes **Wheelchair Access:** Yes

Description of House

Major Gordon W. Lillie—better known as "Pawnee Bill"—personified the rugged frontiersman of the Old West. He was born in Illinois in 1860, came to the Indian Territory in 1875, and became a teacher to the Pawnee Indians. As interest in "wild" west shows grew, Pawnee Bill and six Pawnee Indians joined "Buffalo Bill's Wild West Exposition" in 1883 and began touring the country. In 1886, he met and married May Manning; Manning was a refined Philadelphian who nevertheless joined him in the show and thrilled audiences with her shooting and riding exploits.

Pawnee Bill went on to start his own successful Wild West show and, in 1908, he merged his show with Buffalo Bill Cody's; their show became famous throughout the world. When the tours ended, Pawnee Bill came back to the land he loved and fought to preserve the last of the buffalo herds. He successfully lobbied Congress to appropriate money to establish a bison preserve and built "Pawnee Bill's Old Town and Trading Post" to memorialize the spirit of the Old West. Unfortunately, this complex burnt to the ground in 1944.

Pawnee Bill built this two-story Craftsman and Mission-style home in 1908 out of natural rock on historic Blue Peak; it has over four thousand square feet of living space, electricity and indoor plumbing. He and his wife purchased their furniture around 1910, and most of the pieces still remain. The textiles, kitchenware and table settings, and decorations are also original.

Notable Collections on Exhibit

On display here is a collection of European cut-glass, several paintings by Demning, and numerous Indian artifacts from the early 1900s.

Sequoyah's Cabin

Route 101 in Sequoyah's State Park
P.O. Box 141
Sallisaw, OK 74955
(918) 775-2413

Contact: Oklahoma Historical Society
Open: Year-round, Tues.-Fri. 9 a.m.–5 p.m., Sat. and Sun. 2–5 p.m.; closed state holidays
Admission: Free
Activities: Guided group tours
Suggested Time to View House: 30 minutes
Facilities on Premises: Visitor center and book store
Description of Grounds: 10 acre park with walking trails and picnic tables
Best Season to View House: Late winter-late fall
Number of Yearly Visitors: 80,000
Year House Built: 1829
Number of Rooms: 1

Style of Architecture: Folk, log cabin
On-Site Parking: Yes **Wheelchair Access:** Yes

Description of House

Sequoyah's Cabin—a National Historic Landmark—is probably the oldest original intact log cabin in Oklahoma; it was built by George Guist, later known as Sequoyah. He was born in 1770 in the lower Appalachian region of Tennessee of a Cherokee mother and white father who did not remain with the family.

Sequoyah was raised as a member of the Cherokee Nation and is credited with inventing the Cherokee system of writing. Intrigued by the notion that white men could convey messages by writing, he began experimenting with a written alphabet in 1809 and finally completed a Cherokee syllabary in 1821. Seven years later, Sequoyah was part of the Arkansas delegation of the Cherokee Nation which went to Washington, D.C., to negotiate land trades in the Oklahoma Territory.

Years later, Sequoyah became obsessed with the story of a lost band of Cherokees living west of the Mississippi and set out to find them. Although he found the tribe in 1843, he died soon after near San Fernando, Mexico; the exact burial place remains unknown to this day.

Notable Collections on Exhibit

Inside the log cabin are original tools and furniture handcrafted by Sequoyah, as well as an exhibit showing the history of the Cherokees from the 17th century to the present, and collections of woven handicrafts, pottery, and baskets. There is also a interactive computer program that translates English words into Cherokee.

Additional Information

Sequoyah's Cabin is listed on the National Register of Historic Places.

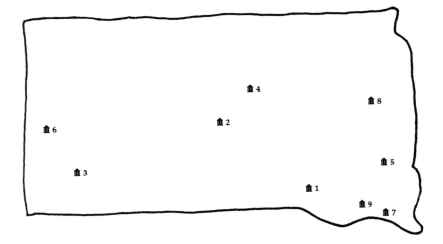

1. **Armour**
   Railroad House

2. **Blunt**
   Mentor Graham House

3. **Custer**
   Badger Clark House or
   "Badger Hole"

4. **Faulkton**
   Major John A. Pickler Mansion–
   The "Pink Castle"

5. **Sioux Falls**
   Pettigrew Home and Museum

6. **Spearfish**
   Historic Booth House

7. **Vermillion**
   Austin-Whittemore House
   Museum

8. **Watertown**
   Mellette House

9. **Yankton**
   Cramer-Kenyon Heritage Home

Railroad House

Armour Historic District on Main Street
Armour, SD 57313
(605) 724-2129

Contact: Douglas County Historical Society
Open: Memorial Day-Labor Day, daily
Admission: Free
Activities: Guided tours
Suggested Time to View House: 1 hour
Facilities on Premises: Small gift shop and
book store
Description of Grounds: County
courthouse grounds
Style of Architecture: National, prairie
railroad frame section house
Best Season to View House: Spring and fall
Number of Yearly Visitors: 1,000
Year House Built: 1886
Number of Rooms: 7

On-Site Parking: Yes **Wheelchair Access:** No

Description of House

This house was built in 1886 by the Chicago, Milwaukee and St. Paul Railroad for their Section Foremen and their families; it was commonly known as Milwaukee Section House #33. Before it was occupied by the first foreman—whose name is unknown—the house was used by workers who were involved in constructing the rail line. It was the first permanent dwelling built in the town of Armour.

Roy Brown was hired as foreman in 1921 and his family lived here until his wife entered a nursing home in 1986. When the railroad had abandoned the property in 1972, the Browns purchased it and were given a life estate to the lot on which it stood. In 1986, it was donated to the Douglas County Historical Society.

The architecture of #33 is very simple and follows the same basic plan used by the railroad for all of its section housing. It has been fully restored to its appearance in the early 1900s. For the most part, the furnishings date to the early decades of this century; some of the pieces belonged to the Brown family. It reflects a typical prairie home in its simplicity and rustic charm.

Notable Collections on Exhibit

There is a very nice collection of vintage clothing on display here, especially babies' and children's pieces.

Additional Information

The town of Armour, South Dakota—population eight hundred and fifty—has a historic district listed on the National Register of Historic Places which includes the Railroad House. The district also includes many large older homes, some of which, though privately owned, may be toured if arrangements are made in advance.

Mentor Graham House

103 North Commercial Avenue
P.O. Box 134
Blunt, SD 57522
(605) 962-6445

Contact: Mentor Graham House Museum
Open: May 1-Nov. 1, 8 a.m.–8 p.m.; groups
by appointment
Admission: Free
Activities: Guided tours, special talks for
school children
Suggested Time to View House: 30 minutes
Description of Grounds: Small yard with
parking lot south of the house
Best Season to View House: Spring-
early fall
Number of Yearly Visitors: 200
Year House Built: c.1884
Number of Rooms: 6

Style of Architecture: National, frame
On-Site Parking: Yes **Wheelchair Access:** Yes

Description of House

The elderly Mentor Graham, a former schoolteacher, lived here in Blunt with his youngest son, Harry Lincoln Graham, and Harry's family. The following obituary notice appeared in the *Blunt Advocate* dated from October 7, 1885: "Mentor Graham died at the residence of his son, H.L. Graham, in this place on Sunday evening October 4th last. Mr. Graham was born in Hardin County, Kentucky, in 1802 and in 1822 moved to Illinois. At seventeen years of age he engaged in teaching and continued in that profession for the next fifty-five years. Abraham Lincoln and Governor Yates were among his pupils...." Mr. Graham was buried in the little cemetery on the Hill but his body was later removed to Farmer's Point, Illinois, where he lived and taught most of his life.

The modest house is essentially one large room in an L-shape with a small upstairs attic. It was saved from certain demolition in 1946 by the efforts of Mr. Ray Pool and the South Dakota State Historical Society. It is hoped that the house will be completely restored and refurnished to appear as it did in the years when Mentor Graham lived here. The house has been listed on the National Register of Historic Places.

Badger Clark House or "Badger Hole"

Contact: Badger Clark Memorial
Society-Custer State Park
Open: Memorial Day-Labor Day, Mon.-Fri.,
10 a.m.–5 p.m., Sat.and Sun., 1–4 p.m.
Admission: Free
Activities: Guided tours, audiovisual
presentations
Suggested Time to View House: 15 minutes
Facilities on Premises: Gift shop
Description of Grounds: Woods trail
leading to the house
Best Season to View House: Summer
Number of Yearly Visitors: 3,000
Year House Built: 1927, "remodeled" 1937
Number of Rooms: 4

**Route 16A, 5 miles east of Custer
Custer, SD 57730
(605) 255-4515**

Style of Architecture: National, rustic cabin
On-Site Parking: Yes **Wheelchair Access:** No

Description of House

This cabin, affectionately called the "hole," was built by Badger Clark—South Dakota's Poet Laureate from 1937 until his death in 1957—who laid the foundation and did much of the construction himself. After Clark spent four years in Arizona for health reasons, he returned to the Black Hills and published his first book, *Sun and Saddle Leather*, in 1910. One of the poems contained therein, "A Cowboy Prayer," brought him national fame and the reputation of being America's Cowboy Poet. His other books are *Sky Lines and Wood Smoke, When Hot Springs Was a Pup* (a history of Hot Springs, South Dakota), and *Boots and Bylines* (published posthumously).

Clark designed the cabin to blend into its lovely pine-covered hillside setting; it consists of four rooms—two bedrooms, a kitchen-dining area, and a living room—with a wide front porch. He even built his porch around a large ponderosa pine rather than have to cut it down. Clark had a multitude of friends and vistors; the porch was a favorite meeting spot during the summer months, just as the living room—with its pink feldspar fireplace built by Clark himself—was the scene of many a gathering in the winter. The poet incorporated many native rocks and minerals into the cabin's foundation and fashioned some of the furniture himself; those pieces he didn't make came with the Clark family from Iowa in the 1880s.

Notable Collections on Exhibit

Among the items on display are paintings of Iowa landscapes by Badger's mother, antique pictures, photographs, family portraits, an Indian arrow, a miner's wrought-iron candle-holders, and a library of more than five hundred books.

Additional Information

The Badger Clark House is listed on the National Register of Historic Places.

Major John A. Pickler Mansion– The "Pink Castle"

South edge of town
Faulkton, SD 57438
(605) 598-4285

Contact: Faulk County Historical Society, Inc.
Open: Memorial Day-Labor Day, daily
1–5 p.m.; other times by appointment
Admission: Adults $5.00; children (10 and
under) $2.50
Activities: Guided tours
Suggested Time to View House: 1 hour
Facilities on Premises: Souvenirs available

Description of Grounds: Prairie yard
Best Season to View House: Summer
Number of Yearly Visitors: 1,000-2,000
Year House Built: Started 1882, completed
1894
Style of Architecture: Folk Victorian
Number of Rooms: 20
On-Site Parking: Yes **Wheelchair Access:** Yes

Description of House

John A. Pickler (1844-1910) joined the Union Army at eighteen, served in the Third Iowa Calvary, and mustered out as a Captain—later he'd attain the rank of major in the 138th U. S. Iowa Calvary. He graduated from Iowa State University in 1870, from the Ann Arbor Law School two years later, and began his career in law and politics; he served in the Iowa Legislature in 1881 and was elected to the 51st U. S. Congress as a Republican Representative from the new state of South Dakota in 1889. It was the first of his four terms in that body; he originated the rural free delivery system, sponsored a woman's suffrage bill, and served as a federal land inspector during the opening of the Oklahoma Territory. His wife, Alice, was also a graduate of Iowa State and held several important positions, including: member of the W. C. T. U. Women's Relief Corps, national chaplain in 1900, and president of the South Dakota Equal Suffrage Association.

The "Pink Castle"—so named because of the salmon-coral color selected for its exterior by local artist Charles Greener—is a large, asymmetrical two-story Victorian structure featuring a full attic and basement, a tower, decorative shingling, two porches, and several bay extensions. A large lamp in the tower was kept lit to guide weary travelers to a place of shelter. Inside, there is a secret room, hand-carved woodwork in the music room and main staircase, two unique stained-glass windows, and a "cubby hole" in the library. The library and music room once belonged to a hotel which had been moved from the ghost town of LaFoon around 1890; when the railroad passed by LaFoon in favor of nearby Faulkton, many of the former town's buildings "took wheels" and moved to the new county seat. The library was one of the finest and largest in all of South Dakota at the turn of the century. Its 2,000 volumes are still on display here.

Notable Collections on Exhibit

The fine library includes Major Pickler's Civil War collection; in addition, one may view a collection of hatpins, banners from the suffrage movement, three victrolas, two pianos, flags, fumed oak and wicker furniture, and children's toys.

Additional Information

The Major John Pickler Mansion is listed on the National Register of Historic Places. It is reported that Susan B. Anthony and Theodore Roosevelt were guests of the Picklers in this home.

Pettigrew Home and Museum

Eighth Street and Duluth Avenue
Sioux Falls, SD 57102
(605) 335-4210

Contact: Siouxland Heritage Museums
Open: Year-round, Tues.-Sat. 9 a.m.–Noon and 1–5 p.m., Sun. 1–5 p.m.
Admission: Free, donations accepted
Activities: Guided tours, audiovisual presentations and special seasonal programs
Suggested Time to View House: 60–90 minutes

Facilities on Premises: Museum
Description of Grounds: Corner lot located in the historic "north end" of Sioux Falls
Best Season to View House: Early fall
Number of Yearly Visitors: 70,000
Year House Built: 1889
Style of Architecture: Victorian Queen Anne
Number of Rooms: 12
On-Site Parking: Yes **Wheelchair Access:** Yes

Description of House

South Dakota's first full-term United States Senator was Richard Franklin Pettigrew, a native Vermonter who grew up in Wisconsin, managed his family's farm in Iowa, moved to Sioux Falls and made his fortune here in real estate. He is credited with much of the community's development, bringing in investors, starting railroads, and even moving members of his family to the town. His success extended into the world of frontier politics and the finer world of philanthropy, where his friendship with Andrew Carnegie resulted in the Sioux Falls library. In his later years, he and his wife traveled the world and collected artifacts as they went. It is said that he purchased this home in 1911 partly to house their collection of fine and decorative art objects.

This impressive three-story house was built in 1889 for the lawyer Thomas McMartin and his wife. Designed by the prominent prairie architect Wallace Dow, it exhibits many Queen Anne-style characteristics: red brick and native Sioux quartzite in contrasting exterior bands, beveled and leaded glass windows, an asymmetrical floor plan, a large entrance hall with a grand staircase, and a variety of interior woods. The fine finishes, marvelous hand-crafted details, and opulent highlights make a fitting backdrop for the wonderful collections amassed by the Pettigrews. The furnishings reflect the period of their residence, 1911 to 1926.

Notable Collections on Exhibit

In 1923, an addition was made to the house for the specific purpose of housing the Pettigrew collections; it opened as a museum two years later. The items on display reflect the interests of the various caretakers of the property: artifacts collected by Frederick Pettigrew, the Senator's brother who excavated Indian mounds as an amateur archaeologist; early stone implements; souvenirs gathered by Senator Pettigrew on his world travels; natural history objects (relating to ornithology) collected by Mary Peabody, the first caretaker; pioneer-era artifacts; antiques; and Congressional records dating from 1797.

Additional Information

The Siouxland Heritage Museums includes both the Old Courthouse Museum (1893) and the Pettigrew Home and Museum. Exhibits and programs depict the history of Sioux Falls and Minnehaha County. Both structures are listed on the National Register of Historic Places.

Historic Booth House

423 Hatchery Circle
Spearfish, SD 57783
(605) 642-7730

Contact: D.C. Booth National Historic Fish
Hatchery
Open: May–Sept., daily; other times by
appointment
Admission: Adults $1.50; students and
children $1.00
Activities: Guided tours, special seasonal
events including Spring Open House,
and Christmas Open House
Suggested Time to View House:
45–60 minutes
Facilities on Premises: Visitor center,
museum and gift shop, fish hatchery
Best Season to View House: Spring-fall
Description of Grounds: Historic fish
hatchery located on Spearfish Creek
Number of Yearly Visitors: 12,000
Number of Rooms: 9

Style of Architecture: Eclectic Colonial
Revival
Year House Built: 1905
On-Site Parking: Yes **Wheelchair Access:** Yes

Description of House

The D. C. Booth Fish Hatchery was established by the Federal government in 1898; it was here that trout were introduced into the Black Hills and fish management was begun in Yellowstone. It is now named after D. C. Booth, the hatchery's first superintendent. Booth's wife, Rudy, taught at the local Normal School and their two children, Katherine and Edward, were both born here.

In 1905, they moved into the well-proportioned two-story frame house which had been built for them and would serve to house all subsequent hatchery superintendents until 1983. The house, with its lovely grounds, formal lines, and two large porches—one front and one rear, became the social and cultural center for the community of Spearfish. Here the Booths entertained numerous important guests; one time, President Hoover came to call. All of the furnishings, whether original or collected, are authentic to the period when the house was first occupied.

The D. C. Booth House, like the Hatchery Building itself with its Victorian detailing and superb corner tower, is listed on the National Register of Historic Places.

Additional Information

When touring the northern Black Hills region, one should also stop at the House of Roses, a twenty-seven-room Queen Anne-style mansion overlooking the town of Deadwood. It too is listed on the National Register of Historic Places; the address is 15 Forest Avenue, Deadwood, South Dakota 57732 and the phone number is (605) 578-1879.

Austin-Whittemore House Museum

15 Austin Avenue
P.O. Box 332
Vermillion, SD 57069
(605) 624-8266

Contact: Clay County Historical Society, Inc.
Open: June-Aug., Fri.-Sun. 1–4 p.m.; other
times by appointment
Admission: Donations accepted
Activities: Guided tours, special seasonal
events including the annual Ice Cream
Social, and Holiday Open House
Suggested Time to View House: 1 hour
Description of Grounds: Landscaped acre
with gazebo
Best Season to View House: Summer
Number of Yearly Visitors: 5,000
Year House Built: 1882, remodeled 1894
Style of Architecture: Italianate, bracketed
Number of Rooms: 12

On-Site Parking: Yes **Wheelchair Access:** No

Description of House

This fine home was built in 1882 for the family of Horace J. and Rachel Ross Austin. Horace had come to the Dakota Territory in 1859 as a surveyor and his wife, Rachel, was one of the first teachers in the Territory.

Their home is a two-story structure in the Italianate style with bracketed eaves and an outstanding lantern (cupola). It features a low-pitched roof with narrow hooded window treatments. In 1894, a major remodeling of the house took place which incorporated several elements of the far more fashionable Victorian Queen Anne style; this remodeling is clearly seen on the porch, in the elaborate spindlework and incised decorative brackets. At the time, the foyer was enlarged and an open staircase installed.

Today we see wall-to-wall carpets showing a spiral design which echoes a similar pattern in the wallpaper friezes commissioned from the originals. The color scheme is dominated by blue and cranberry and the furnishings are authentic period pieces done in walnut and oak.

Notable Collections on Exhibit

In addition to the period furnishings, one may see a collection of vintage clothing, as well as numerous photographs and paintings dating to the 1890s.

Additional Information

The Austin-Whittemore House Museum is listed on the National Register of Historic Places.

Mellette House

421 Fifth Avenue Northwest
Watertown, SD 57201
(605) 886-4730

Contact: Mellette Memorial Association
Open: May-Oct., Tues.-Sun. 1-5 p.m.
Admission: Free
Activities: Guided tours
Suggested Time to View House: 30 minutes
Facilities on Premises: Gift shop
Best Season to View House: Spring-fall

Description of Grounds: Evergreen trees and flower garden
Number of Yearly Visitors: 3,000
Year House Built: 1883
Style of Architecture: Late Italianate
Number of Rooms: 10
On-Site Parking: Yes **Wheelchair Access:** No

Description of House

A. C. Mellette, who had been appointed Territorial Governor by President Benjamin Harrison, was elected to the office of Governor of the newly created State of South Dakota in 1889 by an overwhelming majority of voters. His term was not an easy one, mostly because of the severe drought which ran through the first years of the 1890s; he did everything he could to relieve the suffering of his fellow citizens, and bore the brunt of the effort personally. At the same time, his friend W. W. Taylor, the State Treasurer, defaulted on a large sum of public money. Mellette, as one of the bondsmen, was compelled to cover the defaulted amount by turning over to the state all of his real estate and other tangible assets. Shortly after, the house fell into ruin and was shut up and condemned by the town.

This house is a two-story structure solidly built of red brick in the late Italianate style, featuring a three-story tower which was originally used as a lookout reached by a superb spiral staircase. It is said to be a replica of James Whitcomb Riley's home in Indianapolis, Indiana (which is also listed in this guide). The house is now fully restored and filled with many pieces of Victorian furniture, some of which belonged to the Mellette family.

Notable Collections on Exhibit

Hanging in the house is a self-portrait done by Mrs. Mallette and paintings of her four sons—also done by her.

Additional Information

The Mellette House is listed on the National Register of Historic Places.

Cramer-Kenyon Heritage Home

509 Pine Street
Yankton, SD 57078
(605) 665-7470

Contact: Heritage Home Corporation
Open: June-Sept., Tues.-Sun. afternoon
  hours
Admission: $2.00
Activities: Guided tours, teas and
  receptions, class studies
Suggested Time to View House: 1 hour
Description of Grounds: Fenced garden
  with gazebo used for concerts
Best Season to View House: Spring-fall
Number of Yearly Visitors: 3,000-5,000
Year House Built: c.1886
Style of Architecture: Victorian Queen Anne
Number of Rooms: 17
On-Site Parking: Yes **Wheelchair Access:** No

Description of House

James H. Teller, whose political career included terms as Secretary of the Dakota Territory, Mayor of Yankton, and Chief Justice of the Supreme Court of Colorado, built this house in 1886. It was later acquired by Nelson J. Cramer, a native New Yorker who studied law, married long-time school friend Alice Bullfinch, and moved to Yankton in August of 1872.

This outstanding example of the cross-gabled Queen Anne style was built on Pine Street, a broad avenue lined with stately elms and flowering spirea. It is being preserved by concerned citizens of Yankton, with various city and county agencies, to remind themselves of their town's more gracious turn-of-the-century era. The house features heavy double-hung doors in the front entry, high cove ceilings, both gas and electric chandeliers, original imported German wallpaper in the parlor, and four imported tile fireplaces. All of the period furnishings are from the original family.

Notable Collections on Exhibit

On view in the house are original paintings done by Mrs. Cramer, who had attended art school in New York City, and several hand-painted china pieces.

Wisconsin

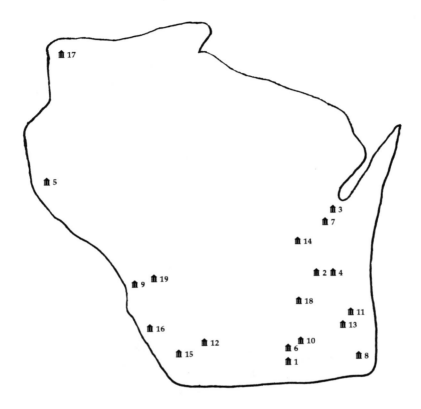

1. **Beloit**
   Hanchett-Bartlett Homestead

2. **Fond du Lac**
   Edwin H. Galloway House and Village

3. **Green Bay**
   Hazelwood Historic Home Museum
   Tank Cottage at Heritage Hill

4. **Greenbush**
   Sylvanus Wade House Inn and the Charles Robinson House

5. **Hudson**
   John S. Moffat Octagon House

6. **Janesville**
   Lincoln-Tallman House Museum

7. **Kaukauna**
   Charles A. Grignon Mansion

8. **Kenosha**
   Yule House

9. **La Crosse**
   Gideon C. Hixon House

10. **Milton**
    Milton House Museum

11. **Milwaukee**
    Captain Frederick Pabst Mansion

12. **Mineral Point**
    Pendarvis House and Trelawny House at Pendarvis Historic Site

13. **New Berlin**
    Winton-Sprengel House

14. **Oshkosh**
    Edgar Sawyer Mansion

15. **Platteville**
    Mitchell-Roundtree Stone Cottage

16. **Prairie du Chien**
    Villa Louis Historic Site

17. **Superior**
    Martin Pattison House– "Fairlawn"

18. **Watertown**
    Octagon House

19. **West Salem**
    Hamlin Garland Homestead
    Palmer-Gullickson Octagon House

Hanchett-Bartlett Homestead

2149 St. Lawrence Avenue
Beloit, WI 53511
(608) 365-7835

Contact: Beloit Historical Society
Open: June-Sept., Wed.-Sun. 1–4 p.m.;
Sept., Sat. and Sun. only 1–4 p.m.
Admission: Adults $2.00; children
(6-12) $.75
Activities: Guided tours
Suggested Time to View House: 45 minutes
Facilities on Premises: Gift shop and
bookstore
Best Season to View House: Spring-fall

Description of Grounds: Picnic tables, a
restored rural schoolhouse, barn and
schoolhouse
Number of Yearly Visitors: 1,300
Year House Built: 1857
Style of Architecture: Transitional Greek
Revival and Italianate
Number of Rooms: 8
On-Site Parking: Yes **Wheelchair Access:** No

Description of House

In 1840 James Hanchett came by ox-cart from Michigan to Beloit and
built his first home in the village at the intersection of School (now East
Grand) and Prospect Streets. Hanchett was a successful contractor—he and
a partner built the first dam across the Rock River in 1844—who lost his
wealth when the Federal government failed to pay him for building a
railroad to Racine because the Civil War threw its bonds into default.

Hanchett then left his home to try his hand at mining. In 1865 he
returned with some promising claims, intending to stay for a short while
before heading east to have them registered. Sadly, he died here in December
of that same year. His wife, Caroline, remained on the farm until 1884, then
moved to be with one of her sons in Chicago; after her death the land was
divided in two and sold. In 1901 the Bartlett family—Rock County residents
since 1845—bought the house and it remained in their possession until 1962.

The Hanchett's second house in Beloit was built out of local limestone
cut from a quarry on their own property, on the northwest corner of Division
and St. Lawrence Streets. It is a fine example of the transitional style which
combines elements of both the Greek Revival (straight lintels over the

windows) and the Italianate (broad eaves). The house is crowned with a lantern (cupola) which provided ventilation during the hot summer months as well as a dignified air.

The furnishings date from the period 1840 to 1884—few pieces belonged to either the Hanchett or Bartlett families—and include: a mahogany gaming table c. 1830, an Eastlake-style settee, a ladies chair c. 1860, and a number of late Victorian pieces.

Notable Collections on Exhibit

In addition to the furnishings mentioned above, there are many other artifacts on display in the house; pieces range from portraits of Beloit's notable citizens to a china wash set in the Alabama pattern with its pink rose design.

Additional Information

The Hanchett-Bartlett Homestead was placed on the National Register of Historic Places in 1977. The barn and smokehouse—built of the same limestone as the house—are original to the property. Limestone, which is a common construction material in the area, is not long-lived and requires constant sealing to prevent ruin.

Other noteworthy historic places to visit in Beloit include the Beckman Mill located at the corner of Mill Pond Road and County "H," and the Rasey House located at 517 Prospect Avenue. For further information, please contact the Beloit Convention and Visitors Bureau at (608) 365-4838.

Edwin H. Galloway House and Village

336 Old Pioneer Road
P.O. Box 1284
Fond du Lac, WI 54935
(414) 922-6390

Contact: Fond du Lac County Historical Society

Open: Memorial Day-Labor Day, daily 10 a.m.–4 p.m.; Sept., Sat. and Sun. 10 a.m.–4 p.m.; group tours by appointment

Admission: Adults $3.00; students (18 and under) $1.00; preschool children free

Activities: Special group tours by reservation

Suggested Time to View House: 90 minutes

Best Season to View House: Year round

Facilities on Premises: Reception center and gift shop

Description of Grounds: Landscaped grounds include eighteen relocated historic buildings including a log cabin and country store

Number of Yearly Visitors: 13,000

Year House Built: 1847, addition 1880

Style of Architecture: Italianate Villa, frame

Number of Rooms: 32, 15 open to the public

On-Site Parking: Yes **Wheelchair Access:** No

Description of House

The farmer Selim Newton built this house in 1847 and lived here until 1868. After that, it served as the home for three generations of the Galloway family: Edwin H. Galloway, lumberman and banker, mayor of Fond du Lac, and member of the Wisconsin legislature; Edwin A. Galloway, who ran a dairy farm here, made major additions to the house, and founded Galloway-West Company (now a division of Borden); and Edwin P. Galloway, grandson of Edwin H., who was born here in 1890 and donated the house and its surrounding acreage to the Fond du Lac Historical Society in 1955.

The house now appears as it did after its 1880 addition and remodeling—a large, white frame, Italianate-style structure with a square tower, lantern, and the characteristic overhanging eaves with decorative brackets. Other features include squared bay windows, a formal entrance hall, natural pine woodwork, and some wonderful interior details—the original hand-painted and stenciled parlor ceiling, frosted and etched glass in all first floor doors, four of the five original iron fireplaces, and a bathroom with its original tine tub. The house is furnished in authentic period pieces.

Notable Collections on Exhibit

In the village, collections may be seen in several of the buildings; the Galloway House features paintings by Mark Harrison and Owen Gromme whereas the Blakely Museum features Indian arrowheads and artifacts and an international assortment of dolls. Other buildings include: the Toy Shop, Photo Gallery, Country Store, Carpenter Shop, and the One Room Schoolhouse.

Additional Information

The Galloway House and Village is listed on the National Register of Historic Places. Approximately halfway between Fond du Lac and Milwaukee lies the little town of Saukville, which contains three superb historic structures: the Halpin Cottage, originally built in 1850 by an Irish immigrant in Five Corners, just north of Cedarburg; the Michael Ahner Log House; and the Karl Zettler Half-Timber House c. 1849 which exemplifies early English and Low Country building methods. All three are located in Saukville's Pioneer Village. The Village is an 11-acre complex well worth visiting; the address is 4880 County "I" and the phone number is (414) 692-9658.

Hazelwood Historic Home Museum

1008 South Monroe Avenue, P.O.Box 1411
Green Bay, WI 54301
(414) 437-0360

Contact: Brown County Historical Society

Open: Memorial Day-Labor Day, daily 1–4 p.m.

Admission: Adults $2.50; seniors $2.00; children $1.00

Activities: Guided tours by costumed docents, historic district walking tours, annual Victorian Holiday events

Description of Grounds: Located on original site with landscaped grounds overlooking the Fox River

Suggested Time to View House: 60–90 minutes

Facilities on Premises: Gift shop, meeting room

Best Season to View House: Spring

Number of Yearly Visitors: 1,500

Year House Built: 1837

Style of Architecture: Greek Revival

Number of Rooms: 12

On-Site Parking: Yes **Wheelchair Access:** Yes

Description of House

Three generations of the Martin family—who had their roots in upstate New York—lived at Hazelwood for over one hundred years. The family patriarch, Morgan L. Martin—frontier lawyer, judge, Territorial representative, mayor, and entrepreneur—was one of Wisconsin's founding fathers; he served as president of the State's Second Constitutional Convention and wrote the final draft of the State Constitution here at Hazelwood. Morgan's wife, Elizabeth, kept a diary of their lives which is now recognized as one of the best sources of information on the pioneering of the state. Other well-known family members include Morgan's daughter, Deborah Beaumont Martin, a regional historian and preservationist who served as the first librarian at Green Bay's Kellogg Public Library, and his brother-in-law, Admiral Melancton Smith, a Civil War Hero and world traveler who lived out his last days at Hazelwood.

Hazelwood is a superb two-story Greek Revival-style house with a four-over-four floor plan, a capacious central hallway which runs from the front entry to the rear, and two pillared porches. The south wing consists of a bedroom and a dining room under which is a basement kitchen connected by a dumbwaiter. The house was built in the eastern United States, shipped by boat over the Great Lakes to Green Bay, and assembled on site. Inside, there are six fireplaces and well-wrought millwork throughout.

Originally furnished in the Greek Revival style, the house was redecorated in 1876 in the then-fashionable Colonial Revival style; this is the period to which the house is presently interpreted. Most of the pieces are American Empire—Sheraton and Duncan Phyfe; sixty percent are original to the family.

Notable Collections on Exhibit

Many of the early pieces of furniture—an Empire sleigh bed, horsehair sofa, and walnut secretary—are of museum quality; there are also many works of art hung in the house and a collection of 19th-century toys on display in the nursery.

Additional Information

Hazelwood is listed on the National Register of Historic Places. It is located in the center of Green Bay's beautiful Astor District and the Fox River Heritage Trail. It now serves as the headquarters of the Brown County Historical Society.

Tank Cottage at Heritage Hill

2640 South Webster Avenue
Green Bay, WI 54301
(414) 448-5150

Contact: Heritage Hill State Park
Open: Memorial Day-Labor Day, Tues.-Sun.
9:30 a.m.–5 p.m.; May and Sept., Sat. and
Sun. 9:30 a.m.-5 p.m.
Admission: Adults $5.00; seniors $4.00;
children (6-17) $2.75; family rate available
Activities: Guided tours by costumed
interpreters, special seasonal and
heritage-oriented events, concert series,
encampments
Suggested Time to View House: 45 minutes
Facilities on Premises: Visitor center, general
store gift shop
Best Season to View House: Late
summer-early fall

Description of Grounds: "Living history"
museum sited on 50 acres with over
twenty-five original or reconstructed
historic buildings divided into four
areas-French Fur Trade 1762, Military
Fort Howard 1836, Small Town 1871, and
Immigrant Farmstead 1905
Number of Yearly Visitors: 55,000
Year House Built: Late 18th or early 19th
century, additions c.1850s and 1930s
Style of Architecture: Colonial French
"piece sur piece" log cabin
Number of Rooms: 13, 3 upstairs rooms not
open to the public
On-Site Parking: Yes **Wheelchair Access:** Yes

Description of House

The Tank Cottage is Wisconsin's oldest standing building and its history
spans the development of this territory from the years of French and British
rule to the era of statehood. It was built around 1800 by Joseph Roy, a fur
trader who had owned land on the Fox River—the cottage has since been
moved from its original site—since 1775. For the first third of the 19th
century it was owned by another fur trader, Jacques Porlier, who also taught
and sat as a judge.

In 1850, the Norwegian immigrant Nils Otto Tank purchased 900 acres
of land west of the Fox River, including the parcel upon which the cabin
stood. Tank was a widowed Moravian minister who'd come to the United
States with his young daughter after serving as a missionary to South
America. He had dreams of founding a Moravian community in this
country, but never received the support he hoped for. The year before buying

this cabin he married Caroline van der Meulen, a former friend of his first wife. Tank did join forces with another minister and start a small religious colony called Ephraim but it only lasted one year before disputes forced its dissolution. Nils Otto Tank died in 1864, and his daughter eight years later. Caroline, who was born in Holland and had many items shipped to her from her wealthy family there over the years, lived on in the cottage until her death in 1891.

The fully restored cottage—it appears as it did in the 1870s—is a one-and-a-half-story structure with side gables and a one-story shed roof addition on each end. The central original section of the building is built in the rare French "piece sur piece" style: full dovetail joints fix the corners where the notched logs meet. The joists, sill, and posts are cut of white oak, while the rafters and vertical boards which run from sill to plate and meet in the mortised joints are white pine. The gable walls are filled with one-inch-diameter branches between the studs to which grass is tied. This forms a kind of lathing upon which river clay is impacted. The whole—called wattle and daub construction—forms a seemingly solid clay wall which provides excellent insulation.

Notable Collections on Exhibit

The Tank Cottage is now a small historic museum housing all the treasures which Tank brought from Norway and, more importantly, all the finery that Mrs. Tank had sent to her from Holland. These include a collection of 18th and 19th century Dutch marquetry furniture and Mrs. Tank's paintings in the style of the Dutch masters, as well as many pieces of jewelry, porcelain, fine metals, and other hand-crafted decorative objects.

Additional Information

Tank Cottage at Heritage Hill is listed on the National Register of Historic Places. It is a "must-visit" for anyone in the Green Bay area.

Sylvanus Wade House Inn and the Charles Robinson House

W7747 Plank Road, P.O. Box 34
Greenbush, WI 53026
(608) 262-5551

Contact: State Historical Society of Wisconsin-Old Wade House State Park

Open: May-Oct., daily 9 a.m.–5 p.m.

Admission: Adults $5.00; seniors $4.50; children (5-12) $2.00; group rates available

Activities: Guided house tours by costumed docents, audiovisual orientation program, monthly frontier craft demonstrations

Best Season to View House: Spring-fall

Year House Built: Wade House-1850, Robinson House-1855

Style of Architecture: Greek Revival

Suggested Time to View House: 1 hour

Facilities on Premises: Visitor center, Wisconsin Carriage Museum and Shop

Description of Grounds: 220 tilled and wooded acres adjacent to Northern Kettle Moraine State Forest with hiking trails and picnic area

Number of Yearly Visitors: 25,000

Number of Rooms: Wade House-27, Robinson House-9, 4 open to the public

On-Site Parking: Yes **Wheelchair Access:** Yes

Description of House

The Wade House Inn was built in 1850 by Sylvanus and Betsey Wade to serve travelers on the Sheboygan and Fond du Lac Plank Road. The Wades—he was from Massachusetts, she from Pennsylvania—had nine children and created their own little self-sustaining community here; their inn is a rare example of a fully restored stagecoach stop in this part of the country. One of their daughters, Julia, married Charles Robinson, who designed the Inn, the Robinson House, and the nearby United Methodist Church—all in the Greek Revival style. The Robinson House shows that its eponymous builder was extremely skilled at adapting a refined architectural style to a frontier setting.

The Inn is a three-story side-gabled structure with a full-width, full-height porch and a second floor balcony accessible through a door. The main floor has two entries—one leading into the center hallway, the second into the guest quarters. As was typical, the kitchen is in the rear. The shuttered windows are in six-over-six arrangements with small, narrow windows set into the frieze at the attic level; the main entry door features sidelight windows. Most of the furnishings are the basic frontier furniture of the mid-19th century; many were left by the Wade family, including a rope bed with an authentic corn-husk mattress.

Notable Collections on Exhibit

Two of the more notable displays are an excellent collection of coverlets and quilts and another of copper lustre "tea leaf" iron stoneware and splatterware.

Additional Information

The Inn and House are both listed on the National Register of Historic Places. They form the centerpiece of the Wade House Historical Complex, a collection of preserved, restored, and reconstructed buildings which reflect the development of the village of Greenbush and its Yankee heritage. In addition to the Inn and House, it includes the Docksteader Blacksmith Shop, the Robinson-Herrlin Sawmill Ruins, and the Wisconsin Carriage Museum. This last houses over 120 vehicles, the largest collection of its kind in the state.

John S. Moffat Octagon House

1004 Third Street
Hudson, WI 54016
(715) 386-2654

Contact: St. Croix County Historical Society
Open: May-Oct., Tues.-Sat. 10 a.m.–Noon,
2–5 p.m., Sun. 2–5 p.m.; open three
weeks before Christmas, same hours
Admission: Adults $3.00; teens $1.00;
children (under 12) $.50; special rates
available
Activities: Guided tours, special seasonal
programs
Suggested Time to View House: 90 minutes
Facilities on Premises: Books and gift items
for sale
Description of Grounds: Beautiful
Victorian-style gardens with carriage
house

Best Season to View House: Summer	**Number of Yearly Visitors:** 5,000
Year House Built: 1855	**Style of Architecture:** Octagon
Number of Rooms: 11	**On-Site Parking:** Yes **Wheelchair Access:** No

Description of House

In 1854 native New Yorkers Judge John Shaw Moffat and Mrs. Nancy
Moffat arrived in Hudson with their daughter Mary. The following year,
they had this Octagon House built for them; this romantic style was very
popular in the mid-19th century, following the publication of Orson
Fowler's book outlining its virtues. It was the first house built on Third
Street. Four generations of the Moffat-Hughes family lived here until 1957.
In 1964 it was acquired by the St. Croix Historical Society.

The Octagon House is topped with a cupola ornamented with finials
and features exaggerated bracketing, pilasters on each of its eight angles,
and an attached screen porch thought to be a later addition. It has been
finished with high Victorian-style color schemes and reproduction
wallpapers. The furnishings—all appropriate to the period of the Judge's
occupancy—complete this superb restoration. It is a wonderful example of
this all-but-forgotten style of architecture.

Notable Collections on Exhibit

On display here are collections of antique dolls and farm implements
from the pre-Civil War period (in the Garden House), and an authentic
19th-century blacksmith shop.

Additional Information

The John S. Moffat Octagon House is listed on the National Register of
Historic Places.

Lincoln-Tallman House Museum

440 North Jackson Street, P.O. Box 8096
Janesville, WI 53547
(608) 752-4519/4509

Contact: Rock County Historical Society, Inc.

Open: May, Sept. and Oct. Sat. and Sun.
11 a.m.–4 p.m.; June-Aug., Tues.-Sun.
11 a.m.–4 p.m.

Admission: Adults $2.50; seniors $2.00;
children (K-12) $1.50; group rate
$.50 per person

Activities: Guided tours, special seasonal
programs

Suggested Time to View House: 90 minutes

Facilities on Premises: Visitor center and
gift shop located in the restored 1855
Horse Barn

Description of Grounds: Formal planted
park with restored orchard

Best Season to View House: Late
spring-summer

Number of Yearly Visitors: 10,000

Number of Rooms: 26

Year House Built: c.1855, west porch
addition 1870

Style of Architecture: Italianate Villa

On-Site Parking: No **Wheelchair Access:** No

Description of House

In 1848 William Morrison Tallman, a New York lawyer whose practice consisted largely of land rights cases, purchased 4,476 acres spanning Green, Grant, Iowa, and LaFayette Counties in Wisconsin for the sum of $10, 495. Two years later he moved with his wife, Emeline—they'd met when Tallman was a student at Yale—and their three children to Janesville where he established a law practice. Tallman was active in Wisconsin politics for years and was well-known as a passionate abolitionist. In 1859, he entertained Abraham Lincoln here; the Tallman House is the only private residence still standing in Wisconsin in which Lincoln is known to have stayed.

Though the building's architect has not yet been positively identified, it bears more than a passing resemblance to an 1852 structure designed by Samuel Sloan. The three-story house, which took two years to complete, features many elements lifted straight out of Sloan's *The Model Architect*, a classic pattern book—the cupola, glass entrance, columns on the south porch, newel post, window hoods, and horse barn. The floor plan consists of a sitting room, dining room, and parlors on the main floor; the kitchen and pantries in the basement; and the bedrooms on the upper two floors.

Interior features include: multi-colored stained-glass windows on the sun porch and doors, marble mantels, enameled grates, porcelain wash basins, walk-in closets with built-in drawers in each bedroom, and an indoor privy in the rear of the house. The furnishings date from the early 1800s to the mid-1880s; almost three-quarters of them belonged to the Tallman family. All are appropriate to the period to which the home has been restored, 1857 to 1878. The Lincoln-Tallman House Museum is listed on the National Register of Historic Places.

Charles A. Grignon Mansion

1313 Augustine Street
P.O. Box 247
Kaukauna, WI 54130
(414) 766-3122

Contact: Outgamie County Historical Society

Open: Memorial-Labor Day, Tues.-Sun.
1–4:30 p.m.; other times by appointment

Activities: Guided tours, special events
including a Civil War encampment
weekend

Suggested Time to View House:
30–45 minutes

Best Season to View House: Summer

Year House Built: Between 1837 and 1839

Number of Rooms: 12

Admission: Adults $2.50; children (age 5-17)
$1.25; family (two adults and children) $6.25

Description of Grounds: Located in large city
park. House grounds have period herb
and vegetable gardens

Facilities on Premises: Small gallery and
gift shop

Number of Yearly Visitors: 5,000

Style of Architecture: Greek Revival

On-Site Parking: Yes **Wheelchair Access:** No

Description of House

Augustin Grignon was a prosperous fur trader who owned land along the Fox River; at the time, Kaukauna was little more than a way station along the river. His wealth derived largely from portaging supplies around the rapids which ran at the foot of his property. In 1830 he left for Butte des Morts and his two sons, Charles and Alex, took over the trading post and built this mansion in the late 1830s—the heyday of the fur industry in the region. As stocks were depleted, the business dwindled in the following decade to almost nothing.

The house the Grignons built on the site of their trading post is a rare example of the eastern Greek Revival-style brought out to the frontier at an early date. It is a two-story frame structure with a full-height entry portico and a full-width half-facade porch with squared Doric columns. Doric pilasters are also visible as framing the downstairs twelve-pane sash windows.

Additional Information

The Grignon Mansion is listed on the National Register of Historic Places.

Yule House

6300 Third Avenue
Kenosha, WI 53143
(414) 654-5770

Contact: Kenosha County Historical Society and Museum

Open: Year-round, Wed.-Sun. 2–4:30 p.m.; closed holidays

Admission: Donation: Adults $1.00; children $.50

Activities: Guides are available

Suggested Time to View House: 60–90 minutes

Year House Built: 1899

Best Season to View House: Spring and summer

Facilities on Premises: Gift and book shop, historical research library

Description of Grounds: Large city yard in established neighborhood

Style of Architecture: Early Colonial Revival

Number of Rooms: 15

On-Site Parking: Yes **Wheelchair Access:** Yes

Description of House

In 1899 George Yule—vice president of the Badger Manufacturing Company and superintendent of the Bain Wagon Company—and his wife, Harriet, built this house. The family lived here until 1923, when Harriet moved to California. Subsequently, the house went through a number of owners who made several changes both in and out before it was acquired by the Kenosha County for use as a museum.

The Yule House is a two-story red brick structure with a pair of two-story bays on the front facade. There is a steeply-pitched gable roof with returned eaves and a fine elliptical window over the front entrance. The porch is made of brick and concrete. In recent years, the house has undergone some alterations, one of which added a wing to the north end of the building.

The furnishings are from the 100-year-old collection of the Kenosha County Historical Society; this superb array of objects illustrates the history and development of the County and all southeastern Wisconsin. Many of these objects came from the William Meers estate.

Notable Collections on Exhibit

In the museum is a large collection of folk art, including paintings, scrimshaw pieces, household implements of etched horn, and needlework samplers. Here one may also view the Meers collection of antique Oriental snuff bottles.

Additional Information

The Yule House is located in the Third Avenue Historical District which includes many historic buildings between Sixty-First and Sixty-Sixth Streets and is listed on the National Register of Historic Places.

Gideon C. Hixon House

429 North Seventh Street
La Crosse, WI 54601
(608) 784-9080

Contact: La Crosse County Historical Society
Open: Memorial Day-Labor Day, daily 1–5 p.m.; open last weekend of November and first weekend of December
Admission: Adults $3.00; seniors $2.50; children (under 12) $1.50
Activities: Guided tours, annual Ice Cream Social, anuual Victorian Holiday Showcase event
Suggested Time to View House: 1 hour
Facilities on Premises: Gift shop

Description of Grounds: City lot near downtown area with meticulous period herb and flower garden
Best Season to View House: Summer
Number of Yearly Visitors: 8,500
Year House Built: 1860
Style of Architecture: Italianate
Number of Rooms: 14
On-Site Parking: No **Wheelchair Access:** No

Description of House

Massachusetts-born Gideon Hixon, a tinsmith by trade, traveled west—first to St. Louis, then up the Mississippi to LaCrosse—and made his fortune in the Wisconsin lumber business. He married a local school teacher and the couple had five boys, all of whom stayed in the family business, which, by the time they reached maturity, included sawmills, flour mills, real estate deals, and banking operations. When Gideon died in 1892, the house passed to his wife who lived here until her death twenty-one years later. Ownership then fell to their oldest son, Frank. It was Frank Hixon's widow, Alice, who gave the house to the Historical Society in 1962.

The original part of the house was built in the Baroque Revival style commonly called the Italianate and fully reflects the fact that its owner was a lumber baron who appreciated fine wood—eleven native Wisconsin woods are used in the house!—and exquisite craftsmanship. Over the years, the family added rooms, including an exotic Turkish Nook, and made improvements to the house, adding gas, electricity, and indoor plumbing, all three of which were extremely rare in this area at the time. The furnishings, which are not appropriate to a 19th-century interpretation, have been removed.

Notable Collections on Exhibit

On display here are many paintings and objets d'art which exemplify the emotional Romantic school, as well as numerous souvenirs from the Hixons' travels through Europe, Asia, and the Middle East. Items include: an Italian triptych, a Reynolds miniature, Imari rugs, a Satsuma vase, and a Chinese teak-and-ivory desk.

Additional Information

The Hixon House is listed on the National Register of Historic Places. In nearby Coon Valley is the Engum House, a fine example of those cabins built by Norwegian immigrants of the mid-19th century in the style of their homeland. The tours are well worth a visit; for information call (608) 452-3524.

Milton House Museum

18 South Janesville Street
(Routes 26 and 59) P.O. Box 245
Milton, WI 53563
(608) 868-7772

Contact: Milton Historical Society
Open: Memorial Day-Labor Day, daily
10 a.m.–5 p.m.; May and Sept.-Oct. 15,
Sat. and Sun. 10 a.m.–5 p.m.
Admission: Reduced rates for schools,
organizations, families and seniors
Activities: Guided tours
Suggested Time to View House: 75 minutes
Facilities on Premises: Country store and
gift shop
Description of Grounds: Museum grounds
include picnic facilities, the 1837 Pioneer
Cabin and 1867 Goodrich House, a
buggy shed and a blacksmith shop
Best Season to View House: Summer
Year House Built: 1844
Number of Rooms: 20

Number of Yearly Visitors: 8,000
Style of Architecture: Hexagonal Grout
On-Site Parking: Yes **Wheelchair Access:** Yes

Description of House

A visit to the Milton House Museum will provide a memorable evocation of life in pre-Civil War Wisconsin. This 1844 structure was built by the
pioneer settler Joseph Goodrich to serve as a stagecoach inn; it is reported
that as many as twenty-five stagecoaches and up to eighteen trains passed
through the town of Milton. Rates at the Milton House were: $.25 per night
for lodging; $.25 for meals; and ten cents for the horses' oats! In addition to
serving travelers, the Milton House was well-known as a stop on the
Underground Railroad—the tunnel which connects the House with the
Pioneer Cabin was used as a hiding-place for escaping slaves.

The Milton House is a hexagonal building with walls from twelve to
eighteen inches thick filled and finished with grout. It is believed to be the
first grout building in the United States.

Notable Collections on Exhibit

In front of the museum is the Milton House Miniature Model. This fully
furnished replica of the original is built on a one inch to one foot scale.

Additional Information

The Milton House Museum is listed on the National Register of Historic
Places. Also located on the grounds in the 1837 Pioneer Cabin. This structure
served as the original Goodrich family dwelling.

Captain Frederick Pabst Mansion

2000 West Wisconsin Avenue
Milwaukee, WI 53233
(414) 931-0808

Contact: Wisconsin Heritages, Inc.
Open: Year-round, Mon.-Sat.
10 a.m.–3:30 p.m., Sun. Noon–3:30 p.m.;
closed major holidays
Admission: Adults $5.00; children (6-17)
$2.50; group rates available
Activities: Guided tours, group tours by
appointment, annual "Victorian
Christmas in Wisconsin"
Suggested Time to View House: 1 hour
Best Season to View House: Spring-early fall

Facilities on Premises: Victorian gift and
book shop located in the Beer Pavilion
Description of Grounds: Large grassy area
with period gardens
Number of Yearly Visitors: 50,000
Year House Built: Between 1890 and 1893
Style of Architecture: Eclectic Renaissance
Revival in the Flemish manner
Number of Rooms: 37
On-Site Parking: Yes **Wheelchair Access:** Yes

Description of House

This magnificent Flemish-style mansion was designed by George Bowman
Ferry for Captain Frederick Pabst, president of the Pabst Brewery from 1889
until his death in 1904. At the time the brewery was reputed to be the largest
in the world. Pabst, who had emigrated to the United States from Saxony
with his parents, started his climb up the ladder of success in 1850 by signing
on as a cabin boy on a Great Lakes Steamer at the age of fourteen. Seven
years later, he earned his Steamboat Pilot's Certificate and became part
owner of the steamship *Huron*. He would retain the title of "captain" for the
rest of his life.

In 1860, he met Philip Best, who owned one of Milwaukee's largest
breweries, and shortly thereafter married Best's daughter Maria. In 1864, he
used the proceeds from a sale of shares in a steamboat to join Best as an equal
partner in the brewery. In 1889, he became president of the company and
changed its name to his own. In addition to his great commercial success,
both in and out of the beer business, Pabst also engaged in many
philanthropic activities on behalf of his city and its citizens.

Two years after Pabst's death, the mansion was purchased by the Roman Catholic Archdiocese of Milwaukee for use as the Archbishop's official residence. In 1976, the estate was sold to a developer who subdivided the property, razed the carriage house, and sold off the mansion to Wisconsin Heritages, Inc., an organization chartered in 1975 precisely to save the state's architectural treasures.

The house was built on Milwaukee's Grand Avenue (now Wisconsin Avenue), a tree-lined street where all of the city's most prominent families had their homes, and stood out among its neighbors because of its unique Flemish Renaissance styling (most American Renaissance Revival styles are Gothic or Eastlake). The marvelous symmetrical facade features a loggia, matching stepped gables with volutes, scrollwork, and a lion insignia carved into a decorative panel, and terra cotta pilasters, balustrades, and friezes decorated with Renaissance strapwork patterns. The mansion is built of tan-colored pressed brick accented with terra cotta ornamentation, red pan tile roofing, and copper flashing.

In addition to the many public and private rooms, the four-story structure also boasts of plant conservatory, musician's nook, and beer pavilion. Perhaps the two most interesting rooms are Captain Pabst's German Renaissance Revival-style study and Elsbeth's (an adopted granddaughter's daughter) French Rococo-style Room. The house is fully furnished in the style of the Pabst family, though only the ladies' parlor, dining room, and music room contain original pieces.

Notable Collections on Exhibit

The Blatz Fine Arts Collection is on loan from the Milwaukee County Department of Parks.

Additional Information

The Pabst Mansion is listed on the National Register of Historic Places. The Beer Pavilion on the east side of the house was originally built for the 1893 World's Columbian Exposition in Chicago and is one of only two surviving structures from that exposition.

Pendarvis House and Trelawny House at Pendarvis Historic Site

114 Shake Rag Street
Mineral Point, WI 53565
(608) 987-2122

Contact: State Historical Society of Wisconsin
Open: May 1-Oct. 31, daily 9 a.m.–5 p.m.
Admission: Adults $5.00; seniors $4.50; adult groups with reservation $4.00 each
Activities: Guided tours, special summer programs
Suggested Time to View House: 60 minutes
Facilities on Premises: Museum store
Best Season to View House: Spring-fall

Description of Grounds: Native Wisconsin woodland ephemerals within dry stone walls and terraces; grounds by guided tour only
Number of Yearly Visitors: 15,000
Year House Built: c.1848
Style of Architecture: National-Folk, Cornish-style stone cottage
Number of Rooms: 4
On-Site Parking: Yes **Wheelchair Access:** No

Description of House

In the 1840s, immigrant miners and stonemasons from Cornwall, England, built these stone cottages for immigrant miners come to work the lead mines here. Mineral Point—forty-five miles north of Galena, Illinois—was at the center of the Upper Mississippi Lead Mining Region in the period from 1827 to 1850.

The cottages—one unit is a row house consisting of three cottages joined at the sides, and two of the six are built of logs as well as stone—housed families who had all come over from the Redruth-Cambourne mining district in Cornwall, families with names like Williams, Thomas, Carbis, Remfrey, Martin, and Cruthers. Beginning in 1935, Robert Neal and his partner, Edgar Hellum, two Mineral Point natives, began to develop the site and rehabilitate the cottages. Furnishings were gathered from the region and the fine stonework was again made visible.

Also on the site, and showing a rather different side of Cornish-style architecture, is the Polperro House. This 1842 "salt-box" structure was also built into the hillside and combines hand-hewn logs construction on a stone foundation.

The Pendarvis Historic Site is listed on the National Register of Historic Places.

Notable Collections on Exhibit

Among the items on display here is a collection of lead and zinc mining tools, tea-leaf ironstone, and Staffordshire china.

Additional Information

Also on view in Iowa County—and definitely worth a visit—is Frank Lloyd Wright's Taliesin, one of the most famous homes in America. It is located three miles south of Spring Green off Highway 23. For further information, please call (608) 588-7900. Taliesin is listed on the National Register of Historic Places.

Winton-Sprengel House

19765 West National Avenue
New Berlin, WI 53146
(414) 679-1783

Contact: New Berlin Historical Society
Open: Guided school tours by appointment
Admission: Donation
Activities: School tours, special seasonal
open house
Suggested Time to View House:
60–90 minutes
Facilities on Premises: Some gifts for sale
Description of Grounds: City park with
picnic table
Best Season to View House: Year round
Number of Yearly Visitors: 800-1,000
Year House Built: c.1870s
Number of Rooms: 8

Style of Architecture: National, farmhouse
On-Site Parking: Yes **Wheelchair Access:** No

Description of House

Over the past one-hundred-and-twenty years, two families have lived in this simple farmhouse; Lewis S. Winton, storekeeper and postmaster of the hamlet of Prospect, Wisconsin, occupied it from 1870 to 1913, when it was bought by Arthur Sprengel and his family. The house and surrounding park has recently been designated the "Prospect Hill Historic District." Prospect Hill was significant as a Yankee settlement.

The house is furnished to the period of the 1880s with many items donated by New Berlin families. One large room upstairs has been made to look like a one-room schoolhouse of the era and the porch is a museum room. When the Winton family lived here, the house had an open porch in the front with pillars and doweled decorative elements; some of this was destroyed when the house was resurfaced with artificial brick siding. The east bedroom windows had been boarded up to conserve heat, but are now reopened and restored. The partitioning of the bedrooms reflects a later period in the life of the house. The bay window shows decorative trim and the house has two arched windows.

Notable Collections on Exhibit

Items on display include: a grandfather clock, a high back chair once belonging to Theadora Winton Youmans, the famous suffragette, a rope spool bed, a hand-made quilt from John Malone, a New Berlin pioneer, and a round floor-to-ceiling corner cabinet from the Louis Winton family.

Edgar Sawyer Mansion

1331 Algoma Boulevard
Oshkosh, WI 54907
(414) 424-4731

Contact: Oshkosh Public Museum
Open: Year-round, Tues.-Sat. 9 a.m.–5 p.m.,
Sun. 1–5 p.m.; closed national holidays
Admission: Free
Activities: Self-guided tours, annual art fair
Sunday after the Fourth of July
Suggested Time to View House: 1 hour
Facilities on Premises: Gift shop
Description of Grounds: City block with
restored period gardens with native
plantings and decorative shade trees
Best Season to View House: Summer
Style of Architecture: Eclectic Period
Revival, Tudor Jacobethan
Year House Built: 1908
Number of Rooms: 22

Number of Yearly Visitors: 60,000
On-Site Parking: Yes **Wheelchair Access:** Yes

Description of House

Edgar Sawyer was born in Crown Point, New York, in 1842 and moved with his family to Wisconsin while still in his infancy. While his father, Philetus, went into politics—eventually winning the office of United States Senator—Edgar tended the family lumber business and amassed a fortune. In 1908, he hired the local architect William Waters to design a mansion in the Tudor Jacobean style. The interiors were designed by Tiffany Studios (beautiful stained-glass windows and woodwork are seen throughout).

In 1924, he donated the house to the City of Oshkosh for use as a museum, and, in 1983, a new wing was added. The house is not furnished because it is used exclusively as a museum.

Notable Collections on Exhibit

The museum collections include permanent exhibits relating the local history and archaeology, the natural history of Wisconsin; these exhibits include collections of paintings, maps, photographs, glass and porcelain, and Indian artifacts. There are also various temporary exhibits held here.

Mitchell-Roundtree Stone Cottage

Jewett and Lancaster Streets
Platteville, WI 53818
(608) 348-5196

Contact: Grant County Historical Society
Open: May 1-Oct. 31, daily Noon–5 p.m.
Admission: Adults $1.00; children $.50
Activities: Guided tours
Suggested Time to View House: 1 hour
Facilities on Premises: Gift shop
Description of Grounds: Sited on 3 acres
Best Season to View House: Year round
Style of Architecture: Folk, English
tidewater style
Year House Built: 1837
Number of Yearly Visitors: 800-900
Number of Rooms: 7
On-Site Parking: Yes **Wheelchair Access:** Yes

Description of House

The Reverend Samuel Mitchell—a soldier in the Revolutionary War under General Washington and witness to Cornwallis's surrender at Yorktown—and his wife built this cottage in 1837. It was occupied by their daughter and son-in-law, Major John Hawkins Roundtree. Roundtree was one of Platteville's founding fathers; when his son Hiram was married in 1848, the lad and his new wife were given the Stone Cottage as a wedding gift. The couple raised four daughters in the cottage—the second oldest, Laura, lived her entire life here. Most of the furnishings on display belonged to Laura and her family.

The cottage is unique in that it is built out of dolomite limestone in a style similar to the tidewater homes built in England in the 14th century. It originally consisted of five rooms: a parlor, sitting room, and dining room on the first floor and the two bedrooms upstairs. In 1890, the house was enlarged to accommodate the growing family; a kitchen was added off the dining room and, above the kitchen, a third bedroom. At that time the original detached kitchen, which lay some fifty feet to the north of the house, was demolished.

Notable Collections on Exhibit

There are numerous family artifacts on display here, including Laura's original paintings and drawings, jewelry, and beautiful examples of needlecraft.

Additional Information

The Mitchell-Roundtree Stone Cottage is listed on the National Register of Historic Places.

Villa Louis Historic Site

521 North Villa Louis Road
P.O. Box 65
Prairie du Chien, WI 53821
(608) 326-2721

Contact: State Historical Society of Wisconsin
Open: May 1-Oct. 31, daily 9 a.m.–5 p.m.
Admission: Adults $5.00; children (5-11) $2.00
Activities: Guided tours, special events, lecture series
Suggested Time to View House: 2 hours
Facilities on Premises: Visitor center and museum store

Description of Grounds: Restored c.1890s landscape grounds
Best Season to View House: Late summer-mid fall
Number of Yearly Visitors: 35,000
Year House Built: 1870, remodeled1885
Style of Architecture: Italianate Villa
Number of Rooms: 26 open to the public
On-Site Parking: Yes **Wheelchair Access:** Yes

Description of House

In 1826 a young clerk for the American Fur Company, Hercules L. Dousman, arrived in Prairie du Chien from Mackinac, Michigan, and proceeded to make a name for himself as an astute entrepreneur, investing in lumber, real estate, fur trading, and the transportation industries. Within twenty years, he had become a very wealthy and influential frontier capitalist and started building his estate. His only child, H. Louis Dousman, built a new house on the property in 1870 and remodeled it greatly in the mid-1880s; it is this structure which has come to be called Villa Louis.

H. Louis Dousman—a bit of a dilettante who owned a stylish house and attached art gallery down in St. Louis—called the estate the Artesian Stock Farm and raised Standardbred trotting horses here. He built a large stable and a race track as part of his operations. When Louis died in 1886, at the age of thirty-seven, his widow renamed the estate Villa Louis in his memory. She was the former Nina Sturgis, whose father, General S. D. Sturgis, had won fame as an Indian fighter and Civil War officer.

The mansion was built on the banks of the Mississippi on the Hopewell Indian Mound; it was constructed of Milwaukee-made "cream" brick and features an enclosed veranda on three of its four sides. The floor plan includes a billiard room, estate office, and guest suite; some of the outbuildings seen are the ice house, a summer kitchen, a laundry building and servants' quarters, and the remnants of Louis's stable. Ninety percent of the furnishings are original to the Dousmans and were in the house during the interpretative period of the 1890s.

Notable Collections on Exhibit

Though there are many fine paintings and objects on display, the heart of the collection lies in the family archives; because the Dousmans were so well-connected throughout the Midwest, this archive provides a marvelous documentary history of the region during much of the 19th century.

Additional Information

The Villa Louis Historic Site is listed on the National Register of Historic Places; the mansion and two additional structures on the site are National Registered Landmarks. The museum runs a fine living history program, historic food program, and hosts many wonderful special events.

Martin Pattison House— *"Fairlawn"*

906 Harbor View Parkway East
Superior, WI 54880
(715) 394-5712

Contact: Douglas County Historical Society

Open: Year-round, daily 9 a.m.–5 p.m.; closed New Year's Day, Easter, Thanksgiving, Christmas

Admission: Adults $4.00; seniors and students $2.00; children (under 6) $1.00; group rate available

Activities: Special programs including Railroad Days, Fourth of July, Ice Cream Social, Christmas Open House

Suggested Time to View House: 90 minutes

Facilities on Premises: Gift shop

Description of Grounds: Wildflower gardens on estate grounds

Best Season to View House: Late spring-fall

Number of Yearly Visitors: 16,500

Year House Built: 1890

Style of Architecture: Late Victorian Queen Anne with Chateauesque elements

Number of Rooms: 42

On-Site Parking: Yes **Wheelchair Access:** No

Description of House

Fairlawn was built in 1890 by Martin Pattison and his wife Grace. Ontario-born Pattison—a lumber baron, banker, sheriff, and mayor—married Grace Frink on May 15, 1879, and the couple had eight children. In addition to his other interests, Pattison discovered the Pioneer and Chandler Iron Ore Mines. Today's Pattison State Park is made up of land on the Black River which he purchased and donated to the state prior to his death in 1917. After his death, Grace moved out to California; in 1920, she gave Fairlawn to the Superior Children's Home and Refuge Center.

The imposing three-story house that the Pattisons built is patterned after a French Chateau; it cost $150,000 and boasts of forty-two rooms, a full attic, and a basement. The exterior is done is fishscale cedar siding with zinc and copper trim. It also features a large cupola and porches around all four sides; the cupola affords a magnificent view of Superior Bay. Inside, fine woodwork—predominantly quarter-sawn oak—is visible throughout. Other interior details include: leaded glass windows, carved mantels, a split fireplace in the family parlor, a unique airshaft for air-conditioning, guillotine doors in the dining room, and pocket doors throughout the first floor.

The first floor of the house is fully furnished with period antiques, some of which belonged to the family.

Notable Collections on Exhibit

On view here is the D. F. Barry collection of Sioux Indian photographs, the Mary Branca doll collection, a collection of Woodland Indian crafts— mostly Ojibwa beadwork, baskets, and tools, and a logging exhibit.

Additional Information

Fairlawn is listed on the National Register of Historic Places.

Octagon House

919 Charles Street
Watertown, WI 53094
(414) 261-2796

Contact: Watertown Historical Society
Open: May 1–Oct. 31, 10 a.m.–4 p.m.
Admission: Adults $3.00; seniors $2.50;
    groups (20 or more) $2.50 each; students
    (6-17) $1.00; children (under 6) free
Facilities on Premises: Gift shop
Suggested Time to View House:
    60–90 minutes
Best Season to View House: Fall
Year House Built: 1854
Number of Rooms: 57

Activities: Guided tours, Christmas Open House
Description of Grounds: Restored "First
    Kindergarten Building" and pioneer barn
Number of Yearly Visitors: 12,000
Style of Architecture: Octagon, brick
On-Site Parking: Yes **Wheelchair Access:** No

Description of House

This solid brick, five-story Octagon House is the largest single-family residence built in Wisconsin before the Civil War. It was designed and constructed by John Richards, a native of Massachusetts who came to Watertown in 1837, then went back east to get married and bring his wife back out with him in 1841. Here he practiced law, farmed some of his 100 acres, operated a grist mill and saw mill, and served as one of the town's early mayors. Descendants of John Richards remained in the house until 1937; at that time, the home and its contents were donated to the Watertown Historical Society.

Richards built his octagonal house in accord with Orson Fowler's popular mid-century treatise, *The Octagon House, A Home For All*. Seven pattern books featuring octagon house plans followed this treatise. This house features full two-story wrap-around porches—these were restored in 1982—and the characteristic center tower. The windows on the first and second floors are shuttered.

Interior details include an impressive cantilevered hanging spiral staircase which rises through the center core of the house from the first floor to the tower; hand-turned spindles made of cherry wood harvested on the Richards farm, an air-conditioning system, and a wood-burning hot air furnace. Approximately half of the furnishings are from the Richards family, including the parlor furniture.

Additional Information

The Octagon House is listed on the National Register of Historic Places. Also on the property is the fully restored First Kindergarten Building which was moved here from downtown Watertown.

Hamlin Garland Homestead

357 West Garland Street
West Salem, WI 54669
(608) 786-1399

Contact: West Salem Historical Society
Open: Memorial Day-Labor Day, Mon.-Sat.
10 a.m.–5 p.m., Sun. 1–5 p.m.; other
times by appointment
Admission: Adults $1.00; students $.50;
family $2.50
Activities: Guided tours, "Garland Days"
weekend
Suggested Time to View House: 45 minutes
Facilities on Premises: Gift shop
Description of Grounds: Fenced yard with
flower gardens
Best Season to View House: Summer
Number of Yearly Visitors: 1,000+
Year House Built: 1859
Number of Rooms: 12

Style of Architecture: National, farmhouse
On-Site Parking: Yes **Wheelchair Access:** No

Description of House

In 1893 this large frame farmhouse and its four-acre property was bought by the well-known pioneer author Hamlin Garland as a homestead for his parents. Garland, who had been born in a log cabin thirty-three years earlier, and gone on to become a sympathetic chronicler of the lives of the poor farmers he had grown up with, also lived here for awhile after his marriage to Zulime Taft, the sister of famous sculptor Lorado Taft. The couple's first daughter was born here in 1903. In 1912, the house was partially destroyed by fire but Garland immediately rebuilt it. After his father's death, the author moved to New York State, then California.

Hamlin Garland's books include *Prairie Folks*, *Wayside Courtships*, and his Pulitzer Prize-winning biography, *The Daughter of the Middle Border*. They are indispensable reading for anyone wishing to understand the life of the poor midwestern farmer at the turn of the century. His ashes are buried beside his parents in Neshonoc Cemetery outside West Salem.

The house was built in 1859; it is a two-story, side-gabled frame structure to which several additions were made. Exterior features include an extended two-story bay and a lean-to porch. All of the windows are in an eight-over-single-pane arrangement.

Notable Collections on Exhibit

On display is a large collection of Hamlin Garland memorabilia including copies of his writings, family photographs, and original furnishings dating from 1893 to the late 1920s.

Additional Information

The Hamlin Garland Homestead is listed on the National Register of Historic Places.

Palmer-Gullickson Octagon House

358 North Leonard Street and Route 16
West Salem, WI 54669
(608) 786-1675

Contact: West Salem Historical Society
Open: Memorial Day-Labor Day, Mon.-Sat.
10 a.m.–5 p.m., Sun. 1–5 p.m.
Admission: Adults $1.00; students $.50;
family $2.50
Activities: Guided tours, June Civil War
enactment
Suggested Time to View House: 30 minutes
Best Season to View House: Summer

Facilities on Premises: Visitor center and
museum with gift shop
Description of Grounds: 1 acre yard with
rock and flower gardens
Number of Yearly Visitors: 1,000
Year House Built: 1856
Style of Architecture: Octagon
Number of Rooms: 8
On-Site Parking: Yes **Wheelchair Access:** No

Description of House

Dr. Horace Palmer, the first resident doctor in Neshonoc, built this octagon house in that town near the La Crosse River. When the railroad was built in West Salem, the population shifted from Neshonoc to this town and the doctor, in order to retain his clients, moved to West Salem too. He also brought his house with him! The procedure took three weeks—the house was split in two where the large wing met the main section of the structure— but the Palmer family continued to live in it the whole time.

In 1876 the house was sold to Dr. Mary Lottridge, the second woman doctor in the United States. Mr. and Mrs. Oliver Gullickson purchased the house in 1921 and their son and daughter-in-law lived in the apartment which had earlier been created out of the former doctor's office. Mrs. Rachel Gullickson was a teacher, historian, nature lover, and world traveler; it was through her efforts that the West Salem Historical Society acquired the house.

The two-story octagonal house is constructed out of oak beams and brick; the brick is lined and the walls are filled with sawdust for insulation. It features a full two-story wrap-around porch and balcony supported by paired columns. The columns and bannister are without ornament, and the fenestration consists of simple sash windows. The attached apartment now serves as a museum.

Many of the original furnishings remain in the house: a Victorian sofa and chairs, a walnut tilt-top table, a wood rocker, a black walnut drop-leaf table, and a bedroom set in the Renaissance Revival style.

Additional Information

The Palmer-Gullickson Octagon House is listed on the National Register of Historic Places. Another house worth visiting when in West Salem is the Historic Salem House, built in 1859 in the Greek Revival style. The house is the former home of the town's founder, Thomas Leonard. He named the town after Salem, Massachusetts, the seat of witchcraft in early America. Leonard believed in witchcraft and incorporated a curious feature in his house: marks cut into the inside of the front door meant to protect against witches' spells.

Index

🏛 *Arkansas*

🏛 *Illinois*

🏛 Indiana

🏛 Iowa

🏛 Kansas

🏛 Michigan

🏛 Minnesota

🏛 Missouri

🏛 Nebraska

🏛 North Dakota

🏛 Ohio

🏛 Oklahoma

🏛 South Dakota

🏛 Wisconsin

🏛 Arkansas

	Photo or illustration courtesy of
Calif House	Eureka Springs Historical Museum
Hawkins House	G.W. Downs/Rogers Historical Museum
Headquarters House-the Tebbetts House	Bob Hamon and John Lewis/ Washington County Hist. Soc.
John D. Trimble House	Eddie Roe/Pioneer Washington Foundation
Pike-Fletcher-Terry House	Arkansas Arts Center Decorative Arts Museum
Sarah B.N. Ridge House	Washington County Historical Society
"Villa Marre"	Quapaw Quarter Association
W.H.H. Clayton House	Fort Smith Heritage Foundation, Inc.

🏛 Illinois

1846 Garfield Inn	Garfield Farm and Tavern Museum
Banta House	M. Stimley/Arlington Heights Historical Society
Brigham Young Home	Larry W. Turner/Nauvoo Restoration, Inc.
Bryant Cottage State Historic Site	Illinois Historic Preservation Agency
Butterworth Center, "Hillcrest"	William Butterworth Memorial Trust
Carl A. Sandburg State Historic Site	Illinois Historic Preservation Agency
Charles Gates Dawes House	Evanston Photographic Studios, Inc./ Evanston Hist. Society
Daniel A. Barrows House	Marla Shaw Schafer/ Galena-Jo Daviess County Hist. Society
David Davis Mansion State Historic Site	Illinois Historic Preservation Agency
Deere-Wiman House, "Overlook"	William Butterworth Memorial Trust
Dr. William Fithian Home	Vermilion County Museum Society
Dunham Hunt House, "Oaklawn"	Dunham Hunt Historic Preservation Society
Ellwood House Museum	Ellwood House Association
Erlander Home Museum	Swedish Historical Society of Rockford
Francis Stupey Log Cabin	Highland Park Historical Society
Frank Lloyd Wright Home and Studio	Don Kalec/Frank Lloyd Wright Home and Studio Foundation
Frank Lloyd Wright's Dana-Thomas House State Historic Site	IHPA/Frank Lloyd Wright/ Wasmuth Portfolio-1910
Frederick C. Robie House	Robie House at the University of Chicago
Governor John Wood Mansion	Historical Society of Quincy and Adams County
Heber C. Kimball Home	Nauvoo Restoration, Inc.
Illinois-Michigan Canal Office and Residence	Will County Historical Society
James Canty Morrison House	Christian County Historical Society
James Millikin Homestead	Alice Flint/James Millikin Homestead, Inc.
Jean Butz James Museum	Highland Park Historical Society
John C. Flanagan House	Peoria Historical Society
John Weir House	Madison County Historical Society Museum
Joseph Smith Homestead and Mansion House	Restoration Trail Foundation
Kruse House Museum	West Chicago Historical Society
Lamon House	Vermilion County Museum Society
Lincoln Home National Historic Site	U.S. Department of the Interior/National Park Service
Lorado Taft Museum	Elmwood Historical Society
Müller House	M. Stimley/Arlington Heights Historical Society
Martin-Mitchell Mansion	Naperville Heritage Society
Oscar Taylor House, "Bohemiana"	Stephenson County Historical Society

	Photo or illustration courtesy of
Pettengill-Morron House Museum	Eugene Voss/Peoria Historical Society
Pulsifer House	Putnam County Historical Society
Ronald Reagan Boyhood Home	Ronald Reagan Home Preservation Foundation
Sarah and Hiram Kimball Home	Larry W. Turner/Nauvoo Restoration, Inc.
Tinker Swiss Cottage	Tinker Swiss Cottage Museum
U.S. Grant Home State Historic Site	Jim Quick/Illinois Historic Preservation Agency
Wilber Mansion	Champaign County Historical Museum
Wilford Woodruff Home	Nauvoo Restoration, Inc.
William L. Gregg House Museum	Westmount Historical Society

🏛 Indiana

1830 Owen House	Historic New Harmony
Andrew F. Scott House	Wayne County Historical Museum
Barker Mansion	Barker Civic Center
Chief Richardville House	Historic Forks of the Wabash, Inc.
David Lenz House	Historic New Harmony
Fauntleroy House	Historic New Harmony
Historic Reitz Home	Reitz Home Preservation Society, Inc.
Home of Eugene V. Debs	Eugene V. Debs Foundation
Howard Steamboat Museum	Voelker/Winn Architects-Louisville Kentucky
James Whitcomb Riley Museum Home	Riley Memorial Association
John D. Oliver House, Copshaholm	Northern Indiana Historical Society
Lane Place Historic Home	Montgomery County Historical Society
Lanier Mansion State Historic Site	Indiana Division of Museums and Historic Sites
Levi Coffin House State Historic Site	Levi Coffin House Association, Inc.
Lilly Pavilion of Decorative Arts, "Oldfields"	Indianapolis Museum of Art
Limberlost Cabin State Historic Site	Lewis G. Hall, Jr./DNR Indiana State Museums Hist. Sites
Morris–Butler House	Dan Francis-Mardan Photography/ Hist.Landmarks Foundation
Moses Fowler House	Tippecanoe County Historical Association
Old French House	Old Northwest Corporation
Posey House Museum	Hoosier Elm Chapter Daughters of the American Revolution
Samuel Purviance House	Gernand Enterprises
Seiberling Mansion	Howard County Museum
T.C. Steele State Historic Site	Indiana Department of Natural Resources
Thomas Downs House	Clark's Grant Historical Society
Thomas R. Marshall House	Whitley County Historical Museum
William C. Grose Home	Jack Phelps/Henry County Historical Society, Inc.
William Conner Estate	Conner Prairie
Wolcott House	Anson Wolcott Historical Society

🏛 Iowa

Bedstemor's House	Danish Immigrant Museum
Brucemore-the Sinclair Mansion	Brucemore, Inc.
Daniel Nelson Homestead	Mahaska County Historical Society, Inc.
Herbert Hoover Birthplace Cottage	National Park Service/ Herbert Hoover National Historic Site
Historic General Dodge House	Historic General Dodge House, Inc.
Hoyt Sherman Place	Des Moines Women's Club
Jonathan Clark Conger House	Washington County Historical Society, Inc.

Laura Musser Mansion	Muscatine Art Center
Liberty Hall Historic Center	Restoration Trail Foundation
Mamie Doud Eisenhower Birthplace SHS	Mamie Doud Eisenhower Birthplace Foundation, Inc.
Masters Hotel	Laura Ingalls Wilder Parks and Museum, Inc.
Mathias Ham House Historic Site	Dubuque County Historical Society
Montauk	State Historical Society of Iowa
Scholte House	Scholte House
Terrace Hill-The Historic Governor's Mansion	Terrace Hill Society
Victorian House Museum	Cedar Falls Historical Society Museum
Wyth House	Cedar Falls Historical Society

🏛 Kansas

1878 Hardesty House	Boot Hill Museum
Amelia Earhart Birthplace Museum	Pat Patterson/Ninety Nines, Inc.
Edward Carroll Mansion	Leavenworth County Historical Society
Eisenhower Family Home	National Archives/Dwight D. Eisenhower Library
Grinter Place	Kansas State Historical Society
Historic Kirby House	Tietjens, Hartenstein and Company
John Brown-Adair Cabin	Kansas State Historical Society
Lebold Vahsholtz Mansion	Lebold Vahsholtz Mansion
Mahaffie House	Mahaffie Farmstead and Stagecoach Stop Historic Site
Mueller-Schmidt House, "House of Stone"	Russell Lupton/Ford County Historical Society
Seelye Mansion	John Avery/Tietjens, Hartenstein and Company
W.P. Brown Mansion	Coffeyville Historical Society

🏛 Michigan

Cappon House Museum	Holland Historical Trust
Carrie Jacobs Bond House	Iron County Historical and Museum Society
Edsel and Eleanor Ford House	Balthazar Korab/Edsel and Eleanor Ford House
Ford-MacNichol Home	Wyandotte Cultural and Historical Commission
Governor Moses Wisner Historic House	Oakland County Historical Society
Henry Ford Estate, Fair Lane	Henry Ford Estate
Honolulu House	Marshall Historical Society
Kimball House	Historical Society of Battle Creek
Robert Yerkes House	Northville Historical Society
Ticknor-Campbell House at Cobblestone Farm	City of Ann Arbor
Voigt House Victorian Museum	Grand Rapids Public Museum

🏛 Minnesota

Alexander Ramsey House	Minnesota Historical Society
Charles A. Lindbergh House	Minnesota Historical Society
Gibbs Farmstead Museum	Ramsey County Historical Society
Glensheen	University of Minnesota
Henry Hastings Sibley House	Sibley House Association/Minnesota Chapter DAR
James J. Hill House	Minnesota Historical Society
Rensselaer D. Hubbard House	Blue Earth County Historical Society
W.H.C. Folsom House	Harry and Kenneth Ekdahl/Taylors Falls Historical Society
W.W. Mayo House	Mayo House Interpretive Society

🏛 Missouri

	Photo or illustration courtesy of
1859 Jail-Marshall's Home and Museum	Jackson County Historical Society
Anderson House	Missouri DNR/Battle of Lexington SHS
Arrow Rock Tavern	Missouri DNR/Arrow Rock SHS
B. Gratz Brown House	Homer L. Jones, Jr./Cole County Historical Society
Bingham-Waggoner Estate	Bingham-Waggoner Historical Society
Campbell House Museum	Campbell House Museum
Chatillon-DeMenil Mansion	Martin Schweig Studio/ DeMenil Mansion Board of Directors
Claybrook Plantation Home	Marla Stephens/Clay County Department of Historic Sites
Eugene Field House	Edson Burch/Eugene Field House Foundation
Felix Valle House	Missouri DNR/Felix Valle House SHS
Garth Woodside Mansion	Garth Woodside Mansion
General John J. Pershing Boyhood Home	Missouri Department of Natural Resources
George Caleb Bingham House	Missouri DNR/Arrow Rock SHS
Hain House	Christos/Friends of Historic Boonville
Harry S. Truman Birthplace State Historic Site	Grant Hoover/Missouri Dept. of Nat. Resources
Harry S Truman National Historic Site	U.S. Department of the Interior/ National Park Service
Historic Daniel Boone House	Hist. Daniel Boone Home/Boonesfield Village, Inc.
Jesse James Farm and Museum	Marla Stephens/Clay County Department of Historic Sites
Jesse James Home	Pony Express Historical Association, Inc.
Krause Mansion	Platte County Historical Society, Inc.
Laura Ingalls Wilder-Rose Wilder Lane Home	Laura Ingalls Wilder Home Association
Lightburne Hall	Lightburne Hall
Mark Twain Birthplace State Historic Site	Art Grossmann/ Missouri Department Natural Resources
Mark Twain Boyhood Home and Museum	Mark Twain Home Foundation
Moses Carver House	George Washington Carver National Monument
Pommer-Gentner House	Deutschheim State Historical Site
Rockcliffe Mansion	Art Grossman Photo/Rockcliffe Mansion
Samuel Cupples House and McNamee Gallery	Roscoe Musselhorn/ Samuel Cupples House Foundaton
Strehly House and Winery	Deutschheim State Historical Site
Thomas Sappington House	Sappington House Foundation
Tower Grove House	Missouri Botanical Garden
Vaile Mansion-DeWitt Museum	City of Independence/Vaile Victorian Society

🏛 Nebraska

E.C. Houston House	Burt County Museum, Inc.
Frank House	University of Nebraska at Kearney
General Crook House Museum	Patricia Pixley/Historical Society of Douglas County
George W. Norris House	Nebraska State Historical Society
Home of William Jennings Bryan, "Fairview"	Bryan Memorial Hospital Foundation
Kennard House, Nebraska Statehood Memorial	Nebraska State Historical Society
Smith House	Jefferson County Historical Society

🏛 North Dakota

	Photo or illustration courtesy of
Custer Home-Fort Abraham Lincoln State Park	Carrie Weiss/ Fort Abraham Lincoln Foundation
Former Governors' Mansion	State Historical Society of North Dakota
Gunlogson Homestead and Arboretum	Robert Gilbert/ North Dakota Parks Recreation Department
Thomas D. Campbell House	Grand Forks County Historical Society

🏛 Ohio

Arthur R. Garford House-Hickories Museum	Lorain County Historical Society
Cary Cottage	Cary Cottage Group
Cassius Clark Thompson House	East Liverpool Historical Society
Christian Waldschmidt House and Gate House	Ohio Society Daughters of the American Revolution
Daniel Arnold House at Carriage Hill Farm	Carriage Hill Farm-Park District
Daniel McCook House Museum	Carroll County Historical Society
Galpin House	Milan Historical Museum, Inc.
Gilbert Flanigan Saltbox Farmhouse	Maumee Valley Historical Society
Hale House at Hale Farm and Village	Western Reserve Historical Society
Harriet Beecher Stowe House	Harriet Beecher Stowe House
Hickok Brick House at Century Village	Geauga County Historical Society
"House of Seven Oaks"	Van Wert County Historical Society
Hower House	Chuck Ayers/University of Akron
James A. Garfield National Historic Site	Western Reserve Historical Society
John Wright Mansion	Alvina Schaeffer/Historic Lyme Village Association
Kelton House Museum and Garden	Lambert Photography/Junior League of Columbus, Inc.
Log House Museum	Historical Society of Columbiana-Fairfield Township
Louis Bromfield's Big House	Malabar Farm State Park
Mac-A-Cheek Castle	Mike Majors/Piatt Castles
Mac-O-Chee Castle	Mike Majors/Piatt Castles
Oldest Stone House	Kathy Heidelberg/Lakewood Historical Society
Oran Follett Museum	Sandusky Library
President Warren G. Harding Home	Ohio Historical Society
"Promont"	Milford Area Historical Society
Rombach Place	Clinton County Historical Society
Rutherford B. Hayes Home, "Spiegel Grove"	Rutherford B. Hayes Presidential Center
Sayler-Swartsel House	Preble County Historical Society, Inc.
Sayles House	Milan Historical Museum, Inc.
Sherman House Museum	M. Stampfle/Fairfield Heritage Association
Taft Boyhood Home	U.S. Department of the Interior/National Park Service
Thomas A. Edison Birthplace	Edison Birthplace Association, Inc.
Thurber House	Thurber House
Wolcott House	Maumee Valley Historical Society

🏛 Oklahoma

Drummond House	Jim Argo/Oklahoma Historical Society
Frank Phillips Home	Jim Argo/Oklahoma Historical Society
Hefner Mansion	Oklahoma Heritage Association Center
Mattie Beal Home	Lawton Heritage Association
Moore-Lindsey House	Cleveland County Historical Society
Overholser Mansion	Oklahoma Historical Society

Peter Conser House	Jim Argo/Oklahoma Historical Society
Seay Mansion, "Horizon Hill"	Chisholm Trail Museum, Inc.
Sequoyah's Cabin	Fred Olds/Oklahoma Historical Society
Sod House Museum	Oklahoma Historical Society

🏛 South Dakota

Austin-Whittemore House Museum	Bruce G. Milne/Clay County Historical Society, Inc.
Badger Clark House or "Badger Hole"	SD State Historical Society/ Badger Clark Memorial Society
Cramer-Kenyon Heritage Home	Heritage Home Corporation
Historic Booth House	D.C. Booth National Historic Fish Hatchery
Major John A. Pickler Mansion	Faulk County Historical Society, Inc.
Mentor Graham House	Mentor Graham House Museum
Pettigrew Home and Museum	Siouxland Heritage Museums
Railroad House	Douglas County Historical Society

🏛 Wisconsin

Captain Frederick Pabst Mansion	Wisconsin Heritages, Inc.
Edgar Sawyer Mansion	Oshkosh Public Museum
Edwin H. Galloway House and Village	Fond du Lac County Historical Society
Gideon C. Hixon House	La Crosse County Historical Society
Hamlin Garland Homestead	West Salem Historical Society
Hanchett-Bartlett Homestead	Beloit Historical Society
John S. Moffat Octagon House	St. Croix County Historical Society
Lincoln-Tallman House Museum	Rock County Historical Society, Inc.
Martin Pattison House, "Fairlawn"	Douglas County Historical Society
Milton House Museum	Milton Historical Society
Mitchell-Roundtree Stone Cottage	Vic Pagenkopf/Grant County Historical Society
Palmer-Gullickson Octagon House	West Salem Historical Society
Pendarvis House and Trelawny House	State Historical Society of Wisconsin/Robert Granflaten
Tank Cottage at Heritage Hill	Heritage Hill State Park
Villa Louis Historic Site	State Historical Society of Wisconsin/Robert Granflaten
Winton-Sprengel House	Libbie Nolan/New Berlin Historical Society
Yule House	Kenosha County Historical Society and Museum

Notes

Notes

Notes

Notes

Notes